# OCR

# Sociology

**AS**

Fionnuala Swann | Viv Thompson

www.heinemann.co.uk

✓ Free online support
✓ Useful weblinks
✓ 24 hour online ordering

**01865 888080**

OCR
RECOGNISING ACHIEVEMENT

Heinemann

Official Publisher Partnership

Heinemann is an imprint of Pearson Education Limited, a company incorporated in England and Wales, having its registered office at Edinburgh Gate, Harlow, Essex, CM20 2JE. Registered company number: 872828

www.heinemann.co.uk

Heinemann is a registered trademark of Pearson Education Limited

Text © Carole Waugh, Helen Robinson, Fionnuala Swann and Viv Thompson

First published 2008

12 11 10 09 08

10 9 8 7 6 5 4 3 2 1

British Library Cataloguing in Publication Data is available from the British Library on request.

ISBN 978 0 435467 38 8

Edited by Caroline Sinclair
Designed by Hicks Design
Typeset by Tek-Art, Crawley Down, West Sussex
Original illustrations © Pearson Education Limited 2008
Illustrated by Asa Andersson & Tek-Art
Cover design by Big Top Design Ltd
Picture research by Sally Cole
Printed in the UK by Scotprint

## Websites

There are links to relevant websites in this book. In order to ensure that the links are up-to-date, that the links work, and that the sites are not inadvertently linked to sites that could be considered offensive, we have made the links available on the Heinemann website at www.heinemann.co.uk/hotlinks. When you access the site, the express code is 7388.

## Photo credits

Cover: © iStockphoto/Les Cunliffe
Ace Stock Limited/Alamy page 126; Adrian Sherratt/Alamy page 235; Allan Ivy/Alamy page 247; Andrew Fox/Alamy page 271; Andrew Fox/Corbis page 63; Anita Bugge/WireImage/Getty page 32; AP/EMPICS page 223; Artiga Photo/Getty page 48; Ben Molyneux Travel Photography/Alamy page 270; Ben Stansall/Getty page 28; Charlotte Nation/Getty page 59; Chris Jackson/Getty page 139; Corbis page 165; David P. Hall/Corbis page 143; David Young-Wolff/Alamy page 150; Dinodia Images/Alamy page xii; Erik Dreyer/Getty Images page 117; Gerhard Steiner/Corbis page 42; Guillem Lopez/Alamy page 22; © Imagesource page 198; Image Source/Rex Features page 16; © iStockphoto page 185; © iStockphoto/Jeff Nagy page 170; James Fraser/Rex Features page 24; Janine Wiedel Photolibrary/Alamy page 38; Jim Spellman/WireImage/Getty page 33; JLImages/Alamy page 35; Jo Hale/Getty page 260; John Powell Photographer/Alamy page 262; PYMCA/Alamy page 252; Kevin Fleming/Corbis page 241; Leon Neal/Getty page 165; Leon Schadeberg/Rex Features page 244; Ludovic Maisant/Getty page 8; Manor Photography/Alamy page 227; Mika/Zefa/Corbis page 68; Mike Hoban/Getty page 6; Nils Jorgensen/Rex Features page 112; Norbert Schaefer/Zefa/Corbis page 124; Pat Behnke/Alamy page 2; Paul Thompson Images/Alamy page 46; ©Pearson Education Ltd/Ginny Stroud-Lewis page 155; ©Pearson Education Ltd/Jules Selmes page 12; Peter Hince/Getty page 23; Philip and Karen Smith/Getty page 247; Photolibrary.com page 207; Photolibrary.com page 214; Rex Features page 49; Rick Gomez/Corbis page 132; Robert Hollingworth/Alamy page xii; Ronnie Kaufman/Corbis page 66; Sonny Meddle/Rex Features page 19; Stuart Aylmer/Alamy page 218; The Photolibrary Wales/Alamy page 18; Travelshots.com/Alamy page 9; Walter Lockwood/Corbis page 35; Westend 61/Alamy page 56

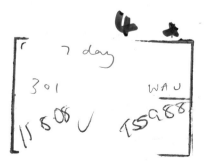

# Contents

# Acknowledgements

The authors and publisher would like to thank the following individuals and organisations for permission to reproduce material in this book.

Page 25 Reprinted from Ward, J. and Winstanley, D. (2005) 'Coming out at work, performativity and the recognition and negotiation of identity', *Sociological Review*, 53, 3, 461–2, with permission from Blackwells; Page 32 Reprinted from Connell, R.W. (2002) *Gender*, Cambridge: Polity Press; Page 81 Reprinted from Oates, C.J. and McDonald, S. (2006) 'Recycling and the domestic division of labour: is green, pink or blue?', *Sociology*, 40 (3), 417–33, with permission from Sage Publications; Page 91 Reprinted from Alexander, C. (1996) *The Art of being Black*, pp 18-20, Oxford University Press; Page 94 Reprinted from Hodkinson, P. (2002) *Goth, Identity, Style and Subculture*, with permission from Berg Publishers; Pages 100–1 Reprinted from Kettley, N. (2006) 'It's cool to be clever: the marginal relevance of gender to educational practices and attainments at AS/A level', *Evaluation and Research in Education* 19 (2), with permission from Multilingual Matters; Page 118 Reprinted from Allan, G. and Crow, G. (2001) *Families, Households and Society*, Palgrave, p. 2; Pages 157, 163, 164 Reprinted from Taylor, P., Richardson, J., Yeo, A., Marsh, I., Trobe, K. and Pilkington, A. (1996) *Sociology in Focus*, Causeway Press, with permission from Pearson Education Ltd; Pages 158 and 167 Figures from *AS & A Level Sociology through Diagrams* by Tony Lawson, Marsha Jones and Ruth Moores (Oxford Revision Guides, OUP, 2000), copyright © Tony Lawson, Marsha Jones and Ruth Moores 2000, reprinted by permission of Oxford University Press; Page 158 Reprinted from Taylor, S. and Field, D. (2007) *Sociology of Health and Health Care*, Blackwell, with permission from Blackwell Publishing; Page 161 John Carvel, 11 October 2007. Copyright Guardian News & Media Ltd 2007; Page 162 Reprinted from McKeown, T (1976) *The Modern Rise of Population*, London: Arnold, in Taylor, S. and Field, D. (2003) *Sociology of Health and Health Care*, Blackwell, with permission from Blackwell Publishing; Page 164 Reprinted from Pill, R. and Stott, N.C.H. (1982) 'Concepts of illness causation and responsibility: some preliminary data from a sample of working class mothers', *Social Science and Medicine*, 16, 45–50, with permission from Elsevier; Page 168 Reprinted from Senior, M. and Viveash, B. (1998) *Skills-based Sociology Series: Health and Illness*, p. 9 published by Palgrave (St Martin's Press LLC Scholarly and Reference Division and Palgrave Publishers Ltd); Page 180 Reprinted from Arber, S. and Thomas, H. (2001) 'From women's health to gender analysis of health', in Cockerham, W.C. (ed.) *The Blackwell Companion to Medical Sociology*, Blackwell, with permission from Blackwell Publishing; Page 181 Reprinted from Sproston, K. and Mindell, J. (2006) *The Health of Minority Ethnic Groups*, Vol. 1, The Information Centre, Leeds (tables 2l.5 and 12.1), taken from Taylor, S. and Field, D. (2006), p. 76), Blackwell, with permission from Blackwell Publishing; Page 187 Taylor, S. and Field, D. (eds) (2007) *Sociology of Health and Health Care*, Blackwell, p.160, with permission from Blackwell Publishing; Page 188 Adapted from Felicity Lawrence, 16 January 2006. Copyright Guardian News & Media Ltd 2006; Page 190 Reprinted from Senior, M. and Viveash, B. (1998) *Health and Illness*, Palgrave, p. 222; Page 194 Figure adapted from Davies, T. (1994) 'Disabled by society', *Sociology Review*, April, reproduced by permission of Philip Allan Updates Ltd; Page 195 Oliver, M. (1990) *The Politics of Disablement*, Palgrave Macmillan; Page 208 Reprinted from Durkheim, E., cited in Aldridge, A. (2004) 'Defining religion', *Sociology Review* 14 (2), reproduced by permission of Philip Allan Updates Ltd; Page 209 Reprinted from Bruce, S. (2002) 'God and shopping', *Sociology Review* (November), reproduced by permission of Philip Allan Updates Ltd; Page 209 Adapted from Aldridge, A (2004) 'Defining religion', *Sociology Review* 14 (2), reproduced by permission of Philip Allan Updates Ltd; Page 225 Adapted from Beckford, J. (2004) 'Religion and postmodernity', *Sociology Review*, 14 (2); Page 236 Reprinted from *Churchgoing in the UK* – © Tearfund UK 2007 (www.tearfund.org); Page 245 Adapted from Arlidge, J. 'The vanishing generation gap', *Observer*, 1 February 2004, with permission from the author; Pages 265 and 266 'Detected offending by age', 'Children and young people cautioned, reprimanded, warned or sentenced for indictable offences' and 'Risk factors associated with youth offenders', Nacro (www.nacro.org.uk); Page 266 Reprinted from *Statistical Bulletin* 17/06, produced by RDS. Wilson, D., Sharp, C. and Patterson, A. 'Young people and crime: findings from the 2005 Offending, Crime and Justice Survey', The Home Office, reprinted by permission of the authors; Page 267 Reprinted from Mori Youth Survey (2004) *Reproduced under the terms of the Click-Use Licence*; Page xi Office for National Statistics, 2004–5, 2005a, 2005b; Page 40 Nasima Begum, 'Employment by occupation and industry – an analysis of the distribution of employment and characteristics of people in the main industry and occupation groups', *Labour Market Trends*, 112 (6), 8 Office for National Statistics; Pages 61 and 63 Office for National Statistics, 2001; Pages 120, 121, 122, 124, 136, 148, 211, 229, 231, 233 National Statistics Online, 2007; Page 148 Crime reduction website. Home Office; Page 172 Derived from Office for National Statistics, Longitudinal Study (tables 1-4); Page 172 Derived from White C., van Galen F., and Chow Y.H. (2003) 'Trends in social class differences in mortality by cause, 1986–2000', *Health Statistics Quarterly*, 20, 25–37 (tables 1 and 2); Page 173 Census 2001, Office for National Statistics/ General Register Office for Scotland/Northern Ireland Statistics and Research Agency, 2001; Page 174 Labour Party White Paper *Prevention and Health*, 1997, p. 39; Page 177 *Health Statistics Quarterly* 34 (2007) 28, 6–17; Page 178 General Household Survey (Longitudinal) Office for National Statistics; Page 182 Health Survey for England, Department of Health; Page 187 'Psychiatric morbidity among adults living in private households', Office for National Statistics, 2000; Page 188 'Psychiatric morbidity among adults', Office for National Statistics, 2000; Page 229 Annual Local Area Labour Force Survey, Office for National Statistics, 2001–2; Page 275 Department for Education and Skills (2005) Education and Training Statistics for the UK 2005 edition.

# Foreword

As experienced teachers of sociology who are also senior examiners, we have been involved with OCR sociology since Curriculum 2000 and have played a large part in the design of the new OCR sociology specification. Over a number of years we have listened to the views of our students with regard to classroom learning in sociology. We have also delivered INSET courses and listened to the constructive comments that teachers have offered about what makes a good textbook. This book is the result of our interaction with both teachers and learners and we hope that it achieves three things.

First, it is designed and written to provide coverage of the entire new sociology specification with a careful blend of up-to-date examples from contemporary British sociology mixed with some of the classic sociological material that informs so much of the contemporary work.

Secondly, it includes activities for use in the classroom, which are designed to encourage students to think sociologically, using the textbook as a springboard but embedding the examples in students' own understanding and experience of the social world. This is our attempt to foster the development of a sociological imagination so that students are encouraged to think sociologically. Experience tells us that these activities will need to be adapted depending on the size and nature of the class, teaching time and teaching preferences.

Finally, the book provides guidance on assessment, which reflects the OCR approach. The Exam Café gives examples of specimen questions, teacher tips, revision checklists and student answers with comments from examiners. These answers are not model answers: they are real examples of what students have written in exam conditions and they should be used as learning tools. Students are encouraged to read them and rework them, taking on board the examiner comments.

This book is written for both students and teachers and we hope that you find it useful and enjoyable.

*Carole Waugh, Helen Robinson, Fionnuala Swann and Viv Thompson,* March 2008

I would like to thank Paul, Alex and Ben for their love and support. *Carole Waugh*

Thank you, Stuart, for always keeping a glass half full.
Thank you, Dan, and thank you, Lydia.
Thanks to all those students I've taught over the years.
Thank you, Carole, for keeping me in a very big loop. *Helen Robinson*

Thanks to Euan and Abigail, for having to share me with a computer! Thanks also to my colleagues at Clitheroe Royal Grammar school – Steve, Andrew and Cath – the most dedicated and inspiring team I have ever worked with, and thanks to my mum – my inspiration, without whose support I could never have done this. *Fionnuala Swann*

For Sarah and Danny, with loads of love and Sheila, sisters first, friends for ever, love and thanks for all you've done over the years. *Viv Thompson*

# Introduction

## How to use this book

The book is divided into three sections. Units 1 and 2 deal with the two units you will study in the specification and the Exam Café provides help and guidance on assessment issues.

The book contains the following features.

## Pause for thought

Each section begins with a 'Pause for thought'. This provides some questions you need to consider before reading the section. They are designed to get you thinking about your experiences of the social world and your views of particular issues. These are useful starting points in lessons or if you are reading on your own. If you can share your views with others in your group this is likely to enhance your understanding, especially if you listen and respond to people who have different views from your own.

## Main text

The text is written at an appropriate level for AS students and contains sociological concepts, studies, theories and contemporary examples. These four ingredients make up the foundation of OCR sociology, and are considered the building blocks to becoming good sociologists. Your ultimate aim is to read, understand and add to this main text throughout the course. The main text corresponds directly to the OCR specification.

## Activities

We have included activities in the main text which are designed to enable you to reflect on what you have read and to give practice at interpreting and applying your sociological knowledge. Some of the activities involve studying photographs, others involve filling in grids or writing short paragraphs using sociological evidence. All of the activities are designed to get you thinking as a sociologist.

## Summary sections

At the end of each section there are summary sections with a list of key words and a missing-word exercise. Each word can be used once only and all of the words should be used. This exercise should reinforce the work you have covered in that section. If you do not do well the first time, you should revisit these activities as this will reinforce the main content you have covered.

## Glossary

A glossary of key terms is included at the end of the book to help with understanding key concepts. It is particularly relevant for gaining a holistic understanding of sociological terminology.

# Exam Café

After each Unit there is an Exam Café section and you will be dipping into these throughout your course. The Exam Café provides lots of ideas to help prepare for your exams.

You can **Relax** because there's handy revision advice from fellow students.

**Refresh your memory** with summaries and checklists of the key ideas you need to revise.

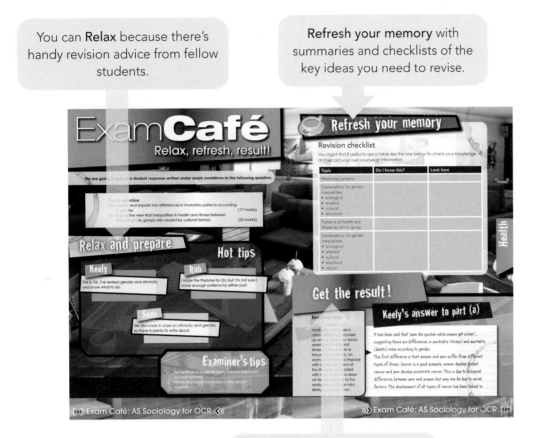

**Get the result** through practising exam-style questions, accompanied by hints and tips on getting the very best grades.

The Exam Café includes sample questions for each section of the text and guidance on how to tackle the questions, together with students' answers and examiner comments. These questions are the same type as those you will have to answer in your final exams. They can all be answered by reference to the material in the main text, although if you can carry out your own reading/research this is likely to improve the quality of your answers. Guidance on the skills assessed in sociology and what the exam requires is given and you should study this carefully before attempting any of the questions.

## What is sociology?

There are many different ways of explaining what sociology is. Before we consider any of these it is useful to look at some of the assumptions people often make about sociology (Figure 1). You may have experienced or be experiencing some of these views at this time in your life.

Sociologists are curious about the world and the way in which it functions. They therefore attempt to study societies in a systematic way. They are particularly interested in the social interaction of individuals and groups. However, sociologists also consider the role of institutions and social processes in explaining the ways in which societies function.

**Some misconceptions about sociology**

**1 Sociology is easy**
If you find studying sociology easy, that is great. However, concepts such as ethnocentrism, cultural capital and globalisation have kept sociologists writing and debating for centuries, so there is a lot to consider. Studying any subject at AS level requires enthusiasm and application and sociology is no exception.

**2 Sociology is common sense**
Some of the topics you will look at relate closely to your everyday life. For example, how do individuals learn social rules or how and why do the British learn to form queues so well? Understanding issues like this can help us to understand how societies function and hold together. To some people these issues are based on common sense, however, by researching them it helps to build up a picture of how life is experienced by different social groups in the contemporary UK. There is more involved than just common sense.

**3 Universities don't accept sociology as a real AS/A level**
This is nonsense. They do.

**4 Sociology is all about debates**
Sociology is certainly about exploring and understanding different viewpoints and thinking about issues in new ways. Sociologists think, discuss and they write. At the end of your course you will be assessed by a written exam and therefore during the course you must learn to write as a sociologist. Debating is a part of sociology but is not all of it.

**5 You have to study sociology if you want to be a social worker**
If you want to be a social worker studying sociology will help you but it is not necessary to have studied it at AS level. Sociology is a useful subject to study at some point in your educational career as it does give you a different way of seeing society. However, studying sociology does not mean that you will be limited to work in social care.

Figure 1 Assumptions people make about sociology

The sociologist C. Wright Mills wrote about the 'sociological imagination'. Mills made a distinction between personal issues and public troubles (Mills, 1959). Personal issues relate to the individual and their immediate life, for example existing on a low income may be a personal issue. Public concerns relate to social structures in society, for example high rates of unemployment may be a public trouble. Mills argues that through studying sociology people learn to develop a sociological imagination where they begin to connect their personal issues to public concerns and they begin to see the relationship between themselves and the wider society in which they live. This enhances their understanding of the society in which they live and, for Mills, the development of a sociological imagination was a key aim of sociology. Mills argued, however, that not everyone could achieve this ability to think sociologically.

By studying sociology you will be introduced to working as and thinking like a sociologist. You will learn the basics of becoming a sociologist and the language that accompanies it. You will be encouraged to use your experience of the social world (personal) and combine it with an understanding of social (public) concerns, therefore attempting to develop a sociological imagination.

## What is OCR sociology?

In the course of this journey, OCR sociology considers the themes of socialisation, culture and identity in the contemporary UK.

◆ Unit 1 looks at the basic concepts associated with the core themes and combines these with considering how sociologists work and collect their data.

◆ Unit 2 offers four topics of which you must study at least one. All of the topics relate to the core themes. Although you only have to study one topic you are likely to become a better sociologist if you study more than one as you will be able to make links between topics and themes more easily.

An outline of the specification, including assessment issues, is set out in Figure 2.

---

**Unit 1: Exploring socialisation, culture and identity**

This unit assesses sociological understanding of socialisation, culture and identity in the context of sociological research.

Assessment is through one 90-minute examination based on pre-released material.

---

**Unit 2: Topics in socialisation, culture and identity**

This unit offers four optional topics from which candidates must study at least one, although you are likely to be a better sociologist if you study more than one.

Optional topics:

◆ Family

◆ Health

◆ Religion

◆ Youth.

Assessment is through one 90-minute examination comprising two questions per option. Each question has two parts: (a) and (b). Candidates must answer two whole questions.

---

Figure 2 OCR AS Sociology at a glance

# What makes good sociology?

One way of understanding the work of sociologists is through the analogy of a restaurant. The good sociologist is like a chef, who is creative and imaginative. All chefs follow basic recipes for making good food but the actual ingredients they use and the way they put them together depends on other factors such as what they are creating, who they are cooking for and the ingredients they have available to them. Sociologists work in a similar way. The basic 'ingredients' that all sociologists use are:

◆ concepts

◆ studies

◆ methods

◆ theory

◆ contemporary examples.

These 'ingredients' provide the basis of good sociology but how they are used and the way in which they are used differs between sociologists. During your AS course you will be learning about and using these ingredients so it is important that you understand what they are.

## Concepts

These are words and terminology that sociologists use to represent some part of sociological reality. Learning basic sociological concepts is the first skill you will acquire in the process of becoming a sociologist, but the process never ends. New concepts appear in sociology all the time. A good example is that of the 'glass ceiling'. The glass ceiling was first used to describe the way in which women were kept out of leading jobs in society. The existence of a ceiling meant something stopped them from climbing further up the career ladder. The fact that the ceiling was made of glass meant that the women could see the leading jobs but could not reach them. The concept of the glass ceiling has become well used in sociology to represent ideas about discrimination and prejudice in the workplace. In a letter to *The Independent* newspaper on 8 January 2007, Viv Thompson, one of the authors of this book, suggested that, as the glass ceiling has been a feature of British life for so long and as we have fewer women in the senior positions of the FTSE 100 firms in 2006 than in 2005, maybe the glass ceiling is 'double glazed.' The glass ceiling and the idea of it being double glazed are both examples of concepts. At a more basic level you will learn about concepts such as norms, values, status and roles in the first part of your course.

## Studies

The second ingredient you can use is the work and research of sociologists in the form of sociological studies. This involves reading about what they have studied and what their studies found. Their findings may be published in the form of statistics or as text for you to read, or a combination of the two. You will spend a great deal of time in sociology lessons reading, learning and considering the work of sociologists. Most sociologists use concepts in their studies and some sociologists generate new concepts through their research.

## Methods

In carrying out their research, sociologists use different methods to collect their data. These methods include questionnaires, interviews and observation. It is important for sociologists to understand the reasons for using particular methods and the implications these methods may have on the findings of the research. A key part of Unit 1 will require you to study the use of different methods in the context of research sociologists have carried out.

## Theory

A theory is all about taking a particular viewpoint or stance. A theory is a way of looking at an issue and all sociologists need to make it clear which theories they have used in their research. This is where sociology involves seeing the world in different ways. There are a number of grand theories which offer different and competing perspectives on social life and if sociologists use these theories in their work then we must bear that in mind when considering their work. You will come across some theory in Unit 1, but theory plays a more significant role in Unit 2 of the course.

## Contemporary examples

By 'contemporary examples' we mean events in society that can inform sociology and may not yet have been studied, or events that are happening as sociologists carry out their research. Contemporary examples that we could use as we write this book include the debates surrounding the television show Celebrity Big Brother. In 2007, the celebrity Jade Goody was voted out of the Big Brother house following accusations of racist bullying against housemate Shilpa Shetty, a leading Bollywood star. This case could be used to illustrate racial discrimination and prejudice, social class and gender issues, or the power of the British media in making and breaking celebrities. Using contemporary examples from the world around you is an important part of your sociology course, but they are not enough on their own to make you good sociologists.

During your sociology course you will become familiar with the different ingredients explained above. You need to use them and blend them in becoming skilled and successful sociologists and the next activity allows you to do that.

The following items all relate in some way to the topic of marriage. You need to study them carefully and then answer the four questions at the end.

## Item A: sociological studies

Figure 3 is a graph showing data about the different living arrangements of men and women in the UK. The graph is followed by some written information from the same studies.

Further evidence from this sociological study tells us that despite the decrease in the numbers of people marrying, marriage remains the main type of partnership for men and women in the UK. In 2004–5, around half of men and women living in the UK were married and one in ten were cohabiting. The average age at which people get married in England and Wales has risen by more than three years since 1995. It was 36 for men and 33 for women in 2005.

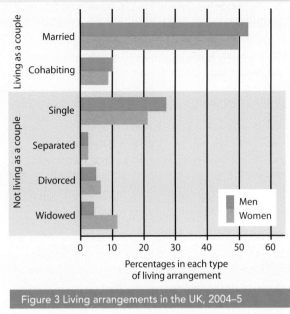

Figure 3 Living arrangements in the UK, 2004–5

(Sources: Office for National Statistics, 2004–5; 2005a; 2005b)

## Item B: sociological concepts

### Cohabitation

This is the word used to describe the situation of two people who live together as a couple but who are not married. Rates of cohabitation increased as marriage rates declined in the 1980s and the 1990s.

### Consumerism

This is another concept used to describe the way in which many people in the UK spend vast amounts of their earnings on consumer (durable/usable) goods. The average cost of a wedding in the UK is in excess of £20,000 and it could be argued that the fact that this is so high reflects the large number of designer weddings.

## Item C: sociological theories

Below are two possible theories about marriage.

One theory is that marriage has a positive impact on an individual's life. Through marriage, individuals form bonds which open up new opportunities for happiness. We can call this a consensus approach as it is based on consensus theory.

A different theory or stance on marriage would be that it creates conflict in an individual's life. By getting married individuals lose their freedom and become controlled in ways that they did not foresee. This is one of the viewpoints that could explain the high rates of divorce seen in the UK during the 1980s and 1990s. We can call this a conflict approach as it is based on conflict theory.

### Item D: contemporary examples

Many Hindus living in the UK have traditional wedding ceremonies. Notice the henna (*mehandi*) patterned hands and the bracelets, which both form an important part of the Hindu marriage (Figure 4).

### Item E: sociological methods

When studying marriage, one of the obvious methods to use are statistics based on the number of marriages taking place each year. These are available from the national statistics website on the internet (see 'Websites' page ii). A different way of studying marriage would be to interview people who have recently got married, or who are planning to be married soon.

Figure 4 A traditional Hindu bride

1 (a) Devise five questions that you would ask a recently married couple if you were researching the reasons why people get married in the UK today.

(b) Why might it be better to interview individuals rather than couples?

2 Study Figures 4 and 5 and explain what they tell us about marriage in the UK.

3 Using the information from items A–E, write a 300-word account (one side of A4) explaining what they tell us about marriage in the UK in the twenty-first century.

This activity has introduced you to some of the skills needed to be successful in sociology. You will be assessed on your knowledge and understanding, your interpretation and application of this knowledge in relation to social issues and your evaluation of sociological

Figure 5 A traditional bride and her bridesmaids in the UK

material and ideas. Students can struggle with the skills of evaluation; you are advised to think about criticisms of ideas, theories and studies throughout this course. All of the sections contain material which can be used to enhance your evaluation; theories can be used alongside each other to show different approaches to the same topic (as in question 1 above on marriage); or specific points of criticism or praise can be used in relation to concepts/studies or theories. Further guidance on developing and illustrating the skill areas is given in the Exam Café.

In this Introduction we have described the main ingredients available to sociologists. You must keep these in mind throughout your study. You are now in a position to work through the main content of the AS sociology course. The starting point for the course is Unit 1, which explores the core concepts of socialisation, culture and identity. You will then go on to study at least one of the topics from Unit 2 in detail. As you progress through the course, remember that the Exam Café and the Glossary are both there to help you.

# Unit 1

# Exploring socialisation, culture and identity

- The formation of culture
- The process of socialisation
- The role of socialisation in the creation of identities
- Exploring the research process
- Exploring the use of quantitative data collection methods and analysis in the context of research
- Exploring the use of qualitative data collection methods and analysis in the context of research
- Exploring the use of mixed methods in the context of research
- Exam Café

# The formation of culture

## Pause for thought

1   If someone is described as 'cultured', what does it mean?

2   Does everyone have a culture?

3   What are important parts of your culture?

Figure 1.1 A Traveller culture

Sociologists use the concept of culture in different ways. It is a contested concept, with no agreed common definition. Williams (1983) used culture to describe a 'way of life', focusing on the beliefs and customs of a society or social group. In the case of the Traveller community in Figure 1.1, they would have their own culture, their own way of life. Sociologists agree that culture is created by society or groups living within a society. This section introduces you to the concept of culture, including different types of culture and the process of how culture is created and how it spreads within a society. We begin by considering how individuals learn and acquire a culture. Sociologists argue that learning a culture involves learning the norms and values of society.

# Norms

A **norm** is a form of behaviour, a common form of behaviour which most people in a society follow. Norms have generally been established over time, passed on from generation to generation and adapted to fit the changing social climate. In this sense, although norms are based on consensus (agreement), they are not fixed and unchangeable. Examples of norms in the contemporary UK include:

◆ wearing a seat belt when in a car

◆ forming queues in an orderly fashion

◆ being quiet when waiting in a doctor's surgery.

Of course, not everyone follows these norms, and when people don't they can be considered 'deviant', meaning going against the norm. Sociologists argue that shared norms play a crucial role in society as a kind of 'social glue' by binding individuals together. Sociologists disagree over where norms come from – whether they come from dominant and powerful groups in society (the rich) or from tradition. To display a norm requires an action, as it is a form of behaviour. Underlying social norms are values.

Fox spent three years observing Englishness and wrote a book based on her observations, trying to understand English culture and to explain what it means to be English. Her book *Watching the English* (Fox, 2004) is a description and commentary on English culture, in which she identifies a number of English norms.

One is the ownership of a mobile phone, which seems to be common practice regardless of class, gender, ethnicity and, increasingly, age. Fox describes how mobile phones are used in a range of different ways, for example youth/teenagers use them as a status symbol, males especially focus on the technological aspects of what they 'can do'. She suggests that women who are alone in coffee bars/social settings may use mobile phones as a form of attachment, a social barrier.

Tea drinking is also considered as an English norm; people frequently suggest that a cup of tea is called for in all kinds of situations from relaxation to dealing with trauma; the cup of tea is considered as having miraculous healing properties.

Activity 1.1

Think of other norms that you would associate with being English or with any other national identity you are familiar with. Share ideas with your class.

# Values

**Values** are general principles or beliefs which the majority of society agrees on. Values develop over time and although largely stable are able to change. Values provide themes which underlie social norms. In our examples above:

◆ wearing a seat belt reflects the value we place on the sanctity of human life

◆ forming orderly queues reflects the values of order and fairness

◆ remaining quiet in a doctor's waiting room reflects the value placed on health and professional advice.

The relationship between norms and values is reflected in Figure 1.2.

Sociologists disagree on whose values become the dominant ones in society; it may be the dominant ethnic group, it may be the values of the rich, or even the politicians who propose the laws of a society.

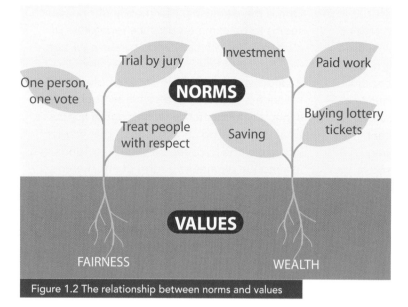

Figure 1.2 The relationship between norms and values

Labels in figure:
Trial by jury
Investment
Paid work
**NORMS**
One person, one vote
Treat people with respect
Saving
Buying lottery tickets
**VALUES**
FAIRNESS
WEALTH

- An ascribed status is given to a person; there is little they can do to change it. It is fixed and very difficult to alter. Being male or female is a good example of an ascribed status; people are born with a sex which is difficult, although not impossible, to change. Individuals such as Prince William also have an ascribed status through his inherited role as the future king.

- An achieved status is earned; it is based on merit/talent or action. In this sense it is changeable and highly likely to change over time. Gaining a job in your chosen area of interest or excelling at a sport are both examples of achieved status, as are becoming a parent or achieving GCSE grades that reflect your effort. An individual such as Madonna has achieved her status through her work as a singer and celebrity, helped along by constant exposure in the media. Achieved status is considered as an important feature of life in the contemporary UK.

Activity 1.2

1 Make a list of five norms in the contemporary UK.

2 Share your list with others. Do you agree that all of these are norms?

3 If you disagree, what is the source of the disagreement?

4 For each norm, discuss the value/s that underlie it.

Activity 1.3

The following three people all occupy a particular status within the contemporary UK. Take each one in turn and make an argument to show how their status could be ascribed or achieved.

- David Beckham
- Paris Hilton
- the Pope

## Status

Status can be held by an individual or by a group. It is based on social position, or standing within society, and has been associated with prestige, honour and social standing. Status relies on the evaluation of social differences, as status can only come from how something/someone is perceived by others. There are positions of high status as well as low status and it is possible to hold both at the same time. For example, someone may have a high status in one setting but a low status in another. Consider a racist activist who is a member of the British National Party (BNP). They may be held in high esteem within the BNP, but occupy a low status position in other areas of social life.

When considering where status comes from, it is useful to distinguish between ascribed status and achieved status.

## Roles

Individuals and groups all perform social roles. A role is a pattern of behaviour; routines or responses acted out in everyday life. We all take on a number of different roles in life and these will change with age and according to the society you live in. Being a student, a sibling or a friend are all roles which bring with them certain expectations. As a student you will be expected to attend classes, participate in learning activities

Copy and complete the table below to identify three roles, apart from being a student, that you play in life.

| Role | Expectations on you | Expectations on others |
|------|---------------------|------------------------|
| Student | Work hard, attend class, be attentive | Teachers: deliver the course, mark your work |
| | | |
| | | |
| | | |

Table 1.1 Roles and expectations

and produce homework. Equally, as a student there are certain expectations you will place on your teacher and school. Roles are closely associated with expected forms of behaviour.

Although roles develop through social processes, we are clearly born into some roles. The role of a son, daughter or sibling is ascribed to people. Other roles develop within the culture we live in and can be embraced or rejected. As individuals take on many different roles, sometimes these roles will conflict with each other, leading to role conflict. For example, there may be times when your role as a student conflicts with your role as a part-time employee. Role conflict is an inevitable feature of contemporary life.

## Culture

The concept of culture is used to describe the beliefs, customs and ways of life of a society or group within a society. However, it is also a contested concept, meaning that sociologists differ in their precise definition of it. Adopting William's (1983) definition of culture as being about 'a way of life' would include all aspects of the way of life of a group within a society: their values, norms, interests and ideas on life. If we define culture in this way it becomes an inclusive definition, able to be applied to many different groups within and between societies. The traveller community shown in Figure 1.1 portrays a particular way of life. Some people would argue that there is a distinct English way of life which differs from the Welsh, Scottish or Irish way of life. Fox's work in Activity 1.1 illustrates some possible features of English culture. It has been suggested

that William's approach to culture is so broad that it becomes meaningless; anything can be part of culture. Woodward (2000) suggests that the culture of society is based on 'shared meanings, values and practices' (p. 22). This definition clearly associates culture with shared norms and values.

Other sociologists have taken a more exclusive approach to defining culture, suggesting that there is a high culture, based on access to and involvement in elite practices. For writers such as Leavis (1933), high culture is something to be protected in society.

1 Working in pairs or small groups, choose a culture from the contemporary UK. Research the norms and values associated with it. The internet, library, family and friends will be rich sources of information.

2 Find some images of the culture and present your findings as either a poster or a blog. Some ideas are given below to help you.

You could choose from the following, or select one of your own:

- a national culture (British, Chinese, English etc.)

- any religious group (Buddhists, Hindus, Quakers)

- a subculture (emo, punk, rap, bhangara)

- a local/regional culture (Geordie, traveller, Scouse, Cornish).

Figure 1.3 shows different features you may want to consider.

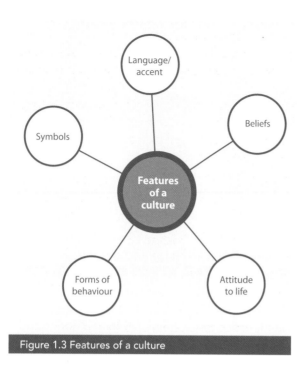

Figure 1.3 Features of a culture

## Different types of culture

Because there are different definitions of culture, there are also different types of culture within society. There are seven different types you need to become familiar with:

- high culture
- popular culture
- cultural diversity
- multiculturalism
- subculture
- consumer culture
- global culture.

## High culture

The concept of high culture is associated with Leavis who was writing in the 1930s. High culture is linked with the elite, upper class in society, those families and individuals with an ascribed status position. It is associated with the arts such as opera, ballet and classical music, sports such as polo and lacrosse, and leisure pursuits such as hunting and shooting. Clearly, high culture is associated with a small elite in society, who, it is argued, operate a system of social closure – not allowing entry to 'outsiders' – thus ensuring that high culture maintains its elite and exclusive position. This is possible as this group have a privileged position in the contemporary UK, both economically and socially.

Some sociologists have questioned whether high culture still exits in the contemporary UK. As more people can now achieve their status and super-rich lifestyles, they can buy access to high culture.

Figure 1.4 Afternoon tea on the lawn at Glyndebourne: high culture

## Popular culture

One of the reasons for questioning the existence of high culture is the rise of 'popular culture'. These two types of culture can be seen as opposites. Popular culture is associated with shallow activities enjoyed and accessed by the masses. Strinati (1995) argues that the media are largely responsible for creating popular culture in the contemporary UK, and that consumption (material goods people buy and use) plays a key role in popular culture. Through digital television and mass communication, the world has become more consumer orientated and popular culture feeds this obsession with images of designer consumer goods and by placing a high value on materialism.

It could be argued that popular culture at times borrows an idea from high culture and popularises it, making it available to the masses. Consider how the sport of golf, once associated with the upper classes, has become more widespread, or how musicians such as Nigel Kennedy and Vanessa Mae have popularised classical music, or how art galleries such as the Baltic in Gateshead or Tate Modern in London provide popular venues for days out for the masses. The use of the Burberry check is another example of how a fashion symbol of the elite has been transformed and popularised.

Some sociologists argue that popular culture is a product of the media-dominated world; that it is a positive force because it brings people of different backgrounds together in a common culture. Others, such as Adorno, take a more sceptical view of it and see it as a way in which the masses can be socialised into being preoccupied with trivial matters, deflecting their interest from important social concerns.

### Activity 1.6

Think of examples to illustrate what popular culture is. Use the following headings and give examples to illustrate each one.

- Newspapers
- Television programmes
- Holiday destinations
- Sports

## Subculture

A subculture is a culture enjoyed by a small group within society. In this sense it is a minority part of majority culture. Subcultures have distinct norms and values which make them a sub-section of society. Examples of subcultures in the UK include youth groups such as emos and skaters, or religious groups such as the Scientologists. New Age traveller groups could also be described as subcultures.

Some subcultures develop in opposition to authority. This is the case with some youth sub-cultural groups, which is explained in depth in Unit 2, Section 5, Youth (pp. 244–278). New religious movements can also be used as examples, where people are searching for more meaning in their lives; these are considered in Unit 2, Section 4, Religion (pp. 207–243).

Membership of subcultures changes over time, as do the types of subculture within a society. In this sense, subcultures can be seen to reflect the changing nature of society and its concerns. Many people associate themselves with subcultures during the period of young adulthood, and then move away from them in time. Other people stay attached to the group in some way for their whole life.

## Cultural diversity

This is a concept relating to culturally-embedded differences within society. A society can be culturally diverse in many ways. Parekh (2006) outlines three types of diversity.

1   When members of society have distinct ways of life while still broadly serving the dominant culture within a society. Groups such as gays and lesbians are trying to open society up, to diversify what is accepted as the norm.

2   Some members of a society rebel against the central principles, rejecting the dominant values. The environmental group 'Reclaim the Streets' is a good example.

3   Communal diversification, where ethnic groups have long-established communities adding diversity to the dominant way of life, such as the Bangladeshi communities living in East London.

There is a huge body of evidence showing that the contemporary UK is a culturally diverse society; class, gender, ethnicity and sexuality are all dimensions of this diversity. Most large cities have areas famous for their distinct ways of life: gay areas, ethnically-diverse areas, ethnically- concentrated areas (such as China Town), areas of high-class housing and areas which are more mixed in terms of housing and business where shops sell ethnically-diverse food and material goods.

Cultural diversity does not necessarily mean the decline of cultural sameness (**homogeneity**). It is still possible for a society to have diversity but agree on fundamental norms and values which bind them together.

## Multiculturalism

There is much debate about the precise definition of multiculturalism. Parekh (2006) sees it as very similar to cultural diversity. Other writers align multiculturalism with different ethnic groups living side-by-side in society. This definition would make the UK a multicultural society with 8.9 per cent of the population coming from minority ethnic backgrounds. Multiculturalism promotes the belief that ethnic groups are all of the same status, having an equal right to preserve their own cultural heritage. Barker (2003) considers a multicultural society as seeking to celebrate difference, through, for example, the teaching of multi-faith religious education and the celebration of a range of ethnically-diverse festivals.

### Activity 1.7

1 Find out about the traditional diet of your parents or grandparents when they were growing up.

2 What types of food do you and your friends eat today?

3 How far has multiculturalism influenced diet in the contemporary UK?

Multiculturalism is related to patterns of migration, in terms of where migrant groups have come from, particularly in the last 50 years.

Figure 1.5 Chinatown: cultural diversity

There has been a debate regarding whether a multicultural society is a positive entity or whether it encourages separatism. A model of multiculturalism has operated in Britain for over 40 years. Some argue that this has resulted in riots and racial conflict in society and that cultural differences make it impossible for ethnically diverse groups to live together without conflict.

## Consumer culture

A consumer culture is clearly related to the things we consume and use in society. It is widely accepted that the contemporary UK is a consumer society. A **consumer culture** is based on cultural and economic factors. Culturally, the society portrays a sense of its identity through the consumer goods available, but the economic conditions within a society are also crucial in the creation of a consumer culture.

Lury (1996) identifies some features of a consumer culture. These include:

◆ the availability of a wide range of consumer goods

◆ that shopping is seen as a leisure pursuit

◆ that different forms of shopping are available – large shopping centres, the Internet, local shops

◆ that being in debt is accepted as a social norm

◆ that the packaging and promotion of goods is a large-scale business.

### Activity 1.8

Take each of Lury's features and consider the extent to which the UK has a consumer culture. Use examples from everyday life to illustrate each feature.

## Global culture

Globalisation is the process by which events in one part of the world come to influence what happens elsewhere in the world. The world has become increasingly interconnected; socially,

Figure 1.6 Piccadilly Circus: global and consumer culture

The formation of culture

politically and economically. Economically, the world's stock markets are connected because of international investment. Politically, world leaders have a particular interest in who they ally themselves with and why. Socially, trends and fashions in the large cities spread quickly to other cities; fashion in Paris is likely to impact on styles in New York and London.

Globalisation means that nations are no longer individual or isolated countries, so that to understand societies and social change we have to look beyond the boundaries of a single country.

A global culture is a key feature of the process of globalisation. A global culture has emerged due to patterns of migration, trends in international travel and the spread of the media, exposing people to the same images from the same dominant world companies. Global culture means the world has become a smaller place, a 'global village' (McLuhan,1989) where cultural homogeneity is a key feature. The concepts of Americanisation and 'McDonaldisation' have been used to raise the possibility that global culture is basically American culture.

Cultures are formed when individuals and groups learn, acquire and respond to social norms and values. We are not born into a culture; culture is developed over time. Some sociologists consider this a process of social discovery; others consider it a process of indoctrination where culture is enforced from above. Institutions such as the media and education play a huge role in the creation of culture. Section 2 considers the process of socialisation which effectively leads to the creation and reinforcement of culture and various identities. Sociologists argue that culture is socially created and reinforced. Cultures differ between societies and they change over time which makes them very important topics for sociologists to understand.

1 Name ten global companies.

2 What do think are the positive features of a global culture?

3 Can you think of any problems with a global culture?

4 Share your ideas with others in the class.

5 Using the ideas from the class discussion, write a 250-word account (one side of A4) outlining and explaining your views on global culture.

## Weblinks

There are websites available which give information on globalisation and global culture (see 'Websites' page ii). You can access further details on some global companies.

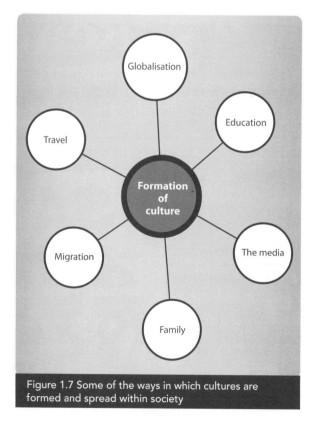

Figure 1.7 Some of the ways in which cultures are formed and spread within society

U1
1

The formation of culture

## Section summary

Use the following key words to copy and complete the summary of this section below. Each word should be used only once.

values   status   culture   high culture   popular culture   norms   consumer culture
culturally diverse   subcultures   achieved status   ascribed status   role
multiculturalism   global culture

_____is a contested concept, which means there is no agreed way of defining it. Sociologists agree that culture is created through individuals and groups learning the _____ and _____ of a society. _____ plays an important part in most cultures, as social standing is important in influencing the _____ an individual plays in society. Sociologists distinguish between _____ _____ and an _____ _____. Both are important features of life in the contemporary UK.

There are many different types of culture in the UK. It has been described as a _____ _____ society where individuality and group differences are freely expressed. The diversity of ethnic groups in the UK has led to the concept of _____ being applied. Similarities and differences between different ethnic groups may be influenced by the _____ _____ in which the world becomes more interconnected.

_____ are groups with their own norms and values; a distinct part of mainstream society. There is a view that the media have played a large part in creating _____ _____ which has challenged the view that culture is something that only the rich/elite can have, known as _____ _____. Perhaps that most accurate use of culture in the UK today is that of _____ _____ which is based on what we buy and consume.

## Exam practice

(a) Define the concept of popular culture. Illustrate your answer with examples.

(8 marks)

(b) Outline and explain two ways in which the contemporary UK is culturally diverse.

(16 marks)

# The process of socialisation

## Pause for thought

1   Who were the most influential people in your life from birth to being 5 years old?

2   Who were the most influential people in your life from when you were 5 years old to 16 years old?

3   Who are the most influential people in your life now?

Figure 2.1 The peer group: an agent of socialisation

From birth onwards all individuals go through a process of **socialisation** during which they learn the norms and values of their society. This section considers that process.

# Biological and social factors

The extent to which individuals are born with natural and unchangeable differences is a well-debated topic. There is an argument that individuals are born inherently different and that natural differences that exist between individuals are fixed and largely unchangeable. For example, males and females are born with different biological features, ascribing a sex to them, and it could be argued that this different biological makeup forms the basis of the social differences that develop between men and women. For example, most women are born with the ability to produce and give birth to children and men are not, which may explain why many women take on the dominant role in childcare in many families.

Sociologists do not ignore the significance of biological influences on a person's life but they are more interested in the role played by social influences. The difference between biological

and social factors is sometimes described as the **nature/nurture** debate, the extent to which natural inborn factors influence an individual's life chances compared with the influence of social factors that society itself creates. This could be viewed in terms of the question: Are we born or are we created?

It is often difficult, if at all possible, to separate biological influences from social influences. In some instances social factors influence seemingly biological factors such as the choice a person makes about the colour of their hair. In other cases biological factors may influence social ones; it may be the case that Mike (see Figure 2.2) has a natural aptitude for maths and numeracy, which partially explains his choice of studying for a degree in that subject. In short, social factors and biological factors are not always easy to distinguish. Sociologists are aware of this and although they more interested in social influences (nurture) they do consider biological factors as and when necessary.

# Processes of socialisation

Socialisation is the process that individuals go through when learning the way of life of a

---

Meet Mike

Figure 2.2 Mike

Mike is a 17-year-old male. He is 5 foot 8 inches tall with dark brown hair and brown eyes. His hobbies include reading science fiction books and playing football. He is taking four A Levels, in Maths, History, Psychology and Sociology, and he hopes to go to university and study for a degree in Maths and Law.

1 Which of Mike's features are a product of biological factors?

2 Which features are likely to be produced by social influences?

3 Are there any of his features that may be a product of both biological and social factors? If so, name them and explain your thinking.

particular society. Socialisation includes the process of nurturing: the way in which individuals are taught and learn the rules and regulations of social life and the norms and values of the group or society they live in. Parents, teachers, friends and work colleagues are all involved in this learning process and they all play a part in ensuring that culture is transmitted from one generation to the next. Understanding socialisation is crucial to sociologists, as it demonstrates the way in which societies are able to function effectively without falling into chaos and disorder. There are two types of socialisation: primary and secondary.

## Primary socialisation

**Primary socialisation** begins at birth and remains with individuals during the early years of life. The period from birth to the age of four or five years old, when most children start full-time school, is generally viewed as the time where family and parents play the most crucial role. For this reason the family is seen as the most significant agent of primary socialisation. However, changes in childcare patterns in recent years mean that day care nurseries and childminders could be considered as primary agents of socialisation too. Arguably, the **media** play an increasingly important role here too, with television channels such as CBeebies and CITV aimed specifically at pre- and school-age children.

## Secondary socialisation

**Secondary socialisation** starts when children begin to be more independent, usually at the point of beginning full-time education. From the age of four or five most children begin to spend longer periods of time away from their primary carers, most notably in school but also in clubs and in after-school care. At this point other social influences become increasingly significant in their lives, friends and teachers in particular. The process of secondary socialisation includes agents such as education, **peer group**, religion, media and, in later life, the workplace. This does not mean that the family is no longer important in how an individual learns the culture of a society but rather that the socialisation process becomes multidimensional.

## Agents of socialisation

The agents of socialisation are the institutions that are significant in the process of learning the norms, values and culture of a society. There are six key agents of socialisation that we need to consider:

◆ family

◆ education

◆ media

◆ religion

◆ peer group

◆ workplace.

The remainder of this section considers each of these in turn and begins to look at the role they play in the socialisation process.

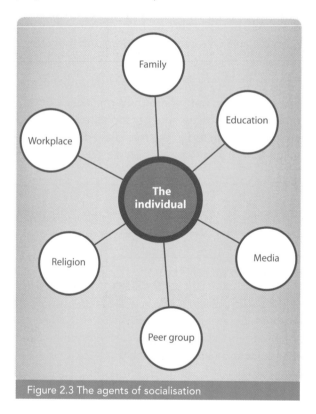

Figure 2.3 The agents of socialisation

## Family

The family is often considered as the bedrock or cornerstone of society. A stable family comprising a man and woman who are married, caring for their own children, is described as a **nuclear family** and has been presented as the ideal family type in the contemporary UK. In 2004, of the seventeen million families in the UK around 70 per cent were headed by a married couple with an average of 1.8 children per family. However, many individuals in the UK do not live in nuclear families. In 2004, one in four dependent children lived in single-parent families. Some individuals live in extended family units where more than two generations of relatives share a home, most commonly with grandparents but also sometimes with aunts and uncles. It is estimated that ten per cent of all families with dependent children in 2004 were reconstituted families or what is commonly known as step families (Office for National Statistics, Labour Force Survey, 2004).

There is a debate within sociology concerning the extent to which the contemporary UK has a diversity of families. There are clearly a number of different family structures and family sizes throughout the UK. However, we should not forget that not all children live in family units. In 2001, 139,000 children were living in other household types in the UK, living with adults who were not their parents, and a further 52,000 under-16 year olds lived in communal establishments such as children's homes (*Social Trends*, 2001).

## Family relationships

Clearly, family size and structure will have an impact on relationships within the family unit and on family life. A family with two parents and one child, with grandparents living 200 miles away will have a different set of family relationships from a reconstituted family who all live in the same geographical area and where two mothers and two fathers are involved in childcare. Maintaining contact with grandparents and extended family is often reliant on technology, with the internet and email providing an opportunity for enhanced communication and relationships.

The following factors have all been identified as having an impact on family relationships.

◆ The extent to which parents balance work with family life. The concept of shift parenting has been used to describe situations where both parents are in paid employment, often working complementary shifts and sharing responsibility for the children around their working lives and shift patterns. These families rarely spend quality family time together, as their lives are based around employment and childcare.

◆ The number, age and even gender of siblings will impact on family relationships.

◆ As life expectancy increases in the UK a different dimension to family life is emerging, as adults are increasingly likely to be involved in caring for their parents into old age for a longer period than in the past.

## Family as an agent of socialisation

The family is the main agent of primary socialisation for most individuals in the contemporary UK. Three ways in which the family socialises the young are given below.

◆ The family teaches the basic norms and values of everyday life. This is often through a process of imitation, where children copy the behaviour of family members, or where children learn the social roles expected of them by looking at **role models** within the family unit. Basic norms such as how to eat food and the time and place for family mealtimes are passed on by the family. These basic norms can reflect wider values, such as the importance of family mealtimes for maintaining close relationships.

◆ Socialisation within the family can also come from the use of positive and negative sanctions, such as praising a child when they behave in the way a parent wants them to, for example giving stickers to young children as a reward. When parents want to discourage inappropriate behaviour they can use negative sanctions, such as withholding computer time.

◆ **Gender roles** within the family are also likely to impact on a child's socialisation. If a young boy sees his father going out to work every day and taking the role of the main wage earner, while his mum stays at home taking the role of homemaker, it is likely to have on impact on how he will view gender roles in family life. This does not mean that he will copy the norm of being the man who is the main wage earner/ breadwinner or that he will share the same value of believing that men are providers and women are carers, but his formative experience is likely to influence his decisions and pathway later in his life.

Figure 2.4 A family at mealtime

Activity 2.2

Study Figure 2.4 and identify norms that are being established. What values might these norms be promoting?

The process through which families socialise their children will depend on a number of different factors. Structural issues such as family size and geographical issues such as where other significant family members live will have an impact, but factors such as social class and ethnicity are also likely to play a significant part in the socialisation process.

# Education

Most children begin full-time schooling at the age of four or five. At this point they begin to interact and socialise with a wider number and type of individuals. Starting full-time school means that children have to learn to adapt to a new set of rules, regulations and cultural expectations. During the eleven years of compulsory schooling (5–16) pupils are constantly reminded of hierarchy and the importance of social order.

Just as there are different family types, so there are a number of different types of school. Most children in the UK attend state-funded schools, although a growing number attend private school (some are also called public schools) paid for by their families, with a small proportion gaining scholarships. There are religious schools, single-sex schools, grammar schools and specialist status schools, among others. The type of school you attend will greatly influence your experience of schooling because expectations, norms and values differ between schools. However, there are two crucial processes of social learning operating in any school and pupils are influenced daily by both: the **formal** and the **informal (hidden) curriculum**.

## Formal curriculum

The formal curriculum comprises the subjects that you are taught in school, including the content of the lessons. During compulsory schooling this is decided by the government in the form of a National Curriculum. Few people would argue with the National Curriculum's emphasis on the foundation subjects of numeracy, literature and science, but many have questioned the type of literacy taught or the lack of practical work in science. Beyond the foundation subjects some critics question why

Table 2.1 shows five qualities that parents may want to see in their children. The qualities include some norms and some values. Copy the table and then state two ways in which a family could socialise their children in order to achieve each quality. The first one has been done for you.

Using the information in Table 2.1, write a paragraph explaining how the process of socialisation works in a family. Include the following concepts in your answer and at least three examples from Table 2.1 (or from qualities you think are important for children to learn).

- Norms
- Values
- Gender roles
- Sanctions
- Imitation
- Role models

| Quality | Example 1 | Example 2 |
| --- | --- | --- |
| To use a toilet | Potty training and using rewards such as stickers to reinforce positive achievement | Imitation of adult use |
| To eat a balanced diet | | |
| To show thanks | | |
| To believe in free speech | | |
| To be a vegetarian | | |

Table 2.1 Qualities that parents may want to see in their children

modern foreign languages are not compulsory and why many history topics focus on British history. The National Curriculum has been described by some critics as an **ethnocentric** curriculum, which means that it teaches British values and culture as being dominant over others (Gillborn, 1990). In education today, the formal curriculum will determine what children learn and to some extent their achievement in school.

## Informal curriculum

The informal curriculum is also known as the hidden curriculum and is responsible for teaching children the everyday rules and regulations of school life. In this sense the informal curriculum plays a crucial role in the socialisation of pupils, as it is responsible for the transmission of the norms and values crucial to survival in a classroom setting. Issues such as the importance of punctuality, what is expected at the beginning of a class, how to queue outside a classroom, the places to gather in at breaktime and the places to avoid are all learnt via the hidden curriculum. They are learnt by talking to other children, listening to stories from older children/ siblings, watching and imitating others. The hidden curriculum will differ hugely depending on the type of school attended but it cannot be escaped. What children learn is not formally taught to them, but it is the way in which the rules, the regulations, the culture and the expectations of the school are passed on.

Sometimes the formal and the informal curriculum overlap, for example with school uniform. Most schools will have a formal uniform policy that pupils must follow. However, it is through informal learning that pupils understand how far they can deviate from the uniform policy. This is particularly the case with a uniform policy which states that blazers and ties must be worn. If

teachers don't enforce such a policy then children learn that wearing these is not compulsory. They have learnt this through the hidden curriculum and it may have an important bearing on how they view other school rules and regulations.

## Education as an agent of socialisation

◆ Subject knowledge is likely to impact on what children learn about the culture of their society. For example, if children were taught that all good scientists were male this would have an impact on how they viewed science and gender issues. The content of lessons therefore plays an important role in the socialisation process.

◆ School rules and policies also play an important part in socialising pupils. Teachers play a crucial role in this process, sometimes acting as role models but also through their use of positive and negative sanctions: rewarding/praising or reprimanding/punishing. Teaching assistants and other staff in school are also important in setting standards and expectations of behaviour from pupils.

In short, education socialises individuals into the culture of a school, which involves learning new norms and values, understanding different social roles and, for most schools, appreciating the importance of achieved status.

### Activity 2.4

Read the following four statements about the purpose of education.

• Education is all about passing exams and getting the highest grades.

• Education is all about becoming a more confident learner.

• Education should encourage people to be creative.

• Education should be about learning to be a good British citizen.

1 Think about each one and write down whether you agree or disagree with it.

2 For each one write a sentence explaining your view.

When you share your views with others you are likely to find that there is a difference in your views, especially if you have attended different schools. The educational experiences you have referred to are also likely to differ, which suggests that education socialises individuals in different ways.

## Media

The mass media is arguably the most dominant agent of socialisation for young people in the UK today. The mass media comprises a number of different media through which ideas and messages are transmitted. Television, radio, film, DVD, internet, text messaging, billboard advertising and the print media (newspapers/ magazines) are all examples of media that collectively are known as the mass media. It is difficult to imagine any individual growing up in the contemporary UK whose life is untouched by the media in one way or another. Research with 11 to 16 year olds in 2004 found that 91 per cent of young people owned a mobile phone (Madell, 2006). In 2005, 16 year olds spent on average two and a half hours a day watching television. When you consider that major multinational businesses all have marketing departments which are responsible for selling the image of products through advertising, you begin to realise the powerful impact that television and advertising can have.

As consumers of media we use them to access information but we also as use them as a means of communicating with each other. The mass media is not a one-dimensional tool sending out messages and images to influence the way we think and act, it is a multidimensional tool that we use and consume.

### The media as an agent of socialisation

The media socialises individuals in a variety of ways.

◆ Through its representation of social groups within society. Sociological research shows how the media representation of social groups changes over time. Research findings show that 20 years ago women in the media tended to be portrayed in a limited number of ways and usually as being of secondary importance to men. Research by McRobbie into a popular 1970s girls' magazine called *Jackie* showed how young women were being encouraged to value romance and

Figure 2.6 Range of magazines in the UK

getting and keeping a man. McRobbie has since used the concept of 'slimblondeness' to describe an archetypal slim blonde female which featured heavily in the media and encouraged young women to copy this appearance. More recently, Currie (1999) analysed the content of teen magazines spanning a 40-year period and noticed a dramatic increase in the importance of beautification in recent years. The growth in the significance of men's magazines in recent years cannot be overlooked. Magazines such as *Loaded*, *FHM*, *GQ* and *Maxim* could be seen as outcomes of the consumer society and men's relationship with it. These magazines are targeting consumer-conscious males.

Similar findings emerge from studies on other social groups such as the elderly, ethnic minorities and the working class.

◆ The media is likely to have an influence on its audiences. This is not to say that individuals believe everything they see, read or hear in the media but rather that images and stories presented in the media will influence attitudes and possibly behaviour to some extent. There are a number of different sociological explanations of the effect of the media in society. Some theories suggest a direct effect, where whatever media we consume influence our attitudes/behaviour straight away. Others suggest a more indirect effect, where media we consume influence us through how our friends/family react to them, or have a drip effect, influencing us gradually over time.

◆ There have been a number of high profile cases in the media where media imagery has apparently led to 'copycat' incidents, that is, the imitation of events/scenes seen in the media. Recently, emo music has been accused of affecting its audience by producing music/lyrics and emotional outbursts on stage that can lead to self-harm. While there may be some truth in this claim, it is not possible to isolate the media as a cause of any one type of social behaviour, and therefore the debate on the influence of the media in society is likely to continue.

◆ The media plays an important role in the creation of the consumer culture. Brand names compete with each other via the media and often use celebrity role models to sell the images of their products. A good example here is the supermodel Kate Moss who famously dated Pete Doherty and modelled for Chanel and H&M, among others. However, following her conviction for possession of a class A drug she was sacked by Chanel and H&M. Clearly, as a supermodel with an iconic boyfriend, Moss had been attractive to a number of companies as she could sell their images to a worldwide, rich audience. But, following drugs charges, Moss became seen as a liability and the companies did not want a supermodel with a drugs conviction as their main face. Since being dropped by these companies Moss has regained her supermodel and super rich status, now

1 Make a list of all of the media you can identify in the cartoon.

2 What kinds of messages might this person be receiving?

Figure 2.7 The media-dominated society

designing and modelling for Top Shop. This case illustrates the power of role models in selling a product (or not), and suggests any media coverage positive or negative may have an advantage in a commercial setting.

# Religion

With many different religious groups in society there will inevitably be clashes over faith. The contemporary UK considers itself as valuing religious freedom and practising religious tolerance, which means that individuals and groups are free to practise their own religions without fear of persecution (providing their activities fall within the law).

The strength of religion in society is a heated topic in sociology. Many writers argue that the UK is undergoing a process of **secularisation**, where religion is losing its influence in society. However, critics of this view point to the strength of many religious groups in terms of membership and religious practice and suggest that religion is not declining but rather is changing. Voas and Crockett (2005) explore the concept of believing without belonging (BWB) in the UK and concluded that there is a strong relationship between religious belief and belonging to a religious organisation.

Most sociologists argue that religion in the UK has become more privatised, a matter of personal choice and sometimes a lifestyle choice. Celebrities such as Madonna and her affiliation to the Kabbalah faith and Tom Cruise's attachment to Scientology have led to an interest in new religious movements. Alongside the main world religions of Buddhism, Christianity, Judaism and Islam there are many new interpretations of faith available in the contemporary UK. There is also a trend in the UK towards the growth of spiritualist and New Age movements, so maybe this is a new type of religion.

---

**Activity 2.6**

Choose one of the following religious groups (or any other that you would find in the contemporary UK):

- Kabbalah
- Scientology
- Rastafarianism
- Zen Buddhism.

For the group you have selected find out the following:

- Where did it originate from?
- What values does it uphold?
- What norms does it follow?
- How does a person join?

---

**Weblinks**

There are many websites on religious groups and movements (see 'Websites' page ii) which you can access for more information and examples.

---

## *Religion as an agent of socialisation*

The extent to which religion influences and even controls members is another heated sociological topic. The following is a list of ways in which religion acts as an agent of socialisation.

◆ Through written rules or through encouraging individuals to follow particular moral codes, different religions promote particular values in society. These values are all supported by norms or patterns of behaviour that religions encourage their members to follow. Most Jewish people do not eat pork (because animals with cloven hoofs are considered 'unclean') and treat Saturday as a rest day. Hindus do not eat beef as they consider the cow to be a sacred animal.

◆ Most religions have a figure of authority or worship who acts as role model to followers. These figures of authority have huge influence over the values of their followers.

◆ Religion can affect males and females in different ways. Consider, for example, different dress codes within religions. Jewish men wear skullcaps and Jewish women don't. Some Muslim women are socialised into the norm of wearing a *hijab* and hiding as much of their body as they can away from men. Other Muslim women are not socialised into this norm but rather choose to wear the *hijab* themselves as an act of empowerment.

◆ There are strong links between religion and ethnicity. Research by Holden (2006) funded by the Home Office examined the attitudes of a large sample of 15 year olds towards race, religion and integration. It found that at a school with predominantly white pupils nearly a third believed that one race was superior to another, compared with a tenth from a majority Asian Muslim school and less than a fifth at a mixed-race school. The study concluded that it would be reasonable to suggest that the Asian Muslim students were the most tolerant. The study also found that many of the students' attitudes came from their parents, suggesting that the role of religion in the socialisation process is related to family background.

◆ In 2006, the British Social Attitudes Survey (BSA, 2006) reported a major decline in religious identity since the 1960s. In 1964, 26 per cent of those interviewed in the survey did not identify with a religion. That figure had risen to 69 per cent in 2006. While religion as a form of social identity has declined, it continues to be strongly related to the values of those who do identify with a religion. On issues such as sex before marriage and euthanasia, religious views clearly influenced other values.

## Peer group

Peer groups are people of a similar age who may also be friends. Peers are probably most influential during the formative years, between the ages of five and eighteen, during the process of growing up and becoming an adult. Peers are important agents of socialisation during this time because most of the time is spent in school together. Skelton and Francis (2003) show how the role of the peer group is essential to understanding the use of playtime in primary schools. Their research shows how playgrounds are dominated by issues of space, where the

Activity 2.7

Study Figure 2.8 and answer the following questions.

1 What religious features can you identify in the picture?

2 Are there any differences between the men and women in the picture?

3 What are all of the people doing?

4 In what way does this image show religion as a source of control in people's lives?

Figure 2.8 Sikh worshippers in a temple in the UK

boys frequently use vast amounts of the space for football, excluding the girls and non-sporty boys. In the same way, girls are seen to exclude boys from activities such as skipping. As children begin to socialise outside school, peers can become even more influential and they continue to have a lasting influence beyond the age of eighteen.

Peer groups can form around issues of rebellion or resistance. For some people resisting the norm and wanting to be individualistic is part of the transitional process of growing up. In these cases peer groups offer an expression of individuality which is difficult to find elsewhere in society. Some youth subcultures such as punks are based on rebellion and resisting the norm (see p. 249). Bennett (2006) studied a group of middle-aged punks in Kent who shared the same interest and enthusiasm for punk music and this gave them the same group coherence they had shared since their young punk days.

## Peer group as an agency of socialisation

Peers encourage each other to conform to shared norms and values; this means that peers can exert pressure on individuals to imitate or to reject group behaviour. Group membership and belonging are important and powerful forces influencing people to conform to fit in.

Within peer groups there are usually significant figures, individuals who have a higher status within the group and who are role models for others. Peer groups are usually based on shared norms and values, for example people who enjoy playing a particular sport or who enjoy a similar type of music.

Sewell (2000) uses the concept of 'cultural comfort zones' to describe how peer groups tend to include people from very similar social backgrounds. In many school canteens/refectories there are groups of students who 'hang around' together and appear to be from the same ethnic background, social class or gender group. Sewell's work focuses particularly on ethnicity, although the same concept could be applied to social class and to groups focused around a sporting interest such as basketball or football. Cultural comfort zones suggest that peer groups form around issues of perceived commonality, what members of the group share in common.

Figure 2.9 An inter-ethnic peer group

Consider your own school or college. Do peer groups form around shared ethnicity (as Sewell suggests) or are peer groups ethnically mixed? Why do you think this happens?

## Peer group pressure

Peer group pressure is an important part of the socialisation process and can be positive or negative. Peer pressure is usually used to encourage conformity, for example pressuring someone to dress in a certain way. Peer group pressure usually means that individuals are encouraged to follow the norms of a group: behaving in a certain way, dressing, talking and often joining in the same activities/hobbies. Clearly, this can involve the adoption of positive norms such as encouraging a healthy lifestyle or involvement in a team sport. On the other hand, peer group pressure can lead to the adoption of negative norms such as encouraging individuals to smoke or to use illegal drugs. Failure to conform to the group's norms can lead to rejection and isolation, which few people want to experience. This is why peer pressure is so influential in the socialisation process.

# Workplace

Most adults experience paid employment at some stage in their lives. Many young people have part-time jobs while they complete their education. The influence of the workplace touches many individuals at some stage in life. However, the changing nature of work and the ability of people to work from home, often through the internet, means that the idea of going to a place of work from 9 o'clock until 5 o'clock is no longer the norm in the contemporary UK. Work has become more flexible than in the past.

It is important to remember that workplaces vary hugely. Consider the difference between the working lives of a teacher who works in a secondary school and a self-employed courier who delivers parcels ordered on ebay. The teacher has a definite place of work, a clear structure to their day and probably a manager or head of department to whom they are responsible. The courier may only be paid for the

work they do each day or week. They are unlikely to have a definite workplace as their work moves around with them and the nature of their work means that they are travelling most of the time. Despite these differences, both workers have to learn the expected norms of their job.

## Workplace as an agent of socialisation

When individuals enter the world of work or when they change their occupation/workplace they go through a process of resocialisation. They have to learn the rules, regulations and associated norms of their new workplace. This includes learning the role(s) for which they have been employed.

Training programmes are usually provided for new members of staff and sometimes mentors will be used to support workers in this process. Also the unwritten rules of the workplace need to be learnt by observing others or through informal discussions with work colleagues. In this sense the workplace can be compared with school, where there is a formal curriculum (lessons) and an informal curriculum (what you learn but are not taught).

In the workplace there will inevitably be dress codes; some workplaces have uniforms, which often portray a clear sense of identity. Consider a police officer's uniform. Few people would

Figure 2.10 A police officer's uniform is easily recognised

be in any doubt of the wearer's occupation and the uniform portrays order and conforming: important values for that job. Other workplaces and occupations may have less rigid dress codes but there will still be ways of dressing appropriately for work and if individuals overdress or underdress this will be noticed.

Workplaces socialise individuals through the same processes as the other agents of socialisation. Through imitation, role models, control and pressuring people, individuals learn where they are placed in the hierarchy of the workplace, how to survive and what they need to do, or who they need to know, to gain promotion.

Ward and Winstanley (2005) studied the process of how workers 'came out' and disclosed their homosexuality in six different types of organisation: the policeforce, the fire brigade, two civil service departments and two banks. They noted that there was more interpersonal activity or informal discussions in the police force and fire service working environments than in the other workplaces. This means that concealing a part of your identity in these workplaces is harder than in others. The study shows how the formal and the informal occupational cultures of police officers and bankers are very different.

## Activity 2.9

Read the following account of a male firefighter describing his thoughts about disclosing his homosexuality to a group of trainee firefighters on a training course, and answer the questions below.

> While I was at a training centre, I didn't want to tell anyone. I'd only known everyone about 10 weeks. I've got enough grief here just trying to get through. Also the male showers were a bit antiquated [old], just one big tiled wall, with shower heads coming out, so it was very open and exposed. And the changing room was just one big room with benches around. I didn't really need the added grief of people all walking out of the shower because I was in there. So I thought I'd just leave it and if anyone asks, I'd tell them. We then had two weeks training in breathing apparatus, we finished that and started the final training.

> At lunchtime I walked into the lockers where all the other lads were sitting and someone started whistling the theme tune from Police Academy, the one they played when they were in a gay bar called the Blue Oyster Club. I walked in, I sat down and they stopped. I thought don't be paranoid, obviously there's a joke going on, you've walked in the middle of it, and you think it's all about you. That Friday, I was in the changing rooms, just cleaning my shoes, and this guy comes in and he's pacing up and down and I could tell he wanted to say something but couldn't. He kept trying to talk to me and he couldn't. It became blindingly obvious what he wanted to ask me, and it's a bit sad really, but I found it quite funny because he was finding it so difficult. Eventually I turned around and said,

> 'What do you want to ask me?'

> 'I can't say.' So I said, 'The answer's yes.'

> There was relief and stuff. That night we all went down the pub.

(Source: Ward and Winstanley, 2005, pp. 461–2)

1 Identify the reasons the interviewee gives for not wanting to disclose his homosexuality at work.

2 What other features of his job and working environment may also explain his reluctance?

# Social control

This section has explained the process of socialisation and how it affects individuals and groups within society. A useful theme in helping to understand the different roles played by the agents of socialisation is social control.

## Formal social control

Formal social control mechanisms are associated with the more formal agents of socialisation. Institutions such as school, university, large workplaces and religious institutions all use formal mechanisms of social control. Formal ways of controlling include written rules or codes of conduct that individuals need to follow. When people deviate from the rules they can expect sanctions to be used. A person who is late for work every day could expect to be reprimanded and warned about punctuality. A student who fails to hand in any coursework for their university course would expect to be sanctioned and would probably fail the course.

## Informal social control

Social control can also be exercised informally. The family, peers and the media all exercise control but without written rules and formal codes of conduct. Instead, they have informal expectations for controlling behaviour. A child who repeatedly comes in late and ignores all curfews on their bedtime could expect their parents to use sanctions such as being grounded or losing time on the family computer, but these sanctions are unlikely to be formally written down and followed. Sanctions from the peer group could involve being left out of group activities because of failure to conform to the group norm. For example, a girl whose peer group all play hockey but who repeatedly misses the practice is likely to be left out of activities related to hockey and may face exclusion from the peer group.

Figure 2.11 could be used to illustrate the difference between formal and informal social

control, but we should not overemphasise the differences as being rigid and fixed. Schools will have formal rules and regulations, but failure to conform to them will rarely lead to expulsion. Teachers use informal methods of social control in the same way as parents to encourage appropriate behaviour. The differences between informal and formal control should not therefore be exaggerated.

The concept of social control is important in understanding how we are socialised into accepting the culture of particular groups in society.

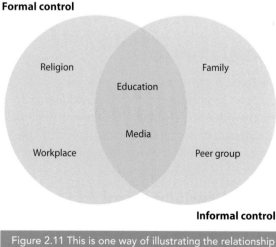

**Formal control**

Religion

Education

Family

Media

Workplace

Peer group

**Informal control**

Figure 2.11 This is one way of illustrating the relationship between formal and informal social control. Can you see any problems with it?

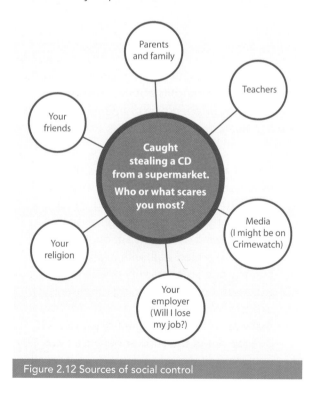

Parents and family

Teachers

Your friends

Caught stealing a CD from a supermarket. Who or what scares you most?

Media (I might be on Crimewatch)

Your religion

Your employer (Will I lose my job?)

Figure 2.12 Sources of social control

identities   primary socialisation   norms   values   family   peers   socialisation   religion
workplace   nature   secondary socialisation   nurture   education   media   cultures   socialisation

There is a debate concerning the extent to which individuals are a product of _____ or _____. _____ is a lifelong process, starting at birth. There are two main types, _____ _____ and _____ _____.

The most important aspect of primary socialisation is the _____. It is responsible for passing on _____ and _____ from one generation to the next.

There are five key agents of secondary socialisation. These are: _____, _____ _____, _____, _____ and _____. These influence the social behaviour of individuals throughout their lifetimes and play a crucial role in the formation of _____ and _____.

## Exam practice

(a) Define the concept of primary socialisation. Use examples to illustrate your answer. (8 marks)

(b) Outline and explain two ways in which an individual's behaviour is socially controlled in the contemporary UK. (16 marks)

(c) Explain and briefly evaluate the view that the family is the most influential agent of socialisation in the contemporary UK. (24 marks)

U1
2

The process of socialisation

# The role of socialisation in the creation of identities

## Identity

### Pause for thought

What do you understand by the following:

- national identity
- identity cards
- identity fraud
- corporate identity?

Figure 3.1 Displaying a national identity

Study Figure 3.1 and identify the symbol of a national identity.

The concept of identity is widely used in the contemporary UK. The example in Figure 3.1 illustrates one of the ways in which identity is used in everyday life. Identity can relate to individual issues and to collective issues. Jenkins (2004) distinguishes individual identity from collective identity. Identity fraud is carried out by individuals taking on the persona of someone else, usually for financial gain. Identity cards are the government's way of tackling issues of citizenship. National identity and corporate identities are more collectively focused, where a group identity and attachment to a shared team, country, company or vision is important. Postmodern sociologists are particularly interested in the concept of identity, seeing it as the main way in which individualism, status and difference is achieved in society.

## What is identity?

Identity is a contested concept, which means there is no agreed way of defining and studying it. A useful way to think about where identity comes from is to use the concepts of sameness and difference.

◆ Identity as sameness is based around the characteristics or features you share with others. This is a crucial aspect of identity because it can push individuals towards adopting particular norms, values or styles. For example, if someone wanted to identify themselves as a goth there are particular places to shop, music to listen to and values to embrace. Identity as sameness is also relevant when you meet someone for the first time. In early conversations and encounters, people try to identify elements of sameness such as shared interests or similar backgrounds. Factors like these are likely to be influential in ascribing an identity to the other person.

◆ Identity as difference can be seen as the opposite, where characteristics or features make you different from others around you. It may be that an individual actively decides to adopt an identity to be different from others. For example, consider a young person who takes an interest in drama and acting as a way of differentiating themselves from the main peer group who are interested in sport. Similarly, we have all seen individuals who we can identify as being different to ourselves, by making simple observations of their behaviour and style.

Woodward (2000) argues that for someone to have an identity, an element of choice is required. Individuals choose to identify with something or somebody, and it is difficult to have an identity unless an individual has exercised some choice in doing so. In this sense, identity is about 'belonging' to something.

Bradley (1996) distinguishes between passive and active identity. A passive identity is one which you were either born into or socialised into. Gender, class, ethnicity and age could all be examples of passive identities. Active identities are those which people actively choose to pursue; being a footballer, a singer in a band or an environmental campaigner are all examples of active identities. However the distinction is not always so clear cut.

Create an individual and give them an identity. Produce a poster clearly showing two things:

- the features of their identity (gender, age etc.)
- how the identity is visible to others.

## Socialisation, culture and identity

Section 3 will consider four forms of identity in detail: gender, social class, ethnicity and age.

In considering these forms of identity, we will look at characteristics of each, how the agents of socialisation covered in Section 2 influence the creation and the reinforcement of these identities, and how culture influences identities, using many of the concepts you were introduced to in Section 1.

# Gender identities

## Pause for thought

1   What have you done in the last week that might be associated with being male?

2   What have you done in the last week that might be associated with being female?

3   How many of the things you did might not be the norm for your gender? Explain why?

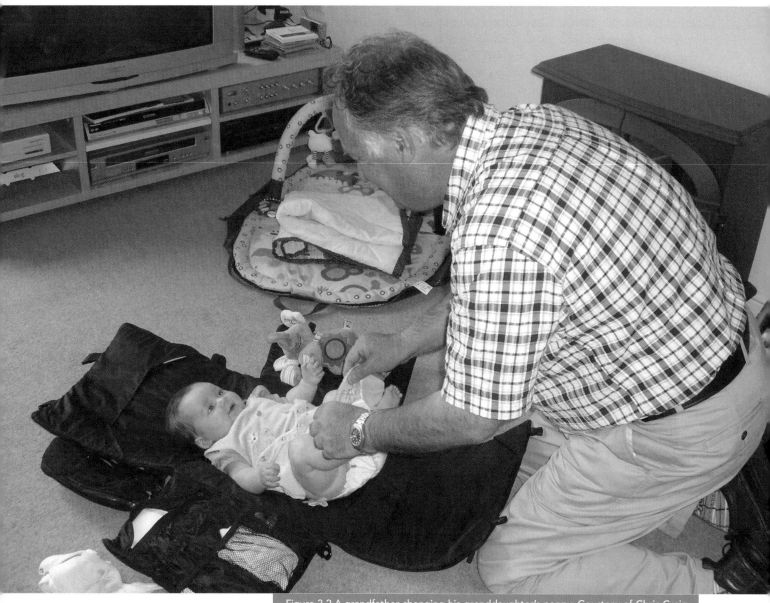

Figure 3.2 A grandfather changing his granddaughter's nappy. Courtesy of Chris Craig

# Sex

Sociologists use 'sex' as a term to classify people as being male or female, based on their biological or physical characteristics. Most people are born with these characteristics: penis and testicles for men, ovaries and, later, breasts for women. There are, however, a few people for whom their sex is unclear. They may, for example, have both male and female sex organs or they may have none. The term intersex, meaning 'between sex', is used to describe people like this. Occasionally, people may feel they have been born as the wrong sex and they sometimes choose to undergo a sex change operation. One of the earliest and most well documented people to have the sex change operation is the travel writer Jan Morris.

## Weblink
For details of Jan Morris's story, see 'Websites' page ii.

# Gender

The term gender is usually used to describe the ways in which men and women may be expected to behave in society. It is a term that describes **socially constructed** behaviour, which means behaviour which is made by, or shaped by, the social world in which we live. Gender is about the construction of masculinity/masculinities and femininity/femininities, of gender identities and gender roles, and is a far more problematic term than sex. For example, in the contemporary UK, the media show images of how women should look, in relation to size and clothes. In the workplace, jobs such as care assistants or plumbers have gender connotations, they are gendered occupations. However, people are questioning these body images and challenging workplace stereotypes.

There are some who take what is described as a biological determinist view of gender, that is, they support the idea that gender is based on biology, and argue that, in all societies, men are essentially aggressive and women essentially

## Activity 3.3

Work in pairs on the following tasks.

(a) Go back to what you wrote in answer to the Pause for thought questions 1 and 2 (p. 30), and take turns to explain whether any of your activities in the last week might be said to be natural.

(b) Think of toys, books, films and language your parents introduced to you that might support the idea that femininities/masculinities are socially constructed. Copy and complete Table 3.1 with your findings.

| Example | Explanation for why it might support the idea that gender is socially constructed |
|---|---|
| Toys | |
| Clothes | |
| Use of language/specific words | |
| Films | |
| Books | |
| Games | |

Table 3.1 Evidence to support the idea that gender is socially constructed

expressive. They contend that these are natural characteristics. However, one of the criticisms of this approach is that it takes little, if any, account of social interaction and the influence of the environment on an individual's gender. Parsons, a functionalist sociologist writing in the 1950s, developed a concept known as sex-role differentiation which went some way towards supporting the biological determinist argument. He suggested that males and females were socialised – initially by the family – into taking on different roles which, he argued, reflected their natural characteristics. He used the term **instrumental** to describe the role that men should adopt, that is, to go out and earn money. He used the term **expressive** to describe the caring role that women should take on, that is, to look after the home and children.

Sociologists such as Stanley and Wise (2002) question this view and argue that gender is socially constructed. In other words, Stanley argues our biological makeup, our maleness/ femaleness, need not lead to what might be described as stereotypical masculine and

feminine behaviours such as aggression or caring. Instead, she argues these behaviours are connected to the way we are brought up and the influences of those around us – our peers, teachers, the media, workmates and religions. These agents of socialisation, she says, tell us how we should behave and, in addition, our masculinity/femininity is based on decisions and choices we make ourselves, the way in which we exercise **agency**.

## Femininities

The concept of femininities covers a range of learned behaviours and ways of expressing these behaviours which may differ according to class, age and ethnicity. For example, Blackman (1995) found the lower middle-class and working-class New Wave Girls in a secondary school were a highly visible group. Membership of the group gave them strength and confidence to use their sexuality to challenge the school's male culture and the sexism of male teachers as well as their male peers. This assertive femininity empowered them and gave them some control and at the same time challenged subordinate or **passive femininity** where women and girls accept traditional ideas about how they should behave, being quiet, demure and submissive.

The role of socialisation in the creation of identities

Figure 3.3 Kylie Minogue, a female icon

Read the passage below adapted from Connell (2002) and consider the arguments put forward by Stanley. Discuss the arguments you could put forward to oppose those who support the idea of sex-role differentiation.

There are masculine women and feminine men. There are women in love with other women, and men in love with other men. There are people who enjoy wearing leather jackets and engineer boots and cultivate toughness and the same people who may on another occasion enjoy wearing pink dresses and are soft and emotional. There are women who are heads of households and men who bring up children. There are women who are soldiers and men who are nurses.

(Source: adapted from Connell, 2002)

On the other hand, Osler and Vincent in *Girls and Exclusion* (2003) found the girls they researched were less willing to pose direct challenges to authority because they didn't want to get into trouble as it could affect their reputation, whereas they found if boys got into trouble they were viewed positively by their peers. Having an attitude and being physical were seen as important parts of a boy's identity and reputation, while, for girls, physical appearance was seen as important. This led them to behave in a way which Jackson (2006b), in her study of lads and ladettes in schools, describes as **normative femininity**. Seidler (2006) argues that for girls from some Asian backgrounds their expectations and perceptions of their femininity is based on the experiences within the family where they learn that their brothers are allowed to do more than they are, and they have expectations placed upon them in terms of how girls should behave. Seidler argues the girls do not want to dishonour their families or go against *izzat* ('family honour') so they often lead a double life: taking a traditional, normative, female role at home and adopting a more questioning femininity outside. Some girls have responded to the dominant ideology of how women should be by forming a sub-cultural ideology of love and romance – an exaggeration of the traditional feminine stereotype. However, McRobbie (2007) suggests that some aspects of female sub-cultural behaviour are more rage against than resistance to the current expectations placed upon girls.

Figure 3.4 David Beckham, a male icon

U1
3

**Activity 3.5**

Identify four types of femininity from the paragraph above and give an example of a well-known contemporary person for each one. Make a poster for the classroom wall of the femininities, leaving space to repeat the exercise for masculinities when you have read the next section.

## Masculinities

Connell argues there are a range of masculinities in the contemporary UK. These are socially constructed sets of expectations about how men should behave, which differ according to class and ethnicity. As with femininities, the emphasis is on the range of masculinities. Traditional or, what Connell describes as, **hegemonic masculinity** is associated with:

◆ male supremacy (power and authority)

◆ heterosexuality

◆ aggression

◆ 'laddish' culture.

The behaviour of hegemonic males is often macho and sexist and includes expectations about what women should do and be and about the technical competence of males, particularly with regard to computer related equipment.

However, recent research, particularly by feminists, suggests that to talk of one homogenous hegemonic masculinity hides the range of experiences and behaviours of what it means to be a 'man' in the contemporary UK (Archer, 2003a). Traditional masculinity is often, but not entirely, associated with working-class males. Nayak (2006) argues that in the 1950s and 1960s they had 'body capital', by which she means they were seen as the main breadwinner, did hard physical jobs and as a result were able to opt out of domestic duties. Their world was the masculine one of work which was public and separate from the private domestic world of unpaid labour inhabited by women. This was a world that was familiar to Willis's twelve 'lads' – young males who, in the 1970s, were doing what the title of his research says, 'learning to labour' (Willis, 1977). For them school was a place to 'have a laff' which meant doing as little work as possible whilst disrupting lessons by 'tut tutting' when asked to do something by a teacher. They knew they were going into the labour market, inhabited by their fathers, of traditional manual work. However, as Jackson (2006) points out, the motives the boys in her study have for their adoption of laddish behaviour is quite complex. She argues they are partly to do with the fear of academic failure and the resulting defensive laddish behaviour which claims it is 'uncool' or feminine to work and partly concerned with social relationships and the desire to 'fit in'. Burdsey (2004) in his research on young Asian footballers also found that 'fitting in' was an important factor in determining the extent to which the footballers were consciously prepared to 'drop' or hide their Asian identity and adopt the laddish behaviour of the rest of the lads.

The idea that it is uncool to work and that working may be seen as feminine, coupled with the need that some Asian boys now have to 'fit in', was found among the working-class Asian boys Archer (2003b) studied in the North West of England. Asian pupils were once deemed to be more focussed and more compliant in school than their white or African Caribbean counterparts, but Archer found at least one 'laddish' group who took pride in messing about and playing up, talking back to teachers and being labelled stupid. Being stupid was seen as positive and in opposition to serious girls. The boys argued that particular teachers and teaching styles encouraged them to behave in the way that they did. They also said it was 'natural' and that boys possessed an innate short temper, aggressiveness and hot-headedness although they realised these traits were in opposition to the school culture. They also said they were not actually stupid just 'slackin' because they didn't want to be seen as a 'boff'. This view of the boys is similar to that of their white and black peers.

Apart from the normative or hegemonic masculinity, Connell identifies three other masculinities:

- complicit masculinity – a masculinity which new men, for example, might be said to adopt in taking on a shared role in the family

- marginalised masculinity – applicable to those for whom the changing nature of the labour market over the last 40 years has meant they can no longer assume there will be jobs for them after school, leaving many with a crisis. Connell uses marginalised masculinity to describe the sense of loss experienced by these young men. This disconnectedness is discussed in the research by MacDonald and Marsh (2005) in their study of the youth of East Kelby on Teeside in the north of England

- subordinate masculinity – which is a term Connell uses to describe a masculinity which is concerned with gay men who are viewed as behaving differently to the expectations of the dominant hegemonic masculinity.

Activity 3.6

Using the posters you have made, create an A5 card for each femininity and each masculinity. On one side summarise, with an example, what the femininity/masculinity is about and on the other think of as many evaluative points as possible. These cards can be used during the course either before the start of a lesson or as revision.

## The creation and reinforcement of gender identities through socialisation

The agents of socialisation help to construct and shape masculinities and femininities. In considering how they do this, it is important to take account of four things.

1   The agents of socialisation are interlinked – a child goes to school, plays with their peers, comes home, watches television and then has tea with their family.

2   The process varies according to social and cultural differences such as class and ethnicity. For example, there may be **racialised masculinities** and class could make a difference.

3 Some sociologists, such as Stanley and Wise (2002), take the view that gender role socialisation is rather simplistic and overly deterministic whilst others argue it involves too many assumptions and generalisations.

4 It is possible to resist the process and exercise some agency, some choice. Resistance and choice means the roles of males and females and the range of gender identities have been and are changing. The rate of change has increased in the late twentieth and early twenty-first centuries.

Seidler (2006) argues young males growing up in the 1950s knew what it meant to be male. They knew they would be likely to do what their parents did – get married, have children and follow in their fathers' footsteps. The sons of miners became miners; doctors' sons went into medicine. They had a traditional view of their identity and role. Sharpe (1976) found girls also had expectations of what they would do with their lives which reflected traditional gender roles. In the early twenty first century, we no longer consider that women have to be the passive, expressive creatures which Parsons (1954) argued was natural. They can choose to remain in education and have a career as Sharpe (1994) found in her second study. We recognise there are choices.

# Family

The family is the place where children begin to learn about masculinities and femininities and to see themselves as the same as, or different to, others in relation to their gender. Children imitate their parents; they identify with their behaviour and internalise what they hear and see. Part of the way they do this is gendered. These gender identities are partially shaped by:

◆ the language used by parents – 'little' girl, 'big' boy, 'brave little soldier', 'pretty', 'handsome' and so on

◆ accepted behaviour – for example, after the age of 12, girls are four times more likely to cry than a boy when something upsets them

◆ the toys they are given – the Bratz, the Mr Men and Miss books, Fifi and Bob the builder

◆ the clothes and accessories they wear – dresses, ribbons, shawls, handbags for the girls; trousers, waistcoats, superhero capes and guns for the boys.

Gendered clothes, toys, language and behaviour are difficult to resist, as is the gendered relationships between mothers and daughters

Figure 3.5 Boy and girl in gendered dressing-up outfits

and between fathers and sons. Mitchell and Green (2002) found evidence that the mother-daughter bond was a strong one for the working-class women they interviewed, especially after the daughter had a baby. They found the young mothers wanted to be seen as respectable, 'good' mothers, not 'rough'. They wanted to be seen as coping and caring and this particular type of femininity of 'good' motherhood was what their mothers, other female family members, as well as female support networks were passing on to them. However, this identity was also shaped by their awareness of their class position, where they lived and their knowledge of the fragility of intimate relationships with the fathers of their children. In her research on masculinities, Archer (2003b) also found the family was of pivotal importance. Respect for the family was a feature of the masculine identity of the Muslim boys she interviewed. They viewed their gender identity in the context of hetereosexualism and a mainstream view of what it means to be male. They described the roles within their families 'mothers [performing] emotional and nurturing roles… and fathers [being] the economic providers' in a very positive way. However, although they described a hegemonic masculinity policed by their fathers, they did not fit neatly into one type of masculinity. Rather, they negotiated a range of masculinities, including 'laddish' masculinities which were differently enacted depending on whether they were at home, at school or with their peers. What Archer

did find was that they saw their gender identity as powerful in comparison with Muslim girls whom they described as weak and passive and whose Muslim femininity was in need of their protection. They anticipated themselves taking on similar roles when they had their own families.

Frosh et al. (2002) found that when boys talked about their parents they described their mothers as more sensitive and emotionally closer to them than their more distant and detached fathers (p.13). This view that family life is still gendered in the twenty-first century is one also held by Charles (2002) who argues men are still seen as the providers and women, although active in the labour market, are still viewed as carers. However, for an alternative view, undertake the first activity in Activity 3.8.

## Mass media

Exposure to the media from an early age helps to reinforce what has already been learned in the family, and constructs for many people a deeper internalised layer of gendered behaviour. Gender stereotypes such as the super hero and the sexy female are found within popular culture. Marsh and Millard (2003) found when young children were asked to consider superhero texts, they were able to pick out ways in which hegemonic gendered activities were embedded in the stories. However, when they were asked to produce their own stories that were not gendered, they found it quite difficult.

Activity 3.7

1 Summarise the research entitled *Dads and their Babies* by Thompson et al. published by the Equal Opportunities Commission (2005).

### Weblinks
The Fathers Direct website (see 'Websites' page ii) will have useful information on this area.

2 Make ten cards with one of the following descriptions on each one. Shuffle the cards and give them to five women from three generations. Ask them to put them in

order of what was expected of them by their families when they were in their early teens.

| Looking after younger siblings | Helping with the washing | Doing the ironing | Getting married | Doing well at school |
|---|---|---|---|---|
| Cooking | Dusting | Vacuuming | Having children | Getting a good job |

3 What differences if any did you find between the three generations? Using the material in the section on gender you have already read, write a brief paragraph summarising how you would explain these differences.

Gauntlett (2002) argues that magazines give advice about how to be attractive to people in relation to gender. He says that television, music, books and magazines provide opportunities for young people to learn how they should dress, behave and interact according to their gender: the thin blonde woman versus the sporty, muscular man with the well-developed six pack. These magazines have details of the lifestyles of celebrities such as David Beckham, with his macho footballer image coupled with his status as a family man, or Kate Moss, a sensitive mother seen as a strong career woman by men and women alike; celebrities who provide role models for young people. Magazine problem columns also give advice on male/female behaviour often in relation to the opposite sex.

Gill and Herdieckerhoff (2006) argue that 'chick lit' – together with 'dad lit', 'mum lit' and 'lad lit' – persuades young women that the body is a key source of their identity. It promotes the idea that whereas chick lit heroines are likely to be financially independent, working outside the home, and sexually assertive, they should also have a sexy body. 'Chick lit' presents the acquisition of such a body as a key source of their identity. In addition, they found that 'chick lit' heroines still need to be rescued by the hero from their single parenthood, or from men who were cheating or conning them, or just from themselves. This is similar to the pre-pubescent young females in *High School Musical* who are given feisty roles while still wearing quantities of make up and are invariably thin.

As far as music is concerned, Storey (2003) claims the early rock and roll music of Elvis Presley and Buddy Holly reinforced aggressive masculinity, portraying a tough and very physically-challenging response to a somewhat uncaring world. In the twenty-first century, the music of Eminem continues to purvey the same message.

The media does not influence us in isolation. For example, recent changes in male fashion with the low slung trouser'd look, which challenges male sexuality and has its origins in Hip Hop, is an example of ways in which the media takes the style of a particular sub-cultural group and helps to shape gender identity.

## Peers

The need to win the approval of our peers becomes increasingly important as we move towards our teenage years and gain some independence from our parents. In relation to gender identity, it becomes important to be viewed as appropriately masculine or feminine allowing us to 'fit in' with peer groups and avoid being teased or, worse, bullied. Just as in the family, the use of language can be gendered. Boys may refer to their 'buddies' or 'mates', girls to their 'best friends' and to those who are 'nice'. In addition, there is still evidence to support the work of Lees (1986) who said that males are able to control females by their use of derogatory language.

The role of socialisation in the creation of identities

---

### Activity 3.8

1  Visit a toyshop and see whether 'favourite' toys for boys/girls are on sale. List the toys which depict either:

   (a)  traditional gender roles or

   (b)  current, so-called 'desirable' characteristics of males and females.

2  Buy a magazine intended for teenage girls/ boys, such as *Nuts* or *Heat*, and randomly select ten pages. How much of the page in percentage terms is devoted to how males/ females should behave with the opposite sex, how they should look as males or females and how they find or catch a male/female?

### Activity 3.9

List the derogatory terms used by males towards females and then those used by females to males. What differences did you notice?

Frosh et al. (2002) found boys identified characteristics such as 'hardness', having a fashionable 'look', holding anti-school values and being sporty as those to aspire to. They were characteristics of a hegemonic nature that would give them a popular status. These characteristics enabled them to point out the differences between themselves and the girls they knew who they did accept tended to be more mature than the boys. The girls agreed and suggested peer

Figure 3.6 A group of young males 'looking cool'

importance outside the home than their ethnic identity.

For some groups of young people, working-class males in particular, place or territory takes on an equal importance to their gender identity. The two are inextricably linked. Their attachment is to one 'safe' area, where the rules are known and the people familiar, in opposition to another place where everything is less certain. Ethnicity also overlaps with peer socialisation and Archer (2003b) argues that, although rather complex, some Muslim boys subverted notions of hegemonic masculinity when they were with their peers replacing them with more distinct racialised masculinities.

Activity 3.10

Using the material in the paragraph above, and your wider sociological knowledge, identify and explain five ways in which peers influence gender identities. You could produce a poster with pictures and photos to illustrate this.

## Education

By the time children enter the education system they will have acquired a sense of their gender identity from other agents of socialisation such as the family, the media and their peers. Given the hours and years most children spend in education, it too becomes an important influence. This influence varies according to class, ethnicity and the stage in the process. A number of factors within the education system affect gender identities. The formal curriculum – subjects taught in the classroom – and the hidden curriculum – the informal messages given out by the way the school is organised, the posters on the walls, the general behaviour of staff and pupils – both give out gendered messages. The patterns of behaviour in playgrounds give out similar messages: the boys taking up space to play football while girls stay on the outside talking, sometimes watching the boys. Frosh et al. (2002) found boys who valued academic success and were committed to work were often seen as more feminine, whereas those who were part of a more anti-school, anti-education oppositional culture, who wanted to have a laugh, were seen as more traditional, hegemonic males. In an earlier study, Mac an

pressure was largely responsible for the 'bad' behaviour of boys when they were in a group. Both the boys and the girls wanted to make their heterosexual status clear. To come out as gay or lesbian was to run the risk of teasing and becoming an outcast.

MacDonald and Marsh (2005) found peer groups were important to groups of disengaged young males, peers who were in the same or similar economic and social situation as each other. These groups helped to reinforce and shape each others' identities and their sense of their masculinity. One of their interviewees, Matty, is quoted as saying 'No matter what you done, if you're in that crowd you just stick with 'em.' (p. 82). What was important to these males was 'being streetwise' and to be 'one of the lads'. Burdsey's (2004) study of amateur and professional footballers also found that, in order to become one of the team, young Asian footballers would often subsume their ethnic identity under a laddish one and join in with the after game activities, such as watching pornographic videos, drinking and talking about girls, in order to become 'one of the lads'. The peer group took on a greater

Ghaill (1994) found teachers sometimes almost colluded with male peer groups who held views that were anti-gay and hostile to women.

In 2001, Skelton found some boys were coming to school with already formed views about laddism to which the teachers responded with tough measures that could be seen as equally macho and hard as the laddish behaviour itself. More recently, Jackson (2006b) found the distinction between masculinities and femininities among young people in school was becoming blurred. She found girls would often take on laddish behaviour – rejecting academic success, messing about in class and generally spending more time on their social life than school work. The term 'ladette' once reserved for the binge-drinking, smoking, cheating, crude and rather overly boisterous post-school-age young women, associated with media women such as Zoe Ball and Sara Cox, is now being used as a term to describe the girls in school who, partly afraid of failure and occasionally afraid of being seen as working too hard, behave in a laddish way.

Some girls are only too aware of the sexism that still pervades some parts of the education system and respond in an assertive femininity way, rather like the New Wave Girls of Blackman's (1998) study 'Poxy Cupid'. They challenged sexism wherever they observed it and engaged in behaviour designed to frighten off even the most misogynist boys, and teachers too.

Gendered behaviour via friendship groups such as the New Wave Girls occurs at all levels and Kehily et al. (2001) found in primary schools that sex gender relationships were articulated via friendship groups. In an extension of this, Renold (2007) found a minority of 10- and 11-year-old boys whom she interviewed went beyond the heterosexual boyfriend/girlfriend gendered behaviour to what she describes as hyperheterosexual identities enabling them to avoid hegemonic masculine behaviours involving anti-gay comments and misogyny.

## Religion

As the contemporary UK has become increasingly secular, the role of religions in the process of constructing gender identities has declined. However, there are some groups for whom religion still plays a crucial role. For Catholics, Hindus, Jews and Muslims, religion helps to shape gender identities that are of a traditional nature. For Catholics, Mary is a role model as a good virgin, a good mother and is seen as pure and sweet in contradiction to Eve who is the temptress who led Adam from the straight and narrow.

Both Catholicism and Islam advocate fidelity and chastity but this is focused on young women and both religions tend to 'overlook' male promiscuity. For young Muslim women, *izzat* ('family honour') ensures that most will adhere to traditional female roles as good daughters who will marry and raise children and not bring any shame upon the family by behaving outside a traditional subordinate female role. However, Butler (1995) found the young Asian women she researched in Coventry and Bradford in 1992 were keen to move beyond the expected role of Asian women from the Indian sub-continent and pursue further and higher education and careers. Although they made clear their religion was important to them, what they were challenging was their culture in terms of gender identities.

The challenge to culture has also been expressed by dress. Woodhead (2007) argues that, for some young Muslim women, religious dress, in particular the veil, has become an important part of their identity and she argues it is seen as what she calls 'Muslim chic' with a slight nod to the wearing of the veil for religious reasons. The issue of whether to wear the veil or not has become one that is articulated in the public domain. Court cases by school girls asserting their right to wear the veil in school, some feminist arguments about the extent to which it is liberating – by moving the focus from how a person looks to what a person says – to the work of the comedienne Shazia Mirza all serve to focus attention of the different identities it affords in terms of gender identities to young Muslim women.

### Activity 3.11

1 Choose two of the sociologists mentioned in the section on education above and summarise what they say in your own words.

2 Write a paragraph summarising two ways in which education socialises young people into gendered roles. Evaluate each way, explaining how it could be possible to resist gender socialisation at school.

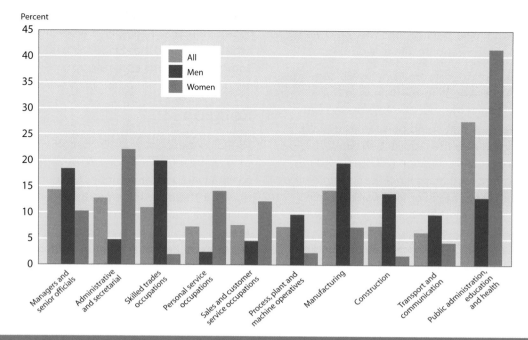

Percent

Figure 3.7 Proportions of people in employment by occupation and industry in the UK, 2003

(Source: Office for National Statistics, Labour Force Survey)

## Activity 3.12

1 Look at back copies of the quality press and consider the key points raised in the Straw debate in 2006 regarding the wearing of the veil.

2 Read *Brick Lane* by Monica Ali, or watch the film. How do the male and female characters resist, or not resist, traditional gender roles?

## Workplace

In the last few decades of the twentieth century, the nature of employment has changed from manufacturing to service industries. The number of part-time, temporary and casual jobs in the labour market has risen and traditional heavy industries, such as coal and steel, employing working-class men, have declined. New technology has bought with it the need for new skills and the global economy has changed the demands for goods and services. At the same time, women have become more economically active and therefore financially independent. All of these changes have contributed to what sociologists such as Mac an Ghaill (1994) argue is causing working-class men, in particular, to face a 'crisis of masculinity'. They have lost their traditional jobs and are unprepared for other skill areas and women are appearing to take jobs men might otherwise have done as the labour market becomes more feminised. Frosh et

al. (2002) argues this has meant young males who might have expected to have traditional gender relations have had to renegotiate more flexible masculine identities.

## Activity 3.13

Look at a range of job adverts. To what extent do you think they are gendered?

McDowell (2003) argues the hopes and aspirations of the white working-class school leavers she studied in Cambridge and Sheffield had orthodox, traditional aspirations which would give them respectability as well as financial security and domestic respectability. The same aspirations were found by other sociologists such as McDonald and Marsh (2005) in Teeside (see section on peer groups, pages 37–38). These aspirations, and the difficulty of attaining them, McDowell argues, is leading to a division between middle-class masculinities with their entrepreneurial masculine roles and those of the working class. It also poses difficulties for the working-class males as they tread a careful pathway between hegemonic 'hard laddishness' and respectable masculinities. The sexualisation of some jobs such as those in the leisure industries means, according to Adkins (1995), women take up subordinated femininities in order to obtain and keep the jobs they financially need.

Watch the film, *The Full Monty*.

1 Identify ten ways in which the changing nature of work affected masculinities.

2 Refer back to the role of the peer group in shaping gender identities. In what ways do peers shape gender identities in the film?

3 Make a timeline covering the last 50 years to show how work has changed, including as much detail as you can. Ask your parents, grandparents and neighbours to help you. Ask them to explain what has changed for them.

A person's gender identity is fluid and shaped and constructed through their experiences that are often quite gendered. The agents of socialisation play a big part, but so too does the individual's ability to resist that process resulting in ever-changing gender identities alongside the more traditional hegemonic masculinities and subordinated femininities.

## Section summary

Use the following key words to copy and complete the summary of this section below. Each word should be used only once.

    sex    shape    the lads    socially constructed    hegemonic    passive    new man
    ladettes    chick lit    laddish    resisting    agency    submissive    the family

Biologists use the term _____ to describe the difference between men and women. Sociologists use gender to describe the _____ _____ or learned behaviour, of males and females. There are a range of masculinities from the _____ masculinity of the traditional, assertive, heterosexual male to the complicit masculinity of the _____ _____ .The emergence of _____ , the female equivalent of laddish culture in the last few years, can be contrasted to subordinate or _____ femininity.

Gender socialisation starts with _____ _____ where the use of toys and clothes begins to _____ a child's gender identity. Gender identities are also shaped by other agents of socialisation including the media and peer groups, from the popular _____ _____ to the need to be one of _____ _____. Socialisation however is not a one-way process and _____ can be exercised. For example, girls do not always choose to be quiet and _____ in school and boys do not always choose to be _____ . There is considerable research evidence of males and females _____ their gender socialisation.

## Exam practice

(b) Outline and explain two ways in which the media may influence femininities.

(16 marks)

(c) Explain and briefly evaluate why some young males may adopt laddish behaviour.

(24 marks)

# Social class identities

## Pause for thought

1   Do you think that social classes exist in the contemporary UK?

2   Which social class(es) do you identify with?

3   What factors did you consider when making this decision?

Figure 3.8 City workers: a middle-class identity?

# Different views of class

There is a strong argument that the contemporary UK is a class-based society. This means that in the UK today social class differences are an important influence on an individual's life. A variety of factors are considered when making a judgement about a person's social class, and you may have considered some of these when you were thinking about the questions on page 42. Factors such as where a person lives, the size of their house, their occupation, speech and dialect, car, education and clothing can all be considered as influencing the identification of social class. The view that social class differences remain crucial in understanding the opportunities and constraints that people have in the UK today is broadly associated with Marxist sociologists (see p. 114).

There is, however, another strong argument, which is that the contemporary UK is an increasingly classless society. This means that in the UK today social class differences either do not exist or, if they do exist, are meaningless because individuals can pick and choose their own identities, cutting across traditional, class-based divisions. For example, a child from what would have been called a traditional working-class background, with a father who is a coal miner and a mother who is a stay-at-home housewife, can move out of their ascribed class position and achieve an occupation and status that has no ties with the working class at all. From this point of view, factors such as housing, occupation, speech and dialect, cars and education are all lifestyle choices that individuals can make regardless of the social class they were born into. The view that differences between people are not as related to social class as they used to be is the one broadly taken by postmodern sociologists (see p. 116).

There will be evidence to support both these views, and it may be that neither of them provides an accurate account of the importance of social class in the UK today, which is a highly complex question. This section will consider what is meant by social class, evidence of different social class cultures and identities, and the role of the agents of socialisation in creating and reinforcing class identities in the contemporary UK.

Study the cartoon below (Figure 3.9) and identify the different cultural signals of the working class and the middle class.

**Figure 3.9 Two class identities**

Social class has been defined in many different ways. Broadly speaking, social class relates to the ways of life of similar social groups. The way of life involves both the culture and the economic (financial) position of a group of people. By culture we mean shared norms and values. By economic position we mean similar financial positions (rich/poor). Both these aspects may influence the way of life.

## Marx and class

The introduction to Unit 2 (pp. 112–116) provides an introduction to Marxist theory and you may want to read this before reading on.

For traditional Marxist sociologists, social class was directly related to a person's economic position and their relationship to what Marx termed 'the means of production'. Traditional Marxists saw two main social classes: the bourgeoisie and the proletariat. The bourgeoisie were the rich, upper class and they owned what Marx called the means of production. The means of production was the key to their economic success, as owning a factory or business meant that any profit would come directly to them.

The proletariat, on the other hand, did not own the means of production and worked for the

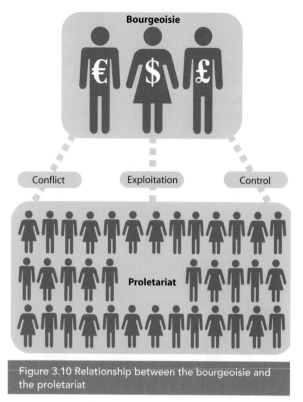

**Bourgeoisie**

Conflict    Exploitation    Control

**Proletariat**

Figure 3.10 Relationship between the bourgeoisie and the proletariat

bourgeoisie. They were paid low wages and had no prospect of promotion or progression: they were treated as wage slaves. The relationship between the proletariat and the bourgeoise was one of conflict, and economic division lay at the base of it.

Marx claimed that over time the proletariat would become aware that they were being exploited by the bourgeoisie. In other words, they would realise that a small group of the rich were getting richer at the same time as the masses of the poor remained trapped at the bottom of the class structure. As the proletariat became aware of the exploitation they would develop a 'class consciousness': an awareness of their exploitation. They would realise collectively that they were the working class and that if they co-operated with each other they could overthrow the small group of bourgeoisie owners by means of a proletarian or workers' revolution. Marx predicted that this would happen when the economic conditions were right and that different societies would reach this point at different times.

Clearly, the proletarian revolution has not yet occurred in the UK and many sociologists would argue that it never will. However, the basic Marxist argument of conflict between rich and poor being based on economic differences is the basis of one of the most important theories in sociology.

Neo-Marxist (new Marxist) writers accept that social class is not always linked solely to finance and the economy and they argue that it is important to consider the role of class culture when considering social class differences.

## Bourdieu and capital

Pierre Bourdieu was a Neo-Marxist sociologist who used the concept of capital (meaning 'resources') to illustrate social class differences. Bourdieu (1986) identified different types of capital that people could possess. Some were ascribed to them at birth and others were achieved in various ways. Some of them are concerned with finance (economics) and some with culture (way of life).

1   **Economic capital** includes income, wealth and financial inheritance. Economic capital can be ascribed or achieved. The social classes with the most economic capital tend to be those with higher paid jobs or those who have a lot of inherited wealth.

2   **Cultural capital** includes cultural attributes often related to education. A knowledge of classical music, classical literature and art would all be examples of cultural capital. This is usually passed down from generation to generation and in this sense cultural capital can be difficult to buy or achieve. It is often thought that children educated in the leading public schools possess most cultural capital as they gain it from their family and their school.

3   **Social capital** includes the resources based on social connections and group membership. This is generated through networking and through relationships with different groups of people. Social capital is largely achieved and is possessed by different classes in different ways. In traditional working-class communities people frequently look out for one another's interests through finding employment for each other or through exchanging services (fixing a car in exchange for plumbing in a washing machine). In higher social classes social capital means the same thing but it often operates through educational institutions or the old boy/girl networks, looking after the interests of each other's children.

1 Using the information on page 44, copy and complete Table 3.2 with two more examples of the different types of capital. One example has been done for you.

2 Using Table 3.2, write a paragraph explaining which social classes you think possess the different types of capital. You should consider the working, middle and upper class.

| Economic capital | Income (wages) | | |
|---|---|---|---|
| Cultural capital | Appreciating classical music and literature | | |
| Social capital | Helping a friend find employment | | |

Table 3.2 The different types of capital

## Summary of Marxist views

◆ Capitalist societies contain two main social classes divided on the basis of their economic position.

◆ The bourgeoisie (rich) own and control the means of production.

◆ The proletariat (workers) are exploited and oppressed.

◆ The proletariat will develop a class consciousness and a revolution will overthrow the bourgeoisie.

◆ Following this class revolution societies will become based on communist ideals of equality.

◆ Neo-Marxist sociologists argue that economics and culture play a role in explaining social class divisions.

◆ Pierre Bourdieu uses the concept of different types of capital to explain social class divisions.

## Postmodern views of class

The introduction to Unit 2 (p. 116) provides an introduction to postmodern theories and you may want to read this before reading on.

Postmodern views of social class take more notice of culture than traditional Marxist theory did. Postmodern views are difficult to generalise from but the underlying argument is that social classes in the UK are fragmenting, splitting up or at least changing. It is no longer clear where the boundaries between being working class and middle class are.

For some postmodern writers this fragmentation is the consequence of globalisation, in which a new international group of workers migrates to the UK and changes the traditional class structures. The example of migrant workers from Eastern Europe could be used to show how the traditional working class are losing their jobs as a new cheaper group of workers is available for employment.

Another group of postmodern sociologists argues that the blurring of the old class boundaries is due to the growth of consumer culture. Consumer culture makes it possible for individuals to pick and choose their own identities based on what they consume. Society is increasingly based on conspicuous consumption and lifestyle choices. Higher wages for many people mean more disposable income is available to buy and to live the lifestyles that individuals want. Lyon (1994) suggested that the postmodern world is a consumer society. In this postmodern view the expansion of popular culture results in the decline of traditional class cultures. Individuals can pick and mix from different styles which were traditionally associated with one distinct social class. Football is a good example here. Once the sport of the working class, football has become a crucial part of popular culture, enjoyed by many in the UK regardless of their class background.

The renewal of many inner city areas can be used to illustrate some of the postmodern ideas. Figure 3.11 shows the Quayside in Newcastle,

Figure 3.11 The Quayside in Newcastle

where buildings such as the Baltic Art Gallery stand alongside the Sage Music Centre, next to designer shops and trendy bars. Visitors to the Quayside may feel that the UK is a consumer-based society with relatively few social divisions. However, if they travel outside this area into other parts of the city, stark images of rich and poor can still be found.

## Working-class culture and identity

Many traditional sociological studies were carried out to explore working-class culture. Studies such as Willis (1977) *Learning to Labour* portray life in traditional working-class communities based around a shared culture. What follows is a list of some features of this culture.

◆ The jobs were based in manual and unskilled labour. The shipbuilding or coal industries dominated the employment opportunities of many northern towns and cities.

◆ There were traditional gender roles within the family: the male breadwinner who provided for his wife and children and the female homemaker who cared for her husband and children.

◆ Boys were encouraged to follow the employment pathways of significant male role models in their families, often gaining employment in the same factories or industries.

◆ The communities were strong and had a feeling of unity, solidarity and togetherness. Working-class communities were supportive and looked after their own kind. Outsiders were often distrusted.

◆ Politically they had strong links with the Labour Party and trade unions, who protected their rights as workers. This meant that a mentality of 'them and us' existed.

◆ They were seen to live for the moment and to want immediate gratification. This meant that the working classes were less likely to save money for the future.

◆ Working-class housing was located in cheaper and less desirable areas. Few of the working class would buy their properties: they were more likely to rent council houses or live in houses owned by the factories, often close to their place of work.

Changes within the working class during the last twenty years have resulted in changing cultures. Observations of the changing working class could highlight the following:

◆ lives becoming more privatised, more home based and less community centred

◆ employment based on the service sector and intermediate occupations, often in office-based work

◆ more shared responsibilities between men and women in the household

- increasing affluence, with more money to spend and a choice of consumer goods to spend it on
- a rise in the number of home owners and people who are socially mobile and aspirational.

The reasons for these changes are complex and include some of the following:

- decline of the heavy industries (coal, steel, shipbuilding), which meant limited employment opportunities in working-class areas that were reliant on the heavy industries
- decline of manufacturing industries in the UK, with work being shipped overseas
- growth of the service sector bringing more non-manual employment opportunities associated with middle-class culture and identity
- changing educational opportunities, which encourage continuation in education up to 18 years and the self-funding of university education through the student loans system
- improved educational opportunities for girls
- social changes, more freedom and individualism, less pressure to follow in parents' footsteps.

### Activity 3.17

Using the information above answer the questions below.

1 Select three of the following factors and show how the traditional working class has changed:

- Employment
- Home ownership
- Importance of community
- Gender roles
- Education and aspirations

2 For each give reason(s) for the change.

Recent studies of the working class have focused less on working-class culture and more on working-class identities. Skeggs (1997) studied the lives of a group of twelve working-class women who had all enrolled on courses in the caring professions at a local further education college in the Midlands. Her research showed how the women tried to distance themselves from traditional working-class norms and values. The women wanted to be seen as 'respectable' and by having careers, owning their own homes and dressing in an 'appropriate' way they tried to disassociate themselves from other working-class women.

### Activity 3.18

Watch either *Brassed Off* or *The Full Monty* and identify features of traditional working-class culture. Do the characters possess economic, cultural or social capital?

Savage et al. (2005) carried out 50 in-depth interviews with people who lived in Cheadle in Manchester. They found a strong culture of manual labour, which gave the area a 'practical flavour': many of the men were employed in physical or manual jobs. Half the men interviewed belonged to a local social club, which formed the basis of their social life and leisure activities, showing a culture of neighbouring. The women in the study organised their social lives around local families or contacts in the area, which suggests the existence of social capital in the area. However, most of the interviewees did not work locally and had to travel to work. Most were home owners, owned their own cars and had access to consumer durables. In terms of class identity: only 21 per cent had a clear and definite view of a class that they fitted into; 41 per cent thought they had no clear social class; 40 per cent viewed themselves as working class; and 18 per cent viewed themselves as middle class.

### Activity 3.19

Write a sociological account of working-class life in the UK using the concepts and studies identified above. Use at least five concepts and refer to at least two studies in your answer.

When you have finished, swap your answer with someone else and check each other's answer for the concepts and studies. Did they use the same ones as you did?

## Summary of working-class culture and identity

◆ Traditional working-class culture was based on features such as community, family, manual work and immediate gratification.

◆ A changed working class is emerging and is increasingly based on privatism, individualism, non-manual work, consumption and social mobility.

◆ The changes are due to factors in education and employment which have made social mobility an achievable goal for many.

◆ Working-class cultures can still be found in the UK but working-class identity is changing.

## Middle-class culture and identity

There have been fewer sociological studies focusing on the middle class than on the working class, possibly due to the debate over who the middle class really are. Traditionally, the middle classes were associated with professions such as doctors, solicitors and teachers. These occupations indicated a high level of educational achievement, the existence of cultural capital and an exclusive professional status which meant that they required extensive professional training. Traditionally middle-class culture was based on:

◆ white-collar or non-manual jobs in professional or managerial roles

◆ high levels of social mobility, with the middle classes aspiring to be successful and move up the social class ladder

◆ strong networks and connections to people in other middle-class professions

◆ deferred gratification: the middle classes believed that if they saved hard in the early stages of their careers they would reap the benefits later

◆ educational achievement and a university education

◆ owning homes in desirable places

◆ cultural capital, foreign holidays and an appreciation of high culture.

Figure 3.12 Call centre workers

However, over time the distinction between the working class and the middle class has blurred. It is no longer easy to see a dividing line between the cultures of the two groups. In particular, it has become increasingly meaningless to talk of a division between those working in manual and non-manual jobs. The rise in white-collar occupations and the call centre culture has meant a huge change in the nature of employment, with an expansion of administrative office-based jobs. These jobs may fit comfortably within the middle-class culture yet economically they have more in common with the low pay and limited benefits traditionally associated with working-class jobs.

As opportunities for further education increase, and as incomes rise for many people in the UK, as organisations such as the NHS and other government bodies grow in number, it is increasingly the case that the middle class has become split into different groups. According to Savage (1992) this split is based on lifestyle and on employment. Savage shows how the lifestyles of the middle class are related to occupational groupings. For example, those working in private sector jobs have more distinctive lifestyles than those working in managerial or government positions.

Wynne (1998) studied a middle-class housing estate in Cheshire and found that the residents of Heathtown possessed economic, cultural and social capital. His work shows a middle-class culture very different from the working-class and manual culture that Savage found in Cheadle.

In another study, Devine et al. (2005) carried out 50 in-depth interviews with a sample of doctors and teachers in Manchester. Both of these professions would be considered as middle class, yet most of the sample did not refer to the concept of social class in their interviews. Devine suggests that they felt uneasy using the label of class as they feared being perceived as superior to others.

The researchers suggest that the concept of social class in the UK is associated with status positions and is an exclusive label, one that seeks to keep membership of higher social classes distinctive and something to strive for in life. This may explain why class identity is changing as some people strive to achieve the exclusive status of being upper class.

### Activity 3.20

Write a sociological account of the ways in which the middle class(es) have changed in the UK, using the concepts and studies identified above. Use at least three concepts and refer to at least two studies in your answer.

When you have finished, swap your answer with someone else and check each other's answer for the concepts and studies. Did they use the same ones as you did?

## Summary of middle-class culture and identity

◆ The traditional middle class was based on professionalism, educational qualifications and cultural capital.

◆ The changing nature of employment patterns means that more jobs are in non-manual occupations which has changed the structure of the middle class.

◆ There has been a blurring of middle- and working-class cultures.

◆ A number of different middle-class lifestyles are visible often related to different types of employment.

◆ It is very difficult to define middle-class culture and is likely that a number of different middle-class lifestyles exist.

## Upper-class culture and identity

The upper class is a much smaller group than either of the other two and in many ways is more coherent and solid. It has been described as being 'socially closed', meaning that those who belong to it are not keen on allowing outsiders a view of their lifestyle, and this makes them difficult to research from a sociological angle. There are two sub-groups within the upper class.

## Traditional upper class

The traditional upper class is made up largely of the aristocracy, who have been born into their wealth and titles. These are rich families who own vast estates and make most of their money from owning land. They are associated with intermarriage, that is, with marrying people from similar social backgrounds. This often increases their social capital as families become related and networks expand. They value tradition, hierarchy and order, keeping the past and national heritage of the country special, which means they have cultural capital. The traditional upper class have economic capital in the form of property and wealth, although they don't necessarily show this wealth in the way the super rich (see p. 50) do. The best example of the traditional upper class is, of course, the royal family.

Figure 3.13 The royal family

# The super rich

The second sub-group within the upper class has become known as the 'super rich'. These are people who have achieved their wealth (and often status and fame) through hard work and merit. In this sense the super rich have economic capital which they have earned. The super rich are, however, associated with a glamorous lifestyle. They are conspicuous consumers, often using the media to their advantage. They value material consumer goods, brand names, labels and live a visibly rich lifestyle. Social capital comes in the form of networking with others in a similar economic position. This is well illustrated by the weddings of the super rich, where the guest lists comprise other rich celebrities. One of the best examples of the super rich are the Beckhams.

For some, upper-class culture is based on inherited wealth and an ascribed status. For others, it is based on achieved status, merit, hard work or good fortune (lottery winners). What unites the two sub-groups of the upper class is their possession of economic capital, whether it is in the form of a country estate which could be sold to make money or in the form of the disposable income of the super rich.

Study Figure 3.14 and identify and label the cultural signs of the super rich.

Which of these would you also identify with other social classes and why?

Figure 3.14 Cultural signs of the super rich

They also all possess social capital through their networks of friends and relatives. The dividing line between the sub-groups comes in relation to cultural capital, which the traditional upper class are born with but which it is very difficult if not impossible for the super rich to achieve.

## Summary of upper-class culture and identity

◆ The upper class is made up of two social sub-groups: the aristocracy and the super rich.

◆ The aristocracy have an ascribed status, the super rich have an achieved status.

◆ Both of the groups have economic capital and social capital. Only the aristocracy have cultural capital.

## Objective and subjective social class identity

A useful distinction to make when considering social class is between objective and subjective social class identities.

Objective social class is based on the view that people can be placed in a social class by using a scale or measurement device. The government currently uses the National Statistics Socio-Economic Classification (NS-SEC), which places individuals in a social class position according to their occupation.

Subjective social class comes from what the people themselves think, where they place themselves and how they define themselves. This may be based on their occupation but is likely to be based on a number of different factors (housing, parents, education, consumption patterns etc.).

Sometimes the objective and subjective class identities coincide, however, in many cases the class you identify yourself with will be different from that which an objective measure places you in.

## Social class identities

A number of different studies have found a high correspondence of the objective and subjective social class at the extremes of social groupings. This means that for people who can clearly be placed objectively in middle-class occupations

(GPs or solicitors) their subjective social class corresponds highly (80 per cent or above). A similar pattern is found in the working classes with jobs that are clearly identifiable as being working class. The problem arises for the large number of people between these groupings, where their occupation does not neatly fall into middle or working class. Occupations such as routine office/administrative jobs, sales, leisure industries or working in what can be termed 'service sector' jobs show a mixed picture of social class identity.

The British Social Attitudes Survey of 2006 (BSA, 2006) found that since the 1960s there has been no decline in the proportion of people identifying with a social class in the UK. There has, however, been a decline in the proportion of the population identifying themselves as working class during this time, although this figure is still high at 57 per cent. The increase in the proportion identifying themselves as middle class may reflect changes in employment patterns and educational qualifications.

## The creation and reinforcement of class culture and identities through socialisation

### Family

The family creates norms and values that can be seen as class based. Everyday events such as mealtimes are sometimes portrayed as being class based. The middle classes are thought to eat dinner in the evening, sitting down together to share a family meal. Working-class mealtimes are often portrayed as being earlier to coincide with the end of the working day for most manual workers. Having meals in front of the television has also been associated with working-class culture. In reality these norms and values are probably breaking down and blurring.

However, the role of the family in passing on cultural capital and economic capital from one generation to the next has not changed. Research from Reay (1998) shows how middle-class mothers are able to influence their children's primary schooling more than working-class mothers. In Reay's research, the working-class mothers had less time to devote to their children due to the demands of balancing housework, childcare and paid employment, but crucially they lacked confidence and understanding of the school system. Some of the mothers had negative experiences of school themselves, making it difficult to assist their child's educational career.

Cater and Coleman (2006) conducted research on 'planned' teenage pregnancies and reported that the risk of becoming a teenage mother was almost ten times higher for a girl from an unskilled family background compared with a professional background. In interviews with 41 teenage mums, they found that many spoke of the norm of settling down early: most of their own mums were full-time mothers, many of whom had been teenage mothers themselves. For the girls in the study, family background, and in particular poverty and disadvantage in childhood, played a major part in their decision to have a baby, which they believed would give them a new identity and purpose. Interestingly, and contrary to the media message, only a minority of the interviewees regretted their decision.

## Education

The main influence education has on social class identities comes from the type of school a person attends. Individuals educated in private schools are surrounded by cultural signals indicating an elevated social class position. Factors such as the crest of a school, or the sports and school trips can be indicators of social class. Even those who are given full bursaries/grants so that their parents do not pay towards their fees will be influenced by this.

The formal curriculum of these institutions may influence a social class identity too. A student who receives weekly Latin lessons, a subject high in cultural capital, is likely to have a different understanding of society than a student who studies vocational courses, with less cultural capital. Power et al. (2003) show a close relationship between children from middle-class backgrounds, achievement at the top public schools and gaining places at the élite universities. She suggests that this is not only a result of high educational achievement, but that these schools actively encourage applications to

Two futures …

Meet a boy called Dan.

- Age – 18
- Education – private boarding school: 10 GCSEs, 3 A levels (Latin, English Literature and History)
- Parental background – army officers posted overseas
- Hobbies – guitar, hill walking and rugby union
- Career – wants to be an army officer

Figure 3.15 Dan

Meet a girl called Anna.

- Age – 18
- Education – comprehensive school: 8 GCSEs, 2 A Levels (Law and English)
- Parental background – mum a hairdresser, dad a mechanic
- Hobbies – socialising with friends, cinema, music and reading
- Career – wants to work in the travel industry

Figure 3.16 Anna

In what ways might the social class identities of Dan and Anna be different? Use the following concepts in your answer:

- economic, cultural and social capital
- formal and hidden curriculum
- norms
- values
- class culture.

the élite universities and see this as a measure of their success. Students attending these schools who do not achieve academic excellence can perceive their experience as personal failure, especially those whose parents work in academia.

Bourdieu (1990) suggested that for middle-class students going to university is like being a 'fish in water' compared with the working-class experience of university, which can be isolating and daunting.

## Media

Media representations of different social classes also influences social class identity. Consider television programmes that focus on working-class culture. Programmes such as *Shameless* show the working class as aggressive, assertive and good at playing the social security system, similar to the ways in which *The Royle Family* illustrated working-class life as being based around a front room and watching television. Research from Medhurst (1999) shows how a group of middle-class students watching *The Royle Family* believed that it was an accurate portrayal of working-class life in the contemporary UK.

We have already mentioned the way in which the media is used by the super rich in society. The Beckhams, for example, are talented at using modelling opportunities to further their own interests.

New media technology also influences social class identities. Brundson (1997) shows how middle-class people saw satellite dishes as being tasteless and a symbol of the working class. Gradually, of course, new media technology can become a part of popular culture, which has probably happened to satellite dishes.

## Religion

The relationship between religion and class identity in the contemporary UK is a difficult one. It is made particularly difficult due to the changing and diverse nature of religious groups and the changing and diverse nature of class identities. There is some evidence that attendance at Church of England ceremonies is higher for the middle classes, although that does not mean that the middle classes are

more likely be religious. There is some evidence that attendance in church provides a degree of status within communities, rural communities in particular. However, religions such as Rastafariansim are likely to have a broader working-class base, as they are often located in the inner city communities of the UK. Perhaps the easiest position to take is that the issue of religion and class identity is under-researched and subject to ongoing change.

## Peer group

Peers play an important part in the class identity, especially in relation to young people. An individual's peer group is related to where they live, the school they attend, the hobbies they share and sometimes to the friends of their parents. Clearly, each of these factors can be related to social class. In this sense social class does influence the formation of peer groups. There is evidence from a number of studies that peer groups in schools often form along social class lines. This could be at the level of a shared sport: a group of girls who play lacrosse are unlikely to be identified with or identify themselves with the working class. Mac an Ghaill (1994) describes different types of masculinities in a school and locates some of these ('Real Englishmen' and 'Macho Lads' as he calls them) clearly within different class positions. For some

Figure 3.17 Working-class skinhead identity

peer groups their social class provides them with a direct sense of identity. In studying a group of white skinheads in an area called Kempton Dene in the West Midlands, Brah (1999) shows how the working-class identity was crucial for this group of males who worked hard at constructing a culture of 'whiteness'.

They followed the norms and values of a key leader called Adam, copying his cultural practices. We can, of course, use the concept of the 'cultural comfort zone' here in suggesting that a key factor in the formation of a peer group is social class and shared culture and identity.

## Workplace

The strong association of manual work with the working class and non-manual work with the middle class means that a link between the workplace and class identities is likely to remain. However, this will change over time as the nature of the workplace changes. Evidence constantly relates an individual's occupation to their class. For example, Savage's (1992) study of middle-class doctors and the evidence from the working-class area in Cheadle where a 'practical flavour' was observed, both indicate a strong relationship between occupation and class identity in the UK.

1 Using the information above, write a 500-word account explaining how social class identities are created and reinforced in the contemporary UK. Use at least three studies and five concepts in your answer. When you have finished, write a list of the studies and the concepts you have used.

2 Swap your answer with someone else in the class and read each other's response. Did they use three studies and five concepts? Were these the same ones that you used?

You may find Table 3.3 a useful way of organising your thoughts, as it encourages you to think of two ways in which each agent of socialisation influences the creation of social class identities.

| Agents of socialisation | First way (include concepts, studies and contemporary examples where you can) | Second way |
| --- | --- | --- |
| Family | | |
| Education | | |
| Peer group | | |
| Religion | | |
| Media | | |
| Workplace | | |

Table 3.3 Influences on the creation of social class identities

## Section summary

Use the following key words to copy and complete the summary of this section below. Each word should be used only once. You need to complete the final sentence in your own words.

classless    family    education    media    religion    workplace    peer group    Marxists
exploitation    class consciousness    cultural capital    economic capital    social capital
postmodern    lifestyle    fragmentation    consumer culture    immediate gratification
community    privatised    middle-class    deferred gratification    aristocracy    super rich
social closure    objective    subjective

Class culture and class identity are socially constructed, which means they are likely to change over time. The two main theoretical approaches to social class come from the _____ and the _____ sociologists.

The Marxists argue that social class is the most crucial social division, and that the relationship between the bourgeoisie and the proletariat is based on _____. Only when the working class become aware of this will a _____ _____ develop enabling a proletarian revolution to take place. The postmodern view is that the contemporary UK is increasingly _____. Society is based on a _____ _____ where individuals can buy the _____ of the social class they want to identify with. This can lead to the _____ of the class structure; it is no longer clear where the social divisions between the classes can be drawn. Some postmodern views describe the contemporary UK as _____.

The neo-Marxist sociologists take issue with this view and suggest that even if the social divisions are less clear than they used to be, it is still possible to identify social classes according to their access and ownership of three types of capital: _____ _____, _____ _____ and _____ _____.

When we look a working-class culture we can see that the traditional culture is breaking down. The concept of _____ _____ has been used to explain the working classes desire to live for the moment. While this is still prevalent in some areas, the working class is increasingly _____. Individualism is replacing _____.

The idea of saving for the future and doing without now in order to reap the benefits later is known as _____ _____. This is associated with _____ _____ cultures and identities.

The upper class is also socially divided into the_____ and the _____ _____. The concept of _____ _____ describes the way in which entry into the aristocracy is limited to those with the right breeding.

In terms of social class identity it is important for sociologists to consider both _____ and _____ measures of identity. Often these will coincide and give the same result, as in the case of most doctors who would be placed objectively in the middle class and subjectively would place themselves there too. Other occupations, however, show less unity and a more complex and fragmented picture of social class identity emerges.

Social class culture and identity is created and reinforced largely by the agents of socialisation; _____, _____, _____, _____, _____ and _____. I think the most significant agent in the creation of class identity is ............... because ... (complete yourself).

## Exam practice

(a) Define what is meant by middle-class identity. Illustrate your answer with examples.                    (8 marks)

(b) Outline and explain two features of working-class culture.                    (16 marks)

(c) Explain and briefly evaluate the view that class identities are created during primary socialisation.                    (24 marks)

The role of socialisation in the creation of identities

## Pause for thought

1     What is ethnic identity?

2     Are people's ethnic identities equally strong?

3     How do ethnic identities change over time?

Figure 3.18 The Notting Hill carnival

# Ethnicity

Ethnic groups are complex. Consider, for example, the African-Caribbean ethnic group. Much can be suggested from such a term, such as the reference to Africa. This may not be where the person is from themselves, but where their ancestors were born; African countries were former colonies of western empires. Secondly, there is the history of the slave trade, the forced movement of people from Western Africa to the Caribbean, which contributes the second half of the concept African-Caribbean. When people migrated from the Caribbean to the UK in the 1950s, many of them were greeted with racism and hostility from the indigenous population. Colonialism, slavery, racism: all of these factors have a legacy.

### Weblinks

For the story of the *Empire Windrush*'s voyage from the Caribbean to England in 1948 see 'Websites' page ii.

You may define your own ethnic group as 'English'. 'Englishness' incudes the old stereotypes of fish and chips, bowler hats and cricket on the village green. There is still the idea of what Curtice and Heath (2000) termed 'Little Englanders', with their narrow-mindedness and desire to exclude others from the notion of being 'English' on the grounds of something such as skin colour. This is complicated by the fact that sometimes ethnic groups can be related to skin colour. The category 'white', for example, is used in some surveys that ask for identification of ethnic group.

An **ethnicity** is not something that only minority groups have; a white majority is regarded as an ethnic group. Of course, being white does not mean the same thing to everyone. For example, being white may be different for different social classes and ages. Hewitt's (1996) research showed that the young, white, working-class people he studied felt a sense of injustice because they could not celebrate their white, working-class culture. Fenton (2003) discusses the overlap between ethnicity, nationality and race and states that in many societies the words are used interchangeably.

## Activity 3.24

Discuss the following questions with two or three other people in your class.

1 What is meant by the term ethnicity?

2 Which ethnic groups (for example, white, Asian, black, Chinese) are present in the contemporary UK?

3 Identify three factors that contibute to an individual's ethnicity.

# Ethnic identity

Modood (2005) describes ethnicity as involving a number of factors, including culture, descent and a sense of identity. Culture includes a shared language, shared food, religion, tradition and values. These factors can be influenced by where a person was born, where they currently live or their ancestory. When people have an ethnic identity it means that they have a cultural attachment to others and often a sense of pride. Some white British people feel that they have no ethnicity, and that ethnicity is something that 'others', notably non-white people, have. However, Banton (2000) suggests that in the contemporary UK ethnicity is becoming increasingly recognised as something everyone has, especially given that questions about it are now included in the Census and are regularly found on official forms.

Ethnic identity is something that an individual can achieve and express to others, for example, through the clothes they wear or their religion's values. An ethnic identity can be applied to an individual as a way of labelling them and their culture as being different. This can involve a process of '**othering**' where the self is seen in a positive way and anything different is defined in the negative. So, in the case of black and white identities, white people may see black people as 'the other', that is, not white, not being like 'us'. Said (1995) explains how this process occurs in the West's construction of the Orient as exotic. It is important to remember that identities can be experienced and/or applied to others and that what a person feels their ethnic identity is may be different from what another person thinks it is.

U1

3

The role of socialisation in the creation of identities

Table 3.4 shows two different ethnic groups that can be found in the contemporary UK. It refers to some characteristics of these groups. However, it is important to bear in mind that these are generalisations, involving stereotyping.

| Scottish | Chinese |
| --- | --- |
| Language: English and Gaelic are the official languages | Language: Chinese, Chinese Mandarin and many locally-used languages/dialects |
| Food: haggis, shortbread, scotch broth, tatties and mince | Food: rice, pork, dumplings, noodles, roast duck |
| Religion: Christianity in the main, but not dominated by any one religious group | Religion: Buddhism and Confucianism (some do not regard this as a religion) |
| Tradition: crofting, heavy industries (e.g. ship building), Highland Games, Scottish dancing | Tradition: patriarchal past, traditional clothing, festivals such as Chinese New Year and spring festivals |
| Values: the Scottish nation | Values: family, education, respect for elders, obedience to authorities, importance of order and harmony |

Table 3.4 Two ethnic identities in the contemporary UK

1 (a) Using the information in Table 3.4, write a paragraph describing either the Scottish or the Chinese ethnic group.

 (b) Explain how this may link to identity.

2 Select an ethnic identity of your choice and research the norms and values associated with that group, using the headings in Table 3.4.

# Ethnicity and nationality

There is an overlap between ethnicity in terms of where an individual was born, where they live and their nationality as stated on their passport. For most people in the contemporary UK these three things coincide, so that most people living in the UK were born in the UK and their passport states their nationality as British. However, when you consider cultural differences the picture becomes more complicated. A person may have been born in the UK and lived there all their life but have parents from China, who were socialised in a different culture, some elements of which will inevitably be passed on to their children. Second-generation Chinese people living in the UK may describe themselves as British Chinese or Chinese British, sometimes depending on where they were born. Some Scottish people would describe themselves as Scottish, others as British. It is likely that some individuals will associate themselves with Scottish Chinese culture. Bond and Rosie (2006) found a marked prioritisation of Scottishness as opposed to a British identity among the Scottish people they studied. What is clear is that ethnicity and nationality do overlap, when a person states their ethnicity it may well say something about their nationality and vice versa.

# Race

Racial differences usually refer to innate biological differences between groups within society, foremost among these being skin colour. However, sociologists argue that society decides which, if any, biological differences are seen to be important in a cultural sense. For example, little attention is paid to eye colour, yet skin colour is often considered as a significant racial difference. Sociologists argue that racial differences are socially constructed, that is, they are made by societies. Sometimes racial differences can form part of an individual's ethnic identity.

A person's ethnicity goes deeper than factors such as skin colour or hair texture. In racial terms the Polish and the British are part of the same Caucasian race, yet there are cultural differences between the two groups which make it meaningless to discuss biological similarities such as skin colour and to ignore cultural ones. Modood (1997) found that African-Caribbeans living in the UK were more likely to mention skin colour as being part of their ethnicity than southern Asians who mostly commented that religion was the defining characteristic of their ethnicity. Jacobson (1997) found that young Pakistanis see Islam as crucial in forming their identity. It affects their diet, dress and general behaviour.

There is a whole history of race relations in the UK and one useful concept in understanding this is assimilation. Assimilation assumes that immigrants to the UK would abandon their culture and adopt that of their 'immigrant hosts', the indigenous white majority. Clearly this has not occurred and it has been debated as to whether assimilation is a desireable/inevitable feature of a multi-cultural society. Due to a number of significant social changes, the distinction between majority/minority culture based on racial differences is of limited use for a society as culturally diverse as the contemporary UK, which has seen the emergence of what are termed new ethnicities. Modood et al. (1997) showed how ethnic identities in the UK are as diverse *within* an ethnic group as *beween* ethnic groups. Hall (1992) describes the emergence of new ethnicities which are aware of, indeed celebrate, difference. A plurality of ethnic identities exists in the UK showing that identities are not fixed.

## Hybridity

The contemporary UK is culturally diverse, and ethnictity forms a large part of that diversity. Sometimes, though, cultures influence each other and new hybrid ones develop. **Hybridity** refers to a mixing of cultures. This can manifest itself in different ways. A good example of this is food and the popularity of the curry house; Chicken Tikka Masala is reportedly England's most popular dish, yet its origins are unclear. Some report it as being imported from Bangladesh cuisine, others say that it was created by Bangladeshi chefs in Brick Lane, East London, who mixed curry with condensed tomato soup to create something acceptable for the English palate. Either way, the fact that all supermarkets stock it and curry houses are found througout the UK shows how different cultures can mix and create something new.

However, individuals do not have to have hybrid identities. Back (1996) researched new hybrid identities and found that they were not fixed.

---

**Activity 3.26**

1 Using the following headings, create a vision of what society in the contemporary UK would be like without a rich ethnic diversity.

- food
- language
- media
- dress/clothing
- religion
- education
- sport

2 What difficulties did this activity raise?

Figure 3.19 Hybrid identities

Young people played with different cultural masks, and different styles. Inter-ethnic friendship and marriages mean that groups borrow ideas from each other and this blurred the distinction between seemingly different ethnic groups. Research by Johal and Bains (1998) focused on what they termed 'dual identities', where, for example, British Asians (Brasians) have a number of different identities depending on who they are with: friends, peers, or at school. Johal and Bains suggest that some of these young people can 'code switch'. This involves behaving one way when with their peers and another when with their families. This code switching was often based around ethnic issues/conflicts in the home and can be seen portrayed in films such as *Bend it like Beckham* and *East is East*.

## Globalisation

The process of globalisation has also encouraged ethnic hybridity to take place. The expansion of the mass media in particular has made it possible for people to consume products from different parts of the world, regardless of where they live. Hybrid cultures can be based on or formed around any issue as Table 3.5 shows.

**Activity 3.27**

1 Complete Table 3.5 by describing other areas of life which display hybrid cultures. Think in particular about what Britain has taken from American culture.

2 Using information from Table 3.5 (and any ideas of your own) write an account of different ethnic hybrids found in the contemporay UK, including where they were formed.

## The creation and reinforcement of ethnic identities through socialisation

Ethnicity is clearly not fixed; it is cultural and is created and reinforced by society. However, as Modood (2005) suggests, even if ethnic identities are changeable, a dominant culture is likely to be visible within particular ethnic groups. From birth onwards, individuals are moulded and shaped

| Issue | Example | Description |
|---|---|---|
| Music | Brasian | A fusion of musical styles from the West and South Asia. Glastonbury had its first Brasian stage in 2004. Brasian artistes include Apache Indian, Jay Sean, Asian Dub Foundation |
| Food | Noodle and Sushi bars | The rise of the noodle as the basis for a meal – a fusion of Thai, Japanese and Cantonese foods – has seen a huge increase in the number of noodle bars across the UK. |
| | Curry | This has almost become a national British dish. The curry house was based on Indian cuisine but was brought into the UK largely by the Bangladeshi people, who own most of them. |
| Clothing | Saris | The traditional Indian sari is stocked in high street stores and worn by women of different ethnic groups. Music and clothing can be inter-linked. For example, white youths wear clothes associated with Hip Hop. |
| Leisure/festivals | Halloween | Traditionally associated with American culture, 'trick or treat' has been adopted by British youth and Halloween has become the third largest money-making festival in the UK. |
| | Diwali | This is the Hindu festival of light. It is celebrated by a range of ethnicities, particularly in schools. |

Table 3.5 Examples of hybrid culture and globalisation

by their social environment. The agents of socialisation play a fundamental part in shaping our ethnic identities

## Family

The family is crucial in creating and reinforcing an individual's sense of ethnic identity. A family surname and first name can protray a sense of ethnic identity, for example the name Gareth Jones suggests a Welsh link. The languages spoken in the family home, the food and clothing selected for children are also important influences.

The values held by the family may be related to ethnicity. Francis and Archer (2006) show how educational achievement is valued by British Chinese families. The family plays a crucial role in the educational success of their children, with families making considerable sacrifices to ensure success for their children, often going without new consumer goods in order to pay private school fees. However, this does not mean that children blindly follow the guidance of their family. It is likely that young people conform to some expectations whilst rejecting others.

Modood et al. (1997) show how young South Asians are less likely than their elders to speak to other family members using a southern Asian language. This may suggests a generational shift with young South Asians identifying more with a British identity. However, caution should be exercised in assuming that traditional values are disappearing. Dench et al. (2006) studied

Bangladeshis living in Tower Hamlets in the East End of London, focusing on whether they were a part of the new East End. Through interviewing white and Bangladeshi residents they built up a picture of the new East End which showed the persistent strength of the extended family for many if not all Bangladeshi families.

There are also structural differences between families from different ethnic groups. Figure 3.20 shows different family types by ethnic group, and it is apparent that some ethnic groups are significantly more likely than others to be headed by lone parents. Patterns such as this and research on family size show differences in family type and structure and these are likely to impact on the number and type of role models within families.

### Activity 3.28

1 Using the data from Figure 3.20 show how family type is linked to ethnicity.

2 In what ways might family type affect the socialisation of children within different groups?

## Education

In school an individual's ethnic identity is shaped by the formal and the informal curriculum. Mason (2005) maintains that many schools are ethnocentric. They evaluate other cultures and

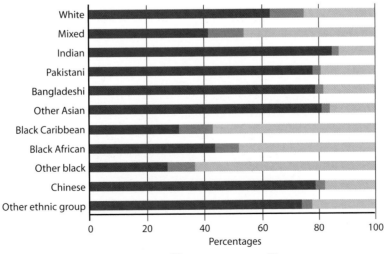

■ Married couple  ■ Cohabiting couple  ▨ Lone-parent

Figure 3.20 Families in the UK with dependent children: by ethnic group and family type, April 2001

(Source: Office for National Statistics, 2001)

practices from the perspective of their own. This can have a signifcant impact on ethnic identity within schools where Johal and Bains (1998) argue that some children wear a metaphorical 'white mask' in order to fit in with the majority culture.

Derrington and Kendall (2004) interviewed children and parents from Traveller communities over a three-year period, aiming to find out the experience of Traveller children in secondary schools and the extent of their ethnic/cultural identity. Some of the Traveller children were clearly proud of their identity. One Year 9 girl said, 'I tell people that I'm a Traveller and I tell them, "If you don't like it, you can lump it".' Other children try to hide their Traveller identity from their peers and teachers. It is suggested that this is for reasons of self-protection, as many of these children had experienced racism, and had a strong desire to gain social approval from the peer group.

The formal curriculum is likely to contain a cultural bias, whether it is by focusing on British history or by emphasising the teaching of some religion(s) more than others. To challenge this, Sewell (2000) offers a curriculum-based perspective on an African-Caribbean viewpoint, which he argues could fit with National Curriculum requirements. However, it could be argued that an emphasis on historical examples, such as slavery, the anti-colonial struggle and the Holocaust, reinforce stereotypes and that a wider perspective is needed to highlight positive achievements. There are major black achievements, for example, not just in music and sport, but in many other fields including business and science.

The UK has a number of faith schools (Christian, Muslim, Hindu), which offer an education tailored towards a particular religion. Whether this is in tune with the value of religious tolerance in the UK is a debated point, and there can be little doubt that faith schools will be ethnocentric to some degree. Faith schools formally link education to religion and can be considered as important in establishing an ethnic identity. It has been argued that Catholic secondary schools, many of which are heavily over-subscribed, contain both a mixed ethnic and social class population, albiet from within the universal Catholic Church.

The informal curriculum can also influence ethnic identities. Wright et al. (2006) discovered that the black girls in her study felt that some teachers treated them unfairly in lessons. From the girls' viewpoint the teachers' actions were racist. Sewell (2000) observed that the black boys in his study tried to resist racism from teachers who often did not believe or understand that some of their teaching practices were actually racist.

**Activity 3.29**

1 Design a positive multicultural curriculum. Assume that you have to study the following subjects and copy and complete Table 3.6 giving examples of activities that would be multi-cultural.

2 How far has your own education been multicultural?

| Subject | Topics to be covered |
| --- | --- |
| Maths/Science | |
| English | |
| Languages | |
| Sport/Drama/Music/Art | |
| History | |
| Religious Education | |

Table 3.6 A positive multicultural curriculum

# Religion

There are clear links between ethnicity and religion in the contemporary UK. Some religions form the dominant factor within ethnic groups. Many people will consider that Muslims are an ethnic group based on one religion, as opposed to being a religion which is followed by a number of different ethnic groups. Similarly, Jewish people are considered as having a religious and ethnic identity which overlaps. Figure 3.21 shows data relating ethnic group to religion.

Figure 3.22 Ethnic identities in school

### Activity 3.30

Study Figure 3.21 and answer the following three questions.

1 Which ethnic group do most Christians belong to?

2 Which religions are most dominant within the Asian ethnic group?

3 Which ethnic group is most likely to have no religion?

The blurring of the distinction between religion and ethnicity is due to the cultural aspects of many religious groups. Food, dress codes, languages and beliefs can all be based on a religion, yet these are also important features in the creation of an ethnic identity. Modood (2005) observes that 100 years ago the African-American theorist Du Bois predicted that the twentieth century would be the century of the colour line. By this he meant that the divide between the black and white communities would be the world's greatest social divide. The twenty-first century may be characterised by the Islam/West divide or the differences between the Muslim and the non-Muslim worlds. Events such as the attack on the Twin Towers on 11 September 2001, the July 2005 bombings in London and the conflicts in Afghanistan and Iraq add weight to this argument and show the significance of religion in ethnic identity in the contemporary UK.

## Peer groups

Some peer groups are made up of people of the same ethnicity; others are multi-ethnic. The ethnic make-up of a peer group is influenced

U1

3

The role of socialisation in the creation of identities

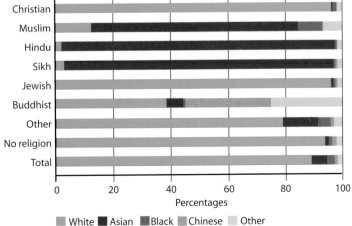

by the schools they attend. Some schools have a multi-ethnic population and others comprise mainly one majority ethnic group. Multi-ethnic peer groups may strengthen ethnic identities due to the realisation of differences within the group. The concept of 'cultural comfort zone' is significant here as it may be that people from the same cultural background feel a sense of comfort in socialising with each other. The sense of sameness and shared group belonging will provide ethnic identification for some individuals but it may have the affect of limiting socialisation with people from different ethnicities.

Alexander (1996) studied the formation of black culture and identity within black British youth. The importance of the peer group was crucial in what she described as the 'art of being black'. The males in her study displayed a strong cultural attachment to being 'one of the boys' regularly attending 'black' clubs which they differentiated from 'white' clubs.

## Mass media

In locations where few minority ethnic groups live or visit, people often rely on media representations for their understanding of different ethnic groups.

Research based on the media representation of minority ethnic groups in the UK has shown that, in the past, they were either ignored or portrayed in a limited number of roles, which frequently highlighted a particular feature of their ethnicity. In soap operas, for example, Asian characters' main story line has been based around arranged marriages and the portrayal of African-Caribbean communities has been

based around social disorder or social problems. Jhally (1992) maintains that being ignored and unrepresented or being stereotyped and misrepresented was a feature of ethnic representation in the British media through the 1970s to the late 1990s. However, recently a change has come about with a new group of ethnic-minority media stars writing the material for and starring in television programmes.

There can be little doubt that the media play a huge role in the creation of ethnic hybrids. A good example is language, with words such as 'bling' and 'chuddies' finding their way into everyday use. Media characters such as Ali G and programmes such as *Goodness Gracious Me* have played a large part in the creation of what can be described as a new dialect. Some call this process Hinglish; a combination of Hindu and English.

Parker and Song (2006) researched the ways in which websites were influencing ethnic identities in the UK. They found that South Asian and Chinese ethnic identities were strengthened by the use of websites targeting these ethnic groups through the organising of social events and providing forums for the discussion of issues related to different ethnic identities.

## Workplace

Modood et al. (1997) found as many differences within minority ethnic groups as between them in the workplace. Some workforces are ethnically diverse and others are dominated by one particular ethnic group. Some minority ethnic groups are more likely than others to experience unemployment. Ethnicity also affects potential earnings and the area of employment in which a person works and succeeds. This may be evidence of discrimination or it may be related to educational achievement or to family and community networks.

Two examples can be referred to. Song (2003) shows how many Chinese living in the UK are employed in the food and catering sector. Clearly this is related in some way to Chinese takeaways and restaurants. Equally it shows the influence of the family on employment opportunities and how important family socialisation is in creating or influencing occupation. Doctors working in the NHS provide a second example of the joint impact of work and family life. Over a third of doctors in the NHS are described as Asian. For

---

**Activity 3.31**

In small groups work on one of the following areas:

- sitcoms/sketch shows

- advertising

- the news

- sport.

Identify some examples that illusrate a positive representation of different ethnic groups.

many Indian families a career as a doctor brings high status and income which will influence their social class and ethnic identities.

Activity 3.32

1 Copy and complete Table 3.7 showing the relevant knowledge for each agent of socialisation.

| | Key concepts | Studies and contemporary examples |
|---|---|---|
| Family | | |
| Education | | |
| Peer group | | |
| Religion | | |
| Media | | |
| Workplace | | |

Table 3.7 Socialisation and ethnic identity

2 Using the evidence in this section write a short essay (approximately 500 words) entitled 'How ethnic identities are created and reinforced in the contemporary UK'.

In considering the process of socialisation and ethnic identity formation it is important to bear in mind that the agencies of socialisation may not all have the same impact. It could also be the case that different groups are affected differently by the same agency. People are not passive; for example, people interpret the media in different ways and within the family there is negotiation. There is the possibility of resistance for all agencies of socialisation, whereby people reject the norms and values.

## Exam practice

(a) Define the concept of multiculturalism. Illustrate your answer with examples.
(8 marks)

(b) Outline and explain two ways in which an individual may express their ethnic identity.
(16 marks)

(c) Outline and briefly evaluate the view that the media are responsible for the creation of ethnic hybrids in the contemporary UK.
(24 marks)

## Section summary

Use the following key words to copy and complete the summary of this section. Each word should be used only once.

code switching    difference    dual identity    ethnicity    globalisation    hybridity
multicultural    nationality    othering    race    white mask

Whereas _____ refers to biological differences, _____ is cultural. Ethnicity is bound up with religion and _____, with a consideration of where a person comes from and where they live now, as well as their culture. The contemporary UK is regarded as a _____ society. Identity formation can involve a process of _____, where other groups are seen in the negative, as not being the same. To see the world as divided into two opposing standpoints such as West versus East or black versus white is inadequate and does not allow for _____ to be fully explored. In a world where we gain ideas from across the globe through the mass media and travel, _____ must also be considered in the formation of hybrid identities.

Some ethnic minority groups practice _____ _____. This is where they change their behaviour with friends and family. With their white peers they wear a _____ _____. This fits with the idea of a _____ _____. The process of new identities being formed when two or more cultures come together is called _____ .

# Age identities

## Pause for thought

1   At what age does childhood end?

2   At what age does middle age begin?

3   When can someone be described as 'old'?

4   What norms and values do you associate with childhood, middle age and old age?

Figure 3.23 Senior athlete

Age is a key source of identity. Age categorisations are found in all areas of life in the contemporary UK, for example the school leaving age, the age at which you can apply for a provisional driving licence, the age at which you can vote and age-related film categories. Age can be considered chronologically (as above) and refers to actual age in years which brings certain roles and status. Alternatively, age can be considered as a stage in life through which people pass, following a life-course from being an infant, through childhood, youth and middle age until old age is reached. Both approaches can be applied to the contemporary UK.

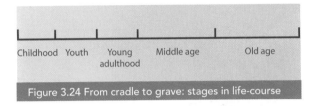

Figure 3.24 From cradle to grave: stages in life-course

There are, of course, some obvious problems with using a life-course approach to age identity, not least that individuals do not follow the same life pattern and the time that middle age starts for one person is not the same for another. Some people aspire to leave the period of 'youth' behind, while for others identifying with 'youth' extends throughout their life. However, it is also problematic to adopt a chronological approach to age identity, as Activity 3.34 shows.

This activity is likely to uncover some conflicting opinions, as age is a controversial topic. It may also show how difficult it is to assume that individuals of the same age can be treated as a coherent group. For example, all 14 year olds are not at the same level of maturity. The reasons behind age-related rules tell us something about the culture of British society. It is likely the reasons you give in the second column of your table will indicate some of the norms and values present in the contemporary UK.

As age is frequently referred to in the UK, it will have a crucial influence on identity. This subsection considers three common age-related identities: youth, middle age and old age. It will consider key characteristics of each category, before exploring how age-related identities are created and reinforced by the agents of socialisation. This subsection raises the question that age-related categories are increasingly meaningless concepts.

## Youth

Youth is associated with people from around the age of 12 to 25 years old. However, clearly people aged 26 are not middle aged. The

Activity 3.33

Think of ten different ways in which an age restriction is imposed in the UK. For each example, discuss the reasons for the restriction and whether you agree or disagree with the rule. You could copy the table below to arrange your ideas.

| Age and issue | Reason | Agree/disagree |
|---|---|---|
| School leaving age – 16 | Time to enter workplace for some young people | |
| Provisional driving licence age – 17 | Safety, aptitude, responsibility | |
| Age-related film categories – 12, 15,18 | Limiting exposure to sexual or violent scenes and bad language | |
| | | |
| | | |

Table 3.8 Age restrictions in the UK

The role of socialisation in the creation of identities

Figure 3.25 Youth identity

concept of youth assumes young people can be identified with a distinct way of life; a period of growing up, rebelling, fun and excitement. Abrams (1959) argued that young people were all part of the same youth culture; at the same transitional stage in their life. During this stage, young people are learning and negotiating the path into adulthood. For some this involves college and training, for others the workplace.

Other sociologists have argued that young people are not a united easily-identifiable social group, and that they differ according to class, gender and ethnicity. Some sociologists consider youth to be based around the concepts of rebellion and resistance (Clake,1976). This could be resisting the norm or rebelling against their relatively low status position in society where money dominates. Subcultural groups such as punks or chavs are often used by the media to represent youth in the contemporary UK and this clearly creates and reinforces an unrepresentative view of youth identity. Youths are often associated with popular culture and the creation of new fashions and styles. This stage of life is identified as being creative and

risk orientated. Postmodern sociologists identify youth culture with a time for experimenting with new styles and fashions, and shopping at the 'supermarket of style', which is a concept used to explain how young people can pick and mix their customs and identity in an 'anything goes' culture (Polemus, 1997). Clearly, the media play a crucial part in the creation and reinforcement of youth identity. Through advertising products and styles of life, youth is given a distinct status obviously different to that of middle age.

However, for most young people, youth is simply a time of growing up. Most youths do not engage in or identify with criminal behaviour or deviant subcultural behaviour. Most youths are identified as being 'ordinary' (Willis, 1990). Section 5 in Unit 2 examines the sociology of youth and contains examples of contemporary and past youth subcultual groups, which you may find useful to consider.

## Middle age

Middle age is a widely-used concept in the UK which is associated with a stage of development lying between young adulthood and old age. Victor (2005) describes it as distinctive phase of life related to people in their forties and fifties, preceding the onset of being considered 'old'. As there are no clear age boundaries or legal positions to help locate when middle age starts and finishes, it may be considered as an attitude of mind; suggesting that there are particular ways in which middle-aged people view life.

Middle age may best be considered as a stage in an individual's life-course, often related to the point at which their children are leaving home. It is also associated with particular norms, values and roles. Norms would include the type of car driven, places to shop for clothes, hobbies and holiday destinations. Values may be concerned with health issues and quality of life. The roles of parent, becoming a grandparent, carer or employee go hand in hand with being middle aged. In many respects, middle age can be identified as having a low status. There have been many cases of age discrimination when people have been told they are 'too old' for particular jobs in their late forties and early fifties. Yet in other ways, middle age brings with it a higher status than either youth or old age (Bradley, 1996).

It could be argued that middle age is experienced so diversely by different people that it is a meaningless concept. Middle-aged men, for example, are often portrayed as hankering after their youth, dreaming of buying a sports car. For women, being middle aged is often portrayed as a time of change; in particular, the menopause. There may also be differences in the way the middle class approach middle age compared with the working class. A common feature is that middle age is a time for reflection, on the past, present and future.

It is likely that people are identified as being middle aged by people in younger age groups. Most children will consider their parents to be middle aged, simply through their status as parents. Parents themselves may not identify with the category as easily. In this sense, being middle aged is associated with the stage in your life-course and the age of the person applying the label.

Activity 3.34

1 Devise a list of terms associated with middle age. This activity would work most effectively as a class discussion.

2 Ask five adults (aged 18 and over) which of these terms they associate with middle age. (They can choose no more than three.)

3 Repeat the exercise with five children from your school/college.

4 Collate your results as a class. Are there any differences between the views of the two age groups?

### Weblink
You can gain further ideas on the opportunities offered in mid-life from the website of Middle Age (see 'Websites' page ii).

## Old age

The point at which a person becomes old is a highly sensitive issue. Chronologically, a case could be made for 'old' being aged 65 or over, as this links directly with the retirement age for men and women. With retirement comes a pension from the state, concessionary travel on public transport and the possibility of free prescriptions. It has been suggested that on your 65th birthday you are unlikely to feel the same as you did the day before. However, according to McKingsley (2001), those aged 85 and over are the fastest growing segment of the population; commonly referred to as the 'oldest old'. This suggests there is a stage of being 'young elderly'. Without a clear age boundary, it may be useful to consider old age as a social category which brings new roles, assumptions, opportunities and barriers.

Victor (2005) suggests old age is stereotyped and identified as a period of:

◆ loneliness

◆ being unable to learn

◆ having poor health

◆ being dependent on others.

He also said that old age was a homogenous category.

People can be identified as being 'old' or may place themselves within the category. Many studies have found that people accept chronological ageing as a fact of life, but they have difficulty fitting themselves into the ill-defined categories of old age or middle age (Bytheway, 2005). Clarke and Warren (2007) interviewed 23 people between the ages of 60 and 96 about their experiences of aging and what they identified with the aging process. They concluded that most of the respondents identified this phase of life in an active and engaged way; they used the concept of 'active ageing' to represent this. Only two respondents found it difficult to 'look forward', claiming it was 'all pointless' and were resigned to 'this is life, you can't change it'. For the others, the older years were identified as providing new opportunities, a time for reflection and hope of experiencing future collaborative events with family members (Christmas, grandchildren).

The concept of old age is changing, however, and is being challenged by people who feel it has become a negative label, used to stigmatise (negatively label) the elderly. Many older people continue to drive, lead active social lives and seek to use their later years to do things they couldn't do when they were younger. This change can be illustrated by reference to the song *My Generation*. Written by The Who in the 1960s, it contains the infamous line of 'I hope I die before I get old'. This seemed to speak for a generation who thrived on youthfulness. This line was adapted by Robbie Williams more recently when he said, 'I hope I'm old before I die' showing how the identification of ageing has changed. More recently the band, The Zimmers, have performed the same song.

Activity 3.35

Below are four statements about age. In pairs or small groups, discuss the meaning of each. What do they suggest about age identity?

1  You're only as old as you feel.

2  I'm young at heart.

3  Life begins at 40.

4  50 is the new 30.

In summary, we have identified the following features within each age category:

◆ old age – dependence, loneliness, ill-health, opportunities, restrictions

◆ middle age – fulfilment, new directions, reflection, money, enjoyment

◆ youth – rebellion, restrictions, resistance, learning, fun.

## Weblink

The Zimmers website (see 'Websites' page ii) provides information and profiles on the band.

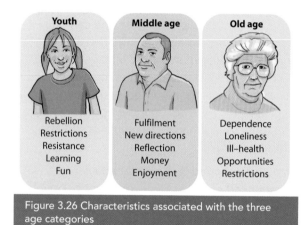

Figure 3.26 Characteristics associated with the three age categories

Laslett (1991) challenged the use of these categories and suggested an alternative three ages of life approach. These were:

◆ First Age is the period of socialisation

◆ Second Age is the phase of work and childrearing

◆ Third Age is the time of independence.

It has been suggested that a Fourth Age now needs to be added as life expectancy continues to increase.

Activity 3.36

Discuss which approach to ageing you think is the most relevant in the contemporary UK: chronological, life-course or the three ages? You need to be able to justify your views.

# The creation and reinforcement of age identities through socialisation

## Family

The family plays an important part in age identity because an individual's position within the family can influence how others see them or how they see themselves. For example, people usually consider their parents to be part of a different generation to themselves, so depending on the way they identify themselves may influence how their identify their parents. This will be passed down from generation to generation. If a child is socialised into thinking that their 60-year-old grandparents are 'old', then they are likely to consider this the norm. Old age is seen as a social problem in many ways. The stereotype of old people as a social problem often comes from within the family. A common theme within many studies is that the family's members assume that the older relative will need and want more care than they actually do. This identification of old age within primary socialisation is likely to have a lasting influence on old age identity.

## Education

From the time of first starting school, age is a determining factor in children's lives. The month a child is born in will determine their year group and their position within that year group as 'old' or 'young'. This remains with the child until they leave school/college. Identification with age boundaries at such a young age is likely have a lasting impression on how people understand the ageing process.

The hidden curriculum will also contribute to age identity. By using phrases such as 'he was an old man when he died', or 'she was a young woman' the identification of age as a social category is reinforced.

## Peer group

Clearly, the peer group is particularly influential during the period of youth. Studies show how peer group pressure is a key factor influencing the norms, values and culture of young people. Most studies of youth culture agree that the role of the peer group is crucial in the identification of a youth identity. Shain (2003) studied how groups of Asian girls developed distinct identities in a secondary school – the Gang Girls, the Rebels, the Survivors and the Faith Girls – as a way of coping with school. Their peers were crucial in who the girls identified with.

## Religion

Much sociological evidence would suggest that religion in the UK is declining, and this is the case for all age categories. Evidence would suggest that the elderly are more spiritual than younger generations. McKingsley (2001), however, found that religion was used as a coping strategy in his sample of those aged 85 and over.

## The media

The media represent different age categories in stereotypical ways. Youths are over represented as deviant and troublesome (Muncie, 2004), middle age is represented as a time of crisis and old age as a time of dependency and loneliness. These representations are important because they influence popular culture so heavily. Thornton (1996) argued that the media are largely responsible for the creation of youth culture and range of youth identities in the contemporary UK. From music to advertising, there is a clear association of style with youth. In recent years there has been a more positive representation of older icons in the media. Helen Mirren is a good example of someone who gains extensive media coverage for her talent and her 'active ageing'. Old age identity in this sense may be changing.

### Activity 3.37

Select a television soap opera or drama and analyse the age of the characters and how they are portrayed (positively, negatively, as a problem, causing problems).

## The workplace

Clearly, retirement does coincide with the identification of 'old age' to some extent. In this sense, the workplace can be considered as the site which prepares people for this potential change in their status. At the other end of the spectrum, the minimum wage for those aged 18 and over creates an age categorisation for young people. The workplace is the most likely site for age discrimination in the UK.

This section has explored various dimensions of age identity and offered some insight into the process through which age identities are created and reinforced. Age has been a neglected area of study in sociology. However, this is now changing and the Third/Fourth Ages are providing researchers with fascinating new insights into the ageing process.

## Section summary

Use the following key words to copy and complete the summary of this section below. Each word should be used only once.

three ages    middle age    chronological    active ageing    transitional    subcultures
life course    youth    oldest olds

Age identity is one of the most recent areas of sociological interest. There are broad approaches to considering age identity, either by age and date which is called_____ or by considering the stage of life a person has reached, this is called the _____ _____ approach. _____ is a time of growing up and learning the social norms and values; it is considered as a _____ stage. Youth is often represented as a time of rebellion and resistance. Youths are often associated with _____. _____ _____ is the time of life for reflection, often associated with career progression or with children leaving home. The period of old age is increasing. There is a distinction between the young olds and the _____ _____. Old age is often represented negatively yet there are signs of people in this category engaging with _____ _____. Research suggests older people find it easier to identify with their chronological age than with the category of being 'old'. A different way of approaching age is through the _____ _____ approach of socialisation, work and childrearing through to the age of independence.

## Exam practice

(a) Define the concept of youth identity. Illustrate your answer with examples.

(8 marks)

(b) Outline and explain two ways in which age identities are created and reinforced.

(16 marks)

(c) Explain and briefly evaluate the view that old age is a meaningless concept.

(24 marks)

# Section 4

# Exploring the research process

## Pause for thought

1    What are your thoughts about the use of guns in the contemporary UK:

    (a)  by the police?

    (b)  by teenagers?

2    Where do you think your ideas have come from?

3    If you had the time and money to do research on the use of guns in society, what difficulties do you think you would need to overcome?

The process of carrying out research and collecting evidence distinguishes sociologists from those who make claims about society based on commonsense opinions, based on personal experiences, values and prejudices. These commonsense opinions are what we hear and read being expressed by friends, family members and the media as we go about our daily business. Personal experiences and commonsense views are important, but without evidence based on research to support them, they remain just that – commonsense views.

The process of doing research will not necessarily be **value free**, that is, free from the biases of the researcher, but where these do affect the research most contemporary sociologists usually 'come clean' and make it clear to readers how they may have been influenced by their values.

## Type of data

The type of data collected by sociologists from their research may be quantitative, qualitative or a combination of the two.

◆    Quantitative data, based on numbers and statistics, are mostly collected by **positivists**. They try to carry out their research in a logical, systematic and objective way using methods similar to those of the natural sciences.

◆    Qualitative data are based on descriptions of events and social interactions and are words. They are mostly collected by **interpretivists**. They take a more open-ended approach to the collection of data, seeking to experience the world from the viewpoint of those they are researching and to look for meanings people attach to their actions.

### Activity 4.1

Look at recent copies of tabloid newspapers. Find one with a headline about gang crime amongst teenagers. Then consider the following question.

'To what extent is the article based on the views of the journalist who wrote it?'

Look for words that suggest the article is based on opinion rather than on fact.

### Activity 4.2

Watch a past episode of the cult television programme *The X Files*. What sort of approach does Mulder take to solving the problem and what is Scully's approach? Which of them is the logical scientific one and who is looking for meanings behind people's actions?

Whether the sociologist is a positivist, an interpretivist or someone using a multi-method approach they will follow a similar process.

## Choice of topic

The first part of the process is to decide what to research; to identify a social phenomenon or a problem to investigate. The decision of what to do may be based on a number of factors.

1   The values and experiences of the sociologist: for example, Hodkinson (2002) carried out research on goths because he had previous experience of the subculture.

2   The sociologist's theoretical position, their view of the world: for example, Plummer's study of working-class girls in 2000 arose from her specific concern with why the education of working-class girls has not been prioritised in the contemporary UK.

3   The organisation employing sociologists in which case the decision of what to research is likely to reflect the values of the organisation. The Child Poverty Action Group is a campaigning charity, concerned to monitor the extent of child poverty. Any research they commission will probably reflect this.

4   The accessibility of the group the sociologist wants to study. Some closed groups, such as young offenders in secure institutions, would be difficult for most sociologists to access. Hodkinson's study on the goths might have been more difficult had he not once been part of the subculture.

5   Practical issues of time and money may determine the choice and extent of a piece of research.

## Research questions

The next part of the process is usually to identify a research question, an aim or, less commonly, a hypothesis. A hypothesis is a claim about what might be the case and is phrased as a statement, for example 'Girls do better with coursework'. Most sociologists, however, start with some sort of question. In *The New East End*, the research questions Dench et al. (2006) posed were concerned with:

◆   the arrival of the Bangladeshis in the East End of London

◆   whether they are now part of the East End

◆   whether the way newcomers become incorporated is different from the way in which previous immigrant groups became part of the area, and, if so, why this should be the case.

There are also those sociologists who start with an aim. For example, Hodkinson's aim in 2002 was to examine the goth scene in the UK. Jackson's aim in 2006 was 'to understand the pattern of behaviours and attitudes that are labelled as "laddish" amongst girls as well as boys' (2006b, p. xii).

## Operationalisation

**Operationalisation** is the process of defining the key terms and concepts which form the basis of the research in order to ensure readers of the research and other sociologists know how the terms are being used. Jackson, needed to explain what she meant by 'laddism' and 'laddettes'. In his research, Hodkinson took goths to mean the subcultural groupings that emerged in the UK at the end of the 1980s which contained elements of punk, glam rock and new romantic fused together (2002). It also means breaking down a research question, aim or hypothesis into something that can be measured.

## Target population

Having decided what to study, sociologists have to decide who the people they potentially want to study are, in other words, their target population. If they wanted to find out whether children from birth to age 10 are given different toys according to their sex, the target population would be all boys and girls from birth to age 10. Since it would be virtually impossible to study all boys and girls of this age group, a sample, or portion, of children would need to be selected: a small number of the bigger, target group.

## Sampling

There are a number of different ways of selecting a sample and the method a sociologist chooses will partially depend on whether they want a sample which is **representative** of their **target population**. This means a sample that fairly reflects that population in terms of social

1   Identify an appropriate sampling frame for each target population in Table 4.1, then decide where it could be obtained from.

2   What problems or difficulties do you think would occur in attempting to obtain any of the sampling frames you have identified?

| Target population | Sampling frame | How could it be obtained |
|---|---|---|
| GCSE students in a local school | | |
| Workers in a factory | | |
| People in local sports teams | | |
| New mothers | | |

Table 4.1 Appropriate sampling frames for different target population

characteristics such as class, gender, age and ethnicity and which, if large enough, will allow the sociologist to make generalisations from their results. That is, the findings or results for the group with whom the research has been done can be applied to other people in the same or similar situation. In some cases there will be a list from which the sociologist can select their sample. Lists that include most of the target population are known as sampling frames. Two of the most useful sampling frames are school registers and the Postcode Address File (PAF)

**Weblink**

The Royal Mail website (see 'Websites' page ii) has information on how to access the Postcode Address File.

# Selecting a sample

There are a number of techniques for selecting a sample and these can be divided into two types:

◆   probability or **random sampling**

◆   non-probability or **non-random sampling**.

## Probability or random sampling

There are three main techniques that come under this broad heading.

1   Simple random sampling – this involves selecting a number of sampling units, which could be either individuals or groups such as a households, from the sampling frame. This selection is usually computer generated.

2   Systematic random sampling – this involves picking one name or unit from the sampling frame and then choosing every $n$th name after that.

If large enough, both of those sampling techniques could mean the sample would be representative of the target population. However, the third technique provides a greater opportunity for a representative sample.

3   Stratified random sampling – this involves dividing the population according to the numbers of people with the social characteristics required, such as gender or ethnicity, and then making a random selection within those groups.

Sampling frames are not always available or even appropriate and even if they are, some sociologists do not use them because of the nature of the sample they are looking for. In relation to any of these situations it is likely that the sample will then be a non-random one.

## Non-probability or non-random sampling

There are three main techniques that come under this broad heading.

1   Quota sampling – this involves the sociologist making a decision about the

numbers of people they want from certain social characteristics and then selecting them personally. The obvious advantage is that the sociologist has some control but they may choose people whom they like the look of or who fit the characteristic very clearly, causing their sample to be skewed or biased.

2 Snowball sampling – this is a useful technique to use when access to a group is difficult and involves a sociologist finding one person they are interested in and then asking them if they know anyone else who might be willing to take part. While clearly useful where access is problematic, this approach could lead to the people in the sample being all rather similar to each other

3 Purposive sampling – this is the technique used by sociologists who are looking for particular people. For example, Hodkinson knew he wanted goths and sought them out. It could also be used where a specific type of person is required, such as a headteacher.

### Activity 4.4

Two other non-random techniques are sometimes used – volunteer sampling and opportunity sampling. Think what each might involve and decide in what circumstances they could be useful.

## Access

Once the sample has been selected, then the sociologist will need to decide how they are going to get access to the people they want to study and whether there is a **gatekeeper** who will facilitate the access. A gatekeeper is someone who knows the people and has it in their power to let the sociologist have access to them. For example, in Jackson's study on lads and ladettes in schools (2006b), the headteachers were the gatekeepers who gave her access. However, access is not always easily obtained, which is why some social groups remain largely unresearched. Gaining access to deviant groups, to those who are illiterate or exclusive as well as those resistant to research can be very problematic and could affect the research design.

### Activity 4.5

Choose three pieces of research you have learned about in one of the identities you have been studying, and decide how the sociologist might have got access to the people they studied and whether you think there would have been a gatekeeper. You do not need to look the research up as long as you know what it was about. If you have understood the research and know who was being studied you should be able to make a sociological 'guess'.

## Primary or secondary data collection

The type of data collected by sociologists could be primary data. Primary data are data collected by the sociologists themselves. They are collected using methods such as interviews, observation and questionnaires which produces data that are new to the sociologist collecting them. Alternatively, they could be secondary data which are data that already exist, which have been collected by other sociologists or other organisations, for example official statistics collected by various government departments or personal documents such as diaries and letters.

Positivists will tend to use methods of data collection which use a standardised measuring instrument such as a structured questionnaire or interview, because this allows the research to be repeated by either themselves or another sociologist and consistent results obtained. These methods are replicable and the data that are collected are **reliable**.

Interpretivists will use unstructured interviews and observation in order to obtain a detailed and in-depth picture of the people being studied. The data collected will then be **valid**, a true picture of the social reality of those being studied. Primary and secondary methods of data collection are considered in more detail in the sections on quantitative data and qualitative data.

## Pilot studies

Some sociologists decide to do a pilot study before they start their main study. A pilot study is a test run to find out whether the research is likely to work and to make changes to the design of the study where necessary. Pilot studies are more commonly used with quantitative methods of data collection to check the sampling and the research device, the questionnaire or interview.

# Ethics

At every stage of the research process it is important to consider what ethical issues might arise. All sociological research intrudes in some way into the lives of those being studied and therefore sociologists should follow the guidelines of the British Sociological Association (BSA). The guidelines are a protocol that sociologists should adhere to. The permission of those taking part should be obtained, their anonymity and privacy assured. In addition, the confidentiality of those being studied should be respected, and their safety, and the safety of the sociologist are paramount. People should have the right to withdraw from the research at any stage of the process.

# Interpretation of data

Whether a sociologist has chosen to collect largely quantitative data, qualitative data or a combination of the two, they have to make decisions about how they will interpret it.

◆ Positivist sociologists, who have collected statistical data from structured questionnaires and interviews, will present the data they have collected in the form of tables and graphs. They will then be able to look for patterns and trends and identify what appear to be significant findings. They will be able to check for similarities and differences in relation to the data. However, it is likely that they will have collected very large quantities of data which means, when it comes to which particular trend or pattern or similarity or difference to comment upon, they will be making a decision which may not be entirely objective (free from bias) and scientific. The decisions on which aspects of the data to comment on may well be based on their own values – on what they see as important in relation to the particular research they have done and what they were hoping to find.

◆ Interpretivist sociologists are likely to have a large amount of data in the form of words which they have collected from their observations and unstructured interviews. This means they will need to select what they are going to comment on. For example, Williamson (2004) could not include all the data he collected from the interviews he conducted and the time he spent with the Milltown Boys. As such he, like other interpretivist sociologists, may well have selected data he considered to be most important or most interesting. This is known as researcher imposition, where the researcher imposes their own views and values on the data collected. Indeed Williamson points out that he became involved in the lives of those he researched by attending activities such as weddings, funerals and parties, which may well have coloured his interpretation of the data he collected.

Whether the sociologist is an interpretivist or a positivist, it is possible to begin overcoming the problem of the data being interpreted from the viewpoint of the researcher. One way is by going back to the people who have been researched and asking them to check whether the interpretation is a fair one or not. This is known as respondent validation, where the respondents are given the opportunity to read what is being said about them and agree or disagree with it.

# Key concepts in the research process

## *Validity*

Validity is the extent to which the research provides a true picture of the social reality of those being studied. It is the extent to which the research does what it set out to do in relation to the individuals or group being studied. For example, Burdsey's research (2004) on the young Asian footballers gives an insight into what they felt about being young Asian footballers. Burdsey did 'get inside their heads' as far as possible in order to portray the world from their point of view and to convey their true feelings and experiences. Data that are high in validity are particularly important to interpretivists, who seek to research the meanings and motives that people attach to what they do and say. In studying young Asian footballers, and the extent to which they wanted to be seen as one of the lads, Burdsey (2004) wanted to understand the decisions they made and to gain an insight into what they felt about being Asian footballers and what informed the decisions they made. By doing this, it can be argued his data is high in validity.

## Reliability

Research may be said to be high in reliability if the method used to collect the data is a standardised one. Questionnaires and structured interviews are both standardised measuring instruments and therefore the research can be repeated by the original sociologist or by someone else and the same or similar results are likely to be found. Positivist sociologists seek to use structured questionnaires or interviews because they claim they are consistent; they can be used again and again and if the results vary it will be not be because the research method is unscientific.

## Representativeness

Representativeness is concerned with whether the group or individuals being studied are a fair reflection of the target population, whether they are typical of it in terms of social characteristics such as age, gender, ethnicity and/or class. Some sociologists are concerned that their sample should be representative and will therefore select it in such a way that it includes all the social characteristics of the target population and that these are in the same proportion as they are in the larger target population. In order for this to be the case, the sample has to be selected using non-random methods and also needs to be reasonably large in order to avoid the sample being skewed by untypical sampling units. If it is both large and a fair reflection of the target population then it will be possible to make generalisations from the data collected.

## Generalisability

This concept is concerned with the extent to which it is possible to apply the findings from the research sample to the wider target population. If the sample is large enough, and if it mirrors the target population, then it is possible to say that the research findings can be applied in that way and that what holds for the sample also holds for the larger population. Again it is positivists who seek to obtain data that will allow them to make such generalisations, although that does not mean the findings from a small-scale study cannot also be said to be generalisable. For example, the research by MacDonald and Marsh (2005) on disconnected youth on Teeside was focussed on Teeside but it would be reasonable to suggest that youths who live in other areas of Britain, where there is high unemployment and general deprivation, are likely to have similar responses to those of the Teeside youths.

Exploring the research process

### Section summary

Use the following key words to copy and complete the summary of the section below. Each word should be used only once.

ethics    common sense    research    replicated    qualitative    generalisations
evidence    quantitative    validity    interpretative    true picture
target population    sample

The difference between_____ _____ and sociology is that sociologists base what they say on _____ . They carry out _____ .

Positivist sociologists collect _____ data, which is data in the form of numbers. Their research can be _____ while _____ sociologists collect _____ data in the form of words, and claim their data gives a _____ _____ of the people they are researching. It is high in _____ .

After choosing a topic, the _____ _____ has to be identified and a _____ selected. If it is large and fairly reflects the people being studied then _____ can be safely made. Throughout the whole process sociologists need to take account of _____ .

# Exploring the use of quantitative data collection methods and analysis in the context of research

## Pause for thought

1 Imagine you are a sociologist and want to study trends in the percentage of GCSE grades achieved by students according to their gender between 1988 and 2008. How will you do it?

2 Imagine you are a sociologist and want to research whether men or women take on most responsibility for recycling within a household. How will you do it?

3 Imagine you are a sociologist and want to research patterns in dating advertisements (personal advertisements, soul seekers) placed in national newspapers to see if there are any differences according to gender. How will you do it?

Quantitative research aims to measure and to generate data that are numerical. Each of the research scenarios in the 'Pause for thought' above would require the generation of numerical data. Throughout this section you will see how sociologists access these data.

Quantitative data deal with measurement and quantification and are usually presented in the form of tables or graphs where the emphasis is on numbers rather than words. Quantitative data are often chosen for social surveys, as surveys usually have a large sample size, although technically a survey can use either qualitative or quantitative methods. Due to the emphasis on numbers, there are specific ways in which quantitative data are collected and analysed, which we will consider in this section.

## Uses of quantitative data

Quantitative data are associated with a theoretical position called positivism. Nineteenth-century positivist thinkers such as Émile Durkheim and Auguste Comte argued that sociology needed to follow the principles and practices of the natural sciences in order to be taken seriously as a new subject discipline. These early positivist thinkers argued that numerical data that natural scientists worked with were value free and objective, and so independent of the researcher's influence. They could be verified again and again through tests to prove (or disprove) a theory or hypothesis, and so were considered highly reliable. This paved the way for sociology to become a prominent social science, working with quantitative data to help explain social phenomena in the same way as natural scientists used numerical data to understand the natural world.

As quantitative data use numbers, they have been and still are associated with solid, objective research with a scientific aura to it. Because of its links with science, quantitative research is thought to be carefully planned and predetermined, with the researchers knowing exactly what they are looking for and how they are measuring it. Figure 5.1 shows the key stages that researchers go through in a research project using quantitative data. Although researchers do not have to stick rigidly to this process, it shows

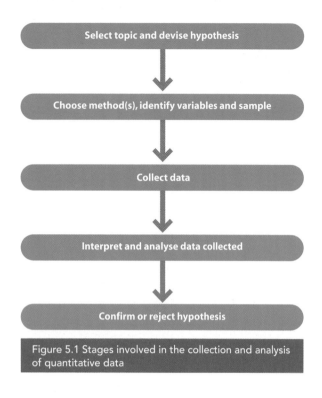

**Select topic and devise hypothesis**

↓

**Choose method(s), identify variables and sample**

↓

**Collect data**

↓

**Interpret and analyse data collected**

↓

**Confirm or reject hypothesis**

Figure 5.1 Stages involved in the collection and analysis of quantitative data

quantifiable data relatively straightforward. Software packages such as Statistical Packages for the Social Sciences (SPSS) will run tests with the data and carry out the statistical analysis for the researcher. This is another reason why quantitative data collection methods are most suitable when carrying out large-scale studies.

Quantitative data are associated with the following:

◆ positivism

◆ large-scale surveys that require large, representative samples

◆ establishing patterns and trends

◆ researching cause and effect

◆ reliability

◆ objectivity and value-free research.

However, nothing is ever as it seems in research and the following points of caution have been made about quantifiable data.

◆ Numbers cannot explain issues: they can only ever paint part of a picture, so quantitative data are often thought to lack validity.

◆ We can never truly establish cause and effect, because variables cannot be isolated when dealing with social issues. For example, if a researcher detects a pattern between gender and income, how can they ever be certain that one variable is the cause of another? It is very possible that other factors impact on the relationship too, such as age and level of skill, for example. In short, in sociological research it is very difficult to establish cause and effect relationships due to the complex nature of social reality.

◆ Researchers are rarely, if ever, value free and objective. The values of the researcher creep into the design of the research project at all stages and although they can be controlled (to some degree) they can never be eradicated. Values such as what is considered as important features or the way in which questions are asked/phrased will inevitably differ from one person to another.

◆ Many of the statistical packages are used by researchers who do not understand them. Using the wrong tests and misinterpreting the data can lead some to question the use of such packages.

how the collection and analysis of quantifiable data is systematic. It begins with a hypothesis to be tested, proven or disproved. It generates data in numerical form and seeks to confirm or reject the hypothesis.

Quantitative data focus on specific factors and study them in relation to other specific factors, often using variables. A variable is a defined property or characteristic of a group, person or situation that can be measured in some way. For example, gender, income, marital status and age are all variables that could be quantified and measured. When the measurements vary between people or groups they can be compared with one another to look for patterns and trends. A pattern is something which is visible within data and which may enable comparisons between groups. For example, there may a pattern in the data between gender and income, or income and age. A trend is something visible over time. For example, a trend may be seen if we compare what was happening in 1997, 2000 and then 2003. Because they work with variables, quantitative data are also useful when researchers want to consider issues of cause and effect, as they can attempt to isolate the variables and test one against another.

Looking for comparisons and correlations between variables makes the analysis of

Read the following description of a piece of research which aimed to collect quantifiable data and answer the questions that follow.

Near the end of 1997, Sheffield City Council launched a pilot scheme to collect paper from households for recycling. The pilot took place in an area which included a mixture of public and private housing stock in order to test the scheme with a variety of household types. The householders were supplied with information about the scheme and given the chance to opt out. Following this information campaign, over 6000 households were issued with blue wheelie bins …

With access to the Council's database, it was possible for us to identify every household that had accepted a blue bin. In order to discover who carries out recycling in the household, we designed a short questionnaire which contained a mixture of open and closed questions, aimed at finding out who initiated the household recycling and how many people took part in recycling as well as their ages and genders. The questionnaire was tested and reviewed by five individuals with expertise in questionnaire design and a further five members of the public …

The sample size was determined by a combination of consideration of the likely final sample size and budget. The questionnaire was sent to a quarter of all households participating in the blue bin trial by selecting every fourth address on the Council's database. This ensured that the households selected were spread across all the streets in the pilot area. In November 2000, some three years after the launch of the pilot scheme, 1532 questionnaires were sent out together with a covering letter and a postage-paid return envelope.

We stress that the aim of this study was not to determine how or why recycling took place in households, nor how or why recycling had developed over time, but simply who started the recycling and who did most of it.

(Source: Oates and McDonald, 2006, p. 24)

1 What were the aims of this piece of research?

2 Identify and explain three reasons why you think a quantitative data collection method was chosen for this research.

# Quantitative data analysis

Quantitative data analysis requires the researcher to scrutinise the data, looking for systematic patterns or trends. Clearly, the statistics compiled by the computer provide the data but it is the responsibility of the researcher to analyse the statistics/numerical data and to consider what they might indicate. This is the point at which the values and expertise of different researchers will begin to influence the findings. What one researcher sees in data another may miss, or discount as irrelevant. For this reason most researchers will work in teams, checking the work of colleagues, or if they do work alone they will seek a second opinion on their analysis.

# Quantitative data collection methods

There are five sociological research methods that you need to be familiar with when studying quantitative data:

◆ questionnaires

◆ structured interviews

◆ semi-structured interviews

◆ statistical data

◆ content analysis.

## Questionnaires

Questionnaires are among the most widely used research methods in sociology. They are lists of questions compiled by the researcher(s), which are subject to self-completion. This means that the respondents themselves fill them in, usually without the researcher present. Questionnaires are suitable for researching topics and questions which require numerical answers and do not deal with highly sensitive issues.

Consider Table 5.1, which shows the findings from the recycling study considered in Activity 5.1. Analyse the data closely and answer the questions that follow. Do this on your own to begin with.

1 How would you interpret the findings from Table 5.1? You should consider the issues of gender, household membership and initiating and sustaining the recycling.

2 Compare your analysis with others. Did you all identify the same patterns? If not, what were the differences?

| | Recycling initiator (started) | Recycling sustainer (kept it going) |
|---|---|---|
| Female | 211 (45%) | 187 (40%) |
| Joint | 120 (26%) | 179 (38%) |
| Male | 76 (16%) | 68 (15%) |
| External person (not a household member) | 13 (3%) | 2 (0.5%) |

Table 5.1 Recycling initiators (who started it) and sustainers (who kept it going) in all households

For example, a researcher who wants to find out the following may consider (and may of course reject) the use of a questionnaire.

1 How many people in a household do the supermarket shopping?

2 How often do they visit the supermarket?

3 How many different types of fruit do they buy in the supermarket?

4 What is the average weekly expenditure on supermarket food?

These four questions all involve a numerical answer and that makes them suitable for questionnaires. None of the questions are particularly sensitive, other than the last one which respondents could choose not to answer. In any case, it may be best answered in a questionnaire, which is anonymous.

The research on recycling used questionnaires as the most appropriate method of research.

## Constructing a questionnaire

Having selected a questionnaire as their chosen method of data collection, a researcher must design the questionnaire, taking great care in doing so. A badly designed questionnaire will produce poor results, which may invalidate a research project. The construction of a questionnaire is therefore a time-consuming and thoughtful craft. The following is a list of the factors that should be taken into consideration.

- The instructions should be clear.

- Where and when to return the questionnaire should be clearly stated.

- The purpose of the questionnaire should be explained.

- Confidentiality should be ensured.

- The questionnaire should not be over long. The length of a questionnaire should take into consideration the target population. Where will they be completing it and how much time would they be able to spend on it?

- Questions should be clear and use language/terminology that will be understood by all of the respondents.

- Questions should not be biased or leading.

- Open questions requiring respondents to write down their thoughts should allow sufficient space for respondents to do so.

- Questions should not offend or upset respondents.

## Question design

The questions have to be clear and concise to ensure that respondents interpret them in the same way. Questions need to be standardised, which means that they should not be ambiguous or confusing.

Questionnaires can contain open-ended and/or closed questions. Closed questions have predetermined answers to choose from, usually by way of a tick box. Open-ended questions ask a question and then require the respondent to write down their own response.

Measurement scales can be used effectively in questionnaires. When a researcher wants to find out the strength of feeling on an issue, a measurement scale can be used. Respondents have to code their answers using a measurement scale such as the one in Figure 5.2.

| Strongly agree | Agree | Neutral | Disagree | Strongly disagree |
|---|---|---|---|---|
| 1 | 2 | 3 | 4 | 5 |

Figure 5.2 A questionnaire measurements scale

## Administering a questionnaire

Alongside the design of your questionnaire you also need to consider how you are going to administer it, which ensures that it reaches a suitable sample of respondents and that you receive a sufficiently high return rate to make the data analysis worthwhile.

There are different ways of administering questionnaires, each with their own advantages and disadvantages.

### Advantages of questionnaires

- Economical, relatively easy to administer, relatively low cost of material, less time-consuming than other methods.

- No chance of researcher face-to-face influence, as the researcher is not present when the questionnaires are filled in.

- Standardised answers to standardised questions: all respondents are faced with the same questions in the same order and format.

- Potential to pre-code the answers and the availability of SPSS makes data analysis potentially more straightforward.

Consider the following short questionnaire. Identify ten potential problems with it.

> Good morning, we are a charity working to prevent the use of animals for tests and trials for cosmetic products. We hope that you will agree that our work is important and spend a few moments completing this short questionnaire.
>
> Thank you.
>
> 1 Male __ Female __
>
> 2 How old are you?_____
>
> 3 Do you buy cosmetic products that have been tested on animals?
>
>    Yes __ No __
>
> 4 What are your views on the government's current policy relating to animal testing? Please explain. _____
>
>    _____
>
>    _____
>
>    _____
>
> 5 Do you agree that more needs to be done to prevent companies from exploiting animals in this way?
>
>    Yes __ No __
>
> Thank you for your time. Please write your name and address below if you would be interested in finding out more about the work of our group.
>
> Name _____
>
> Address _____
>
> _____
>
> _____
>
> _____
>
> Preferred method of contact details (email/telephone) _____
>
> _____

Table 5.2 states different ways of administering questionnaires, with some advantages and disadvantages filled in for you. Copy and complete the table by filling in the boxes.

| Administration | Advantage | Disadvantage | Suitable topic | Unsuitable topic |
|---|---|---|---|---|
| Post | Access a large sample | | | Frequency and experience of domestic violence |
| Internet | | | How much time per day do internet users spend surfing the net? | |
| Hand delivered to households/ organisations | Direct access to respondents | | | |
| Given out face-to-face on the street | | Time consuming | | |

Table 5.2 Advantages and disadvantages of different ways of administering questionnaires

### Disadvantages of questionnaires

- The questionnaire is only as good as the questions it contains. If the questions are misinterpreted then the data will be low in validity.

- Pre-coded, standardised questions can be off-putting to respondents, resulting in a low response rate.

- No chance to check the truthfulness of the answer, again affecting the validity of the research findings.

- Postal questionnaires can be expensive and have low response rates, accessing a sample can therefore be difficult.

## Structured interviews

In many ways structured interviews are like questionnaires, except that they are administered either face-to-face with a respondent or over the telephone. Structured interviews contain standardised questions, which are asked to each respondent in the same order and in the same way. Usually the respondents are offered a list of predetermined answers to select the most appropriate answer from, however, structured interviews can include open-ended questions too. This means that structured interviews lend themselves to collecting quantitative data. Many large-scale government surveys use structured interviews, such as the British Social Attitudes Survey, which conducts interviews annually with approximately 3600 respondents in their homes.

As with the questionnaires it is crucial that the questions are written to access the key information needed for the research. It is worth noting that many research projects use trained interviewers who were not involved in writing the questions for the interview. In any interview the interviewer plays a crucial role, as the tone of their questioning or their body language can play an important part in influencing how a respondent understands and responds to a question.

Interviewers therefore have to be trained to ask questions in a neutral but interested way.

Structured interviews used to be associated with market research companies, where teams of interviewers armed with clipboards stopped unsuspecting passers by and asked the questions on the street. However, in recent years structured interviews have become associated with large-scale surveys where interviews are conducted with respondents, often in their own homes. The data/responses collected are directly input to a laptop computer. This technique has been used in the British Crime Survey and in the British Social Attitudes Survey. The similarities between structured interviewers and questionnaires means that the advantages and disadvantages associated with each are strikingly similar.

### Advantages of structured interviews

- Standardised answers to standardised questions: all respondents are faced with the same questions in the same order and format.
- Potential to pre-code the answers and the availability of computer software programmes makes data analysis potentially more straightforward.
- High response rate as new respondents can be accessed if sample size drops.
- The presence of the interviewer to explain any question (if allowed).

### Disadvantages of structured interviews

- The interview is only as good as the questions it contains. If the questions are misinterpreted then the data will be low in validity.
- Pre-coded, standardised questions can be off-putting to respondents resulting in lower validity or non-completion of the interview.
- Potential for some interviewer effect through body language and tone of questioning.
- Interviews are time-consuming and the cost of paying the interviewers has to be allowed for.

## Semi-structured interviews

In a semi-structured interview the interviewer is again present and has a clear list of issues to be addressed and questions to be answered. However, the questions can be asked in any order and the interviewer has much greater control of proceedings than in a structured interview. The questions are generally open ended due to the flexible nature of the interview but during the course of semi-structured interviews quantitative data could be collected (which is why this method has been included here).

## Statistical data

Statistical data are an obvious form in which to present data generated numerically. Particularly when dealing with large datasets and sample sizes, statistical evidence is likely to be used to illustrate trends and patterns, causes and correlations. Official statistics are compiled and/or commissioned by government bodies, and are owned by the government (under Crown copyright) but are available for use by anyone.

The Office for National Statistics (ONS) is responsible for conducting the Census, where questionnaires are sent to every household in the UK, once every ten years. The data from the Census are clearly quantitative, as the questions are closed, and are used in many government studies. The Census is considered to be representative of the UK population, as it reaches every household and must by law be completed and returned by post (the postage is prepaid). The ONS is also responsible for conducting research into issues such as births, deaths and marriages. These projects again generate quantitative data, using administrative records from local and county-based authorities, as an official record. Clearly, research in these areas is considered reliable and valid due to the fact that it is a legal requirement to register births, deaths and marriages.

A final example of the collection of official statistics is the General Household Survey (GHS), which conducts interviews annually with around 16,000 respondents from 9000 households on a range of social issues. The GHS uses computer-assisted personal interviewing techniques in compiling their largely quantitative data.

Statistical data from all of these sources and many other government departments and organisations is brought together in documents such as *Social Trends*, which is available online and in printed form and presents statistical data from the range of government-sponsored research each year. *Social Trends* is an important source of information in research today.

Non-official statistics are also used by sociologists. These are not owned or compiled by the government but rather by independent companies, researchers or universities. Companies such as Ipsos MORI are independent research organisations that generate statistical data which can be bought or sometimes downloaded. Ipsos MORI carries out work for the government but also for private companies such as Nokia and Toyota. Although not exclusively dealing with quantitative data, much of its research uses large sample sizes and surveys of one kind or another, which makes quantitative data appealing. The company uses face-to-face interview techniques, telephone surveys (using interviews), postal questionnaires and, increasingly, online surveys too. Ipsos MORI makes its money by charging the companies (or government) for the research conducted. Anyone can set up an independent research company and anyone can use their services, which leaves them open to the criticism that their work will always be difficult to replicate and open to potential misuse.

> ### Advantages of statistical data
>
> - As secondary data they are cheap, usually free (official statistics) and relatively easy to access.
>
> - Patterns and trends can be clearly visible.
>
> - They deal with large sample sizes and are considered as representative.
>
> - They can be used and reused to test different variables.
>
> - They are considered reliable as the data generated can be checked year on year.

> ### Disadvantages of statistical data
>
> - Statistical data are open to misuse; they can be manipulated to show what the researcher wants them to show.
>
> - There is potential too for misuse by the government or organisation compiling them, in order to show what they want them to show.
>
> - Some researchers use statistical data but don't understand them, meaning they can be misinterpreted.
>
> - They cannot express reasons for trends, and reduce everything to a number, therefore they are criticised for being low in validity.
>
> - They are secondary evidence, which it is difficult to access in order to verify.

## Content analysis

Content analysis is a method used to analyse the content of any text (Denscombe, 2003). It is a way of quantifying data in the form of sounds, pictures or writing. Content analysis seeks to quantify content in terms of predetermined categories in a systematic and replicable manner. For this reason it has been used extensively in the study of the mass media, where selected text (writing/sound/image) is broken down and analysed, with the researcher looking for evidence to fit into certain predefined categories. Content analysis uses a systematic procedure for textual analysis where a formulaic approach is necessary. The basic procedure for carrying out content analysis is given in Figure 5.3.

Content analysis has the potential to uncover hidden aspects of texts and bring them to the surface. It has been used by researchers studying stereotypical images of girls and boys in children's story books and in the study of the representation of different social groups in the media. Jagger (1998) used content analysis in her study of 1094 dating advertisements in national newspapers. She analysed the dating adverts in four different newspapers over a period of time. Having created categories to place aspects of the adverts in, she found that women were more likely than men to stress economic resources as being important in possible partners. Both men and women placed significance on their bodies and physical appearance.

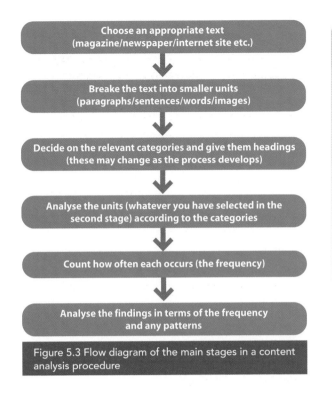

**Choose an appropriate text**
(magazine/newspaper/internet site etc.)

↓

**Break the text into smaller units**
(paragraphs/sentences/words/images)

↓

**Decide on the relevant categories and give them headings**
(these may change as the process develops)

↓

**Analyse the units** (whatever you have selected in the second stage) according to the categories

↓

**Count how often each occurs** (the frequency)

↓

**Analyse the findings in terms of the frequency and any patterns**

Figure 5.3 Flow diagram of the main stages in a content analysis procedure

## Advantages of content analysis

- It quantifies the meaning of text. It can uncover the terminology/ideas being used and the frequency with which they occur.

- It is relatively high in reliability and as it follows systematic procedures it should be replicable.

- It is relatively cheap.

- It can be used on words, images or sound and is of major importance in studying the mass media.

- On straightforward pieces it can provide useful results.

### Activity 5.5

Select a newspaper, magazine or a website page that interests you. The text should include at least four paragraphs and should focus on a current newsworthy issue or event. Carry out some basic content analysis, following the steps below.

1 Decide your unit of analysis (words/ sentences/paragraphs).

2 Develop the categories you are using. Which key words or types of words are used? Think about positive/negative, size, shapes, colours.

3 Count the frequency with which each occurs.

4 Analyse the words and the frequency used. Consider who wrote each piece and write your analysis of it.

## Disadvantages of content analysis

- The initial coding of texts is crucial in establishing the categories to be analysed.

- If the coding is inaccurate then the findings will be considered invalid.

- It could be accused of analysing text out of context, taking words and ignoring the context they are being used in.

- Not considered as a valid method on its own for complex textual analysis.

Exploring the use of quantitative data collection

## Section summary

Use the following key words to copy and complete the summary of this section below. Each word should be used only once.

reliability     cause and effect     questionnaires     structured interviews     numerical
positivist thinkers     objective     natural sciences     variables     patterns
trends     statistical data     content analysis

Quantifiable data are data found in _____ form. This means they can be used for measuring _____ in the data and looking for _____ over time. Quantifiable methods of data collection include _____, _____ _____, _____ _____ and _____ _____. All of these methods share the common characteristic of having relatively little researcher effect, and in this sense they are considered as being more _____ than methods of qualitative data collection. As they focus on the collection of quantitative data, these methods are often used in large-scale studies as a larger sample size can be accessed and different social groups can be targeted making the study more representative than many small-scale qualitative studies.

Methods of quantitative data collection often need to isolate key_____ which are carefully defined characteristics such as gender or age, from which measuring _____ ___ _____ becomes a possibility.

Quantitative data are considered to be high in _____ which means that they can be repeated and the results should be broadly the same. On the other hand, quantitative data lack validity.

From a theoretical view, _____ _____ tend to use quantitative data, as they have been associated with objective findings which hold credibility as in _____ _____. It is a debatable point as to whether such objective findings can be achieved in the social sciences.

Exploring the use of quantitative data collection

# Exploring the use of qualitative data collection methods and analysis in the context of research

Pause for thought

1   If you wanted to research how black British youths experience life in the contemporary UK, how would you do it?

2   If you wanted to research the values associated with New Age Travellers in the UK, how would you do it?

Both scenarios in 'Pause for thought' require the researcher to find ways of accessing and uncovering the experiences and values of social groups. Throughout this section you will find out how sociologists have tackled both scenarios. The central feature of qualitative research is its aim of describing and understanding events or social interactions through words and text. Qualitative data collection methods need to be able to access and uncover the meanings attached to actions, aiming to collect in-depth valid data which present a true picture of social reality. The main methods of research for collecting these data are observation and unstructured interviews.

## Uses of qualitative data

Qualitative data are associated with interpretivist theory. Interpretivists aim to understand the social world through examining the interpretation of the world by its members. In this sense, qualitative data are concerned with explaining social action from the point of view of an individual. Interpretivism does not seek to explain the causes of things, but focuses instead on how things are experienced subjectively by those directly involved. Interpretivists argue that only by studying something in depth can the sociologist

begin to understand the people and situation being studied.

Interpretivism has been influenced by sociologists such as Becker (1963) and the concept of **labelling** and the concept of *verstehen*. *Verstehen* is the German word for 'understanding' and is closely related to the process of achieving empathy: understanding a situation from the viewpoint of another group or individual. In order to do this, sociologists need

### Activity 6.1

If you were asked to research the experiences of young people and substance abuse in your local area, how would you deal with the following issues? You may need to refresh your memory on some of these points, which were covered in Section 4 on the research process (pp. 73–78):

- accessing your sample
- gaining information
- building a rapport
- ethical issues
- social characteristics of the researcher.

to build up a rapport with those who are being studied. This means establishing a solid working relationship where information can be accessed and articulated in a trusting way. The social characteristics (gender, class, age and ethnicity) of the qualitative researcher are very important in establishing a rapport and carrying out successful qualitative research. Consider, for example, the implications of researching the social experiences of living in an old people's home on the south coast of England if the researcher was a young African-Caribbean student from inner London. Figure 6.1 shows the main concepts associated with qualitative data.

**Figure 6.1 Key concepts for qualitative data**

During the last thirty years, there has been more qualitative research carried out in sociology than quantitative research. This is unsurprising given that the main strength of qualitative research lies in its ability to explain social action from the point of view of those being studied. It is especially useful for studying social groups who are difficult to access through questionnaires, such as delinquents or members of subcultural groups. Qualitative data have also been used widely in education where valid studies of the experience of schooling can only come from interviews and observation of school children.

However, qualitative data are not without their critics. Many sociologists consider qualitative data to lack the scientific rigour necessary to make them reliable, arguing that the studies lack consistency and would be difficult, if not impossible, to repeat. Some also point out

that studying a small group of people in depth makes these studies of limited use as they are so unrepresentative. The following points of criticism have been raised about qualitative data.

◆ Small-scale research contributes little to the understanding of the social world, as it is unrepresentative and not able to be generalised to a wider population. For example, studying the social experiences of 15 black youths in London, over the period of a year, is unlikely to be generalisable outside that community.

◆ The research collected cannot provide causal links and offers few ways of solving social problems. Without isolating the cause of something, solutions are difficult to offer.

◆ As qualitative research involves in-depth research with small social groups the social characteristics of the researcher become crucial in the trustworthiness of the data collected. The social characteristics of the researcher will inevitably influence the quality and quantity of data collected. This has led to the criticism that qualitative data themselves are little more than the researcher's subjective understanding and interpretation of a situation.

◆ Large-scale organisations, including many government bodies, find qualitative data of limited use, as the data can lack transparency, in other words, it is not obvious where the findings have come from. Numerical data are often considered to have more rigour even if they lack validity.

## Qualitative data analysis

The data produced in qualitative studies are descriptive words rather than numbers – they are narratives. Vast quantities of data come from interview transcripts and field notes made during observations, and these all need to be analysed in a systematic way to ensure the findings are accurate. Some studies have been known to produce thousands of pages of transcribed notes. Qualitative data analysis is a complex process as the researcher needs to ensure they are interpreting and representing the views of the sample accurately. This involves looking for dominant themes in the text, and involves reading, re-reading and analysing the data.

There are software packages which can help with this process, such as NVIVO and Atlas. However, even with assistance, the analysis of thousands of words of text is a highly skilled and time consuming task. Researchers should also seek a second opinion on their data analysis by either asking the informants to view their data analysis or asking another researcher to check that their interpretation of the data is accurate. This is known as seeking respondent validation.

The collection of qualitative data can be broadly described as following the pattern in Figure 6.2. However, researchers will diverge from this when necessary. For example, it is quite common for the researcher to re-enter the field site (where the data are collected) during the interpretation of the data if they realise they are lacking the required data.

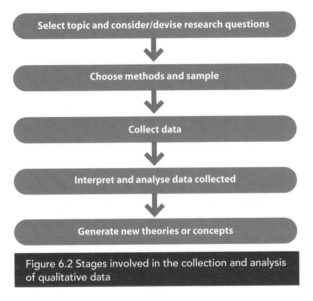

Figure 6.2 Stages involved in the collection and analysis of qualitative data

# Qualitative methods of data collection

The main methods of collecting qualitative data include:

- observation
- ethnography
- interviews
- focus groups
- analysis of personal documents.

The remainder of this section will take each of these in turn, outlining the main features and including the advantages and disadvantages associated with each method.

Read the following description of a piece of qualitative research carried out by a young, female, British Asian sociologist called Claire Alexander. The study was carried out over a twelve month period in London using observation and interviews as the main methods of research.

## The study

The aim was to provide an in-depth, 'street level' account of the creation and manipulation of identity by a group of black British youths, living in London. Alexander was hoping to provide a clear account of black British experience which would take into account the social experiences and aspects of black life.

The participants in the research were predominantly male, partly because black expressive culture at that time was dominated by men, but largely because it was young men Alexander first met. Access to the group was gained through a friend who introduced her to Ricky. Ricky was looking for a flatmate and Alexander moved into his flat at the beginning of the research. Through Ricky she met the rest of the group. Her age, gender and ethnic origin were important aids to the research. As she was broadly the same age as the men, she could fit into their social life. As a woman she posed no threat to the internal structure, and as an Asian she felt that she was considered as an asset to the group's image.

Limitations on time and resources, and the intensity of establishing a strong rapport with the groups meant that the scope of the study remained small scale and sharply focused, and in the end it focused largely on only fifteen youths.

(Source: adapted from Alexander, 1996, pp.18–20)

1 What were the aims of this piece of research?

2 Give two reasons why qualitative data collection methods were suitable in this research.

3 Do you think the data collected in this study would be considered (a) valid and (b) reliable? Explain your answer.

Exploring the use of qualitative data collection

# Observation

Observation is based on the belief that watching and recording activities will produce valid data. The method relies on direct observation of real life situations. It involves the researcher going 'into the field', meaning the natural setting, and observing behaviour without disrupting the situation. The nature of the topic being studied and gaining access and entry to a social setting or group are crucial in successful observations.

Martin (2000) used observation as his method of data collection when he researched the experiences of New Age Traveller communities in the UK. Clearly, however, Martin needed a gatekeeper to give him access to the communities, and without this his study would not have been possible. Some observations are carried out covertly (remaining hidden, the group do not know they are being studied) and others overtly with the group being fully aware they are being researched. In Martin's study he chose to carry out the study overtly living on various Traveller sites in the UK and supplementing his observational data with unstructured interviews.

There are ethical issues involved with covert observation. For example, the participants cannot give informed consent and their right to privacy is encroached. On the other hand, there is evidence that if a social group know they are being researched they may alter their behaviour. This is known as the Hawthorne Effect (so named after a factory 'Hawthorne Works' where a series of experiments took place in 1924–32).

Often the actual topic being studied will influence the covert/overt decision. Martin justified his overt observation in terms of ethics and argued that as he was spending a prolonged length of time in the community, any changes in the behaviour of the group could not be sustained.

Observation is a useful technique for many research topics, and there are different types of observation for the researcher to select from. These can be split into:

◆ participant/non-participant

◆ structured/unstructured.

## Participant/non-participant observation

Participant observation involves the researcher immersing themselves into the lives of a social group for an extended period of time. The researcher would join in the daily life of the people being studied over a period of time. By gaining insider experience, the researcher is able to access and understand the meanings and experiences from the point of view of those being studied. It is a method considered to be high in ecological validity; because the groups are being researched in their own settings. One of the main problems with participant observation is the fear of 'going native', which is where the researcher becomes so absorbed into the social setting of the research they lose the ability to be objective. This is particularly the case when the research is carried out covertly.

The advantages of participant observation include:

◆ limited reaction/Hawthorne Effect

◆ data collected are high in ecological validity

◆ provision of a holistic account, focused on the individual's own point of view

◆ limitation on equipment needed

◆ data collected should be valid.

The disadvantages of participant observation include:

◆ gaining access to the group

◆ going native

◆ difficulty in taking notes

◆ ethical issues

◆ commitment and time

---

### Activity 6.3

1 Think of three reasons why the British Sociological Association considers all covert observational studies to be unethical.

2 Consider each of the following topics and decide whether covert observation would be the only realistic choice of method. For each topic outline the problems of using overt observation.

• The experience of football hooligans in the UK.

• How builders show masculine practices at work on a building site.

• Racism in the police force.

Exploring the use of qualitative data collection

- whether the data are representative
- whether the data are reliable
- risk to the observer, particularly if the observation involves groups who use drugs or violence.

Non-participant observation involves observing from the sidelines, an almost 'fly on the wall' approach where the researcher can see the action and record their data without participating in the groups activities. Non-participant observation is by implication carried out overtly as it is difficult to conceal your identity and presence if you are observing people and recording your data. Some studies of young children in primary schools are non-participant as the data needed can only be recorded by watching. Clearly, the recording of data becomes easier in non-participant observation studies. However, real concerns exist over the extent to which the behaviour of the group is natural if they know they are being watched and observed.

## Structured/unstructured observation

In a structured observation, the researcher knows in advance what they are looking for and seeks to record this data in a systematic way, often through an observation schedule. Structured observations have a framework, and an observation schedule ensures that the same type of data is recorded by different researchers, bringing some reliability/consistency to the findings. In many ways, structured observation can become a frequency count, for example how often an event occurs and how long does it last. Structured observation can generate quantitative and qualitative evidence. A good example here would be research in a classroom when the researcher records how many times a teacher asks questions to girls and to boys, recording this in a chart format.

Unstructured observation does not have a framework and clearly provides qualitative data. The researchers gain access and entry to the field site and observe life as it is in the natural setting, which should produce valid data. There are no preconceived checklists to fill out and the evidence collected is in the form of field notes which are descriptions /accounts of events written through the eyes of the researcher. Martin's study of the New Age Travellers and

Alexander's study of young black Britains both used unstructured observations. The obvious problem with this method is in the recording of the data. When does the researcher write their account and how much does this rely on memory and selective interpretation of events? In these respects, are the data collected reliable?

Activity 6.4

1 Select one topic from the following list and plan an observational study around it.

The choices:

1 Do new religious movements brainwash their members?

2 How far is there a gang culture in the London underworld?

3 Do teachers treat boys and girls differently in the classroom?

4 To what extent does working in the advertising industry encourage young people to achieve size zero?

You need to consider the following issues and to justify your decisions:

- participant/non-participant
- structured/unstructured
- overt/covert
- access/gatekeeper
- time
- how you would record your data
- any other issues that would be important.

2 What would be the main problems to overcome in your study?

## Ethnography

Ethnographic studies use participant observation and often unstructured interviews to provide an in-depth account and analysis of a social group or culture. Both Alexander's and Martin's studies are ethnographies which used participant observation and unstructured interviews to establish their data. Many researchers treat ethnography and participant observation as essentially the same thing. However, in general, ethnography is a description of a group of people or cultures using participant observation

Read the following account of a study of the goth subculture in the UK. It provides an example of what qualitative data look like and the detail involved in writing them. Hodkinson himself described his study as a multi-method ethnography; his main sources of data were participant observation, unstructured interviews and media analysis. Answer the questions that follow.

> A car pulls up outside my home in the English city of Birmingham on a rainy Friday morning at the end of October 1998. The long black hair of its occupants informs me that this is my lift. I run outside towards the car, using my rucksack to shield my recently dyed and crimped purple and pink streaked hair from the rain. The tall, slim male driver, wearing eye-liner and dressed up in tight black jeans and a purple velvet shirt, gets out and helps make space for my luggage in the back of the car, among numerous other bags and various pairs of large black boots. We get into the car, and I am greeted by the three female passengers, and immediately recognise the familiar sound of one of my favourite bands, The Mission, on the stereo. We are five Goths on our way to spend a weekend with over a thousand other Goths in a small North Yorkshire seaside town.

(Source: Hodkinson, 2002, p.1)

1 What do you find out about goths from this qualitative account?

2 Hodkinson was a goth and he had 'insider status' within the goth community. How might this influence the data he collected?

3 Do you think his ethnographic study would be (a) valid and (b) reliable?

The advantages of ethnographic studies include:

◆ direct observation of the people under study

◆ detailed and rich data can be collected over time, increasing validity

◆ strong in ecological validity

◆ provide a holistic understanding

◆ good for achieving empathy/*verstehen*.

The disadvantages of ethnographic studies include:

◆ lack of reliability as the research is difficult to repeat

◆ ethical issues

◆ problems of gaining access

◆ insider knowledge/status may be required for access and can lead to problems in gaining objective data

◆ tendency for ethnographic accounts to become based on stories and perceived as such

◆ small scale and lack of generalisablity.

# Interviews

There are different types of interview use in sociology. Qualitative data can be generated by unstructured interviews and by focus group interviews, both explored in this section. Semi-structured interviews can provide qualitative and/or quantitative data depending on how they are designed. Before exploring unstructured interviews we need to make some basic points about carrying out interviews.

In carrying out any type of interview, decisions have to be made with regard to some key questions.

◆ Should the interviews be conducted one-to-one, or in a group? Group interviews are particularly useful when researching young people due to their collaborative nature.

◆ How will you record the data – tape recording or writing up the field notes? Tape recording the interview may make the respondent feel uncomfortable

◆ Should the interviewer stand or sit, smile, nod or look expressionless? What should they wear to create the right impression?

◆ In what type of location should the interview be carried out?

Consider the following interview scenarios. Using the bullet points at the bottom of page 94, discuss the choices an interviewer might make in each scenario.

1  An interviewer working for a soft drinks company needs data on the best tastes and labels to use in order to increase sales among the 14–19 age group.

2  An interviewer working for the government needs data on the extent of racial harassment in a local town.

3  An interviewer collecting data for their university course on the experiences of student debt.

4  An interviewer wanting data on how masculinities are constructed amongst boys aged 11–14 years old.

## Unstructured interviews

Interviewing is a skill, and carrying out unstructured interviews is particularly challenging. This type of interview is based around a conversation. The researcher has an idea of the topics they want to discuss and a basic structure to follow but the actual questions and sequence of questions develops during the interview. The interviewer is able to probe for deeper answers and prompt the respondents when they need more depth to an answer. The role of the researcher is to be unintrusive and to limit the interviewer effect – where respondents answer in the way they think the interviewer wants them to. The interviewer needs to steer the interview towards covering all of the key points, following up new ideas and encouraging the interviewee to give valid data and stay focused on the topic being discussed. The type of data required is important here as some interviews need biographical information, while others need to explore themes and events. The New Age Traveller study and the goths study mentioned previously both used unstructured interviews as a way of eliciting information.

The advantages of unstructured interviews include:

◆  ability to gain empathy and insight, achieving an understanding through asking questions and responding to answers

◆  flexibility

◆  rapport can be created and sustained through the conversational basis of the interview

◆  the potential for rich valid data on a small group of people

◆  high response rate as interviews are pre-arranged

◆  greater depth of information as interviewer can probe and prompt for further data

◆  additional questions can be asked when they need to be, placing less pressure on the interview schedule. This also allows for questions to check the accuracy and plausibility of respondents' answers.

The disadvantages of unstructured interviews include:

◆  time consuming to conduct and analyse – Martin's interviews with New Age Travellers lasted between an hour and a half and four hours each

◆  interviewer effect – whether respondents answer truthfully or in the way they think the interviewer wants them to

◆  difficulty in data analysis due to length and complexity of transcripts

◆  the social characteristics of the researcher are crucial in accessing valid data

◆  lack of reliability – whether the interviews could be repeated by another sociologist

◆  whether they are representative because time constraints usually restrict the interview to a small number of people

◆  skill of the interviewer in accessing the information without digressing onto different topics

◆  importance of interview setting for achieving ecological validity.

## Semi-structured interviews

These contain some pre-set standardised questions or topic areas and the opportunity for additional questions to be asked when necessary. The questions can be asked in any order and the interviewer has much greater control of proceedings than in an unstructured interview. The questions are generally open-ended due to the flexible nature of the interview, but during the course of semi-structured interviews quantitative data could also be collected if the researcher needed it. Archer (2003a) used semi-structured interviews in her study which explored the identities of Muslim boys and girls in the north of England. Using group interviews to encourage rich, detailed responses, the interviews were scheduled around discussing topics such as 'home', 'school', 'race', 'ethnic identity', 'racism' and 'gender identity'. These interviews, therefore, had more of a structure than unstructured ones but still allowed for flexibility.

## Focus groups

A focus group interview is designed to access information from a particular point of view or small group of respondents. Focus groups usually have between six and nine members and are generally used to explore the views of a specific group of people on non-sensitive research topics. They should not be confused with group interviews which seek to access a range of information from a group discussion rather than in one-to-one interviews. Focus group interviews can be prompted by the use of stimulus material, such as videos or articles. Based on the notion that collaborative interviewing encourages interaction between respondents and is likely to be more valid, they seek to build up responses through group conversations with people who may have similar social experiences. The role of the interviewer becomes that of a moderator; guiding the group discussion depending on the responses given and the aims of the research.

The advantages of focus groups include:

◆ they enables issues to be explored which might otherwise remain unknown

◆ they can encourage a wider range of respondents to be involved because of the group basis

◆ they can be tailored around specific groups' needs.

The disadvantages of focus groups include:

◆ it can be difficult to record and transcribe the data

◆ respondents may not disclose sensitive material

◆ the interviewer effect is not eliminated

◆ the discussions can become dominated by specific individuals.

## Personal documents

There are different types of documents that can be used in sociological research; these can be in written or visual form. Personal documents include letters, diaries and photographs. Letters tend to be used by researchers who need a historical slant to their research. Personal diaries represent a point of view captured at a given point and can be useful for understanding the actions and thoughts of an individual. In the future, qualitative data analysis is likely to involve text messaging and email communication as forms of personal documents. Photographs can capture images from the past and present and can be analysed to provide qualitative data too.

Archer (2003a) included the use and analysis of personal diaries in her study of Muslim boys' and girls' identities.

The advantages of personal documents include:

◆ they are cheap and may be easy to access

◆ they are permanent

◆ their interpretation could be checked by another researcher.

The disadvantages of personal documents include:

◆ whether they are credible and authentic – in other words, whether we can trust the documents

◆ how representative they are

◆ problems in interpreting their meaning.

## Section summary

Use the following key words to copy and complete the summary of this section below. Each word should be used only once.

interpretivists    empathy    personal documents    narrative    unstructured interviews
ecological validity    ethnography    participant observation    social experiences
focus groups    valid

Qualitative data is generally produced in _____ form. This means it can be used for describing and analysing the _____ _____ of different groups. Qualitative methods of data collection include _____ _____, _____ _____, _____ _____ and the analysis of _____ _____ .

_____ is used to describe the in-depth study of a culture or social group using qualitative methods of data collection. These methods are considered as being more _____ than methods of quantitative data collection. Due to their time-consuming nature they involve small numbers of participants whose experiences are studied in-depth.

Methods of qualitative data collection need to achieve _____which means understanding from another person's viewpoint.

Qualitative data are considered to be high in _____ _____ where research is carried out in natural settings. From a theoretical view, _____ tend to use qualitative data.

# Exploring the use of mixed methods in the context of research

## Pause for thought

If you wanted to study the ways in which people from a range of different ethnic groups form queues and the importance they attach to it, how would you do it?

The research scenario above is likely to require a 'mixed methods' approach, because it is unlikely that one method alone would result in achieving the data necessary to gain access to people from *a range of different ethnic groups* to study the *ways* in which they form queues and the *importance* they attach they to do it. The most sensible choice of methods would probably be some kind of observation, some form of interview and possibly a questionnaire.

Sections 5 and 6 in this Unit have outlined the traditional approaches to research methodology. On the one hand, there are methods suitable for the collection of quantitative data, and on the other hand, methods suitable for the collection of qualitative data. Often these two approaches are viewed as being distinct research positions, with clear differences between them (Creswell, 1994). The two approaches are often presented in a list,

in order to emphasise their differences. Table 7.1 is one way of doing this.

These two approaches have been presented as offering the researcher a choice, usually based around a method of data collection, although sometimes the choice is made on the basis of the theoretical positioning of the researcher: positivism or interpretivism. This can result in sociologists being portrayed as fixed in one camp or another. While there are cases of sociologists showing more sympathy for one research methodology than another, there are as many, if not more, sociologists who work with both quantitative and qualitative methods of data collection depending on the nature of what they are studying.

'Mixed methods' is a disputed term within research and has been used to describe sociologists working in various contexts. Some researchers suggest that mixed methods involves using more than one method of data collection, each from different methodological positions, for example using questionnaires for quantitative data with unstructured interviews for qualitative data (Creswell et al., 2002). In researching the educational experiences of ethnic minority students at Oxford University, a group of researchers combined statistical measures of educational achievement with interviews to capture a valid account of the students' experiences. If they had relied solely on the statistical evidence from examination grades, they would have had no text or narrative data to help them explain the patterns and capture the students' experiences.

| Quantitative | Qualitative |
|---|---|
| Numerical data | Narrative/text |
| Sampling procedures | Participation and action based |
| Definition of variables | Empathy/*verstehen* |
| Positivism | Interpretivism |
| Reliability | Validity |
| Statistical data analysis | Narrative data analysis |

Table 7.1 Two methodological approaches

Other researchers argue that mixed methods can be a mixture of methods from within one distinct theoretical position. An example of a sociologist who has used mixed methods in their research is Francis, who used unstructured interviews and classroom observation in her study of gender differences in role-play situations in primary school classrooms (2000). Both methods were collecting qualitative data and were linked with interpretivist sociology.

Due to the existence of the debate regarding what is meant by mixed methods, it is important to have a working definition. In this book, we are using mixed methods as the name for approaches which use more than one method of data collection or which mix and perhaps blend elements of quantitative and qualitative methodology together for the purpose of answering research questions.

# Fitness for purpose

The concept of fitness for purpose is useful when considering the merits of a mixed

Figure 7.1 The researcher 'thinking outside the box'

methods approach. Fitness for purpose means that researchers will select the method(s) most suitable for the collection of the data they require, and as long as the method fits what they need (the purpose) it really does not matter if it produces quantitative or qualitative data. The point to keep in mind about mixed methods is that it enables researchers to break free from the quantitative/qualitative dimension, which can restrict the type of data collected and preclude the flexibility of applying fitness for purpose.

# Methodological pluralism

Methodological pluralism was very popular in sociological research during the 1970s. It treats all methods as equal and assesses the merits of any one given method in terms of how it tackles the research task. The methods used in methodological pluralism should depend on what the researcher wants to discover and nothing more. In practice, this is very difficult to achieve as one research method is usually favoured over another in any research project. Methodological pluralism is in essence exactly the same as mixed methods: it involves using more than one type of data to build up a more coherent study.

# Triangulation

Triangulation differs from methodological pluralism. It involves the use of more than one method or source of data in the study, allowing findings to be cross-checked (Bryman, 2004). Triangulation involves locating a true position by reference to two or more coordinates. In this case, two or more methods of data collection are used and their findings should meet at some point. By using triangulation, the researcher is using different methods (and maybe theories) to be able to check findings against each other. Triangulation should enable the researcher to enhance the quality of the research collected and perhaps bring them closer to true answers.

# Why use mixed methods?

There are many benefits to using mixed methods in sociological research. What follows is a list of some potential strengths and weaknesses of adopting this approach.

### Advantages

- The possibility of adding narrative (words/text) to numbers. This can help add meaning to numbers, rather than relying solely on quantitative data.

- Numbers can be used to add more precision to narrative and pictures (as above but reversed).

- The strengths of qualitative data are combined with those of quantitative data.

- A broader range of research questions can be explored, as the researcher is not limited to asking only 'what', 'how many', 'the extent of', but can also explore 'why' and 'how' issues.

- The strengths of one method can be used to overcome the limitations of another, often enhancing the validity and reliability of the research.

- Can add strength to findings because the data can often be corroborated.

- Mixed methods research is often more generalisable, and it is often possible to collect more data because of the benefits of using methods that complement each other.

### Disadvantages

- Mixed methods research tends to be costly in time, resources and money.

- It demands high levels of skill in the collection and analysis of numerical data and narrative data.

- The researcher must ensure that the methods will complement each other, which often makes the research design process very demanding.

- Careful and skilful data analysis is needed, particularly if the methods produce conflicting results.

- Due to the large amount of data collected, the research can become too complicated and fail to answer the research questions.

- Mixed methods research has in the past been unpopular with social policy makers who prefer the clarity of one-method approaches and results. This may have changed in recent times.

Read the following text and answer the questions below.

Kettley (2006) studied gender and educational attainment using a mixed methods study generated in three sixth forms in England. Kettley wanted to study the extent and causes of gender differences in educational attainment. He used three distinct methods:

- questionnaires completed by 330 students

- unstructured interviews

- non-participant observation.

The GCSE grades held by the students at the start of their course and the AS/A level grades they held at the end of their course were analysed to establish gender differences in attainment. At the start of their sixth form studies the gender gap in attainment was found to be relatively modest and this gap narrowed as the students ended their course. This finding contradicts the very strong media message that the gender gap is increasing. The statistical analysis of the students' grades in this study suggested that gender was of marginal relevance in the educational attainment of men and women.

Unstructured interviews were conducted as well as a period of non-participant observation. The interviews explored the students' practical knowledge of gender and illustrated how they used their everyday experiences when defining masculinity and femininity. Here is part of an interview transcript between Kettley and a male natural science student.

NK: 'What do you think it means to be feminine?'

PX: 'Um, I suppose it would be more of the maternal thing, that sort of thing, you know staying at home and caring for the children …'

NK: 'Okay, what do you think it means to be masculine?'

PX: 'I guess it would be the provider going out to work, um, sort of providing the money for the family and like in the old days when men did everything, worked, provided money and that sort of thing, before women had any rights. I guess it's like a continuation of that.'

Kettley's analysis of this interview states:

This particular relational definition of gender reflected the student's parents' domestic arrangements, his prior schooling and his academic experiences as a natural science student.

(Source: Kettley, 2006, p. 134)

1 Why was a mixed method study the most suitable for Kettley's research aims?

2 Explain how the methods he chose would enable him to produce quantitative data and qualitative data.

3 Use the words below to describe the advantages and disadvantages of mixed methods studies.

- Time
- Cost
- Triangulation
- Validity
- Reliablity
- Generalisability

# Mixed methodology data analysis

Data analysis in mixed methods studies is usually more time-consuming and complex than in studies using only one method. The complexities are particularly difficult if the methods produce conflicting results, or results that do not seem to fit together. As the same techniques of data analysis are used as in single methods studies, however, it is reasonable to state that the mixed method researcher needs to be skilled in the analysis of both quantitative and qualitative data and in blending the results to answer the research questions.

Activity 7.2

Outline a research design proposal using mixed methods for researching how people from a range of different ethnic groups form queues in the UK and the importance they attach to it. Your proposal must specify the following:

- Aims
- Methods
- Access and sampling
- Data analysis techniques.

## Section summary

Use the following key words to copy and complete the short summary of this section below. Each word should be used only once.

triangulation    methodological pluralism    mixed methods    fitness for purpose

_____ _____ research is a catch-all term for studies which use more than one method of data collection. It is also known by the term _____ _____.

_____ _____ _____ involves selecting the method to fit the research question. When more than one method is used in a study in order to check and verify the quality of data collected it is known as_____.

Mixed methods researchers need to be highly skilled in collecting and analysing qualitative and quantitative data. There are disadvantages to mixed methods research; it is time consuming, costly and if the findings from different methods contradict each other it can be very complex to analyse.

# ExamCafé
## Relax, refresh, result!

## Guidance on answering questions in Unit 1 (G671)

You will be assessed on your understanding of the topics covered in Unit 1, structured around some pre-released material. The material will be based on a sociological study relating to one or more of the topics you have covered in Unit 1. The material will give details of a study, and will focus on issues such as the methods used, aims, interpretation of the data and ethics. You will study this material in class with your teacher in the weeks leading up to the exam. You will be given a clean copy of the material in the exam. (You are not allowed to take in your own copy.) You are required to use the pre-released material together with your wider sociological knowledge in the exam.

This exam itself will be comprised of four questions. Parts (a) to (c) will assess your understanding of the relevant subject area. In part (d) you will be asked a question based on the methodology used in the pre-released material. Each question targets specific assessment objectives (AOs) set out in Unit 2.

This Exam Café includes an example of pre-released material, sample questions and a student answer. Some guidelines for answering these questions are set out below.

(a) This assesses your knowledge of a concept. You should show conceptual understanding in your answer through examples (from the pre-released material *and* elsewhere). It is worth 8 marks and you should spend about 5 minutes answering it.

(b) This assesses your knowledge/understanding and interpretation/application of sociological ideas. It is worth 16 marks. You should include studies, concepts, examples and theory (where relevant) in answering the question directly, spending no more than 15 minutes on it.

(c) This assesses your knowledge, interpretation and evaluation/analysis skills. It is worth 24 marks and you should spend approximately 20 minutes on it. As above, the studies, concepts etc. you show are crucial to achieving a good mark. Remember to offer some evaluation of what you write.

(d) This assesses your understanding of methodological issues in relation to the pre-released material. It is worth 52 marks and you should spend between 45 and 50 minutes answering it. You should relate what you write about methods to the research context in the pre-released material and stay focused on what the question asks you. It is very easy to end up evaluating the whole research design when the question may not have asked you to do that. Planning and structuring your answer will help you here.

The Exam Café on page 279 gives specific guidance on the three skill areas of knowledge and understanding, interpretation and application, and evaluation/analysis.

# Get the result !

## Model answer

Here is an exam-style question with a student answer and examiner comments.

## Exploring socialisation, culture and identity: pre-released material

MacDonald, R. and Marsh, J. (2005) *Disconnected Youth? Growing up in Britain's Poor Neighbourhoods*, Basingstoke: Palgrave Macmillan.

*Disconnected Youth?* is a study of the experiences of young people growing up in East Kelby, an economically- and socially-deprived area of Teeside in the north east of Britain. Charles Murray, a New Right theorist, argued that East Kelby was typical of areas where young people were becoming part of a distinct new 'rabble' underclass – an area where young people were choosing to live a life of crime, welfare dependency, single motherhood and long-term unemployment. He argued young males were 'essentially barbarians', work-shy and deviant, and young women threatened the survival of a civil society by being promiscuous, irresponsible and immoral. These young people have been described as lacking status in society. They fall 'under' mainstream society because they neither have secure long-term employment nor are they in education or training.

The aim of the research by MacDonald and Marsh was to find out whether such an underclass of socially-excluded, marginalised youth, who were disconnected from mainstream society, really did exist; whether their lived experiences reflected disaffected and disengaged young people or whether Charles Murray had made assumptions based on an all-too-brief visit to the area. The study aimed to find out how the young people in East Kelby experienced the transition from childhood to adulthood and how their differing circumstances affected that experience.

The research took place between 1998 and 2000 and was carried out in three stages. In the first stage the researchers contacted 40 key people including youth workers, probation officers and social workers. They carried out semi-structured interviews with them in order to gain an insight into the lives of the young people in the area. These key workers, or 'stakeholders' as MacDonald and Marsh called them, also acted as gatekeepers to the young people giving the researchers access to some who would eventually form part of the third stage of their research.

In the second stage Marsh observed groups of young people. She met them in youth clubs, family centres and while travelling around on the buses. In this way she got to know some of them quite well and this enabled the researchers to become familiar to the young people and to be accepted by them. During this stage she 'found' a number of young people who were willing to become part of the third stage. Observing the young people in this participative way gave the third stage of the research, which was semi-structured interviews with 88 young people, some context. These interviewees – 45 females and 43 males – were aged between 15 and 25. They included a range of young people including lone parents, employed and unemployed, students and young offenders. The data collected were largely qualitative and the interviews followed a biographical approach. This means the researchers wanted to explore the experiences of the young people as they grew up in East Kelby and to ask them about their future aspirations. The interviews lasted about an hour although some were longer. They mostly took place in people's homes and were recorded onto audiotape. This enabled MacDonald and Marsh to play back the interviews as often as they wanted which meant they could check they were accurately reflecting what the young people said.

A year later, second interviews took place with 60 per cent of the interviewees. An incentive to persuade all of the 88 young people to be interviewed a second time was offered in the form of a cash prize. Despite this, some either did not want to do another interview or else had moved away or changed address several times and were not contactable.

The sampling technique was a purposive one. MacDonald and Marsh were looking for a range of people with different experiences of social exclusion. Most of them were ethnically white and working class which reflected the population of East Kelby. They were recruited via the key workers, through the second stage of observation and by 'snowballing'. Snowball sampling means some of the interviewees suggested others who might be willing to take part. Although these ways of contacting the participants meant they would not be representative of all marginalised young people, the researchers hoped they would be a sample that was large and varied enough to provide an insight into social exclusion from the point of view of those experiencing it.

There were two sub-samples – one male, one female – chosen from the main sample of 88. Through these two groups the researchers hoped to obtain a deeper insight into the differing experiences of males and females. They also hoped to gain more in-depth information on ways in which peer groups can affect the transition from childhood to adulthood: 'No matter what you done, if you're in that crowd you just stick with 'em' (Matty).

All of the participants were assured of anonymity and confidentiality and the research was entirely overt.

MacDonald and Marsh found the young people of East Kelby had a range of experiences which were linked to the individual circumstances in which they found themselves. They also found they were not deliberately choosing to live a life of crime, welfare dependency, single motherhood and long-term unemployment as Murray suggested. What they did find was that they all experienced poverty and, more particularly, whether male or female, their values and goals were largely those of the respectable working class. They wanted:

- to be in work – 'Getting a job is the main object, isn't it? ... Without a job, you're stuck. Nowhere to go. You're stuck in a dead end, aren't you?' (Leo, 18)

- to have a family within a stable relationship – 'I would like to live with me boyfriend, but not until we've both got jobs and we can both afford it.' (Elizabeth, 19). 'I'd like to have been able to get out, live somewhere nice, show Luke [*her son*] that you don't need to be on the dole and then have kids.' (Claire, young mother)

- to be off benefits; not welfare dependent – 'I ... hate being on the dole ... I just don't like it ... I wanna work... ' (Malcolm, 19).

# Exam questions

(a) Define the concept of status. Illustrate your answer with examples. (8 marks)

(b Outline and explain how any two agents of socialisation influence young people. (16 marks)

(c) Explain and briefly evaluate ways in which working-class culture is created and reinforced in the contemporary UK. (24 marks)

(d) Using the pre-released material and your wider sociological knowledge, explain and evaluate the advantages of using mixed methods to research the lives of young people. (52 marks)

# Jo's answer

(a) Status is based on an individual's social position or social standing within society. Everyone has a status position even if they are unaware of it, and often people have more than one. A person could hold conflicting status positions, for example they could be unemployed and part of the underclass 'rabble' (MacDonald and Marsh) with low status in society, yet they could have a high status within their community. There are two different types of status in society: ascribed and achieved.

(b) The media influences young people in many ways. The media is used and consumed by almost all young people. Madell suggests that 91 per cent of young people own a mobile phone and young people spend over two hours a day watching TV. They are targeted by advertisers keen to create a youth market in trainers, clothes and music. The media creates a consumer culture which young people form part of as they have spare money from part-time jobs and few commitments. The consumer lifestyle influences young people into behaving in ways that will enable them to 'fit in'. This overlaps with the role of the peer group and particularly peer group pressure as an influence on social behaviour. Young people also use the media as a form of communication, especially through MSN and texting. It is clear to see that the media influences young people by both targeting them and as a form of communication.

Another agent of socialisation that influences young people is education. This happens through the formal and the informal (hidden) curriculum. The formal curriculum teaches young people a view of the world through lessons that follow the national curriculum. Some have argued that the curriculum is 'ethnocentric' which means that it looks at society with a cultural slant. If this is the case, then education in the UK may well influence young people into seeing the British way as the 'only way' or the 'right way'. The informal curriculum creates informal rules for young people to follow: where to 'hang out' at lunchtime and the clubs and societies where they might find like-minded people. Young people might also gain a sense of their status within the school communities through informal ways.

**Examiner says:**

Jo gives a clear definition and uses the pre-released material well. The answer would be improved with examples of ascribed and achieved status drawn from the contemporary UK, demonstrating her knowledge of contemporary examples. If the answer contained more details it would be stronger. It displays good knowledge and some understanding of the concept of status.

**Examiner says:**

This answer displays very good knowledge of the use of the media by young people, and how this is a two-way process. Jo also brings in knowledge of cultures and consumption. This answer would improve with some examples to strengthen the explanation.

**Examiner says:**

Jo correctly displays her knowledge of education and related concepts. Both examples in this paragraph need expanding to make them more directly relevant to young people.

(Jo's answer continued . . .)

(Jo's answer continued . . .)

(c) The family influences working-class culture by passing on norms and values from one generation to the next. In this way, social capital can become an important feature of working-class culture – the idea that it isn't 'what you know' but 'who you know' is a feature of traditional working-class communities. The family creates the expectations for individuals to aspire to, whether they are in the workplace or in the home. Cater and Coleman's work on teenage pregnancies showed how some teenage mums actively chose pregnancy because their mums had done the same thing. This shows what could be called 'cultural reproduction'.

Another agent is the peer group and it plays a part in reinforcing working-class culture. Through peer group pressure, the working classes can be encouraged to follow the norms and values of their peers. For males this might involve attachment to hegemonic masculinity and for the females this might involve looking good and taking on a domestic role. People who don't subscribe to the working-class ways can be treated as different and snobbish. Skeggs showed in her study of working-class women that they used education as a way of distancing themselves from the lower working class; a way of gaining a respectable status within their peer group and within their social class. Consumer goods are often very important to the working class who work hard for their earnings and tend to spend them on designer goods. Following the trends of what your peers have may happen although I'm not sure there is any evidence for this.

To evaluate, it's easy to assume that working-class culture is passed on from generation to generation and that the class culture is reproduced. However, the emergence of the new working class, who are socially mobile and privatised, alongside the existence of the traditional working-class communities in some areas shows that working class culture is not united, it is split. It could also be argued that the new working class shares much in common with the lower middle class in terms of culture.

**Examiner says:**

There is a good display of knowledge in this answer; relevant concepts and a study. Jo hasn't explained social capital well, although the point she makes is a good one. The main problem with this paragraph is the neglect of the words 'create' and 'reinforce'. A really good answer would use this material and adapt it to match exactly what the question asks.

**Examiner says:**

Jo rightly, and for the first time, focuses of 'reinforcement' and makes some valid points. Some of what she writes is simplistic and assumes that the working classes follow their peers in various ways. This is clearly not necessarily the case and would make a good point of evaluation. Jo has displayed good practice in selecting agents of socialisation that do not overlap with what she has used in (b). Let's see how Jo ends this section.

**Examiner says:**

This is clear evaluation of the question. It would be improved with reference to the creation and reinforcement of the culture.

(Jo's answer continued . . .)

(d) The use of mixed methods when researching the lives of young people has many advantages. Mixed method studies use more than one method of data collection. This allows a greater quantity of different types of data to be collected (interviews and observation in this study) and it allows the data collected to be checked against each other, improving the validity of the findings by making sure that the research does accurately represent the experiences of young people. This is known as triangulation. MacDonald and Marsh's study is a mixed method qualitative study, which would be supported by interpretivist theory. Interpretivists try to understand the social world by exploring the views of its members and gaining verstehen (empathy) with their views. In this study, using observation and interviews, the researchers were able to access the views of the young people within the natural setting of East Kelby. This is important if the study is to have ecological validity. If the young people had been interviewed or observed in an area not familiar to them, then the reliability of the data would be questioned.

The aim of the research was to see if an underclass existed through exploring the views of the young people themselves. Qualitative methods would have to be used to achieve the detailed data needed. I would argue that mixed methods was essential to the process. By using interviews with key workers the researchers were able to gain access to the young people, which they then observed. Obviously, if they hadn't got access then the participant observation (I am assuming it is PO) could not have taken place. For this reason the mixture of methods was actually essential to the study taking place, because without it access to this marginalised group of young people would be very difficult. Furthermore, the research used two different types of interview: semi-structured interviews (with key workers and students) and further in-depth what seem to be unstructured interviews with a small sample of the young people. By using these qualitative interview methods, rich valid accounts of young people's experiences

**Examiner says:**

Yes, but why?

**Examiner says:**

The study alludes to participant observation and Jo is right to signalling to the examiner how she has interpreted the pre-released material, sometimes it may be necessary to do this. She rightly focuses on the aim of the research and relates this to the question well.

(Jo's answer continued . . .)

can be built up. The interviewer can probe the respondents for the rich detail that is needed to build up a picture of their social experiences. These interviews also allow a rapport to be established between the researchers and a small group of young people which is important as these young people are vulnerable and on the margins of society. They are not going to talk openly about their experiences with people they feel uncomfortable with.

So, to summarise, the advantages of using mixed methods research when researching the social experiences of young people enhances validity, enabling rich qualitative and naturalistic data to be gained which would allow the views of the young people to be expressed in a written narrative form. By using interviews with the key workers, access was gained to the group which allowed the observation to take place and this would not have been possible without using a mixture of research methods.

There are, however, drawbacks to using this approach. The main issue is that the vast amount of qualitative data gained from the three different stages of the research would all be in text form and would need to be analysed. These interviews lasted for an hour and with 88 of them the analysis becomes a huge task. Also, the example of interview transcripts given in the study would all need to be read and analysed by more than one researcher to add credibility to the findings. This would be time-consuming, probably very confusing and may in the end produce a subjective interpretation of the events. The nature of qualitative methods places a great deal in the hands of the researcher who has to access, record and analyse the data in a reliable way. Positivists are critical of qualitative approaches as they are difficult to repeat and gain consistent results. They are also lacking in representativeness. These findings may be accurate for the young people in East Kelby, however, how replicable they are to other social areas is questionable.

However, it is difficult to imagine how the social experiences of young people could be researched without using qualitative methods, particularly in this case where social experiences are clearly linked

**Examiner says:**

This is well contextualised. Jo could explain the process of achieving a rapport in more depth, and how a mixed methods approach helped achieve this.

**Examiner says:**

A good summary paragraph but no real contextualisation. Good display of methodological concepts.

**Examiner says:**

This shows evaluation of the qualitative mixed methods approach, with some contextualisation, which is to be encouraged.

(Jo's answer continued . . .)

to 'differing circumstances' and mixed methods is clearly better
suited to the research than participant observation alone would
be. Quantitative methods may produce more reliable data but the
response rate to a questionnaire would be very low from young people
who have been described as 'the new rabble'.

# Topics in socialisation, culture and identity

- Theoretical introduction
- The sociology of the family
- The sociology of health
- The sociology of religion
- The sociology of youth
- Exam Café

# Theoretical introduction

## Pause for thought

1   Are we as individuals shaped by the society in which we live?

2   How can people change society?

3   To what extent can people choose how to live their lives?

Figure 1.1 Protection or control?

1 Select two of the following statements which you agree with. Give an example to support each of your chosen statements.

- Anyone in society can be successful. It's up to them.
- Men get the best deal in this world.
- People can choose their own identity and lifestyle.
- Workers are exploited at work and don't get paid a fair wage.
- There are lots of differences between members of social groups such as class, ethnic or gender groups.
- Members of society hold shared values that hold society together.
- Opportunities are affected by social class.
- Powerful groups in society justify their position by spreading their ideas.

2 Discuss these with the rest of your class.

# Sociological theory

A sociological theory is a way of seeing something, taking a perspective on it and understanding it from a particular point of view. The theories may be referring to the same thing, but see and understand it differently.

People can have very different opinions on films. For example, one person may complain about the sexist representation of women in a particular film which another person did not see at all. Another may think a film politically biased, whereas someone else may see it as neutral.

Think of a film you've seen and discuss this with other members of your class who have also seen it. Identify two different things about the film that people have picked up on.

People can have an identical experience but interpret things differently. In sociology, theories differ in terms of how they regard society. Different theories have different starting points.

- Some theories begin with society as a whole. They look at the institutions within it, such as the family, education and religion, for example, and then work inwards to the individual and how he or she is affected by the system.

- However, others start with the individual and work outwards to look at how they create meanings and negotiate roles within a system.

# Macro versus micro

Broadly speaking, there are sociologists who see society as a whole, taking a macro perspective, and those who take the individual and their actions as a starting point, taking a micro perspective. Those who use a macro approach have different ideas about the way society is structured and the impact those structures have upon individuals. However, they are all macro approaches because they look at society as a whole, recognise a social system and see external structures that shape the individual.

# The macro theories

The macro theorists include:

- functionalists
- Marxists
- feminists.

## Functionalism

Identify and briefly explain two values people share in the contemporary UK

Functionalists maintain that society has a **common culture** comprising shared norms and values. There is **value consensus**, that is agreement over, and a shared belief in, the same values. We learn this culture through the process of socialisation. The agents of socialisation include institutions such as the family, religion, peer groups, the mass media, education and work, which are all interconnected, working for society as a whole.

Functionalists look at and explain society as a system. To understand how the system works they draw an **organic analogy** which describes these inter-linked institutions as working in much the same way as the organs of the body function together to keep the person alive and performing as a human being. So, functionalists are concerned with what they term the function of these institutions. They want to know what each contributes to society as a whole. The family, for example, has a socialisation function: it teaches children the norms and values of society. A function of religion is to integrate society, to bring people together and create unity. In addition, just as a human being has particular needs that must be met for survival, so too does society. Functionalists call these basic needs functional prerequisites.

Functionalists emphasise the sharing of culture by the majority of society's members. There is agreement over the norms and values which are seen to benefit everyone. The normal state of society is one of harmony because people have this common culture and act accordingly.

## Evaluation

◆ Functionalists present an overly harmonious picture of society.

◆ Marxists regard functionalists as severely underestimating the degree of conflict in society.

◆ Social action theorists raise issues about individual action and choice. They view functionalism as too deterministic, seeing people as products of a system with little room for flexibility and negotiation.

## Marxism

### Activity 1.4

1 Research last year's annual profits of a major bank and a national supermarket.

2 Find out the average earnings of a bank clerk and a supermarket checkout operator.

Marxism takes its name from Karl Marx, who died in 1883. For many Marxists, the starting point for understanding how society works is economic production. Production is fundamental to all societies in order for them to survive; people need food and they need material objects. For production to take place, there has to be technology, raw materials and knowledge. These aspects of production are called the means of production.

However, production also involves social relationships such as those between employer and employee. It is these that shape everything else in society. For Marxists, a person's class is determined by their relationship to the means of production. Owning them puts a person in the ruling class, which comprises the smallest class and is powerful as well as wealthy. The rest of society's members make up the subject class. These are the workers, who have to sell their labour in exchange for a wage.

Marxists regard the relationship between bosses and workers as exploitative. This is not because all bosses are inherently awful people. Rather, it is because in a capitalist society the ultimate goal is to make a profit. Workers represent a large cost for an employer. Hence the boss tries to pay the workers as little as possible while getting the maximum labour out of them. Conflict for Marxists then is inevitable. The experience of work for many workers is of **alienation**. People feel removed from the process of production. Work is meaningless, giving no satisfaction or fulfilment. The workers are not aware of the exploitative nature of their work, though, because it is presented as fair by the ruling class. They spread **ideology** to justify their position. An ideology is a partial picture of society, a way of seeing that is presented as normal, as the only way for things to be.

More recent Marxists put more stress upon cultural and ideological factors, as opposed to the economic one, in affecting how society shapes people.

## Evaluation

◆ Marx has been criticised for the priority he gives to economic factors.

◆ Marx underestimated the growth of the middle classes.

◆ Marxism has been described as a one-dimensional theory.

## Feminism

### Activity 1.5

1 Working in small groups, complete the following sentence:

   'A feminist is .......

2 Compare your sentence with other groups in your class.

3 Are the class findings mainly positive or negative things?

4 Are you a feminist? Justify your response.

There are different types of feminisms, but, in general, feminists believe that women should have equality with men. They see important aspects of society as **patriarchal** – male dominated. Feminists are critical of the power that men hold in society. For example, parliament has historically been dominated by men and is the place where decisions are made about how things should be throughout the country. In the workplace, men have held more powerful positions and have, on average, been better paid. In some families women have experienced violence.

Feminists have fought to change things for women. They see different ways of doing this. For example, some feminists campaign for changes in the law and new social policies. Some things, such as having the same voting rights, might be taken for granted today, but the suffragettes campaigned for women to have the right to vote a century ago. Feminists also sought to change the way that boys and girls are socialised according to their gender. If expectations in terms of what males and females think is appropriate for them to do change, then that can also be a way forward towards equality. Other feminists adopt a more radical approach in order to overturn the patriarchal structures that disadvantage women. Some recent feminists have highlighted the differences between women, questioning the usefulness of categorising the position of, for example, middle- and working-class women in the same vein.

### Evaluation

◆ There have been legal changes that have benefited women.

◆ There are many differences within the categories of 'men' and 'women'.

All of the above theories stress the way in which the individual is constrained by society. Functionalists show how common culture affects our behaviour. For Marxists, the emphasis is capitalism, whereas for feminists, society is patriarchal. The next theory, however, takes a different starting point, with a shift from structure to individual action.

## Social action theory

### Activity 1.6

Consider the following situation. What is happening?

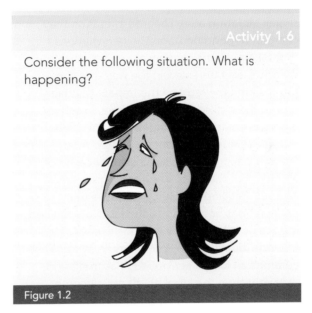

Figure 1.2

In contrast to the theories discussed above, social action theory looks at small-scale interaction. It considers action in terms of what it means for the individual. It also stresses that there are different ways of interpreting things, each of which is valid to the individual concerned. In Activity 1.6 the person could be in tears because:

◆ they are upset about something

◆ there is something in their eye

◆ they are crying tears of joy

◆ they have laughed really hard

◆ they have been peeling onions.

Social action theory sees action as meaningful to the people involved. For example, a person may leave a highly-paid occupation for a lower-paid job which some people may regard in a negative light. However, it could mean something positive for the individual concerned as they want to make a change in career and the lower-paid job represents a move in the right direction. Therefore, what is important is the interpretation for the individual. From this perspective, meanings are not fixed. They are negotiated and change.

Social action theorists focus on the definition of the situation. They examine how things come to be defined and interpreted in the way they are. For example, if a person interprets a situation they are involved in as threatening, it is their definition of that situation that is important, that is, the meaning that they attach to the event. The theorists point out, though, that should a similar situation arise, the interpretation may change, depending upon the negotiations that take place on that occasion. Social action theorists are interested in the way that some groups are labelled and the impact that label has on the individual. For example, in school, a person could be labelled as 'bright'. The individual labelled in that way could then actually become more successful because of a belief that the label was right. This is known as a self-fulfilling prophecy. It means that the expectations according to the label are fulfilled. It does not always work in a positive way for the individual though. For example, if someone commits an illegal activity, such as theft, and is caught then the label 'thief' can become fundamental to how that person sees himself or herself. 'Thief' becomes what is seen as their 'master status'.

## Evaluation

◆ Social action theories are criticised for ignoring the historical and social settings in which interaction takes place.

◆ Not everybody's interpretations are given the same validity. Social action theories do not consider power and its impact.

◆ With regard to labelling, critics argue that not everyone goes along with the label. Some people may resist.

# Postmodernism

### Activity 1.7

What three choices are available to you that your grandparents did not have? (Examples of things you may consider are: relationships, education, travel, consumer goods, food.)

In contrast to the theories examined so far, postmodernists do not believe it is possible to have one general overriding theory about how things are in society. They focus, in particular, on the impact of the media-saturated society of today in which it is difficult to separate media images from so-called reality. We buy magazines about soap stars and have a sophisticated understanding of media messages, so this becomes a **hyper-reality**.

Some postmodernists maintain that people are no longer restricted by their class position, their gender, or their ethnicity. Instead, people can make choices about how to live and what identity to adopt. There is incessant choice available. People can construct their own identity through what they consume.

## Evaluation

People do not make choices in a vacuum. If someone likes the idea of a particular identity, but does not have the means to achieve it, then their identity is not expressed as they wish. They could be restricted by class, if their family do not earn high salaries; or a girl desiring the identity of a celebrity babe may be restricted by her father who will not let her have the body piercing and tattoos she dreams of.

### Activity 1.8

Return to the statements in Activity 1.1. In pairs, identify which theory each statement fits with.

# The sociology of the family

## (i) Key concepts and key trends within the family

### Pause for thought

1   Do people still want to get married?

2   What factors might influence family size?

3   Identify family/household types that you see on television.

4   How important are extended family networks in contemporary society?

Figure 2.1 Wedding day

Sociologists examine families and **households**. This section considers exactly what we mean by these terms. It then explores some recent family trends.

# What's in a name? The family

We all talk about families and share some common understanding of what we mean by the notion of family. It is a term we use in everyday language, without question. However, we do not always mean the same people when we say 'my family'. Allan and Crow (2001, p. 2) explain.

> At times 'my family' can mean my partner and children; at other times, it may be taken to include my children's children too. Alternatively, its reference may be my own natal family, my parents, brothers and sisters, or it may signify a wider range of kin including, for instance, aunts and uncles.

Sociologists stress the importance of precise definitions. We need to be clear on what something means when it is used in research. One useful distinction to make is that between family and household, although a household does, in many cases, comprise a family.

# A definition of family

A key aspect of a family is **kinship**. This refers to ties through blood or marriage. However, there have always been cases of people who are not kin being treated as family members. In addition, Allan and Crow (2001) maintains that things have been made more complex by changing patterns of cohabitation, divorce and remarriage. When does a cohabitee become 'family' and, indeed, family to whom?

In the example in Activity 2.2 you may have considered people's *perceptions* and the issue of *remarriage*. You may have considered the length of the relationship or the level of commitment. If people see themselves as a family, does that count in defining a family? In addition, when people remarry are they still part of the former 'family'? This may particularly be the case where children are involved. Finch and Mason (1993) point out that divorce does not always sever relationships between all family members. In step-families it may be that children do not accept new so-called families as their 'family', however much the newly in-love adults desire it to be so. It seems, then, that ties that are maintained and developed are socially defined. Jordan et al. (1994) found that what was given prominence in defining family was partnership and parenthood. Because of the complexity in defining family, Bernades (1997) prefers to refer to 'families' in the plural rather than privileging one set of arrangements as *the family*. After all, what is a 'normal' family? 'Families' allows for family diversity. It encompasses the notion of there being more than one type of family.

Defining the family is not purely an academic exercise. What is perceived to be a family has important political implications in terms of state policy and the family. For a long time the nuclear family has been given precedence.

Families vary in type and the diversity of family is examined at length in subsection (iii) Here we will look at key structural trends and the importance of extended family networks in contemporary society.

## Nuclear families

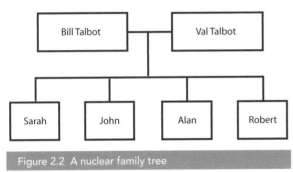

Figure 2.2  A nuclear family tree

The nuclear family consists of two generations, parents and children (Figure 2.2). The adults assume responsibility for the children who are either their own or adopted.

## The ideology of the nuclear family

An ideology presents a partial picture as being normal. Therefore an ideology of a particular type of family, such as the nuclear family, presents that family type as being the most acceptable way of being. It is the nuclear family that has been prevalent in the mass media. For example, in the 1960s Leach (1967) referred to the 'cereal packet image' of the nuclear family whereby the male breadwinner/female housewife with two kids was prominent in media advertising. Two decades on, feminists were critical of the nuclear family and the way that it

was presented as an ideal form. Oakley (1984) illustrates how that nuclear structure was still presented as the conventional family. Barrett and McIntosh (1982) are critical of the way that the ideology of the nuclear family devalues alternative ways of living and makes the people following different routes seem inadequate. They also highlight the negative elements of the nuclear family which does not always live up to the ideal that is presented. It can be an institution of abuse and neglect.

The present New Labour government, although acknowledging family diversity, also seems committed to the ideal of the nuclear family. Smart (1999) argues that the monogamous married couple is still seen as the core element for achieving a stable society. She argues that although New Labour does not condemn alternative forms of family life, it still states that marriage is the best foundation for stable families.

## Extended families

An **extended family** contains kin beyond the nuclear family. This could be through vertical extensions with additional family members from a third generation, such as grandparents, or through horizontal extensions with, for example, a wife's sister.

Much historical evidence suggests that extended families were the most dominant type of family at various stages in the past, where people were heavily reliant on family members for support and when the home was often also the workplace. In a classic study, Young and Willmott (1973) argued that family structures developed through four stages, changing from the extended family to the nuclear family with the process of industrialisation. This reflected the needs of society at the time.

# The importance of extended family ties in the contemporary UK

In the 1980s, Willmott's (1988) research in a north London suburb showed that even when people did not live really close to their extended family there was still a lot of contact and family support. Evidence on contemporary family networks comes from the British Social Attitude Surveys. McGlone et al. (1996) used survey findings and discovered that in the 1990s contact with relatives was still frequent. Extended families were an important source of support: for practical tasks such as helping with jobs, for emotional support, for example at times of illness, and for financial assistance. Park et al. (2001) also used findings from a British Social Attitudes Survey and found evidence of extended kin contact. This survey asked adults over eighteen how often they saw close relatives who did not live with them. More than half saw their mother once a week or more and over two-fifths saw their father as frequently. They were less likely to see their siblings as often. However, siblings were more likely to live further away from each other than to other relatives. Brannen (2003) found that grandparents play an important part in contemporary families, looking after the children and also giving financial support. She found this relationship remains strong after divorce too.

### Activity 2.4

Identify advantages and disadvantages of extended families in contemporary life. Present your findings in a style of your choice, for example role play, PowerPoint, poster.

Hint: Think of roles, relationships and responsibilities for different family members.

Refer back to Activity 2.1. Would you change anything in your answer now?

## Households

A household is a dwelling where one or more persons live. This seems, at first, a straightforward definition. However, how often does a person have to sleep in a house to become part of that household? Do food and tasks have to be shared to qualify as a 'household'? And can a single person be part of more than one household? These are issues to think about as sociologists. A household does not necessarily contain family members, although family units do make up many households.

Sociologists have examined households that are not made up of family members. Heath (2004) examines the growing phenomenon of young adults living in shared households and forming relationships that are not 'family relationships'. However, they are more than 'shared households'. Indeed Roseneil and Budgeon (2004) refer to them as 'families of choice'. Heath's own research with Cleaver (2003) examined shared living arrangements among young people in their mid- to late- twenties. They discovered household sociability and intertwined lives. People enjoyed spending time together in shared living rooms. They socialised together outside the home and participated in shared leisure. Sociability was a key feature. The relationships were valued. Heath argues that sharing households blurs the usual boundaries of expectations that usually go with friendships. Friends in what she terms the 'inner circle' of housemates were different to those in the 'outer circle', for example, sharing clothes and seeing each other wearing little clothing.

## Trends in families and households

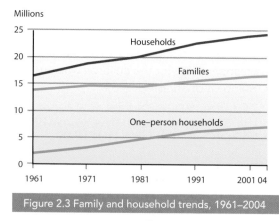

Figure 2.3 Family and household trends, 1961–2004

(Source: National Statistics, 2007)

### Activity 2.5

Look at Figure 2.3.

1 Identify the trends in households and families since 1961.

2 How could you explain these trends?

# Family households

Most individuals in the contemporary UK live in family households in some form for the majority of their lifetime. However, gaining an accurate figure for this is difficult as it is impossible to track every individual throughout their lifetime. In 2004, eight out of ten people lived in a family household, compared with nine out of ten in 1961.

## Key trend – growth in the number of households

The number of households in the UK is growing. By 2006 there were 24.2 million households in the UK (*Social Trends*, 2007). This is a 30 per cent increase from 1971. This increase can partly be explained by the growing trend of single-person households.

# Family size

## Key trend – decline in family size

The average family size in the UK has decreased during the past 30 years, declining from 3.1 people in 1961 to 2.4 people in 2006.

Family size is affected by different things. Three key factors are:

- women's employment – more women are prioritising career over having a number of children
- the cost of childcare – a survey in 2004 by a charity called Daycare Trust, found that childcare costs were nearly a quarter of average household income (Williams, 2006)
- lifestyle choice – a materialistic society based on consumption could mean that people make different lifestyle choices to those chosen in the past. People are spending their money on things other than children.

## Key trend – an increase in the number of young adults living with their parents

In 2006, 58 per cent of men and 39 per cent of women aged 20–24 in England lived with their parents (National Statistics, 2007).

This was an increase of approximately 8 per cent since 1991.

The increase in housing costs has made it difficult for young people to get into the housing market. A lack of social housing is also relevant. The cost of higher education has meant that some young people choose to keep living with their parents while they study.

### Activity 2.6

Interview a member of your class to find out when they intend to leave the home they share with their parent(s). Share your findings with the rest of the class. What are the two main reasons for staying or going?

# Marriage

Thousands

1 For both partners  2 For one or both partners

**Figure 2.4 Marriages in the UK, 1950–2005**

(Source: National Statistics, 2007)

### Activity 2.7

Look at Figure 2.4

1 Identify three trends in marriage.

2 How could you explain these trends?

## Key trend – decline in the number of marriages

The peak for marriages in the UK was in 1972 when about 480,000 people wed. Since the 1970s there was a decline in the number of marriages until the turn of the new century when the numbers started to rise again. However, there has been a more recent change. Between 2004 and 2005, there was an almost ten per cent decrease in the number of weddings in the UK, which was the first fall in three years (National Statistics, 2007).

Some people choose to cohabit rather than, or prior to, getting married. Some people also choose to live alone which they see as a positive lifestyle choice.

Although there are fewer marriages today than there were 30 years ago, in 2005 it was still the case that more than half of all men and women in the UK were married. Marriage is still a relatively popular choice and some people are choosing to do it more than once.

## Key trend – a rise in the proportion of marriages that are remarriages

Remarriages rose by about one-third between 1971 and 1972, following the introduction of the 1969 Divorce Reform Act in England and Wales, and then levelled off. In 2005 remarriages for one or both parties accounted for 40 per cent of all marriages.

## Key trend – marrying later in life

Over the last thirty years people have tended to get married later in life when marrying for the first time. Forty years ago the average age for men to marry was 25; in 2006 it was 31. For women the average age to marry was 23 forty years ago, but it rose to 29 by 2006.

## Expectations of marriage

Expectations of marriage have changed. Allan and Crow (2001) point out that the focus in a marriage is now on the relationship. People expect emotional fulfilment from the marriage. In the past, people, particularly women, might not have had the financial independence to separate from their spouse, but economic freedom has meant that people will not stay together if they are not fulfilled in the relationship.

## Divorce

The divorce rate refers to the number of divorces per thousand of the married population.

## Key trend – increase in the rate of divorce

Divorce rates rose dramatically over the twentieth century, particularly in the second half of the century. The number of divorces reached its height in 1993 when there were 180,000 divorces. The rate began to climb again at the beginning of the twenty-first century. However, between 2005 and 2006 the divorce rate fell by 7 per cent. The divorce rate is now at its lowest since 1984 (National Statistics, 2007).

For 69 per cent of divorces in 2006, the wife was granted the divorce. Unreasonable behaviour was the most common reason for getting divorced.

A rise in the divorce rate can be explained by a number of factors.

◆ Legal changes: each change in divorce law resulted in a large increase in the numbers applying to legally end their marriage.

◆ The Divorce Reform Act in 1969 introduced a crucial new ground for divorce: irretrievable breakdown. This came into force in 1971. Prior to this there had to be a 'guilty party' for a divorce to be granted, for example, adultery or cruelty had to be proved. It is important to bear this in mind when analysing divorce statistics, as it might not be the case that there were fewer people unhappy with their marriage in the past, but

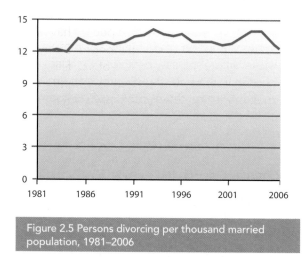

Figure 2.5 Persons divorcing per thousand married population, 1981–2006

(Source: National Statistics, 2007)

that they did not meet the criteria used to allow divorce to take place.

◆ The Matrimonial Family Proceedings Act in 1984 reduced the amount of time couples had to be married from three years to one year, before being able to petition for divorce.

◆ With the Family Law Act of 1996 spouses no longer had to show that one of them was at fault in the breakdown of the relationship. Rather they just had to assert that it had broken down and consider whether reconciliation was possible during a reflection period.

◆ The Child Support, Pensions and Social Security Act of 2000 meant absent parents had to contribute maintenance costs for their children, which was a fixed proportion of their salary.

◆ Cost: for the first half of the twentieth century many ordinary people would not have been able to afford the cost of a divorce. More recently, the rich can afford lawyers and the poor may qualify for legal aid, but for those in between divorce can be very expensive.

◆ Secularisation: a decline in religious belief and practice means divorce is now more acceptable in some cultures. There may be more pressure to stay in an unhappy marriage in a religious community.

◆ Women's economic independence: as women gain economic independence through work their option to leave an unsatisfactory marriage strengthens.

◆ Demographic change: people live longer, so a lifelong marriage is longer than it used to be. This means that people have to work at a relationship for longer. Given higher expectations in terms of a fulfilling partnership, this means there is potentially more risk of the relationship breaking down.

## Divorce statistics – a social construction

In interpreting divorce figures, it is important to bear in mind that the statistics are not necessarily a reflection of *marital breakdown* increasing. People can stay together in unsatisfactory

marriages and indeed there was more social as well as economic pressure in the past to do so. These are termed 'empty shell' marriages. People may stay in unhappy relationships for a number of reasons. For example, for the sake of the children, to keep up appearances, fear of being alone, or apathy. Separation also needs to be born in mind. People may separate without actually divorcing.

# Cohabitation

**Cohabitation** is when a couple in a relationship live together without being married. Cohabitation first arose in the 1970s. It has since become the norm to cohabit before getting married. In 2005, 24 per cent of non-married people aged under 60 years of age were cohabiting in Great Britain. This is about twice the proportion recorded in 1986.

Activity 2.8

In small groups, identify and briefly explain two positive and two negative aspects of cohabitation.

Couples co-habit because of:

◆ a decline of the 'living in sin' stigma that existed in the past

◆ better contraception – Allan and Crow (2001) point out that couples can live together and have a sexual relationship without worrying about pregnancy

◆ a decline in the influence of religion. Co-habiting is an international trend. Other northern European countries such as Austria, Germany and France have similar patterns to the UK. However, trends were slower to increase in southern Europe where there are more Roman Catholics.

# Single-parent families

## Key trend – an increase in single parenthood

The proportion of children living in lone-parent families in Great Britain more than tripled to 24

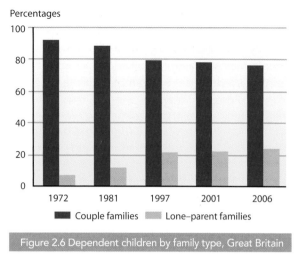

Percentages

Figure 2.6 Dependent children by family type, Great Britain

(Source : National Statistics, 2007)

per cent between 1972 and spring 2006. When considering statistics it is important to realise that they are snapshots. Families do change. For example, a child may be in a one-parent family one year, but then their parent may meet a new partner and remarry or cohabit. Nevertheless, this is a significant statistic. In addition, lone-parent families are not homogeneous. Sometimes a parent classed as a lone-parent family might not actually live with the other parent, but both have regular contact with their offspring. This is where the distinction between families and households is useful, in that families can have significant relationships but not live in the same household. However, not all sources work with the same definitions.

Allan and Crow (2001) identify the two key factors to explain lone-parent households:

◆ increase in divorce – this has made a significant contribution to the rise in lone-parent households

◆ a significant rise in the number of never-married women.

Sometimes lone-parenthood arises due to the death of a partner. However, choice is a key factor in contemporary society.

## Becoming a parent

### Key trend – having children later in life, and in a more compressed time period

In 2005, the average age for mothers at the birth of their first child was 27.3. This was more

than three years older than the average age in 1971 (National Statistics, 2007). Williams (2006) cites Office for National Statistics (ONS) figures showing that women want to have babies later, if at all. In 1980, 70 per cent of women aged 21–23 in England and Wales expected to have a baby in the next five years, but by 2001 this had declined to 40 per cent. He identifies three possible reasons for this:

◆ an increase in the power of women

◆ improved employment opportunities

◆ practical reasons – the cost of childcare. Williams points to the findings of a survey in 2004 by the charity Daycare Trust which found childcare costs had risen to nearly a quarter of average household income.

Hantrais (2006) analyses how family life in the UK and other European countries is undergoing changes. She points out that first births are now likely to occur as women approach the age of 30, compared with 25 in 1980. People are also having children in a tighter time span. Hantrais also draws attention to voluntary childlessness. She gives evidence to show that this has risen in some European countries. For example, the levels of voluntary childlessness among women born in the 1950s and 1960s in England, along with Austria and Germany, is 20 per cent. However, it is under 5 per cent in Portugal.

Figure 2.7 Establishing a career before having a baby

# Single-person households

## Key trend – an increase in one-person households

By 2005 the number of people living alone in Great Britain had more than doubled since 1971, from three million to seven million (National Statistics, 2007).

**Activity 2.9**

In pairs, identify:

(a) categories of people who you think live alone

(b) three possible reasons for the growth in the number of one-person households.

Living alone is a growing trend in all age groups. It remains common among older age groups, with older women making up a large proportion of people living alone. However, the largest growth has been within younger populations (Chandler et al., 2004), particularly in the proportion of men between the ages of 25 and 44 (National Statistics, 2007). Using statistical evidence Chandler et al. predict that the proportion of households with men living alone is expected to rise to 14 per cent by 2021. Chandler et al. explain that growth in the number of younger men living alone, as opposed to the number of younger women, in terms of women being more likely to remain living with the children when relationships break down.

Some of the reasons for the increase in one-person households are described below.

◆ Increasing numbers of people in general are choosing to live alone, as a lifestyle choice. Living alone is seen to give freedom to people to live their lives in their own way. This view can be associated with the postmodernists.

◆ Employment patterns are changing. This means that more people have to move geographical area to find employment and an increasing number of short-term contracts means settling down in one area for life is increasingly difficult. This may explain the increasing number of smaller houses and flats being built to accommodate workers who move in and out of popular areas.

◆ The increase in the numbers of broken marriages and lone-parent families. When partners split up, what used to be one household becomes two. Also the rise in lone-parent families will mean an increase in households as more single adults live in a household without a partner.

Living alone does not necessarily mean a lack of contact between kin or a lack of close relationships. Research by Roseneil and Budgeon (2004) maintains intimacy and care take place between people who do not live together. Research involving interviews with single people in their twenties revealed that over half of the sample described themselves as in a relationship.

## Attitudes of the government towards same-sex couples who want to have children

The New Labour government has been supportive of changing laws so that same-sex couples can adopt children, and that new reproductive technologies should be available both to same-sex couples and to heterosexual couples. However, government messages also indicate that most families have two people of different sexes involved in bringing up their children, and the government does not seem to actively promote same-sex adoption or new reproductive technologies.

**Exam practice**

(a) Identify and explain two reasons for the decline in family size over the past 30 years. (17 marks)

# (ii) The role of the family in society

## Pause for thought

1  Why do people live in families?
2  What contribution does the family make to society?
3  How might families prepare people for their future role at work?
4  How might the way families consume be good for capitalism?

Figure 2.8 A family shopping together

1 Identify three positive and three negative things about living in families.

2 Discuss and compare your responses. Put this work aside to reconsider at the end of the section.

## Theoretical debate

Both functionalists and Marxists see the role of the family as serving society in some way. However, functionalists also regard the family as being beneficial for its members, whereas Marxists' views of the family are more critical. They analyse the role of the family in the context of a capitalist society, stressing the conflict that is generated.

## Functionalism and the family

Functionalists stress the positive aspect of family. In particular, they focus on the positive role of one particular family type: the nuclear family.

Murdoch (1949) claimed the family was a *universal institution*. He studied 250 societies and found the family, in some form, was present in all of them. This suggests that families are necessary in some way, whether it be for societies to survive, for individual well-being, or indeed both.

Functionalists draw an organic analogy. They view a society as a set of inter-connected, inter-related institutions all working together and contributing to society in much the same way as one might consider the parts of a human body all functioning together to make the body work as a whole entity. So for each institution, such as education or religion, or in the case of what concerns us here, the family, they ask what it does for society. They call this contribution to society as a whole its **function**. However, in functioning for society functionalists maintain that the family is also functional for individuals. The two go hand in hand. Functionalists then, present a harmonious picture of the family functioning along with other institutions, to serve the needs of society and its members.

However, functionalists have been criticised for ignoring the dark side of family life. Many families are places of disruption, violence and harm for their members. Sociologists have produced work on what they call the 'dark side of family life' where family members are often abused and where individuals feel unable to live the life they desire because of the everyday stresses and strains of living in small family units. In this sense the functionalists can be accused of portraying an over-rosy picture of family life.

## Functions

Murdoch (1949) identifies four functions of the nuclear family:

- economic
- educational
- sexual
- reproductive.

Murdock explains these functions in the following way.

- Economic: in the past the family was a unit of production. Consider, for example, family farms. Today it is a unit of consumption, buying goods and services for the family.

- Educational: the family is an agency of primary socialisation, passing on shared norms and values.

- Sexual: people are sexually fulfilled by their partners, and expectations of monogamous relationships keep society stable.

- Reproductive: people reproduce in families; they have children, which of course are essential for the survival of humankind.

Think of alternative ways in which Murdoch's four functions of the family could be performed without the nuclear family. What does this suggest about Murdoch's work?

As societies became more industrialised the traditional roles of the family were increasingly taken over by the state. For example, children had to go to school rather than be taught a way of life by the members of the family; therefore the family lost its educational function. However, the functionalists' view is that just because the family has fewer functions to fulfil, this does not give rise to the decline of the family. Parsons (1959) maintains that in modern industrial societies the functions of the family become increasingly specialised. This does not mean that the family has declined in importance – far from it – it simply means that the family can focus on what Parsons sees as its two important functions and fulfil the demands of both.

◆ The socialisation of children: this involves passing on norms and values and appropriate gender roles.

◆ The stabilisation of adult personalities: this involves being supportive to adult family members.

However, there have been criticisms of the work of Murdoch and Parsons. Many of the functions of the family cited by these writers can be provided by sources and institutions other than the family, for example individuals do not require families for economic support. In addition, families do not always function as functionalist writers claim. Families can be dysfunctional for society.

## The 'fit' between family type and society

Functionalists explain the development of the family from pre-industrial society to industrial society in terms of how it 'fits' society. They argue that the family had an extended structure in the past because that was what fitted well with the kind of society at that time. Before industrialisation, a family was a unit of production; it was predominantly self sufficient. Members of the family worked together in a rural economy. The family fulfilled a wider range of functions: as well as the economic purpose, families also carried out an educational function, along with health and political roles. There was no welfare state then, so families provided care for sick family members.

With industrialisation there was a shift towards the nuclear family because, functionalists maintain, this was a better 'fit' with the changing needs of that type of society. For example, in industrial societies it was better to be geographically mobile, to be able to move around to places where there were employment opportunities. It was easier to uproot a small nuclear family than take a large extended family.

According to functionalists, family life can also give a sense of solidarity in a less community-orientated society. For functionalists, the nuclear family is the ideal family form in industrial societies. It is the most functionally appropriate. However, critics believe that alternative family forms are just as valid.

Parsons argues that the isolated nuclear family emerged in industrial societies. This evolved in form as the functions of the family became more specialised. As production became more centred in factories, and the family was no longer a unit of production, then ties with kin wider than the nuclear family are not so essential, giving rise to a more structurally isolated nuclear family unit. Critics argue that extended kin networks are important in modern societies.

Functionalists have been challenged, though, regarding the claim that the family was an extended unit in the past. Laslett (1991) provides evidence from historical research to show that between 1564 and 1821 only 10 per cent of families were extended. This contradicts the functionalist position.

As the nuclear family is not necessarily the most common family type in the contemporary UK, we also need to ask whether functionalist theory can explain the role of other types of families.

## The instrumental and expressive needs of society

Functionalists believe society has basic needs or functional prerequisites that must be met for it to survive. Parsons identifies:

◆ instrumental needs: these refer to the practical, non-emotional needs of society; for example, in an industrial society the economy needs a fit mobile workforce. (More recently we have seen a demand for this workforce to be increasingly flexible.)

◆ expressive needs: society needs people to feel emotionally secure and looked after.

Parsons maintains a useful division of labour occurs when men take on an instrumental role, which takes them outside the family home to be the breadwinner and provider for the family. Women serve a more expressive role taking on the nurturing tasks of caring for the family home and the emotional life of the family.

For Parsons this sexual division of labour is functional all round; it works for society and it works for families. Parsons' account of family life shows it as being enriching and fulfilling, and has been described as the 'warm bath' theory, where fulfilment, well-being, comfort, warmth and rejuvenation are provided by the nuclear family in the same way as a warm bath ultimately rejuvenates people at the end of an exhausting day.

For functionalists, biology determines gender roles. A woman's expressive role is because she is seen as naturally nurturing. However, feminists are critical of familial ideology that presents the nuclear family with a gendered division of labour as natural. They argue that motherhood is a social construction. Women learn that role. Nowadays, men and women do not play different roles in family life. Increasingly women are remaining in the workplace after having maternity leave and men are increasingly taking on more childcare.

In addition, feminists feel that functionalists fail to examine power inequalities between men and women, maintaining that the family is a **patriarchal** institution. Feminists are critical of the way in which functionalists disregard the importance of women's paid work.

Feminists do, though, support the way that Parsons recognises the importance of women's domestic labour. (The problem they see is in the assumption that women should naturally be the ones doing it.)

Functionalists were writing largely in the 1950s and much of their research was based in the USA. However, some of its ideas have re-emerged in New Right thinking in the contemporary UK. These are examined in subsection (iii) on family diversity.

## Marxism and the family

Activity 2.12

Write down three ways that families prepare people for their future role in the workplace.

Marx himself did not provide a developed theory about family relationships and gender inequalities in the home. However, Marxist theorists have taken some of his general ideas and applied them to the family. Marxists are not critical of the family *per se*, but how capitalism has exploited it. They focus on the way family life operates in a capitalist society. In contrast to Murdoch, who regarded the family's reproductive function in a positive light, Marxists explain how future generations of workers being maintained by the family keep capitalism going.

Marxists regard the norms and values people learn through family socialisation in terms of an **ideology**. For example, people learn to conform, not to question authority, to have a work ethic, to prioritise work commitments and the like.

## How families evolved

Engels was a friend and working companion of Marx. He maintained that relationships in early human societies were promiscuous. Marriage and the family developed when people began to own private property. Once people owned property, and at the time it was usually men, then they wanted to be sure that the offspring they passed their property onto when they died were definitely their own. Engels explains monogamous marriage in terms of this. With inheritance, there had to be restrictions on women's freedom. A woman's sexuality had to be controlled so that male family lines continued.

Zaretsky (1976) examines the family in a modern capitalist society where work is alienating, providing little fulfilment. The exploitative nature of capitalism leads to people seeking refuge in the family. However, Zaretsky says the family cannot meet the high expectations placed upon it. In the 1970s, Zaretsky observed how housewives kept capitalism going, performing free household tasks in the home and socialising a future generation of workers (the children) into a way of thinking that suited capitalist requirements. The family is also a unit of consumption. Families buy consumer goods that need to be purchased for capitalism to survive and for the profits gained by the capitalists to be maintained.

Activity 2.13

Identify and briefly explain two ways in which Zaretsky's argument is still relevant thirty years on.

The family's part in consumption is an expanding one. Family leisure time is often spent on trips out to shopping malls where many buy things on credit, building up increasing debts.

Some families are questioning the values of a consumer society, by turning, for example, to a more spiritual life. This can be seen with the growth of New Age movements. However, critics maintain that these new religions themselves are indicative of the very nature of consumer society, where people buy into religion as a consumer product.

## Marxist feminists

Some feminists make use of Marxist theory to explain the oppressions specific to women. Marxist feminists focus upon women's domestic labour and the contribution it makes to the maintenance of capitalism. They show a link between the roles in the family and the way the economy is organised in the wider society. Such writers focus on a nuclear family structure with a sexual division of labour, with men going out to work and women taking care of the family and doing the domestic work. If women did not provide this service free of charge, then, they argue, men's wages would have to be high enough to be able to pay someone else to perform housework. Such a way of organising family roles helps to keep wages down. Marxists maintain that a nuclear family structure serves the needs of capitalism by keeping the worker fit and healthy to carry out his working role.

Marxist feminists show a link between the private sphere of the family and the public sphere of the economy. The roles in the family are not randomly allocated. They link to wider external factors that shape them. However, social action theorists challenge the over-determining nature of the allocation of roles which they argue can be negotiated. For example, men are househusbands in some families.

Some contemporary Marxists argue that Marxism should not be critical of the family. Rather the emphasis should be upon the stresses and strains that capitalist society puts the family under. For example, dual career families may experience conflict in terms of fulfilling the demands of work and family roles. The **work/life balance** can be difficult to maintain in a competitive

economy. On the other hand, families who have low incomes may experience tensions through the pressures of living in relative poverty. Contemporary Marxists stress the need to improve working conditions so that the workplace becomes more family friendly. Some would argue that progress in this area has been made with more flexible working hours. However, critics ask who the flexibility is for, arguing that it acts in the interests of the employer, when it suits them, rather than the worker. Marxists argue that while employers increasingly recognise the need to provide childcare, the attitudes and provision are very different for high- and low-paid workers. Therefore there is a class difference for working- and middle-class families.

Refer back to Activity 2.10. How did your responses compare with the sociological views you have just studied?

## A comparison of functionalism and Marxism

Similarities:

◆ Both are macro theories.

◆ Both are what is inown as structuralist theories; they look at the family in the context of the system as a whole and the relationship between the family and the wider society.

Differences:

◆ In contrast to the organic analogy used by functionalists, whereby the family works for the whole and everyone benefits, Marxists emphasise the kind of society that families are meeting the needs of. For them, the capitalist element of modern societies is what is crucial to understanding how families operate and indeed why they are there in the first place.

◆ For functionalists, the family works harmoniously with other institutions. There is value consensus. For Marxists, conflict is normal.

◆ Functionalists regard what the family does, in terms of passing on norms and values, as a positive thing. Marxists see it in a negative way, maintaining that the family is spreading ruling-class ideology.

Table 2.1 Evaluation of theories

| | Strengths | Criticisms |
|---|---|---|
| Functionalism | Shows the importance of the institution of the family | Ignores the dark side of family life |
| | Stresses the importance of socialisation in the upbringing of children | Overemphasises the harmonious nature of society |
| | Stresses the positive aspect of the family as a support mechanism | The idea of a change from a pre-industrial extended family structure to a nuclear industrial family is too simplistic |
| | | Value of functionalism for family types other than the nuclear family has been disputed |
| | | Fails to examine power inequalities between men and women |
| | | Underplays the significance of women's paid employment |
| Marxism | Shows a link between family roles and capitalism | Marxism is overly deterministic in the way it portrays family roles. People may have more choice in how to organise the family |
| | Focus on gender inequalities by Marxist feminists has aided understanding of the position of women in the family | Critics question the degree to which the family acts as a refuge against capitalism, as highlighted by Zaretsky |
| | Shows a link between control of women and capitalism | Some postmodernists may argue that family consumption can be an enjoyable, liberating experience because of the choice it offers |
| | Shows a link between family consumption and the economy | |
| | Contemporary Marxists show a need for more family-friendly workplaces | |

## Section summary

Use the following key words to complete the summary of this section below. Each word should be used only once.

dysfunction    expressive    function    ideology    isolated nuclear family
instrumental    monogamous    organic analogy    primary socialisation
production    consumption    work / life

Functionalism draws an _____ _____, by which it compares the workings of the institutions in society to the way the organs of the human body work together so that the human body is maintained. They call the contribution that institutions like the family make to the overall maintenance of society its _____. The family carries out _____ _____, teaching children norms and values. Marxists regard these as part of an _____ that prepares family members so they have the right attitudes for the workplace. Critics of functionalism claim that it ignores the negatives of families, the _____, which have a harmful effect on society. According to Parsons, men and women have different roles in the family. Men have an _____ role, while women's roles are _____.

Both functionalists and Marxists examine the family and social change. Functionalists such as Parsons explain a shift to an _____ _____ _____ in terms of it being the best 'fit' in an industrial society. Marxists see the rise of _____ relationships in terms of a need to control female sexuality so that property was passed on through a male line of inheritance. They see a shift in the role of the family from being a unit of _____ to a unit of _____. In a competitive economy it can be difficult to maintain a _____ / _____ balance, where there is conflict between the demands of work and family.

## Exam practice

(b) Outline and evaluate the view that the nuclear family suits the needs of society. (33 marks)

# (iii) Family diversity

## Pause for thought

1   How are families the same as or different from each other?

2   What factors do you think might affect the way families are?

3   How do families change over time?

4   Does society view all families in the same way?

Figure 2.9  How typical?

1 Identify three ways in which families are diverse.

2 Identify three factors that could contribute to an increase in family diversity.

# Diversity

When we talk about something being diverse, it means that there are variations – that things are not all identical, following the same pattern. It is difficult to dispute the fact that families are diverse in the contemporary UK. However, the response to that diversity varies. Some people, for example, celebrate diversity. Others see specific family types as ideal, particularly a nuclear family structure, and regard other types as the source of problems in society.

In referring to family diversity, we could be talking about diversity in terms of a number of different factors:

◆ family structure: nuclear, one-parent, extended, and the like

◆ family size: this can vary within these structures. For example, some single parents have one child, others three, and so on

◆ how a family has been formed. For example, some children may not live with both their biological parents in cases where partners have split up and new families have formed (termed a **reconstituted family**). The way that families came together is an interesting factor in its own right For example, in some families partners are married, others co-habit, others live apart

◆ the kinds of relationships between family members. Some may be caring, some unsupportive

◆ roles vary in families. For example, some families are equal in terms of the division of labour, some are patriarchal, some abusive

◆ sexuality, with more openly gay and lesbian families in the contemporary UK

◆ quality of life. Some families, for example, live in poverty and the kind of family life they have

will be different from that of a family who can afford holidays abroad three times a year.

Households, too, have also become more diverse and not all of these comprise families. Nor do all children live in family households. In 2001, 139,000 children lived in other household types in the UK, with adults who were not their parents. Also another 52,000 children lived in communal settings such as children's homes.

There are other factors to consider in the debate on family diversity.

◆ The extent to which something occurs. For example, the rise in civil partnerships formed by gay couples certainly contributes to family diversity. However, it is also useful to consider how typical these families are in the overall picture of families in the UK. This does not lessen their value or contribution to society. But the extent of family types, or relationship roles and childrearing practices is an element of the debate on diversity.

◆ The range of diversity. For example, if there were only two types of family structure, could that lead to a conclusion that families were diverse?

◆ The issue of families changing. When statistical evidence is used, for example on family structure, it is important to bear in mind that these statistics represent a snapshot in time. Some of those families will change in structure: children grow up and leave home, people divorce, live on their own, share with friends, remarry. In terms of family life and culture, norms and values change. Regarding ethnicity and diversity, this sometimes occurs over generations, for example. Regarding social class, some families experience social mobility and change. For example, some children with working-class backgrounds may change their behaviour from that of their parents or working-class peers. Family trends were examined in subsection (i) and it will be useful to refer to these in relation to the family diversity debate.

Sociological research on family diversity began in the 1980s when the Rapoports' work offered an invaluable insight into this area of sociology.

# How are families diverse?

This section examines the following:

- single-parent families
- beanpole families
- reconstituted families
- cultural diversity
- class diversity
- sexual diversity.

Before we look at these in detail we will look at an early study of family diversity that highlighted some of these types.

In the 1980s, the Rapoports (1982) identified five elements of family diversity. These give a valuable insight into different types of family diversity today. The Rapoports devised the following classifications.

1 Organisational diversity – This refers to family structure, kinship networks and how roles are divided in the home. Families are structured differently; relationships with kin differ; and the ways in which families divide domestic labour varies. Men may do all the cooking in some households, for example, but in others men do none.

2 Cultural diversity – There is ethnic and religious diversity in the contemporary UK which gives rise to family diversity.

3 Class-based differences – Social class affects relationships in families and the socialisation of children.

4 Stage in life cycle diversity – Family life is different for newly-married couples who do not have any children than for those who do have children. Things can change when children grow up and leave home.

5 Cohort diversity – This refers to the period of time at which families pass through stages in the life cycle. For example, if children leave school and go to work when unemployment is high, then that will be different to those leaving when the economy is buoyant.

In addition, regional diversity was revealed in the 1980s through the research of Eversley and Bonnerjea (1982). They found relations with kin wider than the nuclear family to be stronger in rural communities, for example.

The elements of diversity identified by the Rapoports can still provide a useful framework for analysis 25 years on. Regarding what they termed organisational diversity, the structural aspect of this is explored in particular by looking at three family types: single-parent families, beanpole families and reconstituted families. Cultural and class diversity are also examined further and another type of diversity, sexual diversity, is also explored.

## Activity 2.15

Divide up into small groups. Each group should take on one of the following tasks. Feed your answers back to the rest of the class in a plenary session.

### Group A

1 Identify and briefly explain two ways in which culture might lead to family diversity in the contemporary UK.

2 Evaluate how families may not be diverse in spite of cultural differences. Illustrate your answer with two examples.

### Group B

1 Identify and briefly explain two ways that social class might affect families.

2 Evaluate how families may fall out of those class expectations.

### Group C

Invent three families to illustrate organisational diversity. Feed back to the rest of your class using a method of your choice such as role play, poster, PowerPoint presentation.

### Group D

Tim and Sian met through the Internet. They have been together for a year and are ready to commit to a life together after spending time travelling the world.

1 Plot their life on a timeline starting from now until they are very old, identifying significant events to illustrate 'Stages in life cycle'.

2 How typical do you think Tim and Sian's life is?

Have a class discussion on the issues raised.

1 Why do you think extended kin networks could be stronger in rural communities?

2 What changes are taking place in rural communities that might affect families?

# Single-parent families

The proportion of children living in lone-parent families has more than tripled in the last thirty years. Explanations for this trend are highlighted in subsection (i). It is important to bear in mind that statistics on one-parent families are a snapshot and that it can be a temporary phase. Many single-parent families do not set out to be single parents and will often establish new relationships and subsequently new families.

Identify three ways in which people who have been married can become single parents.

Not all single parents have been married. Births outside marriage have become more socially accepted today. In the past there was more pressure to marry when pregnancy occurred; these were referred to as 'shotgun weddings'.

Roseneil and Budgeon (2004) offer some insight into the lives of those who live outside the nuclear family, such as single-parent families. They argue that the conventional family should not be taken for granted as the basic unit of society, as it no longer occupies the centre ground of western societies. They identify the following reasons for this.

◆ The dramatic rise in divorce rates over the past 30 years (and to a lesser extent the number of births to women who are single by choice).

◆ The rise in the proportion of children being brought up by lone parents.

◆ The growing proportion of households that are composed of one person.

◆ The increasing number of women who are not having children.

This final point adds a further element to explore in the family diversity debate.

Allan and Crow (2001) challenge the assumption that lone-parent families have different values to other family types, pointing out that it is not the case that one-parent families reject a two-parent structure. They point out that many single parents do, in fact, form that type of family at some point.

# Beanpole families

Beanpole family structures are extended, but in a particular direction. They are long and thin. Brannen (2003) sees them as being like a beanpole. These are multigenerational families where there is more *inter*generational contact, that is between generations – such as between grandparents and grandchildren – than there is *intra*generational contact, that is within generations – such as those between cousins, for example.

The reasons for fewer intragenerational ties include:

◆ high divorce rates – when partners split up there can be a breakdown of contact between extended family members. For example, if children remain living with their mother, they may not see their father's brothers and sisters as often as before

◆ falling fertility rates – if people have fewer siblings than they used to, there will be fewer relationships on this level than there were in the past

◆ smaller family size – there will be fewer family members to build relationships within a generation, but also these smaller families can be geographically mobile. This can mean, for example, that two grown-up sisters, both with children, can live a long distance away from each other.

The reasons for more intergenerational ties include:

◆ people are living longer – grandparents and even great-grandparents are alive for longer and are more physically fit

◆ provision of practical and emotional support for elderly parents from grown-up offspring – this links to the above point. At some point the elderly may need family support. Some would argue the onus of responsibility is being put back on the family

- grandparents provide childcare for their grandchildren

- an increase in lone parents who may rely on support from their own parents to help with children.

Grundy and Henretta (2006) use the concept of the 'sandwich generation' to refer to women aged between 55 and 69 who, sandwiched between their needy parents and their own children, offer assistance to both. They help their grown-up children with childcare and also care for their elderly parents. Research shows a growing number of women will be in this position of helping in both directions. Women see it as their duty.

Activity 2.18

Why are women rather than men part of the sandwich generation referred to by Grundy and Henretta? Discuss.

## Reconstituted families

A reconstituted family is when families merge together and form a new family. For example, a couple with children split up, the children remain with the mother who later meets a new partner, who also has children. The combining of both groups together forms a reconstituted family. In 2004 an estimated 10 per cent of all families were reconstituted (Office for National Statistics, 2004).

This type of family has a different structure from the conventional nuclear family, although extended families may be a little different from nuclear families in many other ways.

## Co-parenting

Co-parenting refers to situations where children are cared for separately by each of the birth parents for approximately half the time. This situation arises when parents separate. The arrangement could work on a weekly basis, where children spend half of the week with each parent. It could, however, be split over the year, with the children spending time in each family household, perhaps with a less even split in terms of time. The children live in two homes and the structure of each family home can of course vary. For

example, both of the parents could be lone-parent families, or their mother and/or father could have met a new partner, possibly one who also has children, thus forming a reconstituted family.

Smart et al. (2000) researched children's experience of co-parenting. They found that children valued having both parents in their lives. Children tried to treat their parents in a way that they saw as fair too, such as spending time with each parent, almost as if *they* were the parents. Moving between houses was routine for those who had been doing it from a young age. Those who found it a difficult way of living had parents who were hostile towards each other. Some children were enthusiastic about having 'two of everything'.

## Cultural diversity

### Religion

There are links between religion and family. Some religious people are more likely to have children living with them than others. Religion can also influence the way that children are socialised in families.

Activity 2.19

Look at Figure 2.10. The followers of which religion are the most likely to have children living with them?

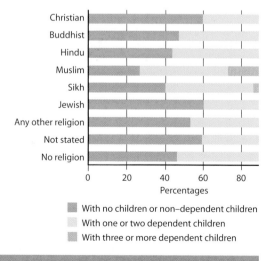

Figure 2.10 Family presence and number of children and religion in Great Britain, April 2001

(Source: National Statistics, 2007)

# Ethnicity and family structure

The 2001 Census shows that in the UK families of Asian and Chinese origin with dependent children living with them are most likely to be married and least likely to be lone-parent families. Mixed, black Caribbean and white families with dependent children have the largest proportion of cohabiting-couple families. Over 45 per cent of black Caribbean, black African and mixed families were headed by a lone parent in 2001. These differences mean that children in these diverse families will be influenced by different role models in the family during the process of socialisation.

Some research on ethnicity and families compares families from different ethnicities within the UK. Other research compares minority ethnic group families in the UK with families in the countries of origin of those ethnic groups.

Berthoud and Beishon (1997) analysed data from the fourth National Survey of Ethnic Minorities by the Policy Studies Institute (PSI). The survey compares different ethnic groups within the UK. The results of their analysis found:

◆ a higher rate of divorce and separation in British African-Caribbean people than in other ethnic groups. There were also more lone mothers in this group, but the mothers were more likely to be in employment than lone mothers in other ethnic groups.

◆ British south Asian people are more likely to marry, and get married at an earlier age, than other ethnic groups. Separation and divorce were rare.

## Change over generations

Research by Modood et al. (1997) shows how young south Asians are less likely than their elders to speak a southern Asian language. This shows a cultural shift over generations.

Singh (2003) reports how changes are taking place within the value system of the Sikh community. The strong value placed on mutual help and assistance within and between Sikh families is being replaced by a value of individualism. Sikh parents are worried by the lack of facilities in Britain for their children to learn Punjabi and fear that their children are taking a pragmatic approach to their family duties. The film *Bend it Like Beckham* highlights some of the cultural

conflict between generations. A young Sikh girl playing football is not what this child's family regard as appropriate. The daughter challenges her parents' values, navigating her way through two cultural systems. The notion of choice is a central aspect of postmodernism. However, critics stress that these choices are not made in a vacuum, as cultural conflict illustrates.

Bose (2003) studied the Bangladeshi community living in Tower Hamlets in London and portrays a picture of a changing community. The community is subject to the dual forces of maintaining traditional Bangladeshi values, such as the importance of kin, women as homemakers, and *izzat* (family honour), and to the changing external environment, which includes dual-career families, individualism and religious choice. A useful example of this is *hijab*, the practice of covering the body and the wearing of a veil which many young women have chosen to do as a central part of their identity, while rejecting the predominantly homemaker role for women in the family. The novel *Brick Lane*, by Monica Ali, now also a film, highlights these dual forces.

Archer and Francis (2006) showed the crucial role played by the family in the educational achievement of British Chinese children. They interviewed thirty pupils, their parents and teachers and concluded that the families used their skills, networks and money to further the educational achievement of these children. Their conclusion was that the educational achievement of British Chinese children is 'hard won', meaning that families made considerable sacrifices to ensure success. However, the children did not blindly follow the guidelines of their families. They were not simply passive. It is likely that young people conform to some expectations whilst rejecting others.

Further recent changes in relation to ethnicity and the family are in terms of divorce and single parenthood of which there are now *some* cases in minority ethnic groups in the contemporary UK. These groups are also having fewer children than before, and expect to have more say in their choice of partner.

## Women and employment

Dale et al. (2004) found differences in women's economic activity between ethnic groups; they also observed changes over time. They found that black women tended to remain in full-time employment when they had children. However, white women and Indian women with children were more likely to work part-time. The economic activity of Pakistani and Bangladeshi women fell significantly when they had a partner and then fell again when they had children.

## Class diversity

Family life may differ according to social class in a number of ways.

### Family structures

Early sociological research on the family had a strong focus on the family and social class. For example, analysis of the maintenance of kinship networks contrasted working-class and middle-class social networks. Middle-class families were more geographically mobile. However, this does not necessarily mean contact with kin dissolves. More contemporary research reveals extended kin to be important in working-class communities. For example, Foster (1990) found extended family members living close to each other in an East End London community. However, extended networks of support remain important across social classes as the evidence on beanpole families highlights.

### Child-rearing practices

There is a tendency for middle-class families to be more child-centred. This could be to compensate for the tendency of middle-class work to be more flexible, but anti-social, thus affecting relationships between parents and children.

### Conjugal roles

'Conjugal roles' refers to the roles between men and women in the household: these can be shared or unshared, the same or different. Oakley's (1974) research showed class to be a relevant factor in the division of labour in the home. (This is examined further in subsection (iv).) Her research showed class to be a factor, with middle-class domestic roles being more shared, but in neither class could they be defined as equal. Contemporary roles are affected by class. For example, middle-class dual-career families are more likely to be able to pay for domestic labour. In terms of money management, Pahl (1989) found that a situation of women controlling the family finances and spending patterns was not a typical arrangement. However, it was more common in working-class families.

## Cultural differences

The children of the upper class/middle class acquire what the Marxist sociologist Bourdieu (1986) termed 'cultural capital'. Their mannerisms and values are distinct from those of other social classes. These mannerisms and values correspond with teachers' notions of what is positive when they go to school. Upper-class children are also socialised into **high culture**, for example, being taken to the opera and experiencing classical music in the home. This contrasts with the **popular culture** of the working class, which might include watching celebrity television programmes, listening to pop music, a day out roller skating or tenpin bowling, and a McDonalds meal. The upper classes learn to speak and express themselves differently. Along with the middle classes, they learn to speak with, what is termed by Bernstein (1961), an 'elaborated code' in contrast to a working-class 'restricted code'.

Postmodernists would, however, be critical of such claims, arguing that there is much more choice available to families, irrespective of their class background. They maintain that people are no longer constrained by their class.

At the other end of the scale is the underclass, comprising people in very low-paid work or the long-term unemployed. Some single parents also fall in this class. Saunders (1996) is critical of this group whom he claims has a work-shy culture. Critics, however, challenge him and point to the difficulties faced by families trying to bring up children in conditions of poverty.

## Sexual diversity

Weeks et al. (1999) stress that there is a large degree of choice occuring in gay and lesbian families. They have what he terms 'chosen families'. Some homosexual relationships have a high degree of choice, and commitment is negotiated in these relationships. The expectations of roles that are pre-set in heterosexual relationships have not been set in the same way for newly evolving gay

Figure 2.11 Sir Elton John formed a civil partnership with David Furnish at Windsor Guildhall in December 2005

relationships. Weeks et al. see this in the context of the wider society where choice is valued and diversity is increasingly accepted. For example, civil partnerships, where same-sex couples are able to obtain legal recognition of their relationship, came into force in December 2005 with The Civil Partnership Act, 2004. There were 5700 civil partnerships formed in the UK between December 2005 and September 2006 (National Statistics, 2007).

## Recent developments

### *The importance of friendship*

Roseneil and Budgeon's (2004) research focuses on people who do not live with a partner. This is a further development to family diversity in the contemporary UK. They carried out in-depth qualitative interviews with 51 people aged between 24 and 60 in three locations in Yorkshire. They found a new emphasis on friendship. Most people were part of complex networks of intimacy and care. Their homes were opened up to their friends, people who are not part of a conventionally defined family.

Friends would stay during periods when they were homeless, unemployed, depressed or lonely. The interviewees chose to de-emphasise the importance of the couple relationship and centre their lives on their friends. Of those with partners, few saw cohabitation as the necessary or desirable next stage.

## Changing households

Subsection (i) highlights the growing trend in the number of one person households and the increase in the number of young adults living with their parents. These are referred to as KIPPERS (Kids In Parents' Pockets Eroding Retirement Savings).

## The importance of choice

By 2001, Allan and Crow (2001) had rejected the notion of a clear family cycle that people pass through, which the Rapoports had found to be an important element of diversity in the 1980s. Allan and Crow attribute this change to the fact that things are more unpredictable in the contemporary UK. There used to be a clearer pattern of growing up, leaving home, getting married, having kids – but this is not so fixed now. They point to the increased choice available in the contemporary UK. People can choose to have a baby before or indeed without getting married, which used to have a stigma attached to it.

# Contemporary views of family diversity

Beck and Beck-Gernsheim (1995) use the concept of individualisation – whereby the individual chooses how to live – to explain the changes that have taken place in the family. This is in contrast to the traditions that people were expected to follow in the past when roles were more clear-cut. They explain such choice in terms of factors such as people having increased educational opportunities and women having better employment prospects, but also that people are more mobile today. They move geographically. They also move socially, potentially experiencing different opportunities to those their parents had.

Such factors mean that love becomes high in importance. People have very high expectations of fulfilment from love in a society which Beck and Beck-Gernsheim argue is more of a risk society than was the case before. This risk society is characterised by uncertainty. People can feel insecure and therefore seek love as a form of emotional security. Love, however, becomes more difficult to sustain when both partners have high expectations of fulfilment.

# Postmodernism

Postmodernists support the view that families in the contemporary UK are diverse. They see variation as normal. They argue that identities have become fragmented and are more individualised, which has impacted upon family relationships. The American sociologist Stacey (1996) uses the concept of the postmodern family. Like Allan and Crow, she argues the family no longer progresses through a range of stages. She supports the view that contemporary families are diverse, stressing that there is no dominant type of family in contemporary society.

A postmodern view of the family is that there is no one dominant type of family. The key is

*choice.* People can choose how to live their family lives. Roles are much more uncertain and negotiable. Femininities and masculinities have undergone change and remain diverse. Pakulski and Waters (1996) claim that contemporary family roles are a matter of choice. The roles interact with consumption and media images.

Postmodernists emphasise the fluid nature of classification groupings such as ethnic or class. They **deconstruct** existing ideas. So, for example, in terms of work done on ethnic diversity, there may be variations *within* the categories used. In terms of class diversity, there may be differences in the way that working-class and middle-class people bring up their children, but postmodernists deconstruct the categories of working class and middle class. Not all working class families are the same.

Lewis (2001) argues that New Labour has a postmodern policy approach to families in that it has developed flexible, diverse and even contradictory policies.

# New Right

The New Right's view of the family is similar to that of functionalism. Like functionalism, the New Right sees the nuclear family as an ideal type and has an overly harmonious conception of this type of family. The New Right is critical of other types of family and is critical of family diversity. For example, it is highly disparaging of single parents, expressing concern about the ability of this type of family to socialise children effectively. It sees an overly generous welfare state as a contributory factor in the growth of lone parents. Some New Right thinkers regard single parenthood in the context of an underclass, characterised by living off benefits, not wanting to work, having short-term sexual relationships and having children with men who do not see their offspring as their responsibility.

Activity 2.20

Critically evaluate the New Right's view of single parents.

The New Right sees divorce as symptomatic of a moral decline in society. The rise in cohabitation is seen in a negative light as undermining the belief that relationships are for life. Dennis (1993) examines the relationship between family type and crime. He argues that the social control that was exercised in the past by traditional families has weakened. Men have become marginalised in families as family roles have changed. He also claims that boys do not have male role models to copy in families where parents split up, pointing to the decrease in negative judgements against men who leave their families. Such boys may turn to delinquent behaviour.

The New Right focuses on what it regards as welfare scroungers and state dependency, blaming the individual for poverty and poor life chances. It can be argued that New Right social policies reinforce traditional family values.

The following are examples of New Right initiatives.

- 1988 changes in taxation – these prevented cohabiting couples from benefiting from better tax allowances than married couples. In addition, couples could not claim mortgage relief as individuals.

- 1993 the Child Support Agency was introduced – this meant that absent fathers had to financially support their children, irrespective of their relationship to the mother of the child. This was a very controversial policy. It was criticised as being introduced as a way for the government to save money, as single parents lost out in benefit payments since receiving maintenance meant their benefits were cut. Allan and Crow (2001) highlight the Child Support Agency's lack of success, pointing out that only about 30 per cent of non-resident parents were contributing towards their child's maintenance by the late 1990s.

Criticisms of the New Right are that it:

- is biased towards traditional family structures

- is intolerant of family diversity

- shifts the blame from structural factors to the individual in terms of social problems and their causes.

# New Labour

New Labour policies do allow for family diversity. Nevertheless, it arguably still idealises a traditional family structure in which heterosexual parents are *married*. Teenage pregnancy in particular is presented as a social problem by New Labour which aimed to increase young teenage mother's participation in education, training and employment.

There are criticisms of New Labour and its policies.

- New Labour expects the family to maintain social control. When children are deviant, by truanting from school for example, parents can be fined. Critics, however, point out that families do not exist in a vacuum. It is necessary to consider external factors such as unemployment and poverty, and not simply blame the family for problems with the behaviour of some young people.

- New Labour is criticised for being contradictory. For example, it acknowledges families have changed, but still promotes marriage and conventional families as the best way forward. Critics argue that this leaves one-parent families feeling inadequate. Also gay and lesbian families continue to experience discrimination.

- Duncan (2006) challenges the assumptions of New Labour that teenage pregnancy is a social problem. He is critical of New Labour's actions which he says have not dealt with wider structural aspects of social disadvantage.

## Weblink

For further information on family diversity, go to the website for Sociology Learning Support (see 'Websites' page ii). You can choose to take part in a number of activities on family and households.

## Section summary

Use the following key words to complete the summary of this section below. Each word should be used only once.

> beanpole    cultural capital    deconstruct    diversity    high culture    intergenerational
> intragenerational    reconstituted    popular culture    sandwich generation

The variance of families in the contemporary societies is known as family _____. It is important to consider its range and extent. There are alternatives to the traditional nuclear family. There has been an increase in single-parent families. Other key developments to the diversity debate are the long, thin, _____ families, where _____ contact is strong, but _____ weaker, and _____ families, or step families, where new families are formed after former families split up. Women are part of a _____ _____, providing support for their grown-up children, and for their elderly parents. Cultural, class, and sexual diversity are also evident. The working class lack _____, favouring _____ _____ over the _____ _____ comprising, for example, opera and classical music that is favoured by the upper class.

Postmodernists highlight the degree of choice available to contemporary families. They _____ categories like class, and stress the differences within these former classifications.

## Exam practice

(a) Identify and briefly explain two reasons for the development of beanpole families.     (17 marks)

(b) Outline and evaluate the view that the contemporary UK contains a range of ethnically-diverse families.     (33 marks)

# (iv) Roles and responsibilities and relationships within the family

## Pause for thought

1  What do you expect from your family?

2  How do relationships between mothers and children compare with those between fathers and children?

3  Do you think you will want to have children one day? Is there a good time to start a family? Do you have any thoughts on who will look after them in their pre-school years?

Figure 2.12 Division of tasks

Sociologists have explored the roles, relationships and responsibilities in family life including:

- those between men and women
- those between parents and children.

Activity 2.21

What do you think the following terms mean: family roles; family responsibilities; family relationships? Share your initial ideas. Now make a note of two of your own ideas about each of these. Put these aside to revisit later when you have looked at what sociological research shows.

## Roles, responsibilities and relationships between men and women

So, how can we analyse family roles, responsibilities and relationships? Sociologists have considered how family relationships are formed, thinking about, for example, the notion of romantic love and the expectations it brings and whether the basis of relationships is changing. Do men and women invest the same **emotion work** in relationships and, if the degree of input is different, what impact does that have?

Sociologists are particularly interested in the part that gender plays in families. Does whether you are male or female make a difference in contemporary families? One useful thing to do is to examine domestic roles, to look at who does what in terms of household tasks. Then there is childcare to consider. Do men and women have different roles to fulfil in terms of taking care of their children and how time is spent with them? And what about the kind of invisible work that goes on in families, like planning what to eat as well as actually shopping for the food and cooking it.

Sociologists have also analysed money management in families to see whether it is gendered, that is, whether it is managed particularly by men or women. This is part of the power dynamics within families that needs to be considered. Power has also been measured

by considering processes of decision making. Domestic violence is also indicative of power.

We will first explore these issues by explaining some of the concepts that sociologists use and considering some of the studies that have been conducted. Then we will look at and evaluate the theories that have been put forward to explain the roles, responsibilities and relationships in family life.

## Adult relationships – intimacy and emotion

Figure 2.13 What's love got to do with it?

Activity 2.22

Study Figure 2.13 and discuss the following.

- Why do people commit to each other today?
- Identify three things you think men and women expect from a contemporary relationship.
- What might you do if your expectations aren't being met in a relationship?

Giddens (1992) examines the shift from families being formed on the basis of reproduction and economics in pre-modern relationships to the importance of romantic love which began to develop in the eighteenth century, through to what he terms confluent love today. Romantic novels were important in spreading the idea of romantic love, with the idea given to women in particular that they would fall in love and be with the loved one forever. However, as Giddens points out, the reality after falling in love for many women was domestic subjection and discontent. Confluent love is different. It need not be forever if the relationship is not working. It fits with Giddens' idea of the pure relationship. In a pure relationship the couple stays together out of choice; it works for both partners. It is the same for all couples regardless of sexuality. The relationship is negotiated and based on openness and mutual satisfaction. Potentially, then, pure relationships could be equal, if that was what both partners aspired to. Yet within contemporary societies there is still this key emphasis upon love, even though, as Allan and Crow (2001) point out, it is still rather vague and imprecise in terms of what we mean by love. They maintain that adolescents are socialised into romantic and sexual love through youth culture: music, magazines, soap operas and the like. However, families too socialise their children about love. The ideology of romance and love is a powerful one.

## Domestic roles and childcare

To see if domestic roles are gendered we can examine the division of labour in the home: who does what in terms of household tasks? We shall consider the practical aspects of childcare here, as much research combines this with domestic roles, but we will explore the relationships between parents and children further in the next part of this subsection.

Activity 2.23

Consider the following family.

Jackie and Steve have three children of nine, four and three. Jackie is a part-time teacher and volunteer at the local play group. Steve is a self-employed property developer.

Working in pairs or groups, complete the activity on this fictional family below. Present your findings either as a poster, through role play or in a summary paragraph.

(a) Imagine a typical day for this family and distribute tasks that need to be done in the home so that the domestic roles are 'equal'. You will need to flesh out the characters. Identify what factors make roles 'equal'. Depending on the type of delivery you adopt to present your findings, either identify and explain them or illustrate them.

(b) Consider the kind of negotiations that might go on in this family regarding roles. Again, depending upon the type of delivery you adopt to present your findings, either identify and explain them or illustrate them.

Examining domestic roles and issues of childcare is quite complicated because of the diversity of families. Some households will have one adult, some two of the same sex, some one of each sex. Some will have grandparents or other relatives living with them who may contribute to chores. Others will have older children who have tasks to do, but it isn't always easy to make comparisons as not all families have children of different sexes, or where they do it might be age, for example, rather than gender that is determining the tasks given. Pre-school children demand more care. However, some families have support from extended kin, others from paid childcare. Some families do not do a lot of domestic tasks themselves. Rather, they pay someone else to do them.

Many of the studies that have been carried out have taken two-parent households and looked at the division of labour between the adults. Other issues to think about, though, centre upon time, both the amount of time someone has available to do tasks alongside commitments to paid work, and also the amount of time spent doing domestic tasks at home. It isn't just a matter of time spent doing jobs either. There is a lot of 'behind the scenes' activity going on in family life – for example, thinking about what to have for dinner, remembering that the cat needs a vaccination, responding to requests from school. What if one partner works very long hours outside the home? How should we allow for that when generalising about who does more in the home? There is also pleasure to consider. Should that be a factor to be weighed up in the domestic roles debate? If cooking is a hobby, for example, how does that compare with laying out fish fingers under the grill for the umpteenth time when a person would really rather be doing anything else that didn't involve feeding people? Should we give equal weighting to all these domestic tasks? Similarly, some people may have one lavatory to clean in their house, others two, three, or even more. So, it is always worth looking closely at what has been taken into account and how: that is, considering the methodology of studies in this area.

## What do early studies show?

In the 1970s, Young and Willmott claimed that roles undertaken by men and women were symmetrical, with a sharing of domestic tasks, childcare and decision making. They found that roles had shifted from what they termed 'segregated conjugal roles' to 'joint conjugal roles'. Segregated conjugal roles refer to a pattern of domestic work divided between men and women. Joint conjugal roles involve more sharing of tasks. The feminist Oakley (1974) was critical of this study because of the way that it had interpreted the findings. Of particular concern was the interpretation of men 'helping' their wives, to mean that roles were 'equal'. Her point was that for there to be *equality* shouldn't men be taking *responsibility* too? A man *helping* his wife is assuming it is her job in the first place! There was also a problem over the *degree* of help that the men had to do before concluding they helped around the home. For example, if they performed one household chore a week then that was recorded as them 'helping'. Oakley's own research showed class to be a relevant factor in the division of labour. Middle-class domestic roles were more likely to be shared, but in no class could men and women be defined as equal.

## Studies from the 1990s: invisible work, emotion work and the triple shift

Invisible work refers to work that goes on in families but is not immediately obvious. Rather, it is carried out behind the scenes. Research by Dunscombe and Marsden (1995) identifies emotion work as an invisible aspect of women's domestic work. Emotion work involves giving love and sympathy, understanding and emotional support. The researchers interviewed 40 white couples who had been married for fifteen years and discovered that it was women who were doing this work. Many of the men did not or were

unable to express themselves emotionally and instead concentrated on their paid employment. This could put a strain on relationships, particularly if women had demanding work outside the home and the majority of domestic work and childcare to do as well. In fact what the study also show us is that women operate a **triple shift**. This means that as well as performing emotion work many women also do paid work outside the home and do housework and childcare as well.

This is an interesting piece of research which introduced a new dimension with its analysis of emotion work. However, it is a small sample to generalise from. An American sociologist, DeVault (1991), focused on a specific aspect of invisible work: feeding the family. She carried out in-depth interviews with 30 women and three men from a variety of classes and ethnicities and found that although women did not do all of the work involved in feeding the family, nevertheless it was the women who were primarily responsible for all the planning and organising of successful family meals.

## ... And more recent research

Domestic work and childcare is clearly demanding and time consuming, but evidence shows that it is still women who bear the brunt of this labour. Much research shows that women are still likely to have more domestic and childcare responsibilities than men. For example, Warner (2005) found that most home-based mothers today work around 100 hours a week. She found the mothers she interviewed were spending 41 hours a week on childcare. But it isn't just women who are predominantly home based who do the most domestic labour. Garrod (2005) argues that it is still the case for professional women. She cites a survey of British business women carried out in 2004 by Bibby Financial which found these women, who were in very demanding jobs, were spending three times as long on domestic work as men. Bibby Financial refers to these women as DIALLs (do-it-alls).

The concept of 'shift parenting' has been used to describe situations where working parents work at different times so that one of them is available to look after the children. This does, of course, mean that the family rarely spends time together as a whole unit.

## Lesbian households – how does sexuality affect domestic life?

Dunne (1997) found that, in the lesbian relationships she studied where the couple had children, there was more negotiation and flexibility in terms of which partner looked after the child than in heterosexual relationships. Lesbian couples were more likely to take turns in reducing hours in paid work to suit the demands of childcare. Dunne explained this with the argument that in heterosexual relationships it is still primarily the male who earns more, which affects the organisation of things in the home. Also there are fewer norms regarding lesbian relationships so there could be more freedom to choose how to live as a result. Similarly, Gabb (2005) found that gendered parental roles are constantly reviewed and reworked within lesbian parent families.

What concerns Gabb, though, is the lack of status of what she terms 'other mothers'. These are the partners of the biological mothers in lesbian relationships. Her research in Yorkshire, using semi-structured in-depth interviews, revealed a discomfort with being referred to as the *mothers* of the children, even though they shared 'motherly' roles and responsibilities. These 'other mothers' defined themselves as the non-mother in relation to the 'mother', which gave them a sense of uncertainty. Gabb points out their lack of social, legal or 'birth' rights, so that should these families split up they have to rely on the good will of the biological mother to have access to their children. The children themselves easily dealt with the roles of their parents, frequently referring to the 'other mother' by her first name. (For example, one child interviewed said she had a mother and a 'Janis'.)

### Weblink
The Equal Opportunities Commission (EOC) website (see 'Websites' page ii) provides information on studies of family roles and responsibilities.

## Power in families

Activity 2.24

1 Identify and explain three ways that you could measure whether someone has power in a family relationship.

2 What do you think is the source of power? Discuss this in groups and then compare your ideas as a class activity.

### Decision making

One way of measuring power in relationships is to look at who makes decisions. In the 1980s, research by Edgell (1980) on middle-class families found a difference in terms of the areas in which men and women made decisions. Men made what were deemed important decisions about things such as whether the family should move house or what car to buy. They also were in charge of key financial decisions. Women, however, made decisions about domestic issues, spending on children's clothes and interior design. These were seen to be unimportant areas of decision making. Therefore it seemed that men had more power. But is this still the case today and is the study valuable? The sample used was small, just 38 couples. They were all middle class, so we cannot generalise about other groups from these findings.

Research in the 1990s found some change. One factor that did have an impact was male unemployment. Leighton's (1992) research, also on middle-class couples, showed that wives made more financial decisions if their husbands were unemployed. Further research on dual-career families by Hardill et al. in 1997 found a small shift towards more egalitarian relationships. However, men did still dominate decision making in most households.

### Money management

Another way of measuring power is to look at who controls the family finances. Pahl (1989) interviewed 102 couples with at least one child under 16, both with some form of income. She interviewed them both separately and together about money management and classified them according to different kinds of money management systems. She found the most common form of money management was husband-controlled pooling where money was shared but the husband had more influence in how it was spent. Wife control was the least typical, but more common in working-class families. Further research by Vogler and Pahl (1994) found that when cutbacks had to be made, women were more likely to reduce spending on their own food and clothing so their husbands and children did not suffer so much. However, they see a move towards more equality with regard to money management as more women participate in full-time employment.

## Violence

Use of violence is another sign of power in a relationship. The Home Office defines domestic violence as:

> Any incident of threatening behaviour, violence, or abuse (psychological, physical, sexual, financial or emotional), between adults who are or have been intimate partners or family members, regardless of gender or sexuality.

Dobash and Dobash brought domestic violence to people's attention in the 1970s. More recently, their research stresses that women who experience violence are not hopeless or helpless. Many were actively seeking help and held positive views about themselves (Dobash and Dobash, 2000).

In terms of the extent of violence, this is a difficult thing to measure. Not all research uses the same definition. Also statistics may lack validity because victims are reluctant to come forward. What the Council of Europe (2002) did find, with an analysis of ten separate domestic violence studies, was consistency in findings. These showed that one in four women experience domestic violence over their lifetimes and that between six and ten per cent of women experience domestic violence in a given year.

Weblink
You could visit the Women's Aid website (see 'Websites' page ii) to find further information on domestic violence.

## Children and control

More contemporary research takes a different angle on power dynamics. Gatrell (2006) argues that children are a focus for power among couples. She suggests that power relations between married/cohabiting parents are similar to divorced ones where couples compete for access and control of children. Her interviews with 20 highly-qualified professional working couples with pre-school children revealed a level of ambivalence in two-thirds of the men about their partners' careers, which meant they were denied privileges they could have had in a patriarchal relationship. For example, one interviewee agreed intellectually with the way things should be in an equal relationship but felt irritated that his partner did not iron his shirts and at the fact that there was never any food in the house. Gatrell raises the possibility of men being threatened by women's employment because it challenges male privileges. Consequently, men try to defend their dominance by asserting themselves in an area previously considered to be women's: childcare.

# Roles, responsibilities and relationships between children and parents

### Activity 2.26

Identify three expectations of what a father's role should be. Prioritise them in order of importance. Compare these with the role of an actual father of your choice. This could be someone you know, or someone in the media. Discuss your work with other students.

Weblink
Visit the Families Need Fathers website (see 'Websites' page ii) to find information on the role of the father in the family.

### Activity 2.25

1  Research the financial cost of domestic violence in the UK. Can you think of other costs that aren't financial?

2  Find another sociological study on domestic violence. Share your findings with your class.

# Fathers

In terms of fathering in general, it appears that *attitudes* towards the father's role are changing. But does that mean a shift in practice? Research shows there has been a shift away from the expectation that fathers should be breadwinners. Dermott (2003), for example, examines the demise of the breadwinner father to be replaced by what she terms 'the intimate father'. Her research involved 25 semi-structured interviews with fathers with at least one child of primary school age who were all in professional/managerial roles. She looked at how these men combine employment and family life. Their paid work was not seen as central in their role as a father. Instead, these fathers sought 'intimate fathering'. To be a good father there was an expectation of emotional openness and a close relationship with one's children.

Similarly, Thompson et al. (2005) found that only 39 per cent of the fathers they studied viewed being a breadwinner as the most important aspect of fatherhood. In their research on fathers' involvement in the first year of their child's life, they found that 80 per cent of the fathers they surveyed said they would be happy to stay at home to look after their child. It could be, though, that social class affects expectations. Research by the Equal Opportunities Commission (EOC) in 2002 still shows that, although fathers play a range of roles in contemporary families, most still see themselves primarily as breadwinners. The key factor affecting the maintenance of traditional gender roles was women's lower average pay. However, the research also identified men's lack of confidence in their own caring skills as relevant. This fits with Thompson et al.'s work. Even though men were willing to stay at home to care for children, 65 per cent of them still thought that women were 'naturally' better at childcare. It seems, then, that the ideologically traditional ideas linger.

The EOC study *Dads on Dads* (Hatter et al., 2002) carried out by MORI identifies the four types of dad listed below.

- **Enforcer dad**: He is not involved with the day-to-day care of children. Being a role model and setting out clear rules are what he sees as important. These are usually older dads who are traditional in terms of gender roles.

- **Entertainer dad**: He plays with the children whilst his partner gets on with all the domestic chores.

- **Useful dad**: He helps out, but is led by the mother in terms of what needs doing.

- **Fully involved dad**: He is equally involved with running the home and the family, at least for some of the time. Mother and father roles are interchangeable in this family.

# Social policy

You might wonder what social policies have to do with how people organise their family roles and the types of relationships people have. Think about policies to do with paid time out of work when a woman has a baby, or policies on whether there is a right to flexible working practices, and you can begin to see the link. If a woman is given more time off work than a man and guaranteed to be able to go back to her job at the end of her maternity leave, then in many cases the man will not have the same relationship with the baby or take on as much of the caring of that child. It is only since April 2003 that new fathers have been entitled to two weeks paid paternity leave. If employers do not have to allow employees with families to work fewer hours and one partner's job pays a lot more, that can affect decision making in families about which partner works full time.

Garrod (2005; 2007) highlights how issues concerning relationships between parents, children and society are increasingly the focus of debate among policy makers and politicians. She raises some interesting questions regarding the role of the state and family life. To what extent, for example, do state policies reflect changes in social institutions, initiate change, accelerate it, or lag behind it? One aspect of family life that the state has taken a recent active interest in is the age at which people become parents. Garrod (2007) cites an interview with the then prime minister, Tony Blair, who identified a need for state intervention to prevent babies born into 'high risk families' becoming problem teenagers. Such intervention might take the form of making teenage mothers attend parenting skill classes.

Duncan (2006) also highlights the way in which teenage parenthood is presented as a social problem. Teenage pregnancy is seen as being

Figure 2.14 A pregnant teenager

teenage pregnancy and poor outcomes in terms of education, employment and income. He points out that becoming a mother does not necessarily *cause* any of these. Rather it could be due to *pre-pregnancy* social disadvantage. He also looks at qualitative research on young parents' values and experiences. These studies show that many young mothers are positive about their parenting experience. Indeed, many feel stronger, more responsible and more competent as a result of it. Bell et al. (2004), for example, found an increase in self-esteem and a sense of security and stability. There is less research available on young fathers but where there is, it is positive. These young fathers are also socially disadvantaged to begin with, but fathering does not worsen this. Evidence shows it can be a turning point for these young men.

Activity 2.28

Select one policy from each political party and think about how it might affect family roles and relationships. Report your findings to the class.

Activity 2.27

Garrod asks whether state intervention is designed to *discipline* those involved, or *support* and *aid* potentially vulnerable young parents. Where do you stand on this debate? Discuss this with other members of your class.

caused by ignorance and low expectations according to the government's Social Exclusion Unit. The policy response to this from New Labour was to aim to halve the under-18 conception rate by 2010 and increase teenage mothers' participation in education, training and employment.

Duncan, however, challenges this assumption that teenage pregnancy is a social problem. He is also critical of Labour's actions, which he says have not dealt with wider structural aspects of social disadvantage. Using his own research and also citing the work of others, he presents a case for the positive side of teenagers becoming parents. He examines statistical evidence on the social outcomes of teenage motherhood and warns of the danger of assuming that there are causal links between

## Sociological explanations
## Functionalism

Functionalists explain the roles, responsibilities and relationships within the family as being as they are because they are **functional**, both for society and the individuals within it. For example, partners have sexual fulfilment from each other and the emotional attachment that goes with that brings the family together as a unit. Families need to socialise their children into the culture of their society. Someone needs to work to earn money. Functionalists maintain that fathers are best suited to a more instrumental role of breadwinner, whereas mothers are naturally inclined to an expressive role of childrearing. Adult personalities, according to Parsons, are stabilised by the family. The man can return to work soothed and calmed by his wife's love and support. This is also referred to as the 'warm bath theory', as he is refreshed by his family. Fun is had by all, both parents playing with the kids.

### Evaluation

◆ Functionalists present an overly harmonious picture of the family where partners care for each other and fulfil each other's needs and children are socialised believing in society's values and conforming to the norms.

◆ Functionalists ignore the dysfunctions of families, that is, the harmful, negative aspects of family life. There is what has been termed a 'dark side of family life'. There is conflict within families. Domestic violence and child abuse occur between family members.

◆ As families change it becomes more difficult to understand family roles and relationships from a functionalist perspective which does not allow for the diversities in families that we find in the contemporary UK. Nevertheless, the nuclear family is still presented as the ideal.

◆ Feminists are critical of the way that women's needs are neglected by this approach. Their theories are discussed below.

## Marxism

In the 1970s, Zaretsky analysed family life from a Marxist perspective. Like Parsons, he thought that the family could provide fulfilment away from the world of work. However, he was critical of the exploitative nature of the capitalist system. He argued that capitalism needs housewives to reproduce and socialise the future workforce, to bring up children who will do as they are told by those in authority. Zaretsky also explained family roles and relationships in terms of the family being a unit of consumption in a capitalist society. Families purchase goods as a unit. People do not, for example, buy a washing machine to share with their neighbour.

### Evaluation

◆ It is certainly the case 30 years on that the family is a unit of consumption, when there are now expectations to consume more and more products produced on a global economic scale.

◆ Somerville (2000) points out that Zaretsky ignored the negative aspects of families, such as domestic violence and incest.

## Feminism

Feminists stress the negative aspects of the family for women. Generally they argue that relationships between men and women in the family are still patriarchal, that the family is male dominated. Feminists generally want equality between men and women, but differ in terms of their explanations of the causes of women's oppression in the family. Some feminists are Marxist, explaining women's situation in terms of capitalism. Haralambos and Holborn (2004) cite two studies that can be used to illustrate this theory: Ansley, who looked at the housewife in the 1970s, and Barrett and Mcintosh. Ansley (1972), for example, explained the traditional housewife role in terms of the support she provided her husband by acting as a safety valve. By this she meant that the frustrated feelings her husband had towards his job would be absorbed by her, soothed away, rather than being stored up and acted upon against the exploitative capitalist system. Perhaps, in modern times, some men could perform this role as more women work in the paid economy? On the other hand, with dual earner households, perhaps both partners are too exhausted to comfort anyone, and some may experience job satisfaction. Barrett and Macintosh use the concept of the anti-social family. As well as being critical of the way that women are exploited and the gains made by capitalists at the workers' expense, they also challenge the way that any alternative ways of living are devalued. In addition, the negative aspects of the family, violence and abuse are overlooked. Other feminists adopt a more liberal approach. For these feminists, legislation and policy is crucial. So they might say, for example, if there were more policies implemented to enable women to have flexible working patterns to fit with the demands of childcare, then that would be a way forward. Somerville (2000), for example, refers to the increased choices women have and the way that social policies can help working parents. Radical feminists see the structures of society at large as being patriarchal as well as the unit of the family. They say that sexism is embedded in the system and patriarchal ideology presents women's triple shift as normal. Postmodern feminists emphasise the differences between women and want to get away from the notion of a female essence, whereby all women are seen as sharing a common experience of being a woman, to an understanding of the differing circumstances of women. For example, they question the usefulness of trying to explain the situation of a black working-class woman in the same way as a white middle-class one.

### Evaluation

◆ Critics say that feminists do not allow for the fact that some women may enjoy domestic work and carrying out a caring role in the family.

◆ Critics say that feminists ignore the positive aspects of family life for women.

◆ Critics say that feminists discount any progress that has been made in the move towards equality.

# Demographic changes
# An ageing population

There is an ageing population in the UK, which means that an increasing proportion of the population are elderly. By 2020, according to Age Concern, half the population of the UK will be over 50 years old. This has implications for family roles and relationships. Family structure is also affected by an ageing population. There is an increase in **beanpole families**, that is, multigenerational families with few members in each generation.

Activity 2.29

Identify two positive and two negative aspects of having an elderly relative living in your household.

Care of the elderly when they need it is a burden falling increasingly on women. Grundy and Henretta (2006) maintain that women see this care as their duty. They refer to a 'sandwich generation' of women aged 55 to 69 who, as well as caring for their elderly parents, also provide childcare support for their children by looking after their grandchildren. There are different ways of viewing this issue. It could be seen in a positive light in the sense of people having support from and giving support to their families. However, a less rosy picture could see this as restrictive, limiting the roles of women to caring for others.

An ageing population is often seen as a social problem, for example some writers refer to the burden of care in which the elderly can put a strain on both state and family resources. Allan and Crow (2001), however, challenge some popular stereotypes of the elderly and the family. The elderly are not all dependent. They stress that the elderly population is fitter and more self-reliant than popular stereotypes would have us believe. Later-life experiences are also diverse. There are differences based upon class or ethnicity, for example. They also found that elderly people are not generally neglected by their families. Most elderly people have regular contact with their children and when there are grandchildren this can revitalise family relationships. Grandparents can provide support for dual-career couples.

Postmodernists stress the choices available to us in the contemporary world. The elderly do not have to conform to stereotypical lives. However, these choices can be restricted, particularly for those elderly people living in poverty.

The family as an institution and the state do not operate in isolation. State policies have a direct implication for family life. Lishman (2005), director-general of Age Concern England, argues that ageing should be seen as an opportunity rather than a burden. This could certainly be the case if state policies on housing, education and health focus on improving the lives of the elderly, which could then have a positive impact on family life in an ageing population.

## Family size

Families are getting smaller. This trend is examined in subsection (i). The issues raised there can be linked to roles, responsibilities and relationships in the contemporary family.

Return to your original thoughts on family roles, relationships and responsibilities from Activity 2.21.

1 Now that you have studied the sociology on this area, copy Table 2.2 and complete it.

2 Have your initial ideas been confirmed by the evidence or changed?

Discuss these points with the rest of your group.

Table 2.2 Time to reflect

| Original idea | Evidence to support idea | Evidence against idea |
|---|---|---|
| Example: women do more housework than men | | |
| | | |
| | | |
| | | |
| | | |

## Section summary

Use the following key words to complete the summary of this section below. Each word should be used only once.

ageing population    anti-social    beanpole    child-centred    confluent    conjugal roles
dark side    decision making    DIALLS (do-it-alls)    dysfunctions    emotion work
functional    intimate fathering    invisible work    money management    other mothers
pure    safety valve    sandwich generation    shift    symmetrical    triple shift

Giddens maintains that a shift has taken place from romantic love to what he terms _____ love. He talks about a contemporary relationship with the potential for equality where couples stay together when it works for both parties. He calls this a _____ relationship. Research has been carried out on _____ _____ to see whether they are becoming more equal.

Willmott and Young found families to be _____ _____ in the 1970s, but Oakley challenged their findings. Dunscombe and Marsden found that women work a _____ _____ of housework and childcare, paid work and _____ _____. Not all domestic labour is visible. De Vault examines the processes behind feeding the family, one example of _____ _____. Vogler and Pahl are interested in a particular aspect of family responsibilities: _____ whereas Edgell analysed the process of _____ _____ in order to learn about power in relationships. Bibby Financial found that professional women were _____, spending three times as long on domestic labour than men. With some parents working different hours, families spend little time together. This is known as _____ parenting. In lesbian relationships Gabb found that what she termed _____ _____ lacked the status of biological mothers.

Families have become more _____ in terms of the focus upon children. Expectations about relationships between fathers and children are changing. Some men are not content to be just a breadwinner. Dermott identified _____ _____, which included emotional openness, communication and a close relationship between fathers and their offspring.

There are different theories about the family.

Functionalists see the relationship between the family and society as _____. However, they are criticised for ignoring the _____ of the family, the _____ _____ of the family where abuse and violence occur. Marists are more critical. The Marxist feminist Ansley sees women's supportive role acting like a _____ _____. Barrett and Mcintosh refer to the family as _____ .

Finally demographic changes, such as an _____ _____ have had an impact upon family life and family structure, with a growth in _____ families which are multigenerational. An ageing population is affecting the family. A _____ _____ of women is caring for elderly relatives as well as supporting their children with childcare.

## Exam practice

(a) Identify and explain the consequences for family life of an ageing population. (17 marks)

(b) Outline and evaluate the view that the roles between men and women in the family are not equal. (33 marks

# The sociology of health

## (i) Key concepts and the social construction of health and illness

### Pause for thought

1 What evidence can you give to support the statement that 'Good health is valued in contemporary UK society'?

2 Discuss why health and illness may mean different things to different people.

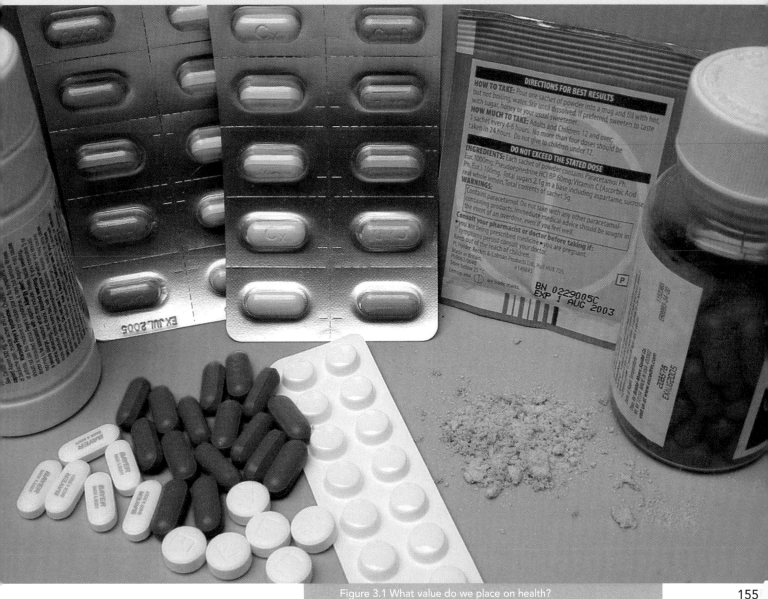

Figure 3.1 What value do we place on health?

# Health

When people meet each other, their greeting is often 'How do you feel today?' or 'How are you?' These are commonly asked questions, yet you probably don't find them straightforward to answer. In order to decide whether you are healthy or not, you need to define what is meant by health. Write down your answers to the questions below.

1  Think of someone you know who is very healthy. Who are you thinking of? How old are they? What makes you say they are healthy?

2  At times people are healthier than at other times. What is it like when you are healthy?

3  Compare your definitions with others. What are the main similarities and differences?

These questions were part of a survey of 9000 individuals carried out by a team of researchers at the University of Cambridge. The results, analysed by Blaxter (1990), will be examined in a later subsection.

We hear a lot about 'health', 'healthy living', 'healthy lifestyles'. Messages about our health, and the health of the nation, are delivered through our families, the media, politicians and even supermarkets. Thirty years ago, people may have defined health primarily in terms of doctors, hospitals and drugs. Today, people have a much broader image of what it means to be healthy. In your answers to the question, 'What is it like when you are healthy?', you may have drawn upon a range of images from healthy eating, taking vitamins and regular exercise, to therapy, sensible drinking and healthy social relationships. Information and knowledge about health (and illness) are not just the property of health 'experts', and the sociology of health is not confined to the narrow area of medicine.

According to the World Health Organisation (WHO), health is 'a state of complete physical, mental and social wellbeing and not merely the absence of disease or infirmity'. This all-inclusive definition focuses on a positive view of health, rather than regarding health merely as *not* being ill. As a definition, however, it has encountered some criticism. It could be argued that it is overly idealistic and too broad as, in reality, most of us are not completely physically, mentally and socially well at any one time. If we use this definition, we are unhealthy if we have a headache or if we feel a bit fed-up. Another problem with this definition is that it sees health in *absolute* terms in that it fails to take into account the notion that, within any given society, people understand different things by the concept of health – that it can change over time and between cultures. According to Dubos (1987), good health involves being able to function effectively. This implies that being healthy or ill are relative experiences/concepts. From this standpoint, health means very different things to different people and the health of an individual can be judged against, for example, their gender, age and occupation. For example, a young, male professional athlete may well have a very different conception of health and wellbeing compared with an elderly, wheelchair-bound female. This view that health is a relative concept will be explored in the subsection on the social construction of health and illness (pp. 162–166).

Illich (2002) proposes a much more critical definition of health. He argues that we can only function effectively and experience health and wellbeing if we can come to terms with and accept our less than perfect physical and mental condition. Illich argues that healthy people consciously accept the inevitability of ageing and, ultimately, death. From this point of view, we are healthy when we accept that we are inevitably going to feel ill, pain and sickness and we take responsibility for this. Illich is strongly critical of modern medicine and the way in which it has robbed people of the capacity to deal with their own wellbeing.

The definition of health, then, is not a simple matter. If an absolute definition is used (such as the one offered by the World Health Organisation), it fails to recognise that what counts as health and healthy varies between individuals, groups and societies. In this sense, there is no universally agreed definition of health.

1 Carry out a brief survey on definitions of health. Ask different groups of people (divided up by, for example, gender, age, ethnicity or class) about their definitions of what being healthy means.

2 Do your results support the view that there is no universally-agreed definition of 'health'?

## Disease, illness and sickness

**Disease** refers to a specific biological or mental abnormality which usually involves medically diagnosed symptoms, such as high blood pressure, and is a medically recognised condition, such as diabetes or measles. More generally, however, disease can refer to 'any pathological (unhealthy) condition, bodily or mental, whether caused through illness, accident or injury' (Taylor et al., 1996).

**Illness** refers to the subjective experience of *feeling* unwell or ill – a person's own recognition of lack of wellbeing. It is possible both to have a disease and not feel ill, such as being HIV positive, and to feel ill and not have any disease, for example, feeling a 'little bit under the weather'. Illness is often referred to as **morbidity** and death as **mortality**.

Sickness is a social role and as such it involves certain rights and obligations. Just as your role as a student gives you the right to an education and the duty of, for example, doing your homework and listening to your teacher; the role of a 'sick person' gives them the right to have time off work/school, but a duty to seek medical help.

Definitions about health are inevitably tied up with definitions about illness and disease. As the previous discussion about definitions illustrates, many people see being healthy as the opposite of being ill. Rather than thinking of health, illness and disease as distinct and separate categories, it may be useful to see them as a continuum, from perfect health at one extreme to death at the other. Of course, this does not mean that all individuals start with perfect health at birth and slowly move along the scale until they reach inevitable death. Some individuals are born

1 Copy Table 3.1 and complete the shaded area with examples to illustrate the relationship between disease and illness. Use the words listed underneath (two in each category) as a starting point and then add some of your own.

Table 3.1 The relationship between disease and illness

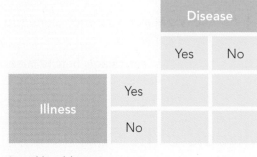

Good health
Nausea in early pregnancy
Flu
Happiness
Chlamydia (sexually-transmitted infection)
Carrier of typhoid
Feeling tired and lacking in energy
Measles

Figure 3.2

2 Look at Figure 3.2. Describe how it shows the relationship between illness, sickness and disease.

with **chronic illnesses**; some rarely experience symptoms of illness; and most symptoms never develop into acute or chronic diseases. Figure 3.3 illustrates the health–death continuum.

| Health—death continuum | HEALTH | PRE–SYMPTOMATIC | SYMPTOMS NO ACTION | SYMPTOMS NON–MEDICAL ACTION | ACUTE | CHRONIC | TERMINAL | DEATH |
|---|---|---|---|---|---|---|---|---|
| Example | | Pathological cell division | Smoker's cough, Hangover | Head cold | Infectious diseases | Diabetes, Arthritis | Some cancers | |

Figure 3.3 The health–death continuum

(Source: Lawson et al., 2000)

1 For each point along the continuum, add another example.

2 Discuss how, at each stage, health/illness could be measured.

3 Using the diagram, write one paragraph to explain how the health–death continuum supports the view that health and illness are relative concepts.

# Models of health

The different meanings we give to 'health' and 'illness' are important as they can shape the way in which we define causes of ill-health, and the strategies used to solve it. If health is defined in medical, scientific terms then it is seen as being about the absence of disease where ill-health arises from identifiable and treatable biological or physical causes. On the other hand, if health is defined by people's own feelings and awareness then definitions are relative and social factors are involved in both defining and causing ill-health. These two competing models of health are often referred to as the bio-medical and social models of health.

# Bio-medical approaches

The bio-medical model (sometimes referred to as the medical or mechanical model) takes a scientific approach to understanding health and illness. It is the dominant view of illness in Western societies and gained prominence in the late nineteenth century in Britain. This view of health and illness is held by most official health practitioners, such as doctors and surgeons, and is the main approach found in the National Health Service.

Assumptions of the medical model.

◆ Health is biological normality.

◆ Illness and disease are caused by an identifiable factor, usually biological (such as a faulty gene or a virus), and this disease occurs randomly in the population.

◆ Disease can be identified and classified into different types, for example diseases of the nervous system, diseases of the circulatory system.

◆ Illness is a temporary condition producing a physical symptom.

◆ Illnesses are identified and classified by medical officials, not lay people.

◆ Diagnosis of symptoms is objective, requiring very little debate between the doctor and the patient.

◆ Illness and disease can be treated and cured; often by removing the identified cause. Scientific medicine is seen as the way to solve health problems.

◆ The health of society is seen as largely dependent on the state of medical knowledge and the availability of medical resources.

This biomedical model of health underpins the organisation and delivery of health care in contemporary societies. As Taylor and Field (2007, p. 26) note:

Medical research is focused primarily on biochemical or genetic processes underlying disease. Most medical work involves diagnosing and treating abnormalities within the body, and the education and training of most health professionals, particularly doctors, revolves around understanding the human body and intervening in the disease process.

I will soon find out why this car has broken down. It's got a poor maintenance record which has no doubt contributed to the problem.

Figure 3.4

1 Explain similarities between Figure 3.4 and the bio-medical model of understanding health and illness.

2 Think back to a time when you have been ill. Did you seek medical advice? Was diagnosis and treatment based on the medical model?

3 Research and find out about three diseases and illness in contemporary society. For each one, note down the cause and the treatments/cures available.

### Weblink
The Department of Health website (see 'Websites' page ii) contains a wealth of resources, news and policy issues in relation to health and illness.

## Evaluation of the bio-medical model of health

The main strength of the bio-medical model is that is emphasises the importance of trying to find a cause of illness and disease. There is a huge amount of evidence which supports bio-medical solutions to disease, ranging from successful operations (mending broken bones, kidney transplants, Caesarean sections) to cancer screenings and immunization programmes. Sheeran (1995) has noted the increasingly successful practical application of the principles of medical knowledge in the West. However, the sociology of health and illness has been built up around a critique of the medical model of understanding health and illness, and has raised several important criticisms.

◆ **Defining health**: The objective, absolute definition of health used by the bio-medical model can be criticised for failing to recognise the relativity of health and illness. As the previous section has shown, what counts as 'being healthy or ill' is socially constructed. Furthermore, if a positive definition of health is adopted, then ill-health is a normal experience. Self-report studies show that over 95 per cent of people say they have one or more symptoms of illness.

◆ **The cause of ill-health**: The focus on treating symptoms by applying scientific or medical solutions ignores the wider social conditions which may have caused the illness or disease in the first place such as pollution or poverty. Furthermore, research has shown that ill-health is caused by multiple factors and, rather than illness being randomly distributed, there are definite social patterns by social class, gender and ethnicity.

◆ **Medical treatment**: The medical model focuses on treatment (e.g. through drugs, surgery, medical technology) but this is very expensive. When the NHS was first established, it was predicted that, after an initial wave of curing existing illness and disease, the system would focus on preventative measures. This, however, has not happened. The NHS has become firmly based on curative medicine and only a very small percentage of its total expenditure is given to health promotion and prevention strategies. The implications of a curative based system is that the real causes of ill-health are never addressed. Furthermore, doctors have been unable to cure the major causes of death in the twenty-first century. Infectious diseases, such as smallpox and typhoid have been replaced by degenerative illnesses, such as strokes and cancers and it is often argued that health policy should focus on combating the risk factors associated with chronic illnesses, such as smoking and excessive alcohol

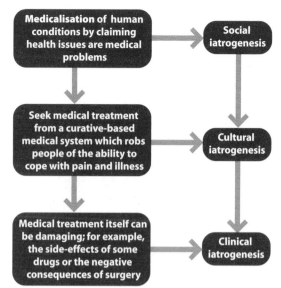

Figure 3.5 Iatrogenesis

and successful definers and providers of health care. According to Foucault (1973), the medical profession gained dominance by creating and controlling a new scientific language to describe the body which gives the profession status. A critical examination of the role of the medical profession is discussed in a later subsection. A much more critical examination of the role of doctors and medicine has been offered by Illich (2002) who claims that medicine does more harm than good. Illich calls this **iatrogenesis** which means doctor-caused illness. Illich argues that the medical profession has a vested interest in ensuring there is plenty of disease.

Activity 3.6

1 Discuss how the following natural human conditions have become medicalised: pregnancy, worry, bad behaviour among children, ageing.

2 Take one of the examples from question 1 and carry out some research to show how it has become medicalised. You could use secondary sources (health websites, newspaper articles) and primary sources (e.g. interview someone who has experienced pregnancy). Present your findings to the rest of the class.

3 Read the newspaper article below. How could you use this article to evaluate the claim that 'Medicine and medically-based health care are helpful in curing illness and disease'?

intake. Medicine is almost completely ineffective against some new diseases like AIDS or new-variant CJD and there is still no cure for the common cold.

◆ **The role of doctors**: The medical profession has established itself as the only legitimate

Scores of NHS patients were killed during Britain's deadliest outbreak of a hospital superbug, a damning report by the government's health watchdog reveals today. The Healthcare Commission attributed the deaths of 90 patients at the Maidstone and Tunbridge Wells hospitals in Kent to infection from *Clostridium difficile*, which causes severe diarrhoea and has taken over from MRSA as the main threat to patients. The report found 1,100 patients contracted *C. difficile* at the Trust's three hospitals between April 2004 and September 2006. The Commission concluded that 90 patients 'definitely or probably' died as a result of infection. Today's 124-page report blamed the Trust's board for giving too much attention to balancing the books and meeting government waiting-time targets – and too little to service to patients and infection control. 'Patients, including those with *C. difficile* were often moved between several different wards, increasing the risk of spreading infection,' it said. The investigation began after the *C. difficile* outbreaks, when the Trust claimed to have corrected its infection control problems. But the inspectors took photographs of contaminated bedpans, overflowing buckets of needles and sharp instruments, and food stored in medical refrigerators.

The Commission said the Trust failed to protect patients because the board was unaware of the first outbreak and was slow to react to the second.

(Source: Carvel, 2007)

4  Search for other examples of clinical iatrogenesis. Any Internet search engine will lead you to a huge range of examples.

5  Can you think of, and write down, two criticisms of Illich's view?

# The social model of health

The social model is an umbrella term which includes a range of ideas and strategies about health and health care which have largely been developed in response to criticisms of the

medical model. From this perspective, health and illness are not biological facts; they are relative concepts which vary from time to time, from place to place and from person to person. The medical profession has the power to define a person's state of health, and they tend to treat people as passive objects rather than as 'whole' persons. The social model advocates that lay definitions and judgments are just as valid as professional assessments; for example, much illness is diagnosed and treated in the family and lay people have their own valid interpretations and accounts of their experiences. From this point of view, illness is a personal, not medical, experience.

The social model of health emphasises the social causes of health and ill-health, and how society influences health. As Nettleton (2006) points out, health and disease are socially patterned. Illness is not randomly distributed; there are clear social patterns in terms of class, gender, ethnicity. This suggests that it is social and environmental factors that make some groups more vulnerable to disease than others.

### Activity 3.7

1  List five social or environmental factors that may influence health.

2  If health care policy was based on a social, rather than a medical, model of health how would ill-health be tackled?

One of the most significant criticisms of the medical model is that medicine has been largely ineffective in curing illness and disease. McKeown (1976), a medical historian, has demonstrated that the decline in mortality which has occurred within western societies has had more to do with nutrition and hygiene and patterns of reproduction (social factors) than it has with vaccinations and medical treatment. By tracing the history of the infectious diseases which were the major causes of death in Britain in the last century, he demonstrated that deaths from most infectious diseases (including the prime killer, tuberculosis) were falling long before there was effective medical treatment.

According to McKeown, the major reason for the declining death rate was that people became stronger and thus more resistant to infectious disease. This was due to better nutrition,

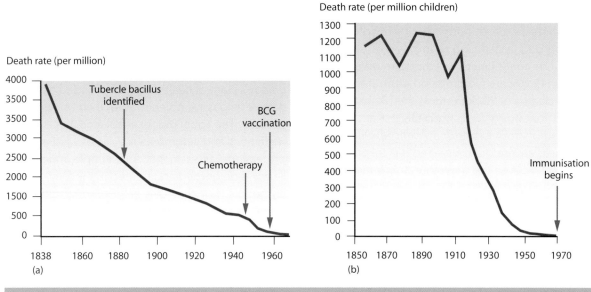

Death rate (per million)

Death rate (per million children)

Figure 3.6 Decline in the death rate from (a) tuberculosis and (b) measles due to medical advances

(Source: McKeown, 1976)

improvements in public health and changes in people's behaviour, especially greater use of contraception and improved personal hygene. McKeown developed his work into a critique of modern health care. He argued that we are spending far too much money on the treatment of disease and not enough on prevention and health education.

## The social construction of health and illness

The term 'social construction' comes from the work of two interactionist sociologists, Berger and Luckmann (1966). Their argument is that both our everyday concepts and the so-called 'taken for granted' features of our world are created through social interaction. Take, for example, the action of winking. A definition of winking is to close or open one or both eyes quickly. But this does not take into account the meanings attached to the action of winking. It is only through interaction with others together with the social context you are in, that winking takes on a meaning. Depending on the context, winking could suggest to someone 'I know your secret', or 'I find you attractive'. We also know that winking is socially constructed because it means different things in different societies. For example, in some Latin American cultures, winking is a romantic or sexual invitation. In Nigeria, Yorubas may wink at their children if they want them to leave the room. Many Chinese consider winking to be rude. In Hong Kong, it is important

not to blink one's eyes conspicuously, as this may be seen as a sign of disrespect and boredom.

What these examples show is that actions can only be interpreted through the meanings that people give them. When we say that something is socially constructed we don't mean that it doesn't exist. Rather, the important characteristics of something (for example, crime statistics, disability, childhood) are defined by the attitudes, values and norms of behaviour that surround it in any given society or part of society, and that these actually shape the reality of that thing. From this perspective, the meanings of the words 'health' and 'illness' cannot be taken for granted as they mean different things to different people.

### Activity 3.8

In pairs, look back through the text on this page and find examples of how health and illness are socially constructed. Share your findings with the rest of the class.

There are many dimensions to the view that health and illness are socially constructed and this is summarised in Figure 3.7. If health and illness were objective, scientific, absolute facts, then everyone would interpret symptoms in the same way; all societies would have the same methods of diagnosis and treatment and illness would be randomly distributed. Sociologists point out that this is not the case.

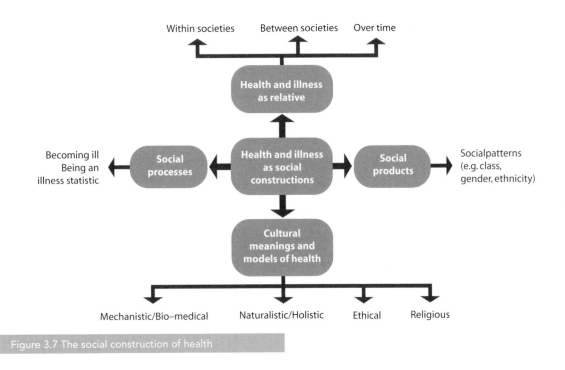

Within societies   Between societies   Over time

**Health and illness as relative**

Becoming ill
Being an
illness statistic ← **Social processes** ← **Health and illness as social constructions** → **Social products** → Social patterns (e.g. class, gender, ethnicity)

**Cultural meanings and models of health**

Mechanistic/Bio–medical    Naturalistic/Holistic    Ethical    Religious

Figure 3.7 The social construction of health

# Health and illness as relative

To say that health and illness are relative is to say that definitions of what is healthy and what describes illness are not given facts; they vary from person to person (within societies), from society to society (cross-culturally), and over time. A person's ideas about health and illness are related to and reflect their theories of disease, illness and treatment. As Taylor et al. (1996) note, 'Ideas about health and illness vary because they are created, passed on and modified as part of the process of living together in societies. As such, they are social constructions. And it is because they are social constructions that the concepts of health and illness are relative' (p. 423).

# Health as relative: within societies (lay definitions)

Health and illness can be said to be relative concepts if people have different definitions. In the Health and Lifestyles survey, Blaxter (1990) surveyed a random sample of 9000 individuals about their definitions of, and views about, health. One of the criticisms of the bio-medical model of health is that, by focusing on disease, it ignores lay people's views and experiences of their own health. Doctors are qualified professional definers of health and their patients are not as expertly informed. However,

as Blaxter points out, since health must in part be subjectively experienced, lay people may actually be better informed. Blaxter found that individuals have many different definitions, which she classified as negative or positive. Negative definitions of health see health as being free from symptoms of illness, or not having a disease/disability, whereas positive definitions associate health with physical fitness or as psychological or social wellbeing.

Blaxter found some social patterns in definitions of health. She noted, for example, that the way in which health is defined differs according to age and gender. Younger men tended to speak of health in terms of physical strength and fitness, whereas young women favoured ideas of energy, vitality and ability to cope. In middle age, concepts of health become more complex, with an emphasis on total mental and physical wellbeing. Older people, particularly men, think in terms of function, or the ability to do things, though ideas of health as contentment, happiness, a state of mind – even in the presence of disease or disability – are also prominent.

In addition to Blaxter, other studies have shown that definitions of health not only vary between individuals but also between groups of people. Williams (1983) carried out a study of elderly people in Aberdeen and he identified three lay concepts of health from his interview data:

In pairs, decide whether the quotes in Table 3.2 reflect positive or negative definitions of health. Copy and complete the table.

Table 3.2

| Typical quotations in response to the questions in Activity 3.1 (see page 156) |
| --- |
| 'I think health is when I feel fresh in the morning and ready to take on what the day has to offer!' |
| 'A healthy person is the right weight and has shiny hair and strong nails.' |
| 'Health is when you don't feel tired or lethargic.' |
| 'He must be healthy because he does lots of exercise like cycling to college every day.' |
| 'Being healthy is never needing to go to the doctor.' |
| 'I am a healthy person because I have lots of energy to do all the things I want to.' |

◆ health as the absence of disease

◆ health as a dimension of strength, weakness and exhaustion

◆ health as functional fitness.

There is also some evidence to suggest a relationship between types of belief and social class. For example, D'houtard and Field (1984) in a study of 4000 people in France, found that respondents from non-manual backgrounds had more positive conceptions of health than those from manual backgrounds, who revealed more negative definitions. In the UK research has found that working-class women are more likely to hold functional conceptions of health (the ability to participate in normal social roles). For example, a study by Pill and Stott (1982) quotes one woman as saying that 'the good mother' just keeps going: 'Being married ... well, I haven't really had much wrong with me and I think it is partly down to the fact that I haven't got time to worry about anything being wrong. Not only that, I think with a family you can't afford to be ill' (pp. 49–50).

The relationship between beliefs and social class, however, should not be overstated. Calnan (1987) did not find clear distinctions between the classes. When asked about their own health, both working and middle-class women were likely to offer negative definitions of health.

A secondary analysis of Blaxter's data to compare the health beliefs of Asian, African-Caribbean and white groups (Howlett et al.,1992) found that, compared with white respondents, Asians were more likely to define health in functional terms, and African-Caribbeans were more likely to describe health in terms of energy and physical strength. They were also more likely to attribute illness to bad luck. This supports the argument that groups in society with the least power are more likely to hold fatalistic views on the causes of illness. A study of two Cantonese-speaking communities in the UK (Prior et al., 2002) found that health was related to happiness and inner contentment. To be happy was both equated to, and a necessary feature of, being healthy.

# Health as relative: between societies

What health means and how it is recognised varies between cultures. Although most societies differentiate between health and illness, they differ widely in their beliefs about the causes of, and solutions to, illness. Furthermore, societies differ in the levels of discomfort and pain which are accepted as normal and different societies may interpret similar symptoms very differently. As Taylor et al. note, 'whether a person feels healthy or ill is determined within a cultural context' (1996, p. 423).

# Health is relative: over time

Another aspect to health and illness as relative concepts can be seen when we examine changing conceptions within one society over

- A skin rash is a medical condition in the UK, but in one South American tribe the absence of a rash can prevent someone getting married.

- In some West African societies, rolls of body fat on females are regarded as both healthy and desirable. Wealthy men frequently send their daughters to 'fatting houses' to make them plump.

- Zulu women of South Africa are believed to 'pollute' humans, animals and crops if they have contact with them during menstruation.

- 'Drapetomania' was a mental abnormality black slaves were said to have if they attempted to run away from their natural masters, their white owners.

Using Figures 3.8 and 3.98 together with the facts outlined above, write a response to support the view that health and illness are culturally defined concepts.

Figure 3.9 A size zero model

Figure 3.8 The hour-glass shape

time. For example, until 1957, homosexuality was classified as a mental illness and men who 'admitted' to being homosexual often had to undergo 'treatment' such as aversion therapy. Such a belief would not be tolerated in today's society where sexual equality is now enshrined in law. A further example is offered by Helman (1978) who examined the beliefs that people had about 'catching' colds, chills and fevers. He found that folk beliefs state that you are more likely to 'catch' a cold if your head, neck and feet are uncovered. Catching a cold was seen as the result of carelessness: it was everyone's responsibility to dress properly, avoid going out with wet hair etc.

### Activity 3.11

1 Carry out a brief survey of people's opinions about 'catching colds'. Try to ask people from two generations. Do they offer folk explanations (see Helman above) or do they follow the bio-medical explanation of colds as viral infections? Are there any differences between the two generations?

2 Find out about illnesses, such as sweating sickness, dancing mania, ptosis (detached colon), neurasthenia, which used to be prominent but have now all but disappeared. Prepare a brief presentation to give to the rest of the class outlining the causes, symptoms and solutions of such illnesses.

# Health and illness as social products

Further support for the notion that health and illness are socially constructed comes from examining the social distribution of illness. If illness were purely biological, it would be randomly distributed among the population. However, as the section on health inequalities shows, illness is patterned according to factors such as social class, gender and ethnicity.

## Cultural meanings and models of health

Another aspect of the social construction of health and illness is in the existence of different models for understanding health and illness. Different cultures provide different interpretations of health and illness, partly because they have different ideas about how the body works. For example, among Hindu practitioners of yoga, the body is believed to house a number of *chakras* or energy centres, unrecognised by western science. The bio-medical model is just one way of defining and understanding health. Other models are summarised in Table 3.3.

**Weblinks**

The websites on alternative medicine (see 'Websites' page ii) will allow you to research a little further into the types of complementary therapies that are generally available.

Table 3.3 Models of health and illness

| Health-illness model | Examples of cultural beliefs |
| --- | --- |
| Equilibrium | Chinese medicine states the body has energy channels (yin and yang) that have to be kept in balance.<br>Humoural theory states that it is an imbalance in the four humours, blood, phlegm, black and yellow bile, which causes illness. |
| Religious | Possession by evil spirits. For example, health returns if you lie down and pretend you are dead, then the spirits will leave. Another solution could be exorcism. In societies which follow this model, the priest/shaman is the protector of health. |
| Ethical | Illness is a punishment for wrong-doing, or the result of someone casting a spell on you. |

Search for examples of alternative or complementary therapies and find out about how their ideas about health, illness and the body differ to the bio-medical model.

# The social processes of becoming ill

Like health, the very definition of what symptoms constitute an illness is culturally relative. A young person may define shortness of breath and

| Factors influencing the process | Stages in the process of becoming a patient | Removal from the process |
|---|---|---|
| Cultural differences in tolerance to conditions, e.g.<br>• Italians and Jews are more demanding and dependent on doctors<br>• In some societies the practice of couvades operates in which women show no distress in childbirth, but their husbands are allowed to get into bed and groan | All people | |
| Cultural explanations for ill-health, e.g. religious or scientific<br>Speed of onset of symptoms<br>Perceived risk | Those who have unpleasant bodily sensations, are uncomfortable or unhappy | No problems |
| Costs and benefits of being labelled as ill, e.g. absence from work or other obligations<br>Interference with social, personal or physical activity | Interpret their condition as possible illness | Interpret their condition as normal, e.g. period pains, hangovers |
| Availability and costs of doctor<br>Faith in Western medicine<br>Giving symptoms a specified time to improve | Self–diagnosis as ill | Assume it is trivial and will go away |
| Availability of diagnostic facilities<br>Stereotypes of patient, e.g. malingerer, or based on gender and age | Decision to consult doctor | Self–medication |
| Judgement of seriousness<br>Fashion in medicine, e.g. anaemia and low blood pressure are not now routinely treated | Doctor diagnoses illness | Doctor diagnoses no illness |
| Level of specialisation<br>Competence of the doctor | Decision to treat or refer | No action taken |
| Effects of label<br>• Legitimisation of illness<br>• Help to get appropriate treatment<br>• Stigmatisation,, e.g. AIDS<br>• Change in people's behaviour towards person, e.g. physical impairment can make people treat the patient like a child | Illness given a label | |
| Social reaction creates a self–fulfilling prophecy, e.g. passivity and compliance of blind person is the result of treatment by those who see blindness as a psychological adjustment rather than as a technical handicap | PATIENT | |
| | Patient becomes a patient! | |

Figure 3.10 The social process of becoming a patient

(Source: Lawson et al., 2000)

difficulty in walking as an illness, but a 90-year-old may not. Sickness is defined as reported illness. As Figure 3.10 shows, there are a number of factors which influence whether a person becomes defined as officially ill. What this shows is that the process of becoming an illness statistic is socially constructed and, therefore, morbidity statistics cannot be taken for granted.

What counts as illness?

1 Rate the cases in Table 3.4 according to the extent to which you consider each one to be an illness.

2 Compare your answers with those of others in your group/class. Which factors did you agree as being (a) definitely ill and (b) definitely not ill? Why?

3 Write a paragraph to explain how notions of illness are socially constructed.

Table 3.4

| Set of symptoms | Definitively not ill | | | | Definitely ill |
|---|---|---|---|---|---|
| Pregnancy | 1 | 2 | 3 | 4 | 5 |
| Severe hangover | 1 | 2 | 3 | 4 | 5 |
| Migraine | 1 | 2 | 3 | 4 | 5 |
| Breast cancer | 1 | 2 | 3 | 4 | 5 |
| Lack of appetite resulting in serious weight loss | 1 | 2 | 3 | 4 | 5 |
| Broken leg | 1 | 2 | 3 | 4 | 5 |
| Wrinkles | 1 | 2 | 3 | 4 | 5 |
| Severe memory loss | 1 | 2 | 3 | 4 | 5 |
| Acne | 1 | 2 | 3 | 4 | 5 |
| Shouting at oneself in public | 1 | 2 | 3 | 4 | 5 |
| An 80-year-old woman whose eyesight is failing | 1 | 2 | 3 | 4 | 5 |
| A 14-year-old boy who finds it very hard to hear | 1 | 2 | 3 | 4 | 5 |
| An overweight man with high blood pressure and shortness of breath | 1 | 2 | 3 | 4 | 5 |
| A man who wants a sex change | 1 | 2 | 3 | 4 | 5 |
| A woman who started smoking knowing the habit could damage her health and who now has lung cancer | 1 | 2 | 3 | 4 | 5 |
| An alcoholic | 1 | 2 | 3 | 4 | 5 |
| A young man who claims he is Napoleon | 1 | 2 | 3 | 4 | 5 |
| A teacher who has been off work for 6 months claiming not to have the energy to get out of bed | 1 | 2 | 3 | 4 | 5 |
| A 25-year-old woman who has become bald | 1 | 2 | 3 | 4 | 5 |

(Source: Senior and Viveash, 1998)

# The social process of becoming a patient

Figure 3.11 supports the view that morbidity figures reveal only the tip of the illness iceberg. The majority of illnesses are not shown in the figures because a large number of people do not report every illness symptom to their doctors. The idea that only a proportion of illness (maybe as little as 6 per cent) is revealed by the morbidity figures is known as the clinical iceberg.

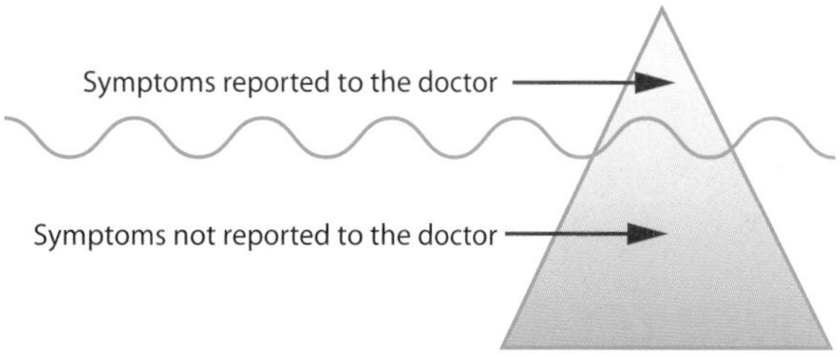

Symptoms reported to the doctor

Symptoms not reported to the doctor

Figure 3.11 The clinical iceberg

## Section summary

Use the following key words to copy and complete the summary of this section below. Each word should be used only once.

absolute    bio-medical    constructed    construction    culturally    cure    disease
healthcare    healthy    iatrogenesis    idealistic    immunisation    infectious
lay    models    morbidity    mortality    obligations    personal    relative
role    social    statistic    subjective    time    wellbeing

Today, people have a whole range of ideas when it comes to interpreting what it means to be _____. The World Health Organisation defines health as total physical, social and mental _____ but this has been criticised for being too _____ and seeing health as an _____ concept. Most sociologists point out that health is a _____ concept as it means different things to different people. The opposite to being healthy is being ill and it is useful to distinguish between _____, which refers to a specific mental or biological abnormality, sickness which is a social _____, involving specific rights and _____, and illness which is the _____ experience of feeling unwell.

As there hare different definitions of what it means to be healthy and ill, there are also different _____ used for understanding them. The _____ model takes a scientific approach to understanding illness and this model underpins the organisation and delivery of _____ in many contemporary societies. This model, however, has been criticised for failing to recognise the social _____ of health and illness. Furthermore, this model does not focus on non-medical causes of ill-health and the NHS has become largely focused on _____ rather than prevention. Illich offers a highly critical view of medicine and the medical profession; he claims that medicine can actually cause illness and he calls this _____. The _____ model of health, on the other hand, sees health and illness as social, not biological, concepts and it advocates that _____ interpretations are just as valid as professional ones. From this viewpoint, illness is a _____ not a medical experience. McKeown argues that the medical model fails to recognise that the decline of _____ diseases started much before the introduction of _____. He argued that the decline in _____ (death) and _____ (illness) were the result of social factors, rather than medical intervention.

Many sociologists argue that health and illness are socially _____ which means that they are defined by the attitudes and values of a society. From this viewpoint, health and illness are relative experiences; they vary both between and within societies, over _____ and cross _____. Even the process of becoming an official illness _____ is socially constructed, as there are a number of factors which influence whether a person becomes defined as officially ill.

## Exam practice

(a) Identify and explain two features of the bio-medical model of health. (17 marks)

(b) Outline and evaluate the view that health and illness are socially constructed. (33 marks)

# (ii) Patterns and explanations of ill-health in society

## Pause for thought

A recent report concluded that life expectancy in Glasgow is lower than it is in Iraq. Discuss why this might be the case

Figure 3.12 The reality of poverty

## Patterns of ill-health

Consider the following statements, all statistics published between 2005 and 2007 from research into health inequalities in the UK.

◆ There is 11 years difference in life expectancy between those who live in the poorest parts of the country and those who live in the most affluent areas.

◆ Annually, some 7500 deaths among people younger than 65 could be prevented if inequalities in wealth narrowed to their 1983 levels.

◆ A baby girl born in Leeds is more than twice as likely to die in the first year of life as an infant girl growing up in a Dorset town.

◆ Men aged 16–44 are less than half as likely as women to consult their GP, resulting in later diagnosis of serious illnesses.

◆ Babies born to immigrant Pakistani mothers are more than twice as likely to die in their first week of life as the babies of British-born mothers.

Social inequalities in health have long been a feature of British society and the sociology of health often revolves around measuring and explaining such inequalities. This subsection will be sub-divided into examining evidence for, and explanations of, health inequalities related to social class, gender and ethnicity, although it must be remembered that class, gender, ethnicity and, indeed, age will all interact to produce different health experiences for individuals. For example, the health experiences of, say, a white middle-class, middle-aged man and a black, working-class young woman may be very different.

## Measuring health inequalities

Most studies of health inequalities rely on mortality (death) and morbidity (illness) data. The incidence of deaths or illness refers to the number of cases in a given period. The prevalence refers to the total number of cases at a certain point in time. Incidence and prevalence are normally presented as rates (for example, the number of deaths per 100,000 of the population) rather than crude numbers, as this makes comparisons more meaningful. Data on mortality are taken from death certificates, which include information on sex, age, area of residence, occupation or last occupation, and cause of death. Data on morbidity is more problematic, as the previous subsection on the social construction of illness statistics has shown.

### Activity 3.14

For each of the following ways of gathering morbidity data, identify and explain one strength and one weakness of each in terms of whether it is a valid measure of illness.

- Levels of absenteeism at work
- GP consultation rates
- Surveys of self-reported illness

## Health inequalities and social class

The overall health of the population has improved over the last century, with life expectancy increasing and infant mortality falling. In terms of life expectancy, a man can expect to live 30 years longer today than if he was born in 1901, and a woman 31 years longer (Office for National Statistics, 2005). However, despite significant improvements in the absolute health of the UK population, there has been very little reduction in the 'health gap' between rich and poor since the 1800s. As Nettleton (2006) comments, the poor die at a younger age than the rich and are more susceptible to major diseases and chronic illness. Official statistics published during the last twenty-five years reveal massive inequalities in health. The most recently published government review of the research evidence, the Wanless Report (2002), again confirmed the existence of health inequalities and sought to explain them.

## Measuring social class and health inequalities

Any research centred on social class needs to address the way in which social class will be operationalised. This can be problematic for a number of reasons. The main issue is that there is no universal agreement about how social classes are defined and measured. Subjective approaches focus on what social class an individual thinks they are in. The problem with this measure is that different people will understand different things by the term 'class' and this makes any comparison very difficult. Objective measures of social class have tended to focus on occupation as a key indicator. Officially, the Registrar General Scale has been used since 1921. This is based on five groups defined by occupational skill. Changes in the labour market and the nature of work led to a new measure, which came into used with the 2001 Census. This is called the National Statistics Socio-economic Classification (NS-SEC). The seven main classes are based on job responsibilities, including degree of control over the content and pace of work and supervisory duties. An eighth class includes the long-term unemployed and those who have never worked.

### Activity 3.15

1 Carry out some research to find out about the RGS and the NS-SEC social class classifications. What social class would you be in, based on the occupation of your highest-earning family member?

2 In pairs, discuss why occupation is a useful indicator of social class?

3 Can you think of three criticisms of using occupation as an indicator of social class?

## Social class and mortality

The pattern of social class inequalities in health is well documented. Consider the following statistics.

- About 50 per cent more babies are stillborn or die in the fist week of life in unskilled families than in professional families.

- The risk of dying before the age of 5 is more than twice as great for a child born into social class V (unskilled manual workers) as for a social class I child.

- ◆ Children from poorer backgrounds are five times more likely to die as a result of an accident than children from better-off families.

- ◆ The death rate in social class V is about twice that of social class I.

- ◆ A person born into social class I lives, on average, about 7 years longer than someone in social class V.

- ◆ Men and women in social class V are twice as likely to die before reaching retirement age as people in social class I.

- ◆ About 90 per cent of the major causes of death are more common in social classes IV and V than in other social classes.

Regional inequalities in health are closely related to poverty and social class. Shaw and Davey Smith (2005) examined the relationship between poverty and life expectancy by comparing affluent and poor areas of the UK between 1992 and 2003. They found that health inequality is increasing, with life expectancy continuing to rise faster in the most advantaged areas of the UK.

### Activity 3.16

1 What overall trends in life expectancy and mortality can you see Tables 3.5 and 3.6?

2 What evidence can you find to support the statement that health inequalities are widening between some social groups?

Table 3.5 Life expectancy at birth by social class in England and Wales

| | Occupational social class | 1972–1976 | | 1997–2001 | | Differences between 1972–1976 and 1997–2001 at birth | |
|---|---|---|---|---|---|---|---|
| | | Men | Women | Men | Women | Men | Women |
| I | Professional | 71.9 | 79.1 | 79.4 | 82.2 | 7.5 | 3.1 |
| II | Managerial and technical/intermediate | 71.7 | 76.9 | 77.8 | 81.7 | 6.1 | 4.8 |
| IIINM | Skilled non-manual | 69.4 | 78.0 | 74.6 | 81.3 | 7.4 | 3.3 |
| IIIM | Skilled manual | 69.3 | 75.1 | 73.3 | 79.3 | 5.0 | 4.2 |
| IV | Partly skilled | 68.3 | 75.0 | 73.3 | 78.6 | 5.0 | 3.6 |
| V | Unskilled | 66.4 | 73.8 | 71.0 | 77.6 | 4.6 | 3.8 |

(Source: adapted from Office for National Statistics Longitudinal Study)

Table 3.6 Trends in mortality by social class and gender, 1986-1999

| Social class | 1986-1992 | | 1993-1996 | | 1997-1999 | |
|---|---|---|---|---|---|---|
| | Men | Women | Men | Women | Men | Women |
| I and II | 460 | 274 | 376 | 262 | 347 | 237 |
| IIINM | 480 | 310 | 437 | 262 | 417 | 253 |
| IIIM | 617 | 350 | 538 | 324 | 512 | 327 |
| IV and V | 776 | 422 | 648 | 378 | 606 | 335 |
| Ratio | 1.69 | 1.54 | 1.71 | 1.44 | 1.75 | 1.41 |
| IV + V : I + II | | | | | | |

(Source: White et al., 2003)

The sociology of health

# Social class and morbidity

Evidence shows that working-class people, especially the unskilled, go to the doctor more often and for a wider range of health problems than people in professional jobs (Browne and Bottrill, 1999). In 2001, for the first time a question on self-assessed general health was included in the UK Census. Each person in a household was asked to rate their health over the previous twelve months. The possible responses were 'good', 'fairly good' or 'not good'. Poor self-assessed health has been found to be a powerful predictor of admission to hospital, disability and subsequent mortality. Self-assessed health draws together an individual's perception of all aspects of their health and wellbeing. However, while self-assessed health status is recognised as a good measure of health-related quality of life, concerns remain about the reliability of subjective assessments. These are known to vary systematically across population sub-groups (by ethnicity and social class) and over time. They reflect difference in illness, health-seeking behaviour, expectations and cultural norms for health.

There are clear differences in self-assessed health by occupation. Moving down the occupational hierarchy, self-assessments of health worsen. While just over 80 per cent of higher managerial/ professionals see themselves as having good health, only 65 per cent of those in semi-routine occupations take the same view of their health. Approximately half of the long-term unemployed/ never-worked group see themselves in good health. Among those who were 'economically active', those working full-time and those who were self-employed were more likely to report themselves as being in good health than those working part-time. Three in five unemployed people reported their health as good (62 per cent), a rate of 14 percentage points lower than the average for the economically active group (Bajekal et al., 2006, p.12).

Figure 3.13 shows how limiting long-term illness varies by NS-SEC and gender. It shows a clear gradient in the proportions reporting limiting long-term illness even after controlling for age differences. Whereas fewer than 10 per cent of people in the managerial and professional group report such a limitation, the figure is closer to 15 per cent among those in semi-routine and routine occupations, and over 40 per cent amongst males

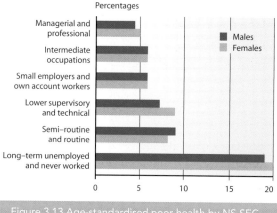

Figure 3.13 Age-standardised poor health by NS-SEC and gender, 2001

(Source: Census 2001, Office for National Statistics/General Register Office for Scotland/Northern Ireland Statistics and Research Agency, 2001)

who are long-term unemployed or have never worked. Such class differences are apparent not just in relation to physical health, but also in terms of mental health. Neurotic disorders are reported by 20 per cent of those in the unskilled manual category, compared with just 9 per cent in the professional category. This means that those in the lowest social class are over twice as likely to suffer from a neurotic disorder as those in the highest social class (Coulthard et al, 2004).

# Explanations for social class inequalities in health

Since the publication of the Black Report in the 1980s, explanations have tended to be categorised into one of four explanations: artefact, social selection, cultural and structural/materialist.

## Artefact explanations

These explanations see both class and health as artefacts (artificial; not natural) of the measurement process and, therefore, it questions whether social class inequalities in health are real. This approach argues that the relationship between social class and health is spurious and the evidence is not necessarily valid. For example, researchers who focus on the health differences between class I and class V could be accused of selecting two relatively small classes at the extremes of the social scale, and therefore exaggerating the differences. Also, the fact that measurements of social class have changed over time means that making valid comparisons over time is difficult.

Furthermore, the way that illnesses are diagnosed and the way in which deaths are classified vary over time and space; in other words, health statistics are a social construction.

Activity 3.17

Look back over the section on the social construction of health and illness. Pick out two examples which show that using health statistics to examine social class differences is problematic.

However, most researchers accept that class differences in health are real and numerous studies show that a social gradient is present across all social classes. For example, in a study of Whitehall civil servants, where occupational status was precisely determined, there was a clear mortality gradient; that is, the lower the rank/grade, the higher the mortality rate. The other point about the artefact explanation is that by accepting it, we would deny the link between class and health, and this would mean that no social policy would be needed to deal with this problem, as it is non-existent.

## Social selection explanations

These explanations suggest that good or bad health causes social mobility (movement up or down the class hierarchy). Those who are healthy are more likely to be upwardly mobile, and those who are unhealthy are more likely to move down into a lower class. From this viewpoint, the working class appears to be relatively unhealthy simply because people in higher classes who suffer ill health move down into the working class. Think about this in relation to education. You may well know people at school who suffered high levels of illness and consequently had a lot of time off school and failed to gain many educational qualifications. There is some supporting evidence for this explanation. Wadsworth (1986), using data from the 1946 British National Birth Cohort, has shown that males who had a serious illness in their childhood are more likely to end up in a lower social class. Thirty-six per cent of males of non-manual origin who were seriously ill moved down the social scale, whereas only 23 per cent of those who were not ill had a similar experience. Illsley (1980) found that upwardly mobile females in Aberdeen were

healthier, taller, had a better physique and had lower perinatal death rates in their first pregnancies than those who were downwardly mobile. Connelly and Crown's (1994) report on homelessness and ill-health suggested that schizophrenics are overrepresented among the homeless because of social selection – it is the schizophrenia which puts people at risk of becoming homeless. There are, however, a number of limitations to the social selection explanation.

## Cultural explanations

These explanations state that inequalities in health are attributable to differences in norms, values, attitudes, lifestyles and behaviour of the different social classes. According to Annandale and Field (2007), people in lower social classes have more negative definitions of health and lower expectations of health, seeing health in fatalistic terms. These health beliefs are related to health behaviours. A range of HMSO reports conclude that people in lower social classes indulge in more unhealthy behaviours, such as smoking, drinking alcohol, eating more fat and sugar, and taking less exercise. Such behaviours are linked to a variety of conditions, including heart disease, cancers, strokes, bronchitis and asthma. Let us take the example of smoking. In the UK the proportion of smokers has reduced in both manual and non-manual groups. However, those in manual groups have been consistently more likely to smoke than those in non-manual groups and the relative difference between manual and non-manual smokers has increased. For example, in 1974 men in Great Britain from manual backgrounds were 24 per cent more likely to smoke than men in non-manual groups. In 2000, they were 52 per cent more likely to smoke. At the extreme, cultural explanations can be seen as 'victim blaming'. These lifestyle factors are seen to be in the control of the individual; health inequalities can be solved if unhealthy people change their behaviour and adopt healthier lifestyles. Such a view has been commonplace in government policy over the last 40 years, as can be seen from the following statement: 'Much ill-health in Britain today arises from over-indulgence and unwise behaviour. Not surprisingly, the greatest potential and perhaps the greatest problem for preventive medicine now lies in changing behaviour and attitudes to health' (from the Labour Party's White Paper, Prevention and Health, DHSS/DES, 1977, p. 39).

Evaluating the social selection explanation.

1 Match the sentence starters on the left to the sentence endings on the right.

2 Put them in a rank order, from what you consider to be the most significant criticism to the least.

| Sentence starter | Sentence ending |
|---|---|
| Social mobility cannot explain most of the differences as most ill-health occurs… | is education |
| A more important factor than health in explaining social mobility… | as there has been no opportunity for them to experience social mobility |
| Illness does not necessarily lead to downward mobility as… | in middle life when a person's social class position is already established. |
| It cannot explain the cases of illness among infants and children in lower social classes… | some people are able to adapt to illness and continue with their careers. |

1 Working in groups, choose one of the health-related behaviours listed below:

- smoking
- drinking alcohol
- poor diet
- lack of exercise.

Carry out some research to find evidence of class differences in your chosen health-related behaviours.

2 Devise a health promotion campaign with the aim of reducing health inequalities, from the cultural/behavioural perspective.

The cultural/behavioural model has a number of limitations. Firstly, such explanations essentially place the blame on individuals themselves but, in reality, people's lives are likely to be affected by their culture *and* by the material circumstances they face. In fact, it can be difficult to separate these factors. As Townsend (1999) has pointed out, some people have more freedom than others to 'choose' a healthy lifestyle. In this sense, behaviour cannot be divorced from its social context. People in lower social classes adopt unhealthy behaviours as a rational response to the situation they find themselves in. According to Blackburn (1991), improving the income of low-income families is a key factor in improving their eating patterns.

Weblink

Look at this government website which has a section on health statistics (see 'Websites' page ii). Search for 'focus on health' or 'focus on inequality'.

Look back at the statistics on smoking on page 174. Write one paragraph to explain how factors other than culture, norms and values may influence a person's decision about smoking.

U2

3

The sociology of health

Another criticism of the cultural view is that some studies have shown that, even when such health-related factors as smoking, heavy drinking, lack of physical exercise, poor diet and obesity are controlled, differences in the mortality rates of the different social classes remain.

## Structural/materialist explanations

These explanations suggest that social class differences in health are caused by the structure of society and the different working and living conditions of the different social classes. It is the way society is organised, and not individual lifestyle choices, that disadvantages poorer social groups.

### Activity 3.21

1  Explain how the following material factors could lead to ill-health:

- long working hours

- dangerous working environment

- damp housing

- low income or unemployment

- stress.

2  Suggest one solution to each of the material factors listed above.

Accident rates are highest among those in the more dangerous manual occupations. Martin et al. (1987) argue that those who live in poorer housing conditions tend to have higher rates of respiratory disease. From a materialist view point, the poor diet of the working class is more to do with lack of income rather than cultural choice. In 1988 and 1995, Lobstein (1995) compared prices and foodstuffs available in an affluent and a poor part of London. It emerged that healthy food actually cost less in the more affluent areas of London than in the poorer areas, while unhealthy foodstuffs were slightly cheaper in the poorer areas than in the more affluent areas. Therefore, poorer people were more likely to have to pay more for healthy foodstuffs.

## Reducing inequalities in health

In the 1980s and 1990s, government health policy emphasised 'unhealthy behaviours' which contribute to ill health, and health improvement policies focused on changing individual behaviour, rather than the wider social environment. However, current research and policy stress the interaction between structural factors and individual behaviours. The Acheson Report (1998) was commissioned by the New Labour government to document health inequalities and a subsequent government policy document, *Saving Lives: Our Healthier Nation* (Department of Health 1999a), stated two key aims regarding the health of the population:

◆  to improve the health of the population as a whole

◆  to improve the health of the worst off in society and to narrow the health gap.

The second of these targets will be challenging, given the evidence that income inequalities have actually increased since 1997 (Shaw, 2002). Most official reports into inequalities in health, from the Black Report and the *Health Divide*, to *Our Healthier Nation*, point to poverty being the major cause of ill health. Evidence shows that over the last twenty years, the number of people living in poverty grew significantly and the gap between the 'haves' and 'have nots' has continued to widen. The problem is that the Labour government has not addressed wealth and income redistribution.

## Patterns of gender and health

## Gender and mortality

Since the end of the nineteenth century, women have had a higher life expectancy than men. In the UK, life expectancy for men is 77 years and for women 81 years (*Social Trends*, 2007). Men continue to have higher mortality rates than females, although the gap is narrowing: mortality rates decreased by 24.3 per cent for males but only 18.1 per cent for females between 1996 and 2006. At all ages, women's death rates are much lower than men's. Almost two-thirds of deaths before the age of 65 are male, and, after that age, there are almost twice as many women as men in the population.

Table 3.7 Leading causes of mortality in England and Wales, by sex, 2006

| Underlying cause of death | | Number of deaths | Percentage of all deaths |
|---|---|---|---|
| **Males rank** | | | |
| 1 | Ischaemic heart diseases | 46,316 | 19.2 |
| 2 | Cerebrovascular disease | 18,744 | 7.8 |
| 3 | Malignant neoplasm of trachea, bronchus and lung | 16,964 | 7.0 |
| 4 | Chronic lower respiratory diseases | 13,007 | 5.4 |
| 5 | Influenza and pneumonia | 11,511 | 4.8 |
| 6 | Malignant neoplasm of prostate | 9061 | 3.8 |
| 7 | Malignant neoplasm of colon, sigmoid, rectum and anus | 7467 | 3.1 |
| 8 | Malignant neoplasm of lymphoid, haematopoietic and related tissues | 5777 | 2.4 |
| 9 | Dementia and Alzheimer's disease | 5282 | 2.2 |
| 10 | Aortic aneurysm and dissection | 4774 | 2.0 |
| *All deaths* | | *240,889* | *100.0* |
| **Females rank** | | | |
| 1 | Ischaemic heart diseases | 36,272 | 13.9 |
| 2 | Cerebrovascular disease | 29,650 | 11.3 |
| 3 | Influenza and pneumonia | 17,212 | 6.6 |
| 4 | Dementia and Alzheimer's disease | 12,912 | 4.9 |
| 5 | Malignant neoplasm of trachea, bronchus and lung | 12,350 | 4.7 |
| 6 | Chronic lower respiratory diseases | 12,281 | 4.7 |
| 7 | Malignant neoplasm of female breast | 10,942 | 4.2 |
| 8 | Heart failure and complications and ill-defined heart disease | 6567 | 2.5 |
| 9 | Malignant neoplasm of colon, sigmoid, rectum and anus | 6547 | 2.5 |
| 10 | Diseases of the urinary system | 6181 | 2.4 |
| *All deaths* | | *261,719* | *100.0* |

(Source: *Health Statistics Quarterly*, 2007)

## Causes of death

As Table 3.7 shows, the leading cause of death for both sexes was ischaemic heart diseases which accounted for approximately one in five male deaths and one in seven female deaths during 2006. Cerebrovascular diseases (strokes) were the second leading cause of death for both sexes and accounted for a higher proportion of female deaths than males. A further five causes of death appear in both the male and female top ten underlying causes but not at the same ranks. Men are more likely to suffer heart disease, cancer and HIV/Aids. They are twice as likely to die in accidents as women and three times more likely to commit suicide.

---

### Activity 3.22

Examine Table 3.7 and answer the following questions.

1 State one cause of death which ranks in the male top ten, but not in the female top ten.

2 Find one cause of death which is ranked more highly for females than it is for males.

3 Can you explain why there are a higher number of deaths for females than males, yet men have a higher mortality rate?

## Gender and morbidity

It has been noted as a general trend that 'men die quicker, but women are sicker'. Women are the major users of health care services and apparently experience more illness than men. As Table 3.8 shows, the rate of self-reported long-standing illness per thousand of the population in 2005 was 273 for males and 282 for females. Interestingly, from birth to fifteen years, it is males who have a higher rate of self-reported illness. Women go to the doctor about 50 per cent more often than men between the ages of 16 and 44 and data on stays in hospital show higher female rates than males (Office for National Statistics, 2005b). Women are more likely than men to experience neurotic disorders (e.g. depression and anxiety) and receive far more prescriptions for tranquillisers, sleeping pills and anti-depressants. However, alcoholism is three times more likely in men than in women and men are four times more likely to be registered drug addicts than women.

Table 3.8 Self-reported illness, by sex and age in Great Britain, 2005

| | Long-standing illness | Limiting long-standing illness |
|---|---|---|
| **Males** | (rates per 1,000 population) | |
| 0-4 | 140 | 46 |
| 5-14 | 181 | 72 |
| 15-44 | 175 | 90 |
| 45-64 | 401 | 233 |
| 65-74 | 554 | 342 |
| 75 and over | 583 | 402 |
| *All ages* | *273* | *150* |
| **Females** | | |
| 0-4 | 93 | 28 |
| 5-14 | 160 | 67 |
| 15-44 | 209 | 114 |
| 45-64 | 407 | 245 |
| 65-74 | 589 | 370 |
| 75 and over | 545 | 401 |
| *All ages* | *282* | *163* |

(Source: Office for National Statistics, General Household Survey (Longitudinal), 2004–2005)

## Explanations for gender inequalities in health

### Biological explanations

These focus on genetic and physiological differences. For example, evidence suggests that boys are the weaker sex at birth, with a higher infant mortality rate. At the time of birth, boys are, on average, developing mentally some 4-6 weeks behind girls. There is also some evidence to support the view that women seem to have a better genetic resistance to heart disease (Waldron, 1983). In terms of illness, the biological model would point to conditions associated with pregnancy, childbirth, contraception, abortion and menstruation to explain higher female morbidity rate. However, the problem with focusing exclusively on biological explanations is that it only deals with a proportion of illnesses and disease, and is therefore limited. Furthermore, although underlying genetic, hormonal and metabolic differences exist, they can be modified by social processes and therefore it is the *interaction* of biological and social factors that needs to be examined. As Annandale and Field (2007) note, secretion of oestrogen is affected by environmental and lifestyle factors. Most sociologists point out that biological explanations cannot explain the wide and shifting mortality gaps between men and women.

## Artefact explanations

The difference in morbidity rates according to gender are largely based on self-report studies of an individual's illness. This has led some commentators to suggest that the higher levels of ill-health reported by women reflect their subjective beliefs, rather than objective reality. However, a study by Macintyre (1993) found that men were more likely to over-rate their symptoms compared with women so, in fact, morbidity statistics may well be an underestimation of gender differences. Other arguments in support of the artefact approach would point to women's higher attendance at GP surgeries as a consequence of their nurturing role. Women may seek more medical help than men, but this is often on the behalf of others, such as children and relatives. Men are not necessarily healthier than women; rather they consult doctors less than women. Another criticism of the apparent higher morbidity statistics for females is offered by Macfarlane (1990) who claims that if we exclude visits necessitated by pregnancy or menstruation for women between the ages of 15 and 44, then more men than women actually visit their doctors.

## Cultural/behavioural explanations

Traditional male gender roles and masculine norms may well encourage behaviours that pose serious risks to health and increase the likelihood of an early death. Their higher consumption of alcohol and drugs are among the major risks for suicide which is now the most common cause of death among young men in the UK (Taylor and Field, 2007). Gender role socialisation for females means that they are less likely to engage in risky behaviours, for example, reckless driving and dangerous sports. Furthermore, there is evidence that women may be more likely to follow healthy diets than men as attention to health and the body helps to define femininity. It must be noted, however, that females are also at greater risk of eating disorders, and the consumption of alcohol and drugs and engaging in risky leisure activities are increasing among younger women in the twenty-first century. Behavioural explanations may also account for why women seek help from the doctor more often. Some researchers believe that women are socialised into being more aware of health than men which might lead women to define themselves as ill more often. Seligman (1990) refers to this as 'learned helplessness', meaning that it is more socially acceptable for women than for men to admit they are ill.

### Activity 3.23

1 Do you agree that women have more health awareness and are more likely to seek a doctor's help? Discuss this as a class.

2 Can you think of anything that may limit women's likelihood of visiting the doctor?

It has also been argued that men are less likely than women to recognise or seek help for illness because independence and stoicism in the face of pain are defining features of masculinity. Illness and injury are often seen as a kind of weakness to be overcome rather than given in to. This has led to the suggestion that if men were to heed health education messages and made greater use of health services this would improve their life expectancy. Levels of social support may also explain higher mortality rates amongst males. A study by Perren et al. (2004) found that men living alone were less likely than women living alone to have relationships which involved providing and receiving favours, a difference which the authors conclude may increase the risk of older men living alone becoming socially isolated.

U2

3

The sociology of health

## Structural/materialist explanations

It is women's role as carers that causes ill-health. Women are the main carers of children and, increasingly, elderly and disabled relatives. According to the charity Carers UK, many carers fall into poverty and suffer severe financial hardship as a direct result of caring. This caring and domestic role may make women feel isolated, stressed and depressed, and may result in illness. Popay and Bartley (1989) have researched the health inequalities of domestic labour. The 'labour conditions' of the home – air pollution, noise, damp, temperature extremes, access to lavatory and access to first aid facilities – were found to impact on a person's health. With the exception of noise, overall, women seem to work in more favourable conditions in the formal labour market than they do in domestic labour settings. This is particularly significant given their findings that women with children who also work in a full-time job spend significantly more hours doing housework than men. The unequal distribution of power and resources within the home may explain the health status of men and women. Research has shown that women spend relatively more of their personal income on household goods – especially food – than do men (Graham, 2002). Women's poor health may be due to poor employment conditions. A large percentage of women in paid employment do part-time work, which tends to be poorly paid and have fewer perks (for example, sick pay) and this may force women into poorer living conditions. Poor pay may lead to poverty (with inadequate diet, unsatisfactory housing, and stressful living conditions) as well as limiting occupational pension provision in old age. For Arber and Thomas (2001), it is the social structural differences within society which are the most important causes of gendered health inequalities. For example, women are more likely to be single parents, which in turn is associated with material disadvantage and with poorer health for both mothers and their children. Arber and Thomas conclude that, 'Women in most societies are more likely than men to be poor, have less education, and live in disadvantaged material circumstances. The feminisation of poverty in the US and UK has been widely acknowledged, and is particularly associated with lone motherhood and older women' (2001, p.108).

Higher male mortality rates could also be explained by material factors. Men are more likely to work in dangerous environments and are more likely to suffer accidents at work. Structural changes in the economy may contribute to higher male unemployment levels, which is associated with stress, increased alcohol and drug use and suicide.

### Activity 3.24

Below is a list of illnesses. Devise a chart for recording:

- each illness
- what the cultural and material/structural factors that could contribute to each one are
- whether women or men are more likely to be affected.

1 Lung cancer

2 Obesity

3 Repetitive strain injury

4 Asthma

5 Depression

6 Coronary heart disease

## Ethnic inequalities in health

A key difficulty when examining the impact of ethnicity on health is derived from the problem of defining ethnic origin. The term 'ethnicity' has been used in a wide range of ways and, consequently, direct comparisons between ethnic groups and levels of health have been problematic. Indeed, it is only since the 1991 Census that respondents have been asked to specify their ethnic group. Despite this, many sociologists argue that this should not be used as an excuse not to investigate the health experience of ethnic minorities, and the available evidence does suggest marked inequities in the UK in the health patterns of ethnic minority groups, compared with the white majority.

Evidence suggests that members of minority groups die from much the same diseases as do the majority population: cancer and circulatory disorders. However, significant differences have also been identified. For example, Africans and African-Caribbeans tend to have increased incidence of stroke and high blood pressure. African-Caribbeans, Indians, Pakistanis and Bangladeshis are more likely to suffer early death from liver cancer, diabetes and tuberculosis. Asians (Indians and Pakistanis) suffer more heart disease and are more likely to die from it. Indians and African-Caribbeans are more likely to be compulsorily admitted to hospital for mental illnesses. All ethnic minority groups tend to have a higher rate of stillbirths and neo-natal mortalities and higher mortality rates caused by accidents, poisoning and violence.

Table 3.9 shows the prevalence of self-reported, long-standing illness and limiting long-standing illness within minority ethnic groups. It shows that there is considerable variation between minority ethnic groups, some with higher rates than the general population and others with lower rates.

Carry out an analysis of Table 3.9. What are the biggest variations in reported illness between the different minority ethnic groups?

Table 3.9 The prevalence of long-standing illness and limiting long-standing illness within minority ethnic groups in England, 2004 (%)

| | Black Caribbean | Black African | Indian | Pakistani | Bangladeshi | Chinese | Irish | General population |
|---|---|---|---|---|---|---|---|---|
| Men (boys)* | | | | | | | | |
| Long-standing illness | 39 (21) | 24 (11) | 37 (18) | 35 (18) | 30 (14) | 22 (17) | 47 (23) | 43 (24) |
| Limiting long-standing illness | 24 (7) | 10 (5) | 23 (6) | 20 (7) | 24 (5) | 9 (10) | 26 (7) | 23 (8) |
| Women (girls)* | | | | | | | | |
| Long-standing illness | 44 (22) | 24 (7) | 30 (9) | 41 (13) | 31 (10) | 24 (13) | 44 (17) | 24 (20) |
| Limiting long-standing illness | 28 (8) | 12 (2) | 19 (3) | 30 (6) | 21 (3) | 10 (3) | 23 (4) | 27 (7) |

* Boys and girls aged 15 and younger

(Source: Sproston and Mindell, 2006)

U2

3

The sociology of health

## Artefact explanations

It is worth noting here that the 'evidence' of ethnic inequalities in health remains an extremely complex field of sociological enquiry complicated by inconclusive and sometimes ambiguous evidence. Nevertheless, health differences (such as those noted already) do exist and various explanations have been proposed about the causes of such inequalities.

## Biological explanations

Biologically speaking, a range of findings indicate that, to a large extent, the pattern of disease amongst immigrants tends to follow that of their own country. This has been particularly well-documented for sickle-cell anaemia, prevalent among African / African-Caribbeans, and Tay-Sachs disease, found predominantly in the Jewish population. However, as serious as these conditions may be, their treatment must be viewed in the light of health care strategies. Some researchers have suggested that there is a covert racism in health care, which operates by marginalising diseases which are specific to non-white ethnic groups by paying relatively little attention to them. Or, at the very least, there have been claims that the health professionals have been slow to recognise that ethnic minorities may have special health needs. The fact remains that inherited diseases only account for a small percentage of the health problems of the ethnic minorities and genetic explanations are unable to account for the wider racial and ethnic patterning of health status.

## Cultural explanations

Some sociologists have argued that the differing patterns of health can be accounted for by cultural explanations which are associated with a range of factors – distinct lifestyles, perceptions of illness and illness-behaviour, traditions and cultural values. Cultural explanations tend to focus on patterns of health-related behaviours such as diet, smoking, exercise, child-rearing practices and low uptake of screening services. For example, perinatal mortality is high for Asian mothers and it is often blamed on their low attendance rate at ante-natal classes. However, it is important to note how many Asian women feel intimidated by doctors and are reluctant

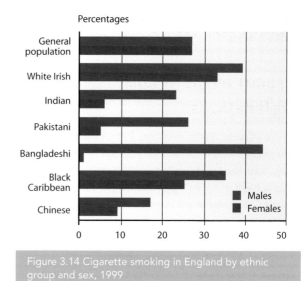

Percentages

Figure 3.14 Cigarette smoking in England by ethnic group and sex, 1999

(Source: Department of Health, 1996)

to be examined by a man. In a similar fashion, the relatively high rate of heart disease suffered by Asians is sometimes attributed to the used of cooking fats such as ghee. As Figure 3.14 shows, 44 per cent of Bangladeshi men smoke cigarettes, followed by 39 per cent of Irish men and 35 per cent of black Caribbean men. This compares with 27 per cent of men in the general population and 17 per cent of Chinese men (*Health Survey for England*, Department of Health, 1999b).

However, one of the most glaring failings of these findings has been the tendency to make sweeping generalisations; for example, 'Asian' and 'Caribbean' cultures are often discussed as if there were no social class, regional or religious variations. It must also be noted that some cultural effects appear to weigh in the favour of minority groups. For example, mortality rates from lung cancer and chronic bronchitis are lower in people from the Indian sub-continent than in the white population due to lower levels of smoking and alcohol consumption. As Figure 3.14 shows, only a tiny minority of Bangladeshi women smoke. In addition, very few women of Asian origin drink alcohol. Many sociologists now recognise that the analysis of health issues which focuses on cultural factors alone ignores other important factors such as poverty and stress. It is all very well to 'blame' individuals for making unhealthy lifestyle choices, but can such choices be viewed as distinct from cultural beliefs and structural factors? Do people know what the 'healthy choice' is? How free are people to choose their lifestyle? It is, therefore, crucial not to consider culture as an all embracing and defining force, but to examine how it combines with material conditions.

# Structural/materialist explanations

The structural/materialist explanations examine the quality of people's material surroundings/living conditions as explanations of ill health. Unemployment has been linked to ill-health and it is well documented that black people and Pakistanis experience high unemployment rates. Furthermore, Amin (1992) claims that some ethnic minorities are concentrated in more hazardous work and thus are exposed to more accidents and work-related illnesses.

Investigations into ethnicity and housing have revealed that some ethnic minorities live in poorer accommodation and in poorer inner-city areas. A survey of homeless households placed in B&B accommodation showed that most of the people were from ethnic minority groups. The health problems and hazards experienced by people living in B&B accommodation has been well documented (Lissauer, 1994) and include higher rates of depression, more frequent hospital use and a lack of coherent provision of GP services.

Moreover, there are significant variations in terms of income between ethnic groups. For example, the mean income of Pakistani and Bangladeshi households which are in social classes I and II is less than the mean income of 'white' households who are classified as being in social classes IV and V (Davey Smith et al., 2002). It is claimed, therefore, that it is not ethnicity itself that accounts for the differences, but the socio-economic factors that are experienced by those in particular groupings.

The advantage of the material explanation is that is does not 'blame the victim' for their illnesses but examines the way society is organised. However, this explanation should consider the relationship between gender, age and region along with material circumstances as factors affecting ill-health. Whichever factor is emphasised as being linked to ethnic inequalities in health (biology, culture, material structure), many commentators now argue that these inequalities have been compounded by the racism experienced by many ethnic groups, which has resulted in ethnic minorities receiving a poor level of care from the NHS. According to

Littlewood and Lipsedge (1982), for example, black patients are:

- twice as likely to be detained involuntarily for mental illness
- likely to receive heavier doses of drugs
- more likely to be seen by a junior doctor.

Furthermore, a study by Bowler (1993) on the views of midwives on maternity wards found that they held a number of stereotypes of Muslim Asian women which may have affected the quality of care which these patients received. It is also the experience of racism which affects health status. For example, Karlsen and Nazroo (2004) found that those people who were worried about racial harassment were 61 per cent more likely to report that their health was less good than those who did not.

A major issue when trying to select a single explanation or account for a particular health pattern is the question of whether different explanations can be separated. In this sense, material factors such as income might influence the decisions people make about how to behave. However, the links between health and material factors have been well documented (the Black Report; the *Health Divide*). Poor housing conditions, overcrowding and unemployment clearly have an impact on health, and time and time again, studies have indicated that Caribbean and Asian groups are more likely to be subject to these adverse conditions. Poverty, unsuitable working conditions and low incomes are, of course, direct measures of material deprivation and have long been identified with ill health. All these considerations have been found to be more prevalent among black groups, although the relationship to health has been hard to verify and studies have drawn attention to the gender and regional variations which considerably complicate the picture.

Ultimately, most sociologists specialising in health and medicine would argue that the real root of the problem lies in material and environmental conditions. However, even this assumption is too generalised. The way ahead must, at the very least, include recognition that ethnic inequalities in health is a basic feature of social stratification in today's world.

## Section summary

Use the following key words to copy and complete the summary of this section below. Each word should be used only once.

access     artefact     behaviour     carers     choices     construction     correlations
depressed     doctor     doctor     domestic     expectancy     family members
feminisation     gap     gender     genetics     health     learned helplessness
living conditions     longer     masculine     mobility     morbidity     mortality
NHS     Pakistani     poor     poverty     risky     roles     smoking
socialised     unemployment     V     valid     values     victim

Illness and disease do not strike randomly amongst the population and any examination of health trends will show that health is patterned according to class, _____ and ethnicity. In terms of social class, although life _____ for everyone has improved over the last century, there has been very little reduction in the health _____ between rich and poor. In terms of _____, a person born into social class I lives, on average, about seven years longer than someone born in social class _____. In terms of _____, evidence shows that working-class people are more likely to visit the _____ and are more likely to define themselves as having _____ health.

There are four main explanations of these class inequalities in health. _____ explanations argue that the evidence of class inequalities is not _____ and that health statistics are a social _____. Social selection explanations argue that it is good or bad _____ which causes social _____. People who experience poor health, will move down the social class scale. The cultural model argues that inequalities in health can be attributed to the norms, _____, attitudes and _____ of the different social classes. For example, the working classes are more likely to partake in unhealthy behaviours such as _____, eating fatty foods and doing little exercise. This model has been criticised for blaming the _____ and taking emphasis away from wider social factors which may cause health inequalities. The structural model of health argues that it is the different working and _____ _____ the different social classes which causes inequalities in health. For example, long working hours, dangerous working environments, low incomes and _____ causes higher morbidity and mortality rates among the working class.

In terms of gender, it has been noted that women live _____ than men, but they also visit the _____ more often. Biological explanations focus on _____ and physical differences between males and females to explain these health inequalities. The artefact explanations focus on examining why women seemingly suffer higher morbidity than males. This explanation points out that just because women visit the doctors more than men, this doesn't mean they suffer more illness; it may be that they have easier _____ to the doctor as they are often responsible for taking other_____ _____. The cultural model suggests that the higher male morbidity rate may be explained in terms of traditional male gender _____ and _____ norms, which means they are more likely to engage in _____ behaviours. Also, women are _____ into seeking help from doctors; a process which Seligman refers to as _____ _____. According to the materialist/structuralist model, it is women's role as _____ that causes ill-health as it may cause women to feel isolated and _____. Also, women's poor health may be related to poor conditions in the home as they take responsibility for _____ labour. Moreover, women are more likely to be poor; a consequence of the _____ of poverty.

In terms of ethnicity and health, there is considerable variation between mortality and morbidity patterns and artefact explanations point out the difficulties of establishing _____ between ethnicity and health. Cultural models stress lifestyle factors and behaviour _____, such as use of fats in cooking. Material explanations point out that unemployment causes ill-health and some ethnic groups, particularly black and _____ groups suffer from this. Finally, many commentators point out that the problems which some ethnic minorities face are compounded by _____ which has resulted in ethnic minorities receiving a poor level of care from the _____.

Exam practice

**(a)** Identify and explain two differences in morbidity between males and females. (17 marks)

**(b)** Outline and evaluate the view that class inequalities in health are caused by cultural factors. (33 marks)

# (iii) The social construction of mental illness and disability

## Pause for thought

Look at Figure 3.15. Do you see this person as healthy or ill? Why?

Figure 3.15 Who do we see as healthy?

185

# Mental illness

## Defining mental illness

These are typical examples of the kind of comment in recent newspaper headlines:

'Stigma of mental illness ruins lives'

'Prisoners 10 times more likely to suffer mental illness'

'People with mental illness face widespread discrimination'.

'One in four students suffer mental illness'

Mental illness is very common. According to MIND (the national association for mental illness), about one in four people in the UK have a mental illness. There is a great deal of controversy about what mental illness is, what causes it, and how people can be helped to recover from it. The severity of various conditions can be seen as being on a continuum, ranging from anxiety and mild depression through personality disorders to severe psychotic disorders.

U2

3

The sociology of health

### Activity 3.26

Take one of the mental disorders listed below and carry out some research to find out what the disorder is and what the symptoms are. If you can, find out what the stated causes and solutions are.

- Panic attacks
- Anxiety disorders
- Obsessive-compulsive disorder
- Phobias
- Post-natal depression
- Manic depression (Bipolar disorder)
- Schizophrenia

## Explaining mental illness

There are many different theoretical approaches to mental disorders but a broad distinction can be made between biological, psychological and sociological perspectives (see Table 3.10).

- Biological theories argue that mental disorders are symptomatic of an underlying bodily malfunction and should be managed by medical treatments.

- Psychological theories suggest that some mental illnesses and behavioural disorders may be a product of personal experiences that distort rational thought processes. They are, therefore, diseases of the mind, rather than the body.

- Sociological approaches focus on relationships between individuals' experiences of mental disorder and wider patterns of social organisation. However, a different sociological view questions whether mental illness actually exists.

# Structural theories

Structural theories of mental illness argue that mental illness does exist and its causes can be identified. Unlike the medical model, however, the causes of mental illness are to be found within society and not in the individual's body. Research shows that specific mental disorders, such as schizophrenia and depression, are not distributed randomly in populations but are consistently linked to social variables.

## The relationship between social class and mental illness

Class and mental health are closely correlated. As Rogers and Pilgrim (2005) note, poorer people are much more likely to experience mental ill-health.

Table 3.11 shows that, compared with no disorder, those with a psychiatric disorder are *more likely* to be economically inactive and are *less likely* to be employed. However, it is important to note that the majority of people with psychiatric disorders are employed and it may not be unemployment which is linked to mental illness, but *inadequate* employment, that is, work which is poorly paid, insecure and with unsatisfying tasks. Stansfeld et al. (2003) found that work is the main determinant of inequalities in depressive symptoms in men.

Table 3.10 Models of mental illness

| | Medical | Psychological | Social |
|---|---|---|---|
| Definition/diagnosis | Diagnosed by doctors in terms of clearly-defined criteria and are symptoms of underlying bodily disease | Diagnosed by doctors or therapists. Precise diagnosis difficult. Mental illnesses are diseases of the mind | Diagnosis problematic. Often owes more to social factors than clinical evidence. Behaviour 'labelled' as illness may be response to difficult situation |
| Causes | Uncertain, but growing evidence of genetic predisposition and biochemical causes | Often cause by experiences in patients' past, especially childhood | Triggered by social circumstances that create stress, lower self-esteem and sense of control |
| Treatment | Medical, surgical and nursing care | Psychoanalysis to help reveal subconscious conflicts or cognitive disorder. Behaviour modification | Individuals may require help and treatment initially, but condition will not improve unless changes made in the life situation |
| Goal | To restore patient to health through treatment, or at least control symptoms and prevent condition getting worse | To give patient insight into origins of problems and help develop strategies for combating them | To help reduce rates of mental illness by revealing social influences |

(Source: Taylor and Field 2007)

Table 3.11 Characteristics of adults with psychiatric disorders, by employment status (percentages)

| Employment status | Female | | Male | | All | |
|---|---|---|---|---|---|---|
| | With a disorder | No disorder | With a disorder | No disorder | With a disorder | No disorder |
| Employed | 55 | 62 | 61 | 75 | 58 | 69 |
| Unemployed | 3 | 2 | 4 | 4 | 4 | 3 |
| Economically inactive | 41 | 36 | 35 | 21 | 39 | 28 |

(Source: Office for National Statistics, 2000)

Furthermore, the neighbourhood can be an influence on mental health. People who report living in neighbourhoods with high levels of crime, vandalism, graffiti, danger, noise and drugs are more mistrustful of those around them, and feel powerless; factors which can contribute to mental illness (Ross et al., 2001). The link between poverty and mental health has been well-documented. A study in Scotland found that financially-deprived young people were twice as likely to commit suicide as their peers in more affluent localities (McLoone, 1996). Reading and Reynolds (2001) found that anxiety about debt was the best predictor of depressive symptoms in poor families.

Read the following newspaper article.

### Rise in mental illness linked to unhealthy diets

Changes in diet over the past 50 years appear to be an important factor behind a significant rise in mental ill health in the UK. The Mental Health Foundation says scientific studies have clearly linked attention deficit disorder, depression, Alzheimer's disease and schizophrenia to junk food and the absence of essential fats, vitamins and minerals in diets. Poor diets are linked to problems of behaviour and mood. A nutritionalist working for the nutrition and mental health programme in Rotherham, South Yorkshire, said the mental health patients she saw generally had the poorest diets she had ever come across. 'They are eating lots of convenience foods, snacks, takeaways, chocolate bars, crisps. It's very common for clients to be drinking a litre of cola a day. They get lots of sugar but a lot of them are eating only one portion of fruit or vegetable a day, if that.'

(Source: adapted from Lawrence, 2006)

1 How could you use this article as evidence against the medical / biological view of mental illness?

2 How can this article be used to support structuralist explanations of mental illness?

Table 3.12 Prevalence of neurotic symptoms (%), by gender (people aged between 16 and 64 years)

| Diagnosis and rate (past week) | Female | Male | All |
|---|---|---|---|
| Sleep problems | 34 | 24 | 29 |
| Fatigue | 33 | 23 | 28 |
| Irritability | 24 | 20 | 22 |
| Worry | 23 | 18 | 20 |
| Depression | 12 | 11 | 12 |
| Concentration and forgetfulness | 11 | 9 | 10 |
| Depressive ideas | 12 | 9 | 10 |
| Anxiety | 10 | 9 | 9 |
| Somatic symptoms | 9 | 6 | 7 |
| Worry about physical health | 7 | 7 | 7 |
| Obsessions | 4 | 5 | 6 |
| Phobias | 6 | 4 | 5 |
| Compulsions | 4 | 3 | 3 |
| Panic | 2 | 2 | 2 |

(Source: Office for National Statistics, 2000)

U2 3 The sociology of health

# The relationship between gender and mental illness

There is a significantly higher proportion of women diagnosed as mentally ill compared with men, although there are differences in proportion, depending on the diagnosis. Some diagnoses are inevitably limited to women, such as post-natal depression. Also, anxiety states, depression and post-traumatic shock disorder are more likely to be diagnosed in women than in men. Blaxter (1990) found that, throughout the life span, women report greater psychological illness than men, including depression, worry, sleep disturbances and feelings of strain. However, some diagnoses are overwhelmingly male, such as anti-social personality disorder (Tyrer, 2000).

Because women live longer than men, higher female prevalence rates for both dementia and depression in old age also make a contribution to female over-representation. How, then, can this apparent overrepresentation of females in mental illness be explained? Rogers and Pilgrim (2005) suggest three possible answers.

Social causation – society causes excessive mental illness. Such explanations often focus on the link between the stress of women's lives and mental illness. For example, women's domestic roles lack structure and so they have time to 'brood' over emotional and personal problems. Stress may also be caused by the caring role which women fulfill, which may mean that they have a lack of privacy and high demands placed on them. Brown et al. (1995) found that the probability of depression increased when women felt trapped and humiliated.

Artefact – female over-representation is a social construction. It has been argued that women are more likely than men to seek professional help, both because of greater knowledge about issues of health and illness and because they are socialised into discussing emotions more freely. This results in higher consultation rates, and, therefore, women appear to have higher rates of mental illness. As has been noted previously, women may make contact with GPs when taking their children to be seen for minor ailments. However, there is also some evidence to suggest women with young children may put their children's health needs before their own, which inhibits them from entering the sick role (Rogers, et al, 1999).

Social labeling – women are labelled as mentally ill more often than men. Some feminist researchers argue that women are all too often labelled as 'mad' by patriarchal society. Women become vulnerable to being labelled as mentally ill when they fail to conform to stereotypical gender roles as carers or if they are too aggressive towards men. This is reinforced by a patriarchal medical and psychiatric profession which views females as inferior and more prone to neurotic illnesses (Barrett and Roberts, 1978). Feminists also point out that women are prescribed minor tranquillisers and anti-depressants in far greater quantities than men. The prescription and use of such drugs are viewed as a means of 'social control' because they transform social problems into medical ones.

# The relationship between ethnicity and mental illness

In a national survey of British people and mental illness, Nazroo (1997) concluded that those of African-Caribbean origin are more likely to suffer depression than the majority of the population, but less likely to suffer anxiety. People of South Asian origin have lower rates of depression than the majority population. People of African-Caribbean origin are significantly over-represented in treatment for psychotic disorders, with one and a half times the rate of admission for treatment compared with the majority population (Koffman et al., 1997). Recently, Tolmac and Hodes (2005) found that black adolescents are still over-represented in mental health services, especially if they were born outside the UK and had refugee status. Rogers and Pilgrim (2005) note that those of African-Caribbean origin are more likely that white people to have contact with psychiatric services through the police, courts or prisons.

The cultural and material model used to explain ethnic inequalities in general health and illness can be applied to the study of mental illness.

Decide whether the following explanations for ethnic inequality and mental illness are cultural, structural or artefact.

- Asian groups have lower rates of distress because they are more psychologically robust and have fatalistic attitudes to suffering.

- Asians avoid contact with the psychiatric services because of the stigma attached to psychiatric conditions.

- Some ethnic groups suffer higher levels of material deprivation.

- Stress, derived from racism, affects mental health.

Thinking about abnormality and mental illness

Look at Table 3.13.

Table 3.13 Defining mental illness

|  | Very abnormal | | Not abnormal | | Mentally ill |
|---|---|---|---|---|---|
| A man shouting at himself in the street | 1 | 2 | 3 | 4 | |
| A man shouting at himself in his own home | 1 | 2 | 3 | 4 | |
| A crowd shouting at a football match | 1 | 2 | 3 | 4 | |
| A cleaner who believes she is the Queen | 1 | 2 | 3 | 4 | |
| A young boy who claims to have an imaginary friend | 1 | 2 | 3 | 4 | |
| An adult who claims to have an imaginary friend | 1 | 2 | 3 | 4 | |
| A woman who hears voices in her head telling her to be quiet | 1 | 2 | 3 | 4 | |
| A woman who hears voices in her head telling her to kill men | 1 | 2 | 3 | 4 | |
| Someone who claims to be heterosexual | 1 | 2 | 3 | 4 | |
| Someone who claims to be homosexual | 1 | 2 | 3 | 4 | |
| A man who claims to be a messenger from God | 1 | 2 | 3 | 4 | |
| A man who feels constantly depressed | 1 | 2 | 3 | 4 | |
| A woman who feels that she cannot face housework anymore | 1 | 2 | 3 | 4 | |

(Source: Senior and Viveash, 1998)

1 Copy Table 3.13. For each of the cases listed in the table, decide and circle on a scale of 1–4 how abnormal it is. Tick the end box if you think it is a mental illness.

2 Is there any agreement as to which cases you defined as very abnormal?

3 Which cases did you see as being caused by mental illness?

4 What does this exercise tell you about the social construction of abnormality and mental illness?

# Interactionist theories of mental illness

Where structural theories see mental illnesses as being real, with a cause that can be treated, interactionist theories challenge the existence of mental illness. Where structural theories examine the way that mental illness is unequally distributed across the various social groups in society, interactionists explore the reasons why certain forms of behaviour are viewed as mental illness and why certain people come to be labelled as mentally ill.

Calling conditions mental *illnesses* may be a reflection of the dominant medical model, which primarily sees mental disorders as symptomatic of an underlying bodily malfunction. According to Foucault (1973), to use the term 'mental illness' reflects a way of thinking. The use of language such as 'symptoms' and 'disease' reflects the power of the medical profession to define mental disorders as a medical, biological issue. Few people assume that mental illnesses can be 'caught' in the same way as some physical illnesses, so why do we use the same type of bio-medical language to describe them? To use the word 'illness' is to shape the way people think about the behaviour. Foucault calls this *discourse*: a way of thinking expressed through language. Perhaps mental illness is just an unusual way of behaving which has nothing to do with being ill or having a 'problem with the mind'.

Another aspect of the Interactionist perspective is to note that definitions of mental illness are really about what is and isn't accepted as *normal* behaviour. Mental abnormality is behaviour which departs from accepted social norms and this rests on what people see as normal and socially-acceptable behaviour. At one time, those whose behaviour departed radically from social norms were variously labelled as 'idiots', 'lunatics' or even 'possessed' by demons and spirits. In modern societies, however, such people are more likely to be seen as suffering from mental disorders and in need of care and treatment.

One way of supporting the view that mental illness is socially constructed is to examine the way in which definitions and treatments for abnormality and mental illness have changed over time. Figure 3.16 shows the range of ideas held on the causes of abnormal behaviour over nearly 2500 years.

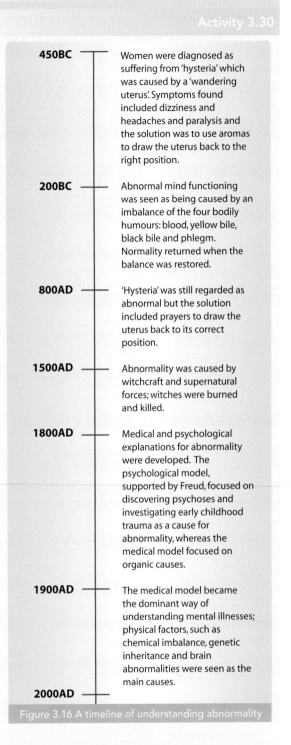

**Activity 3.30**

**450BC** — Women were diagnosed as suffering from 'hysteria' which was caused by a 'wandering uterus'. Symptoms found included dizziness and headaches and paralysis and the solution was to use aromas to draw the uterus back to the right position.

**200BC** — Abnormal mind functioning was seen as being caused by an imbalance of the four bodily humours: blood, yellow bile, black bile and phlegm. Normality returned when the balance was restored.

**800AD** — 'Hysteria' was still regarded as abnormal but the solution included prayers to draw the uterus back to its correct position.

**1500AD** — Abnormality was caused by witchcraft and supernatural forces; witches were burned and killed.

**1800AD** — Medical and psychological explanations for abnormality were developed. The psychological model, supported by Freud, focused on discovering psychoses and investigating early childhood trauma as a cause for abnormality, whereas the medical model focused on organic causes.

**1900AD** — The medical model became the dominant way of understanding mental illnesses; physical factors, such as chemical imbalance, genetic inheritance and brain abnormalities were seen as the main causes.

**2000AD** —

Figure 3.16 A timeline of understanding abnormality

1 How have explanations of mental illness changed over time?

2 Discuss how mental illness is viewed today. Is it still primarily viewed in bio-medical terms? Have psychological explanations become more prominent?

U2

3

The sociology of health

From an Interactionist view point, mental illness is relative and socially constructed. What may be regarded as abnormal or 'mad' in one society or at one point in history, may be seen as perfectly normal in another.

Activity 3.31

Discuss how the following examples illustrate the relative nature of defining mental illness:

- being an unmarried mother
- homosexuality.

## Being mentally ill

Scheff argues that there is no such thing as mental illness; it is just bizarre behaviour which cannot be explained by other means. People who behave bizarrely are not mentally ill; rather their behaviour does not make sense to others.

## Mental illness as social control

The dominant medical profession have the power to define the behaviour of those with less power as abnormal or mentally ill. Take the example of hysteria. This was increasingly used as a diagnosis between 1879 and 1914 – coinciding with the rise in women's movements. It illustrates how a wish for privacy, independence and assertiveness amongst 'hysterics' was seen and diagnosed as abnormal by patriarchal psychologists. Modern feminists see similarities in the diagnosis of premenstrual syndrome and menopausal 'psychological problems'. Szasz (1971) argues that the label 'mentally ill' (mad) has been used as a method of social and political control. For example:

- dissidents in the former USSR were sent to mental asylums
- slaves in southern USA who ran away were labelled as having the mental illness of drapetomania.

Therefore, those whose behaviour the powerful do not like have, in many parts of the world, been diagnosed as mentally unwell. From this viewpoint, the label 'mental illness' is nothing more than a convenient means to deal with socially disruptive problems. For example,

'people *shouldn't* be afraid of open spaces, therefore agoraphobics are ill and need treatment to normalise them'.

Activity 3.32

How could you use a Marxist framework to comment on the relationship between mental illness and social control?

Criticisms of the view that mental illness is socially constructed:

- Szasz ignores the real personal suffering that mental illness causes and the relief that can be given by psychiatric treatment (Realist view).
- The view fails to address the way people are labelled as 'mad' and the effects which this label may have. It is to this that we now turn.

## Interactionist perspective – inside the asylum

Goffman (1968) examined the way in which the mentally ill were labelled in the mental institution.

Activity 3.33

1 Match each one of the following examples to one of the concepts in stage 3 of Figure 3.17: responding to the label mentally ill.

- Accepting new role and following the rules.
- Refusing to cooperate with staff.
- Keeping head down.
- Accepting mental illness and becoming dependent on the institution
- Becoming introverted.

2 Watch a film about people's experiences of entering a mental institution and see whether you can see Goffman's three stages being applied. Examples of such films include: *One Flew Over the Cuckoo's Nest* and *Girl Interrupted*. The film *The Shawshank Redemption* contains a good example of institutionalisation, but it is in the setting of a prison, not an asylum.

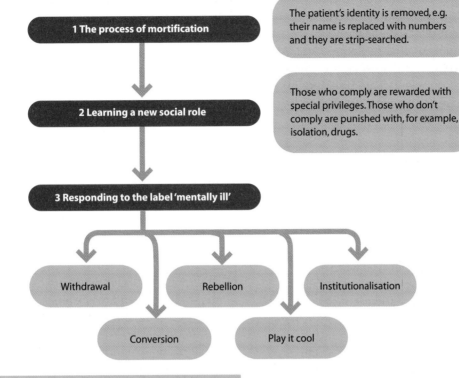

| 1 The process of mortification | The patient's identity is removed, e.g. their name is replaced with numbers and they are strip-searched. |

| 2 Learning a new social role | Those who comply are rewarded with special privileges. Those who don't comply are punished with, for example, isolation, drugs. |

3 Responding to the label 'mentally ill'

Withdrawal | Rebellion | Institutionalisation

Conversion | Play it cool

Figure 3.17 The process of learning to be mentally ill

He argues that the mentally ill do not get *cured* in hospital, rather they learn to *act* mad and this reduces any chance of returning to the outside world. Once a person has been labelled as sick they go through three phases. Figure 3.17 summarises this.

Rosenhan (1973) conducted an experiment to investigate how people come to be defined as insane. The experiment involved eight 'sane' people (stooges) entering twelve different psychiatric hospitals in the USA, claiming to 'hear voices' and requesting psychiatric diagnoses and help. On being admitted, all volunteers stopped pretending and behaved normally. None of these volunteers were recognised as fakes. All were diagnosed as schizophrenic.

### Activity 3.34

1 Explain how Rosenhan's experiment supports the interactionist view that mental illness is not real; it is a social construct.

2 In what ways could Rosenhan's experiment be seen as unethical?

## The sociology of disability

The topic of disability is useful for applying the medical and social models which were addressed in subsection (i). Disability studies is a relatively new area within sociology but social disadvantage among disabled people has recently become a key focus for government debate. Government policy led to the passing of the 1995 Disability Discrimination Act (DDA), giving disabled people certain legal protection from discrimination in several areas. In 1999, the Disability Rights Commission was set up to work towards the elimination of discrimination against disabled people (it merged into the Equality and Human Rights Commission in 2007, along with the Equal Opportunities Commission and the Commission for Racial Equality). However, disability rights activists have argued that government policy is 'based on a flawed understanding of the needs of disabled people, which seems to blame them for their disadvantage' (Hyde, 2001, p. 8).

## How extensive is disability?

The DDA defined a disabled person as 'anyone with a physical or mental impairment, which has a substantial and long-term adverse effect upon their ability to carry out normal day-to-day activities'. This definition avoids the misconception that disability mainly concerns mobility impairments or is largely congenital. At least 8.5 million people in the UK (approximately 10 per cent of the population) are disabled, of whom 6.8 million are of working age (Office for National Statistics, 2002).

## Defining disability

Sociologists argue that our understanding of social issues is partly shaped by the words we use. If words have developed negative connotations, then these words themselves become a tool for prejudice. The word 'handicapped', for example, has largely fallen out of use because of its association with begging ('cap-in-hand'). Other terms which were originally used to describe impairments are now rejected as they are used as a form of insult; terms such as 'spastic' or 'cripple' are examples. As the text below shows, even the way in which we understand the term 'disability' is open to debate.

### Definitions

**Impairment** – any disturbance or interference with normal psychological, physiological or anatomical structure or functioning. For example, a spinal injury, a hearing impairment, lacking part of a limb.

**Disability** – physical or mental impairment which has a substantial and long-term adverse effect on the ability to carry out normal day-to-day activities.

**Disabelism** – The disavantage or restriction of activity caused by society which takes no or little account of people who have physical impairments and this excludes them from participation in the maintatream of social activities

## The medical model of disability

From this perspective, disability has been primarily understood as a medical problem, rather than as a social issue. It tends to focus on

the *individual* limitations that result from impairment. Disabled people are seen as being in need of care by medical personnel. This model focuses on the physical impairment that leads to the disability (e.g. the physical loss of hearing that leads to problems with hearing). From this viewpoint, disabled people are disadvantaged because their impairment prevents them from doing things that other people take for granted.

However, this model is not without its criticisms:

◆ It fails to recognise the *social* barriers which prevent social participation. By focusing on the characteristics of individuals, it offers only a partial explanation of disadvantage.

◆ It endorses policies which are likely to be ineffective and may even reinforce disadvantage and social exclusion. For example, employment policy has focused on individual rehabilitation, rather than removing discriminatory barriers.

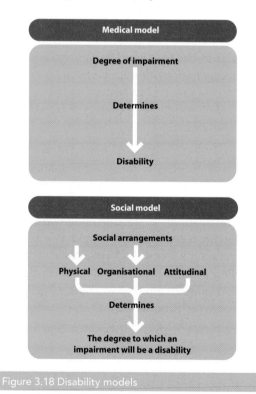

Figure 3.18 Disability models

(Source: Davies, 1984)

## The social model of disability

This model challenges the idea that disability and handicap are caused by impairment.

According to Hyde (2001), people with impairments are excluded by a social environment which is inaccessible and discriminatory. For example, disabled people are often prevented from traveling to work, not by their inability to use buses, but because public transport has been designed for the exclusive use of people without impairments.

Thus, inability to take part in social activities can be explained primarily in terms of social barriers. As Oliver (1990) states, it is the inability of the social environment to cater for people with disabilities rather than the impairment itself which causes disability. In this sense, disability is socially constructed. This is reinforced by Shearer

If the social model had been used to frame the Office of Population Census and Surveys (OPCS) disability survey questions, it would have looked very different. Oliver (1990) turns the assumptions in the individual, medical model of disability around by rewriting the questions. Can you rewrite the rest of the questions from the point of view of the social model?

Table 3.14 Turning the assumptions in the OPCS questions around with the social model

| OPCS question | Oliver's answer |
| --- | --- |
| Can you tell what is wrong with you? | Can you tell me what is wrong with society? |
| What complaint causes your difficulty in holding, gripping or turning things? | What defects in the design of everyday equipment like jars, bottles and tins causes you difficulty in holding them? |
| Are your difficulties in understanding people mainly due to a hearing problem? | Are your difficulties in understanding people mainly due to their inability to communicate with you? |
| Do you have a scar, blemish or deformity which limits your daily activities? | Do other people's reactions to any scar blemish or deformity you may have limit your daily activities? |
| Have you attended a special school because of a long-term health problem or disability? | Have you attended a special school because of your education authority's policy of sending people with your health problem/disability to such places? |
| Does your health problem/disability prevent you from going out as often or as far as you would like? | Are there any transport or financial problems which prevent you from going out as often or as far as you would like? |
| Does your health problem/disability make it difficult for you to travel by bus? | What is it about the local environment that makes it difficult for you to get about in your neighbourhood? |
| Does your health problem/disability affect your work in any way at present? | |
| Does your health problem/disability mean that you need to live with relatives or someone else who can help or look after you? | |
| Does your present accommodation have any adaptations because of your health problem/disability? | |

(Source: Oliver, 1990)

(1981) who states that, for example, not being able to run for a bus would not be a disability if buses waited for their passengers! According to Davies (1994), the social model argues that people with impairments are disabled by society, by the way society's institutions operate and by the attitudes and beliefs non-disabled people hold about disabled people.

The stigma associated with being different may restrict opportunities for relationships, education and employment.

## Stigma and disability

◆ 'Stigma' is when people with certain characteristics are regarded as inferior or deviant by many members of 'normal' society.

◆ A person with a disability is often not seen as a person but as a disabled person without, for example, normal feelings.

◆ Disabled people are often viewed with a mixture of pity and fear (social reaction).

The influence of the medical model on official policy and government research into disability is suggested in Table 3.14 which is taken from one of a series of surveys of disabled people in the UK carried out by the OPCS. The questions clearly suggest that the inability of the individual to take part in social activities can be explained in terms of an underlying impairment.

Criticisms of the social model include:

◆ There is a lack of reference to the role of impairment in restricting social participation. For example, people with profound mental impairments may find it difficult to take part in social activities, irrespective of how these activities are defined and organised. Many disabled people themselves argue that having an impairment is a major part of their life.

◆ Many people accept that they have impairments, but do not wish to be labelled as 'disabled'. In a recent government survey of people claiming benefits, fewer than half chose to define themselves as disabled (Department for Work and Pensions, 2002). Many people rejected the term because they saw their health problems related to illness rather than disability. However, Barnes (2003) has pointed out that in a society where disability is stigmatised and associated with abnormality, it is not surprising that some people with impairments choose to reject the label 'disabled'.

### Weblink

There is a wealth of research into different aspects of disability available to read from the Centre for Disability Studies, University of Leeds (see 'Websites' page ii).

### Section summary

Use the following key words to copy and complete the summary of this section below. Each word should be used only once.

abnormal    African-Caribbeans    asylum    constructed    control    depression
disability    discriminatory    disruptive    environment    ethnicity    four    Goffman
impairment    individual    label    medical    neighbourhoods
patterns    social    society    stress    women

### Mental illness

Mental illness is very common and approximately one in _____ people experience a form of mental illness. Structural theories of mental illness argue that there are identifiable _____ according to gender, class and _____ and that these are caused by _____ and not biological factors. In terms of social class, it has been found that poverty and living in deprived _____ are strongly linked to mental illness. In terms of gender, _____ are more likely to report symptoms of mental illness. This has been explained in terms of the higher _____ levels faced by women, or that women are more likely to consult doctors and given the _____ of being mentally ill. In terms of ethnicity, _____ _____ are more likely to be diagnosed as suffering from _____ and have more contact with psychiatric services.

Interactionist theories challenge the existence of mental illness and examine they ways in which some behaviour is seen as _____ and given the label of mental illness. In this way, mental illness can be seen as socially _____ as definitions and interpretations vary over time. Mental illness can also be seen as a form of social _____ whereby applying the label of mental illness is nothing more than a means of dealing with socially _____ problems. Writing from an interactionist perspective, _____ examined the ways in which the label of mental illness was applied and accepted by patients in an _____.

## Disability

There are two main models for understanding disability: medical and social. The medical model defines disability as a _____ problem. It focuses on _____ limitations that result from _____. From this viewpoint, it is the impairment that causes _____. On the other hand, the social model challenges the view that disability is caused by impairment. It is the social _____ which is inaccessible and _____ which causes disability. From this point of view, people with impairments are disabled by _____

## Exam practice

(a) Identify and explain two differences in morbidity between males and females. (17 marks)

(b) Outline and evaluate the view that class inequalities in health are caused by cultural factors. (33 marks)

# (iv) The role of health professionals in society

## Pause for thought

1 Why do we trust doctors?

2 How can the medical profession be seen as agents of social control?

Figure 3.19 What is the role of the health professional?

As societies have modernised, formal health care systems have been developed and there is little doubt that the medical profession came to dominate the provision of health care over the last century in the UK. We tend to offer high status to the medical profession and they are certainly one of the most prestigious and well-paid occupational groups in society. One substantial area of the sociology of health is the examination of the role of the health profession in society. Debates have focused on:

◆ how the medical profession gained its status

◆ whose interests it serves

◆ what its sources of power are

◆ what its role in promoting social control is.

Activity 3.36

1 Do you trust doctors? Discuss why.

2 What evidence and arguments can you think of to support the view that doctors have high status in contemporary UK society?

3 In pairs or small groups, brainstorm all the different parts of the medical profession – GPs are just one part of a wider professional group.

There are four main sociological perspectives which can be applied to an understanding of the role of the medical professions.

1  Funtionalist theories – which see the medical profession as serving the interests of society as a whole;

2  Weberian theories – which have examined the strategies used by the professiona in order to achieve and maintain their high status position.

3  Marxist theories – which see the medical profession as reflecting and supporting the interests of the dominant ruling class.

4  Feminist theories – which see the medical prefession as reflecting the interests of men and controlling female health.

# Functionalist theories of the role of the medical profession

The functionalist theory of the role of the medical profession has largely stemmed from Parson's analysis of the sick role. Parsons (1951) saw sickness as a social state and a potential threat to social order. He argued that too much sickness could be deviant for society, as people would not be complying with the work-centred norms of modern societies. For this reason, Parsons argued that a 'sick-role' is crucial for the wellbeing of society. People can only be legitimately defined as 'sick' if they conform to the elements of the sick role. Acquiring the sick role involves certain rights and certain duties or obligations. To acquire the sick role, people must:

◆  define sickness as undesirable and want to get better

◆  not expect to take care of themselves

◆  be willing to seek medical help and co-operate with medical professionals

◆  be exempted from their normal activities (e.g. work or school).

Activity 3.37

Carry out a mini survey using questionnaires/interviews to discover if people do adopt the 'sick role' when they have had an illness. Try to find out what they were/weren't allowed to do when they were suffering from an illness.

Parsons recognised that the medical profession has a significant role to play in promoting the sick role and ensuring that sickness doesn't become deviant. The medical profession promotes **universalism**; it also stands for **affective neutrality**. From this view point, doctors act as official gatekeepers to the sick role and they also have certain rights and responsibilities.

Rights:

◆  The right to carry out an examination of patient's physical and personal life.

◆  Authority over the patient and autonomy in practice.

Obligations:

◆  Patient's needs must be put first, before self-interest

◆  Emphasis is on restoring health, through specialist help and expertise.

From a functionalist view point, the medical profession have high status and rewards because they perform the vital function of controlling illness and helping vulnerable people. Functionalists see the medical profession as primarily altruistic. Doctors serve the public interest rather than pursue private gain. The Hippocratic Oath is indicative of this social commitment. Doctors swear to do all they can to help the sick regardless of material interest. Doctors, therefore, must not only be competent but they must also be totally trustworthy and the reason why we define them as such is because, as a profession, they share a number of traits.

- They have learned theoretical knowledge about the body which allows them to make objective and detached assessments and decisions about the causes of illness and the best cures.

- They are fully trained; entry to the profession is highly competitive and only the most talented will be allowed access to the training. Training takes many years of study and application, tested through rigorous examination and assessment.

- The profession has a strict code of ethics which ensures that doctors do not abuse their power and that decisions are always made in the interests of the patients.

- They are regulated and controlled by the General Medical Council, which maintains a register of qualified practitioners and disciplines those guilty of professional misconduct.

Criticisms of the functionalist theory:

- The model cannot be applied to many chronic illnesses from which patients cannot recover.

- Doctors' interventions may well cause illness, rather than cure it.

- Patients do not always take a passive role and they don't always follow the medical advice they are given.

- Doctors are not objective.

- Some patients can become more knowledgeable about new or rare conditions than their doctor.

- Studies of illness behaviour (the processes by which people come to define themselves as ill) have shown that only a minority of symptoms are brought to medical attention (Young, 2005).

- It does not recognise a range of possible doctor-patient relationships and it assumes the relationship is always consensual.

- There is some evidence that the general public's confidence in doctors as altruistic has been severely shaken.

### Activity 3.38

1 Separate the criticisms of the functionalist theory into criticisms of the sick role and criticisms of the doctor role.

2 Now match the explanatory statements which follow with each of the criticisms.

- A study by Punamaki and Aschan (1994) found that only a minority of patients followed the specific advice of doctors.

- Doctors have their own specific career interests and there are limits to what they can cure.

- There is so much health advice available to lay people, that doctors' diagnoses and treatment strategies may not always be acceptable.

- Illich (1976) claimed that Western medical treatment can cause damage to patients.

- There are differences between the knowledge, interests and expectations of doctors and their patients that may lead to tension and conflict (Taylor and Field, 2007).

- A number of public scandals such as the Harold Shipman serial killings, the controversy surrounding the removal of children's organs at Liverpool's Alder Hey Children's Hospital and the recent deaths from hospital-acquired infections, undermine the functionalist argument.

- Therefore, what Parsons is really talking about is a 'patient' role, rather than a 'sick' role.

- People suffering from these types of illness may well need to maintain normal social roles to help in the rehabilitation process.

## The Weberian approach

Rather than the medical profession serving the interests of society as a whole, this approach sees the medical profession as benefiting its *own* interests. This approach stems from the work of Weber who, writing in the early twentieth century, argued that occupational groups use strategies to increase their amount of status and power. Historical evidence supports the view that the 'success' of the medical profession in gaining power and influence came primarily as a result of organisation and campaigning. For example, the 1958 Medical Registration Act established the General Medical Council which was authorised to keep a register of 'suitably qualified' practitioners. In reality, this meant that many of the homeopaths were excluded.

Friedson (1970) applied a Weberian perspective to analyse how the medical profession gained its dominance and status. He argued that the professions act in order to gain **social closure** through professional dominance. Doctors, as a profession, have forced other competing providers of health care into subordinate positions and consequently have managed to promote high status and rewards for themselves. Millerson's traits of a profession can be seen as techniques of closure (see Activity 3.42).

Activity 3.39

Millerson (1964) identified the traits of a profession which included:

- theoretical knowledge
- specialised education
- formal examinations
- an independent body (representative and regulatory).
- professional code of behaviour
- the aim of the 'public good'.

For each one of the traits listed above, explain how it can be seen as a technique of closure.

Turner (1987) develops this Weberian approach. He argued that professionalisation by doctors is no more than a strategic means of retaining certain types of privilege that results from this monopoly. This has been achieved by enlarging the degree of social distance between doctors and patients (keeping the patient mystified). He examined how doctors have managed to emerge as the highest status health care professionals and argues that they have done this partly through a process of occupational domination.

According to Turner, occupational domination has been achieved in three different ways.

1 Subordination – forcing other health care occupations to undertake tasks as delegated to them by doctors (e.g. nurses, midwives).

2 Occupational limitation – the medical profession force other groups to limit their activities to a particular part of the body (e.g. dentistry).

3 Exclusion – preventing competing occupations from performing health care practice (e.g. homeopathy).

However, there have recently been several challenges to the autonomy of the medical profession.

◆ There has been a shift in morbidity from infectious to degenerative diseases, most of which do not have any medical 'cures'. Related to this is an increasing emphasis on preventative medicine as these degenerative diseases are linked to lifestyle factors.

◆ There has also been a challenge from within the medical profession with the increasing professionalisation of the paramedical occupations such as nursing. Also, de-professionalisation has taken place as doctors have lost their monopoly over medical knowledge within a better-educated society; for example, the growth in alternative models of health.

The popularity of alternative medicine and therapy is explored later in this section.

## The Marxist perspective

Marxists argue that the medical profession serve to promote the interests of the capitalist ruling class. This is achieved through the following structures.

1 Drugs/pharmaceutical companies

2 Private medicine

3 Gatekeeper role (defining, legitimising and access)

4 Maintaining a fit and healthy workforce

5 Ideological role of medicine

Using the paragraph below, link each of the structures (1–5) above to its relevant explanation.

Navarro (1979) argues that the professions play a key role in social control in capitalist societies by hiding the real causes of ill-health, which are poverty and material deprivation generated by the capitalist system. Biomedicine defines illness as a result of individual misfortune or failure to follow a healthy lifestyle. No consideration is given to the wider social context which has generated most illnesses. From this point of view, medicine and the medical profession plays an ideological role as medical science can provide the answers and solutions to what are really problems generated by the inequalities of capitalism. False class consciousness is reinforced as the health care system promotes the view that it cares. Navarro rejects the Weberian argument that prestige comes from occupational closure. Instead, he argues that doctors are rewarded with status, high financial rewards and monopoly over medical knowledge in return for them acting as agents of social control for the ruling capitalist class. Navarro argues that the medical profession serve as a gatekeeper and control the workforce; it defines who is 'officially' ill and, in this sense, it acts as an 'agent of social control'. Sickness is primarily defined as inability to work. The medical profession must maintain a healthy workforce as this will serve to increase productivity and profit. Furthermore, the medical profession is a major consumer of the products of capitalism; high tech medicine requires a massive industry. McKinley (1984) argues that doctors themselves are merely workers within a vast medical industry that produces marketable health care products in an effort to generate more profit for the bourgeoisie. Medicine, then, is just another capitalist commodity. Private medicine is explained by Marxists as being both an example of medicine as a commodity and as an example of social inequality – a 'two-tier' system where the rich can afford private health care.

Write an explanation of the Marxist view, including the following words: reproduction of the labour force; legitimising the sick role; capital accumulation/consumerism; ideology; legitimation; inequality.

Critics of the Marxist perspective have pointed out that they ignore the real beneficial work that doctors do in helping people from all social classes who are ill. Also, interactionists argue that Marxists ignore the doctor-patient interaction: patients might not simply accept the dominant ideology; they might not believe that their symptoms are biologically caused but might well think the cause lies in social factors, such as work and poverty.

# Feminist perspectives

Feminists see medicine and medical knowledge as a means of maintaining patriarchal control over women. According to Abbott and Wallace (1990), medicine seeks to control women who deviate from traditional femininity. They cite the following examples.

◆ Female contraception (such as the pill and the intra-uterine device) carry significant health risks which men would not be expected to tolerate. Radical feminists argue that contraception is big business which generates massive profits for pharmaceutical companies. It in therefore in the interests of such companies to restrict women's ability to choose how they control their own fertility. Feminists question why the majority of contraceptive advice is directed at women, whereas male contraceptive measures have fewer side effects and yet are not so widely used.

◆ Control over childbirth has been taken away from women. Pregnancy is a natural condition which has been medicalised. As Abbott and Wallace (1990) note, pregnant women are treated as potential problems; they are required to make regular ante-natal visits and they are almost forced to have a hospital birth where mainly male doctors control the management of labour and childbirth. According to Oakley (1984), obstetricians tend to see pregnancy as a medical problem, whereas women see it as a natural process. According to feminists, induction of labour and Caesarean section operations are often seen as a matter of convenience for hospitals, rather than for the good of the mother and baby.

◆ Post-natal depression, menstruation and the menopause have been neglected by bio-medicine. There has been very little medical research into these conditions; feminists suggest that very few male doctors take these conditions and their effects on women seriously.

◆ The giving of tranquilizers to housewives with depression does nothing to address the real causes of the problem; that is, the fact that the mother-housewife role is not valued by society.

Doyal (1985) has shown how the development of the medical profession has involved the wrenching away of medical knowledge from women by men. Before the 1858 Medical Registration Act, women used to be the key health care providers but they soon became just 'helpers' in a male-dominated profession. Even though midwifery is still a mainly female profession, obstetricians and gynaecologists are generally male. In fact, men still make up the majority of consultants and the medical profession is a prime example of occupational vertical segregation – the higher up the medical occupational scale, the more men dominate.

Radical feminists see the medical profession as legitimising inequalities and controlling women. The Victorian disorder 'hysteria' was increasingly diagnosed between 1870 and 1914. This happened to coincide with the rise of the women's movement and, as Showalter (1991) pointed out, this illustrates how a wish for privacy, independence and assertiveness amongst 'hysterics' was seen and diagnosed as abnormal by medical psychiatrists.

Activity 3.42

How would feminists explain the relationship between eating disorders such as anorexia nervosa and the medical profession?

One major problem with the feminist perspective is that it ignores the harm that medicine can exercise over men as well as women. It has been recently noted, for example, that there has been very little publicity or awareness campaigns for prostate and testicular cancers which are increasingly contributing to the male mortality rate.

# The postmodernist approach

Postmodernists note that the bio-medical model of health has gained dominance over all other theories of health, including alternative therapies. However, postmodernists argue that, in a rapidly changing and fragmented world, no single approach to health and illness can be seen as the 'truth'. People now have access in the world of mass communication to a huge variety of models of health from which they can choose. Consumers now buy into or out of private health care, state health care, alternative medicine and so on. Consumer society contributes to the fragmentation of health views and health care. As Senior (1993) notes, people may 'shop around' for what they feel is the best explanation of their illness.

Postmodernists argue that no single theory (meta-narrative) can reduce all experiences to the biomedical view of illness. As Senior (1998) argues, all theories are simply ideas which compete to become recognised as the illusory truth. Postmodernists claim that power can be acquired through language. Foucault argued that words and phrases can affect the way people think. This is the power of discourse. Medical discourse is dominated by doctors who are able to medicalise human behaviour. Thus being overweight becomes 'obesity', being sad becomes 'depression' or being worried becomes 'anxiety'. This medical scientific discourse shapes the way people view society. According to Foucault (1973), knowledge cannot be separated from power, so definitions of health and illness depend on who has the power to define the state our body is in. In medieval times this might have been the priest; nowadays it is the doctor. For Foucault, though, those in power can exercise social control in very subtle ways. Technology can be used to maintain surveillance over people's behaviour (for example, through CCTV) but in the postmodern world, surveillance is not necessarily exercised by others but by individuals themselves, through self-surveillance. Dieting and exercise force individuals to monitor and regulate their own bodies; an increasing number of self-diagnosis health kits are on sale (such as blood pressure and cholestrol testing kits). It may well be that doctors will play less of a role in social control while individuals exercise self-control.

Activity 3.43

How would Marxists, feminists, functionalists and postmodernists interpret the trend of more people requesting cosmetic or plastic surgery?

## The rise of complementary medicine

2000 BC: 'Here, eat this root.'

1000 AD: 'That root is heathen. Here, say this prayer.'

1850 AD: 'Prayer is superstition. Here, drink this potion.'

1940 AD: 'That potion is snake oil. Here, swallow this pill.'

1985 AD: 'That pill is ineffective. Here, take this antibiotic.'

2000 AD: 'That antibiotic is artificial. Here, eat this root…'

As subsection (i) has shown, there are various different models and explanations of health and illness, and historical evidence shows that societies differ in their ways of understanding health issues. While the bio-medical model has been prominent in Westernised societies throughout the last century, there is increasing evidence that this model is being challenged. One of the most serious challenges comes from the increasing popularity of what have been termed alternative medicine and therapy.

Sales of alternative medicines in the UK are increasing. In 2007, sales figures suggest that

Britons will spent £191 million in 2007 on alternative treatments, up 32 per cent in the previous five years. Mainstream stores such at Boots and Tesco now stock alternative therapies. In the UK there are over 100 alternative medical treatments available with over 90,000 practitioners. These treatments, especially those of Eastern origin, tend to focus on the patient as a whole person. Many claim to work by using the body's own healing powers. Others stress the use of natural herbal remedies. The most popular alternative treatments are acupuncture, homeopathy, osteopathy and herbalism. Herbal remedies such as green tea-based treatments and Echinacea account for 63 per cent of the complementary medicines market. Sharma (1992) has described the ten most popular practices. In descending order, these are:

1 Herbalism

2 Osteopathy

3 Homeopathy

4 Acupuncture

5 Chiropractic

6 Spiritual healing

7 Hypnotherapy

8 Reflexology

9 Naturopathy

10 Aromatherapy

Activity 3.44

1 Carry out some research into one of the above alternative medicines/therapies. If you can, talk to an alternative therapist in the town where you live.

2 How could you use the range of alternative therapies to support the view that health and illness are socially constructed?

Before exploring the popularity of alternative medicine in more detail, it is important to consider the terminology used. The term 'alternative' has often been used interchangeably with other terms, such as 'complementary' or 'holistic', each which have its own precise definition which have been usefully summarised by Hunt and Lightly (1999).

- **Alternative medicine** – medical practices that are different from accepted forms; used instead of orthodox medicine.

- **Holistic medicine** – embodies a particular attitude to health: the patient's health is regarded as integral to the human organism and there needs to be an understanding of the physical, emotional, psychological, social and spiritual aspects of the client.

- **Complementary medicine** – implies a recognition of the potential relationship between various health care choices and can include many orthodox and non-orthodox healing strategies. It marks a shift from seeing alternatives as in opposition to modern medicine to recognising that they can support orthodox treatment.

- **Orthodox medicine** – the bio-medical model of understanding health and the body which is widely accepted in Western societies.

Definitions of alternative medicine are ultimately tied to the role of scientific bio-medicine in having the power and authority to label such forms of medicine as 'alternatives'. It seems that people are so socialised to have faith in the dominance of bio-medicine that alternative treatments are considered to be on the fringe of respected medical practice. As Bivins (2007) notes, 80 per cent of the world's population are estimated to use non-Western forms of medicine, yet the privileging of the bio-medical model ensures that these systems continue to be regarded as primitive and unscientific. The problem, as Bivins (2007) sees it, is that bio-medicine claims a monopoly of absolute, universal knowledge. The only options available for other forms of medicine, from acupuncture to herbalism to homeopathy, are to set themselves in opposition, or to take up the subservient role implied by the term 'complementary'.

## Explaining the growth of alternative medicines

Hunt and Lightly (1999) offer five, broadly interrelated reasons for the increasing popularity of alternative medicine.

1  People find it hard to accept that orthodox medicine sometimes fails and so resort to an alternative. This explanation suggests that people are becoming increasingly frustrated with orthodox medicine, partly as a consequence of having increased expectations of what it can achieve.

2  People are increasingly critical of the effects of the orthodox services. Surveys show that people are concerned about the unpleasant side-effects of drugs and the interventionist nature of medical practice. Illich's theory of iatrogenesis, discussed earlier, is relevant here.

3  There is a growing dissatisfaction in people of all ages with what is available in the orthodox medical sphere; for example, the long waiting lists for treatment and the failure to cure chronic illness. As Bivins (2007) notes, the popularity of bio-medicine suited a population under permanent threat of infectious disease. Today, though, patents' needs have changed. Chronic and degenerative conditions have risen inexorably and this has led to disenchantment with the perceived ineffectiveness of 'industrial' medicine. This is linked to the view that alternative therapies may be preferred as they allow much more input from patients, thus empowering them in diagnoses and searches for cures. People feel that they are listened to and treated as individuals, which is a major departure from the approach of orthodox medicine.

4  Some people have religious or philosophical arguments against certain Western medical practices. Modern bio-medicine subscribes to the principle of the mind-body divide, whereas many alternatives focus upon the dimensions of healing and health related to the psychological and spiritual needs of the patient.

5  There is a growing proportion of the population which simply needs to be different and experiment. For example, alternative medicine is part of a cultural current which embraces New Age therapies, the holistic health and wholefood movement, and the quest for the 'natural' in therapy, childbirth and food.

Whatever the reason is, there is no doubt that alternative medicines are becoming ever more popular. According to research by Thomas et al. (2003), in the UK, 47 per cent of people have used complementary and alternative medicine (CAM) at some times in their lives and 10 per cent use some form of CAM each year. Users tend to be older, female and over 90 per cent is purchased outside the NHS. At least 10 per cent of hospital physicians also use CAM as part of their clinical practice. It has been estimated that one in two practices in England now offer their patients some access to CAMs.

## Section summary

Use the following key words to complete the summary of this section below. Each word should be used only once.

alternative    altruistic    bio-medical    capitalism    care    control    critical    deprivation    gatekeepers    ideological    legislation    male-dominated    mass communication    Oakley    patriarchal    power    profession    responsibilities    rewards    ruling class    sick role    side-effects    social closure    society    status    truth    workforce

The medical profession have gained high _____ in UK society over the past century as they gradually came to dominate the provision of health _____. Functionalist theories see the medical profession as benefiting the whole of _____. According to Parsons, illness is potentially threatening, so the _____ _____ is necessary to promote social stability. The role of doctors is to act as official _____ to the sick role and this is accompanied by specific doctor rights and _____ _____. Functionalists see the medical profession as primarily _____: doctors serve the public interest rather than pursue private gain. The Weberian theory points out that occupational groups use strategies to increase their amount of status and _____ in society. Friedson argued that the medical profession act in order to gain _____ _____ through professional dominance: through various _____ they have forced other health care providers into subordinate positions and have managed to promote high status and _____ for themselves. The Marxist perspective argues that the medical profession serve the interests of the dominant _____ _____. It plays an important social _____ function by hiding the real causes of ill-health (poverty and _____ ) generated by the system of _____ .

The medical profession also play an _____ role by falsely promoting the view of 'caring capitalism'. Marxists also point out the medical profession maintains a healthy _____ which will help to increase capitalist productivity and profits. The feminist view sees medicine and medical knowledge as a means of maintaining _____ control over women. They note that medical care has been wrenched away from women and given to a _____ _____ profession. For example, _____ points out that many mothers feel that pregnancy and childbirth has become medicalised. The postmodernist approach argues that no single theory of health and illness can be seen as the _____. People now have access in the world of _____ _____ to a huge variety of models of health from which they can choose.

There is some evidence that the Western _____ model of illness and the power of the medical _____ are being challenged by the rise in complementary or _____ therapies. There may be a variety of explanations for the increase in complementary medicine; for example, people's increasing _____ view of the medical profession and the _____ of medical treatment.

## Exam practice

(a)  Identify and explain two features of the bio-medical model of health.  (17 marks)

(b)  Outline and evaluate the view that health and illness are socially constructed.    (33 marks)

# The sociology of religion

## (i) Key concepts and the changing nature of religious movements in society

### Pause for thought

1 What is a religious belief?

2 How many different types of religious institution and movements can you think of ?

3 What are the aims of fundamentalist movements?

Figure 4.1 Religion in the park

### Activity 4.1

1 Write down five things you associate with religion. Now complete the sentence, 'Religion is…' Discuss your points with the rest of your class.

2 (a) Consider the following examples of behaviour and decide which ones are instances of religious behaviour.

- Praying in your home
- Reading the Qur'an
- Sitting in a yoga pose
- Using crystals for healing
- Waving a scarf at a football match and singing the team song
- Taking a revered cuddly toy into an exam
- Attending mass on Christmas Eve
- Throwing salt over your shoulder

(b) Discuss your decisions with members of your class.

## Defining religion

What does it mean if we say we are 'religious'? Indeed, is it enough to *say* we are 'religious' if we do not actually *do* anything on account of it? If we hold beliefs, how is it decided whether these beliefs are religious? Who decides – is it the believer himself or herself, a senior practitioner within that religion, or the sociologist studying the religiosity of the society? What does it mean if we follow religious practices, such as attending a ceremony at a religious building on a regular basis, only because our mum insists upon it or because we fancy the person sitting two rows in front? It is certainly not a straightforward task to define or measure religion.

### Definition: religiosity

Religiosity refers to how religious a society is, looking at, for example, beliefs and practices.

## The classical sociologists

Durkheim (1912) defined religion as:

a unified system of beliefs and practices relative to sacred things, that is to say, things set apart and forbidden – beliefs and practices which unite into one single moral community called a **Church**, all those who adhere to them

(Source: cited in Aldridge, 2004, p.8)

At the essence of Durkheim's definition is the sacred. If something is sacred you are in awe of it; it is really special and powerful. Anything can be sacred. Different religions have different sacred things. For Durkheim, sharing something as sacred unites people.

### Activity 4.2

One example of the sacred for Hindus is the cow.

1 Find three other examples of sacred things from different religions.

2 Consider what having sacred things does for people.

Weber (1922) approached his study of religion with an open mind. He did not set out with a clear definition of religion. For Weber, it was important to understand the meaning of religious beliefs and practices *for those taking part.*

## Contemporary definitions

These can be split into two broad types. Aldridge (2004) refers to them as:

◆ inclusive definitions

◆ exclusive definitions.

## Inclusive definitions

These are much broader than exclusive definitions which are explained below. They are functional. This means that they consider what the religion does for its followers (providing solutions to ultimate problems, for example) and how it guides them. Inclusive definitions avoid referring to the supernatural, or a transcendental order or other worldly powers.

These definitions can be applied to systems of beliefs and practices which unite groups of people.

An example of an inclusive definition is provided by Geetz (1966). Geetz maintains that religion enables people to explain human existence by giving it meaning. Religion is used in a broad sense here to refer to beliefs and practices that people have to give them a sense of control over their lives.

The strengths and weaknesses of inclusive definitions include:

### Strengths

◆ Inclusive definitions encourage us to think beyond the major religions, such as Christianity.

◆ Inclusive definitions are less likely to be ethnocentric.

◆ Inclusive definitions encourage analysis of what the purpose of religion is within a culture.

### Weaknesses

Some sociologists find these too broad.

◆ Bruce (2002b) is critical because he is interested in whether religion is losing social significance; he feels that to include examples such as the popularity of the World Cup as a sign that religion is still prominent is not useful.

◆ Hamilton (1995) finds the reference to the ultimate problem of human life that inclusive definitions use problematic. He questions what this problem is and also asks who is to say what it is – the sociologist or the believer?

# Exclusive definitions

These are narrower than inclusive definitions. They are also in the main **substantive**, which means that they say what religion is. Sociologists generally use these types of definition in their work. They refer to beliefs practices and institutions that lean towards powers or beings that are not of this world, the superhuman or the supernatural. They are deliberately restrictive, excluding such things as being devoted to a football team or idolising a celebrity, having a strong political commitment or seeking meaning through consumerism as being 'religious'.

An example of an exclusive definition is provided by Bruce:

> beliefs, actions and institutions that assume the existence of supernatural entities with powers of action, or impersonal powers or processes possessed of moral purpose.
>
> (Source: Bruce, 2002b)

The strengths and weaknesses of exclusive definitions include:

### Strengths

◆ Sociologists generally favour them. Aldridge (2004) points out that they are closer to what we normally understand religion to be, excluding secular activities like being a fan of a rock group.

### Weaknesses

◆ Aldridge (2004) says the greatest danger is that they will be too narrow, so they only apply to some religions in some social contexts.

U2

4

The sociology of religion

Table 4.1 Advantages and disadvantages of being defined as a religion

| Advantages of being defined as a religion | Disadvantages of being defined as a religion |
|---|---|
| Tax concessions | Legal restrictions e.g. Transcendental Meditation rejects the religion label as it restricts what it can do in secular organisations |
| Gives social acceptance | Associations with authority and narrow mindedness. Some movements prefer to be called spiritual rather than 'religious' |
|  | Fear of being seen as a 'weird' **cult** |

(Source: adapted from Aldridge, 2004)

- Self and Starbuck (1998) point out that not all religions involve belief in supernatural or superhuman beings.

- Aldridge (2004) believes that there are advantages and disadvantages to being defined as a religion (Table 4.1).

Activity 4.3

Find five religious images. Make them into a collage. Explain what makes them religious.

# Religious belief

Activity 4.4

1 Carry out a brief interview. The aim is to find out what the interviewee believes in. Keep the questioning as open as possible. Begin with 'What do you believe in?' Report your findings to the group. Compare and discuss your findings in terms of people being religious today.

2 In terms of measuring religiosity, what else would you need to find out about?

In the 2001 UK Census, 71.6 per cent of respondents identified themselves as Christian. A further 2.7 per cent identified themselves as Muslim, which was the largest non-Christian religious group. But what does this really mean? Because someone *says* they are a Christian or a Muslim, do they have to actually *do* anything, or *believe* in anything to be 'religious'? Is it a clear cut thing – 'yes, I'm religious', or 'no, I'm not', or are there degrees or levels of being religious? Is there room for any doubt in the beliefs of someone who is defined as 'religious?

Some sociologists, for example Davie (1994), maintain that what is happening regarding religion is a shift to 'believing without belonging'. This means that religions such as Christianity are not disappearing. Rather, they are retreating from the public sphere. Religion is more privatised. However, other sociologists, such as Bruce (2002b) disagree. They argue that religious belief – along with religious practice – is declining. The debate about the strength of religion in

contemporary society is examined in the final section on Religion.

Day (2007) adds a useful new dimension to the debate about religion and belief in the contemporary UK. She aimed to find out what people believed in. In fact this was her opening question, deliberately leaving the interpretation of 'belief' open. She conducted qualitative research with more than 200 people, including 68 semi-structured interviews. Day was interested in why some respondents who said they were 'Christian' when offered the choices that were given in the Census weren't even sure that God existed. She classified her findings into the following categories.

- **Adherent Christians** – They declared their faith in interviews, believed in God, attended church, believed in Jesus as divine and believed that they would go to Heaven when they died.

- **Natal Christians** – They said they were Christian because they were baptised. They identified themselves as a Christian because of their birth place and family.

- **Ethnic Christians** – They saw Christianity as a way of affiliating to an ethnic group and distinguishing themselves from other ethnic groups.

- **Aspirational Christians** – They referred to Christianity in terms of being good and respectable.

Day's research contradicts the 'believing without belonging' and 'privatisation' theses. She concludes that religion, far from disappearing, is often used publicly as a marker of group identity.

## Children and religious belief

Garrod (2006) gives useful insight into children and religious belief with her analysis of a report published by the National Children's Bureau for the Joseph Rowntree Foundation in 2005. It examined children's perspectives on believing and belonging. Garrod explains how the school is one of the few places where children from different religions and ethnic backgrounds meet regularly and where friendships are formed that cut across these boundaries. The researchers devised a threefold typology to organise children's experiences:

1   **Religious identity** – which particular religion they identified with

2   **Social practice** – included formal learning about the religion and the ceremonies, public rituals and festivals linked to it

3   **Belief and spirituality** – included the children's thoughts and personal practices.

Using this typology, the children were identified as belonging to one of the five following groups:

◆   **Highly observant** – carry out religious practices; committed to beliefs

◆   **Observant** – religious observance compulsory in their lives; accepting, even if they find it boring

◆   **Occasionally participating** – enjoy religious festivals and feasts, for example

◆   **Implicit individual faith** – have personal spirituality; practise prayer, meditation and rituals

◆   **Not religious** – little interest or understanding of religion; may mock the religious.

The children were aware of group identities forming around religion and that it also meant some children were excluded. The children also use religion and ethnicity interchangeably.

# Religious membership

## What do statistics show?

In 2001, the Census collected information about religious identity. The topic was new to the Census in England, Wales and Scotland although the subject had been included in previous Censuses in Northern Ireland.

Just over three-quarters of the UK population reported having a religion. More than seven out of ten people said that their religion was Christian (72 per cent). After Christianity, Islam was the most common faith with nearly 3 per cent describing their religion as Muslim (1.6 million).

Table 4.2 The UK population by religion, April 2001

|  | Thousands | Percentage |
|---|---|---|
| Christian | 42,079 | 71.6 |
| Buddhist | 152 | 0.3 |
| Hindu | 559 | 1.0 |
| Jewish | 267 | 0.5 |
| Muslim | 1591 | 2.7 |
| Sikh | 336 | 0.6 |
| Other religion | 179 | 0.3 |
| All religions | 45,163 | 76.8 |
| No religion | 9104 | 15.5 |
| Not stated | 4289 | 7.3 |
| All no religion/ not stated | 13,626 | 23.2 |
| Base | 58,789 | 100 |

(Source: National Statistics, 2007)

## Problems with statistics

Statistics on religious membership are problematic for a number of reasons.

1   Statistics are a social construction. The process of their compilation needs to be borne in mind.

2   There are problems with the reliability. The way that statistics were recorded in the nineteenth century and today are not the same, so material is not replicable.

3   There are problems with the validity. Different religions use different criteria to record membership. It is important to think about who is compiling these statistics, and for what purpose.

4   There are problems with interpretation. It is easy to show statistics of people being members of a religion, but what does that mean in terms of religiosity? For example, people may be members of a religion beacause of a desire for companionship. Martin (1969) argues that the high church attendance figures in Victorian times were a reflection of the fact that people then had a need to be seen in church rather than being a sign of them being deeply religious.

The sociology of religion

---

**Activity 4.5**

Describe what Table 4.2 shows on religion in the UK. How might you explain these findings?

# Religious commitment

Activity 4.6

Identify and explain two means by which individuals could show their religious commitment.

In order to measure religious commitment one thing sociologists may examine is religious participation and membership. However, the reliability and validity of statistics is questionable, as outlined previously. Along with attending a place of worship, other religious practice could be to do with dress. The wearing of the *hijab* has lead to much debate in the contemporary UK, yet what this does illustrate is the way in which religion influences what we wear. There are numerous examples of religion and dress.

Activity 4.7

Give three further examples of religion commitment illustrated through dress.

Prayer could be another sign of religious commitment. So too could following a religious code of conduct.

Activity 4.8

Give three examples of religious commitment shown through following a religious code of conduct.

Religious *practice* alone, though, may not be enough to really prove religious commitment. It may not indicate *belief*. There can be belonging without believing. Thus there could be a problem in assuming that someone is committed to a religion on account of their practice alone. The other thing to consider is religious belief, although this, too, is problematic. It is difficult to assess the significance of *private* beliefs and practices. Some activities may go on in private, even if a person does not attend a church. Also, when surveys are carried out about religious belief there can be methodological problems, as Hamilton (1995)

highlights. He says that people have a propensity to say 'yes' to the type of questioning that asks whether they believe in God.

# Different types of religious institution and movements

## Early typologies

A typology classifies according to ideal types. An ideal type is a a perfect version of something, which is probably never reached. This means that things do not always fit perfectly into them. However, they can be useful to generalise from and make comparisons. When comparing religious organisations, it is helpful to consider things such as the following:

◆ membership

◆ organisational structure

◆ scale

◆ the relationship to the wider society

◆ demand on members

◆ attitude to others.

## Comparisons between religious organisations

Both Weber and Troeltsch, writing in the late nineteenth century, have differentiated between a church and a sect. Weber contrasted a church and a sect in terms of membership, for example. The church is inclusive; membership is ascribed at birth, unless you choose to opt out. Sects, however, are exclusive; people have to choose to join. However, there are strict entry criteria.

In the 1920s, Niebuhr was the first to compare the characteristics of denominations and sects in his study in the USA. One of the criteria used was the demand placed on members. With denominations there may be some small restrictions placed upon activities. Methodists, for example, are discouraged from drinking alcohol. However, the demands made by sects are more severe. Some expect their members to withdraw from society. Some sociologists find these classifications are too simplistic when they are applied to contemporary society.

# Key features of religious organisations

Niebuhr (1929) said that denominations develop from sects as they get more members, gain more respectability and gain second generation members. Denominations are seen as part way between church and sect.

According to Troeltsch (1931), sects are the opposite of churches in many respects.

Table 4.3 Key features of religious organisations

| Key features | Churches | Denominations | Sects |
|---|---|---|---|
| Membership | Universal appeal; membership is from all social classes, but particularly from the upper class | No universal appeal; membership is disproportionately from the middle class | Membership is mainly from the lower classes |
| Organisational structure | A complex hierarchy of paid officials; for example, the Roman Catholic Church has the Pope at the top of the hierarchy, with cardinals, archbishops, bishops and priests below him. Churches are bureaucratic organisations | A hierarchy of paid officials; bureaucratic organisations | No hierarchy of paid officials; many have a charismatic leader |
| Scale | Large scale; national or international | National or international | Relatively small and strongly integrated |
| Relationship to wider society | Churches accept the norms and values of society and closely related to the State, particularly in medieval times, for example | Deonominations do not identify with the State | Sects challenge society's norms and values; they are opposed to the State |
| Demand placed on members | Level of involvement varies; membership with little participation is possible. | Little pressure on members | Members may be expected to withdraw from society; deep commitment expected |
| Attitude to other religions | Claim to have a monopoly of religious truth | Do not claim a monopoly of religious truth; co-operate with other religious organisations showing tolerance of other religious beliefs | Claim a monopoly of religious truth |
| Examples | The Anglican Church, the Roman Catholic Church | Methodists, Baptists | Jehovah's Witnesses, the Amish |

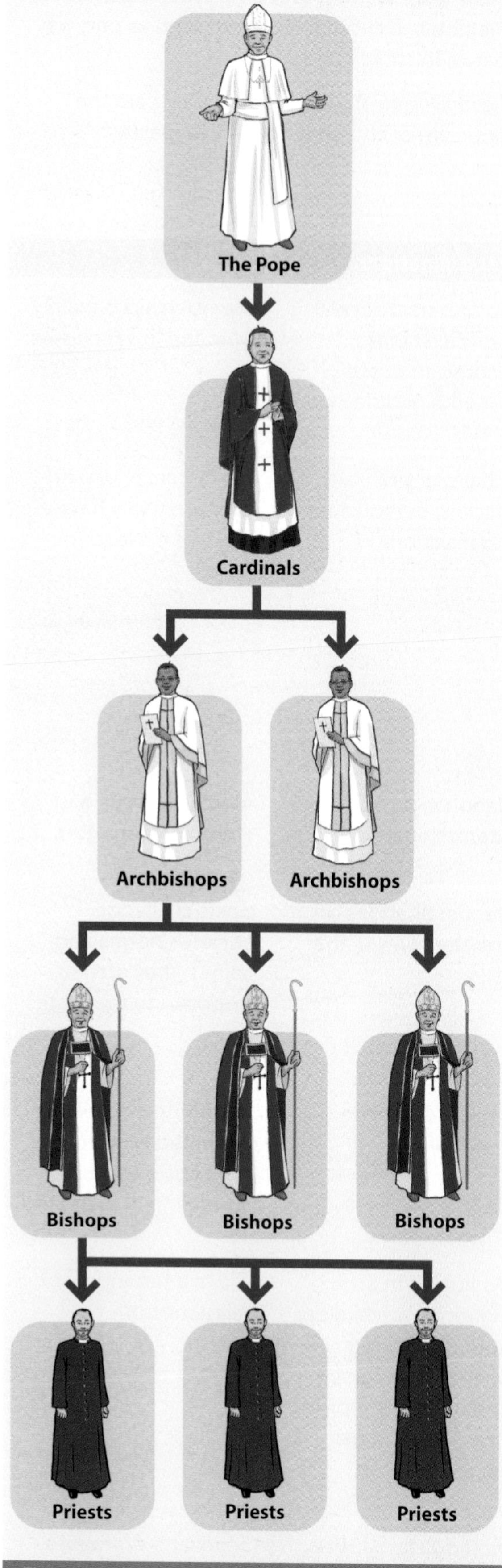
The Pope
Cardinals
Archbishops
Archbishops
Bishops
Bishops
Bishops
Priests
Priests
Priests
Figure 4.2 The structure of the Roman Catholic Church

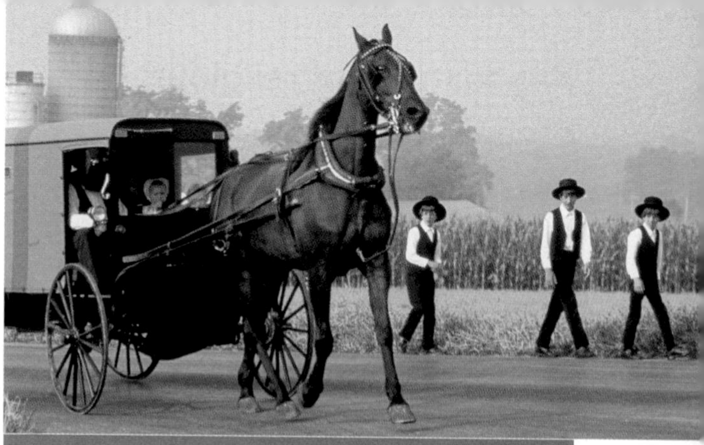
Figure 4.3 The Amish community

## Usefulness of the church-denomination-sect typology in contemporary society

### *Criticisms*

- Stark and Bainbridge (1985) say it is difficult to make the distinctions and to try to do so is confusing. For example,when did Methodism become a denomination? The characteristics drawn up in a typology are never going to be found in every religion. They go so far as saying that typologies of religions should be abandoned.
- The typology is ethnocentric, relying on Christian examples.
- The point about second generation sects becoming denominations is challenged. Aldridge (2000) claims that to contrast the features of a church with a sect is useful for analytical purposes, but criticises Niebuhr's claim that second generation sects become less dynamic.

## Are churches different now?

- There is criticism of the view that the church and the state are still closely linked. Bruce (1996), for example, argues that this relationship has fragmented.
- Religious pluralism in the contemporary UK means competition for support from the state.
- Christianity has moved on with the introduction of Alpha courses.

## Activity 4.9

1 Find out about the Alpha organisation.

2 Who is it aimed at?

3 What does it offer?

4 How many people attend the courses in the contemporary UK?

### Weblink

The Alpha organisation website (see 'Websites' page ii) has further information on their courses on the Christian faith.

# What about new religious movements?

## Activity 4.10

1 Find three facts about new religious movements.

2 Put these facts together with others found by your colleagues to make a poster.

### Weblink

INFORM is a charity set up by Eileen Barker (see 'Websites' page ii).

New religious movements (NRMs) are different from churches, denominations and sects. NRMs can be based on religious, ethical or spiritual groupings that have not yet been recognised as being mainstream. Examples of NRMs include: Unification Church (Moonies), Scientology and the Krishna Conscience. The relationships between NRMs and sects is a point of debate in the sociology of religion, as they share many common characteristics.

In the 1970s, Wilson defined characteristics of a sect as including being:

◆ voluntary

◆ exclusive

◆ a source of identity

◆ expulsion being possible

◆ based on individual conscience.

However, a number of these characteristics could equally apply to NRMs, which are voluntary (despite claims by some that they brainwash their members) and a source of identity, and there is also the possibility of being expelled from the group.

In the 1980s, Barker (1985) suggested a different way of viewing these newer movements which focused on where they originated from. For example, the Krishna Conscience has its roots in Hinduism; the Children of God has roots in Christianity.

Wallis (1984) devised a classification scheme for looking at NRMs (Table 4.4) which has become an almost ideal typology that groups and movements can be considered against, not unlike the typology used to differentiate between church/denomination/sects. Wallis differentiated groups according to their relationship to the outside world: whether they reject it, affirm it or accommodate it. He suggested three ideal types:

◆ world-rejecting

◆ world-affirming

◆ world accommodating.

It is clear that the emergence of NRMs and religious sects have altered the basic structure provided by the church/denomination/sect typology. This is probably a result of a greater diversity of religious groups in society: religious pluralism. Barter (2007) argues that the definition of a denomination used by Neibuhr is still relevant to Methodism today, which suggests that some use can still be made of this typology.

## Activity 4.11

Find three features of Methodism that match Niebuhr's characteristics.

### Weblink

The Methodist Church of Great Britain has a website which provides more information about Methodism (see 'Websites' page ii).

U2

4

The sociology of religion

215

Table 4.4 Wallis's new religious movements

| | World-rejecting | World affirming | World accommodating |
|---|---|---|---|
| Features | • Very critical of the outside world. They alone have the truth.<br>• Members must show uncritical obedience to leadership.<br>• No salvation outside of the faith.<br>• They are millenarian movements. | • Accept the world as it is. They claim to help people succeed in it and also show how to cope with the stress of individual achievement in a competitive world.<br>• Many offer expensive training<br>• They emphasise the 'true' self.<br>• They offer strategies for coping with the loneliness of modern life, emphasising self discovery authentic relationships with others. | • Usually offshoots of an existing church or denomination.<br>• Offer stronger direct experience of God, including the belief that the Holy Spirit can touch congregations and enable them to speak in tongues, which are thought to be angelic languages. |
| Examples | Hare Krishna; The Unification Church (the Moonies) | Transcendental Meditation (TM); Scientology | Neo-Pentecostalism |

# New Age movements

'The **New Age**' is a term used in relation to a number of ideas that developed in the 1980s. Drane (1999) explains the appeal of the New Age in terms of the modern scientific world being unable to satisfy people who, feeling disillusioned, try to develop their own spirituality. But exactly what is the New Age? Aldridge (2000) identifies a number of key themes, some of which are listed below.

◆ **Rejection of scientific methodology** In contrast to scientific objectivity, New Agers embrace the subjective.

◆ **Questioning of professional expertise** Science is only one belief system. Professionals are seen as having closed minds blind to the wisdom of ancient traditions and disempowering their clients.

◆ **Rejection of organised religion** New Agers reject religions with authority structures, opting for emotional intensity.

◆ **Commitment to ecology** New Agers are green and revere the Earth.

◆ **Affirmation of feminine imagery** Many New Agers dislike the way that organised religions treat women. New Age has rekindled interest in the Goddess which it uses in a feminist context.

## Spirituality

According to Heelas (1996), the central feature of the New Age is a belief in self-spirituality. This involves looking within, beyond your conscious self, to discover hidden spiritual depths.

It is possible to engage with the New Agers on different levels. People vary in terms of the degree of commitment they have. Some, for example, are deeply committed and give up their conventional lives for the counterculture. Others take it seriously, but follow it alongside their conventional lives. Finally, others take it less seriously, merely dipping into it.

Heelas and Woodhead (2005) explain why religion is giving way to spirituality. Their research shows that people prefer to call themselves 'spiritual' rather than 'religious' in contemporary times. However, they recognise the need for a clear understanding of what is meant by such a concept. They identify a cultural shift from life-as to subjective-life. Life-as involves conforming to external authority, fulfilling one's objective roles and duties and obligations. Subjective-life is about subjective experiences, living according to your inner experience; it is about passions and emotions, dreams and states of mind. They find the distinction between life-as and subjective-life useful in distinguishing between religion and spirituality; religion being bound up with life-as, and spirituality with subjective-life. Heelas and Woodhead use the term 'holistic milieu' to refer to activities that are 'spiritual but not religious' and anticipate its growth based on their findings of what is referred to as the Kendal Project.

Voas and Bruce (2006) are critical. They argue that the evidence is far from conclusive. They question the activities regarded by Heelas and Woodhead as having a spiritual dimension. They maintain that some people participating in actions such as t'ai chi and yoga would regard these as leisure activities. They also argue that there is nothing new about contemporary alternative spirituality.

Davie (1994) regards the presence of the New Age movement as a sign of the continuing significance of the sacred, but in a new form. She maintains such movements are alternatives to and rivals of conventional religiosity.

# Religious fundamentalism

Self and Starbuck (1998) explain the origin of the term **fundamentalism**. It was first used in the debates among American Protestants in the 1920s. Traditional protestant truths were re-established under Protestant fundamentalism when they were threatened by liberal interpretations. Fundamentalists demand strict adherence to their religious beliefs and practices. Davie, however, is critical of the way that the term is often used in a disparaging way insinuating fanaticism.

Fundamentalism involves the reassertion of traditional values when they are seen as under threat. Bruce (2000b) sees it as an attempt to reassert a culture threatened by modernisation. It has been used in relation to Islam where traditional patterns of belief have been challenged. Other characteristics include democracy, a high level of commitment from followers, considering religious authority and doctrine to be absolute and often being led by charismatic male leaders.

Two examples of religious fundamentalism would be:

## Christian fundamentalism in the USA

Ammerman (2003) identifies the Moral Majority, part of a revival of Christian fundamentalism in the 1970s. This was a movement which was critical of things developing in America at the time, such as divorce, internet pornography, adultery in the White House and the like. It aimed to bring God to the centre of American society.

## Islamic fundamentalism

Armstrong (2001) explains the rise of Islamic fundamentalism as a consequence of western ideas failng to work in Muslim countries. She argues that the failure of modernisation in some countries led to a reassertion of religion. She maintains that fundamentalist movements believe they are under threat from the West with its secular values so they have to fight to survive.

For Armstrong it is the failure of modernisation that has lead to fundamentalism.

### Section summary

Use the following key words to copy and complete the summary of this section. Each word should be used only once.

adherent Christians    aspirational Christians    'believing without belonging'    church    denomination    ethnic Christians    exclusive definitions    functional    fundamentalism    inclusive definitions    life-as    New Age    natal Christians    sacred    self spirituality    sect    subjective-life    world-rejecting sect    world-affirming sect    world-accommodating sect    substantive

Considering definitions of religion, the _____ is at the core of what Durkheim identifies as an essential aspect. Aldridge identifies two types of contemporary definitions: _____ which are

_____, and _____ which are _____. Sometimes people may hold religious beliefs without being a member of a religious organisation, what Davie terms _____ _____ _____. There are different types of religious organisation. Troeltsch showed that many features of a _____ were the opposite of a _____. Niebuhr described the features of _____, which fall between large-scale churches and small-scale sects. Wallis differentiated between three types of sect, according to their relationship to the outside world. These three ideal types are _____, _____, and _____. In 2007 Abby Day carried out some research the findings of which contradicted the belief without belonging thesis. She found four types of Christians_____, _____, _____ and _____.

Heelas ands Woodhead argue that there has been a cultural shift from _____ to _____. Regarding the _____ _____ which grew in the 1980s, Heelas identifies a central feature as _____ _____.

The term _____ refers to a reassertion of traditional values when they are under threat.

## Exam questions

(a) Identify and explain two ways in which religion has been defined. (17 marks)

# (ii) The role of religion in society

## Pause for thought

Figure 4.4 A funeral service

There is theoretical debate within sociology regarding the role of religion in society. Does religion promote stability and consensus, for example, or is it a source of conflict? Does religion act as a mechanism of social control that benefits particular groups in society or does it socialise people into a commonly-agreed set of norms and values? Is religion a force for social change or is it a conservative force?

This subsection not only examines the ideas of the classical theories, functionalism, Marxism, and Weberianism in relation to those debates, but it also considers their relevance in contemporary societies. Moreover, it explores the more recent postmodernist contribution to an understanding of the role of religion. Many of the examples used in this subsection are drawn from religious situations around the world, which do of course play a role in the culturally diverse UK. Some examples taken from the contemporary UK are given towards the end of the subsection.

Some sociologists do question the value of trying to apply the insights of the classical sociologists to religion in contemporary societies. Nevertheless, as Beckford (2003) points out, there is a case for them helping us to deal with important questions about religion today and apply their thinking to new issues. Beckford acknowledges, though, that it is challenging to make sense of the role of religion today. This is because of the range, diversity, and changing nature of religions in contemporary society. If religions are diverse, for example, is it possible to generalise about the role of religion per se? In addition, there is the complexity of defining what religion actually means as discussed in subsection (i).

# Functionalism

Activity 4.12

Identify and briefly explain two ways in which religion brings people together.

Subsection (i) explains how functionalists draw an organic analogy. They compare the way that institutions in society, such as the family, education and religion, are interconnected – working for society in much the same way as the organs of the body work together to keep the whole body functioning. Religion is a secondary agent of socialisation. Functionalists regard this institution in a positive light, stressing the good things it does for society and for the individuals within it. They maintain that religion is functional for society and also serves the needs of the individual. These functions are examined below.

Thus religion is one of the agencies of socialisation, although one which is arguably declining in importance as societies become more secular (less religious). It provides a set of moral beliefs and practices for people to commonly adhere to. Therefore it unites them, reinforcing what Durkheim termed 'the collective conscience'. Society needs people to hold these shared values and morals. Religion has a role in maintaining stability and consensus. It preserves the *status quo*. It provides a sense of belonging to something that the community shares. For functionalists, religion is a conservative force. It has a role in maintaining things as they are and for functionalists that is good, because it maintains stability.

Both Durkheim (1912) and Malinowski (1915) examined small-scale pre-industrial societies in order to theorise about the role of religion. Durkheim analysed Australian Aboriginal tribes. He maintained that they illustrate the central role of religion, which is to bind people together. For Durkheim, religion creates unity. He regards the world as being divided into the sacred and the profane. The sacred is religious, the profane everything else that is non-religious. Sacred things in themselves are not special. Rather it is what they represent. The sacred is symbolic. The Australian aborigines practise totemism which involves worshipping sacred objects such as animals or plants that are used in ceremonies and rituals to bring the clan together. So, for example, in respecting a creature, this becomes a totem. The creature is sacred. Durkheim maintains that in worshipping the totem, people are actually worshipping society itself because the totem symbolises the society and its values.

Activity 4.13

In pairs, identify sacred symbols in contemporary society.

According to O'Dea (1966) the essence of religion transcends everyday experience. People need it because there is:

- **contingency** – life is full of uncertainty

- **powerlessness** – we can do little to remove uncertainty in our lives

- **scarcity** – things are distributed unequally.

Religion helps people cope with these issues.

### Activity 4.14

Take each of the above points of contingency, powerlessness and scarcity and give an example of how religion helps people deal with these problems.

O'Dea (1966) moves some of the earlier functionalist views forward. For example, he does not see religion as inevitable. He also recognises that what have been seen as the functions of religion are not always fulfilled by this institution in modern societies. Another development is the acknowledgement that religion may have dysfunctions too.

## The function of religion

- Maintenance of social order: according to Durkheim, religion reinforces the solidarity of society. Religion enables social integration to take place through, for example, collective worship. For Malinowski, religion provides reassurance at potentially stressful events.

- Socialisation: functionalists argue that religion plays a crucial part in teaching the norms and values of society. Religion has a key role in maintaining value consensus. It creates and passes on the shared values of society. For example, many religions pass on the value of the sanctity of human life. Parsons examines religion in the context of the cultural system that guides peoples' behaviour. Religion is entrenched in the norms and values of society. For example, people are socialised to follow the norm to be faithful to a partner and think that extra marital affairs are wrong. This is linked to Christianity, for example, where one of the Ten Commandments says it is wrong to commit adultery.

- Provision of support: religion can be a comfort to people in their daily lives.

- Ceremonies give emotional security and a fixed point of reference when ideas that people hold conflict.

- Promotion of group goals over and above individual ones. This can be particularly important in societies that have become more individualistic.

- Provision of standards: religion can offer a code of conduct for people to follow in terms of what is appropriate.

- Provision of a sense of identity: this is highlighted with Mitchell's (2006) work. Although not writing from a functionalist perspective, in examining the religious content of ethnic identities, Mitchell shows how religion can be an important aspect of identity. She maintains that the religious dimensions of such identities have been under-theorised, arguing that religion often constitutes the fabric of ethnicity. She also points out that the religious ideas learned when we are children can help us make sense of situations later in life.

- Gives aid at times of crisis and transition from one status to another. Malinowski explains how religion can help people at stressful times in their lives, such as when people die or become ill, and when going through potentially traumatic events. According to Malinowski (1915), religion can help people to understand what could otherwise be inexplicable, such as an unforeseen disaster. It enables people to get through bad experiences. Through religious rituals social solidarity is restored as people are able to deal with the stresses that might otherwise threaten it.

## Evaluation of functionalism

- Functionalists underplay religion's dysfunctions. There are many examples of conflicts between religions and within religions.

  ◇ between Hindus and Muslims in India.

  ◇ between Protestants and Catholics in Northern Ireland.

  ◇ between Sunni and Shiite Muslims

As Beckford (2003) points out, conflict is strongest where religious and political and social divisions coincide.

- Durkheim can be criticised on methodological grounds. He studied a small number of Aboriginal groups which may well not be representative.

- Durkheim is challenged over his claim that in worshipping God, one is also worshipping society itself, which some regard as too much of a leap.

- The relevance of Durkheim in contemporary societies where religious diversity is raised.

- Malinowski is criticised for exaggerating the importance of religion in helping people deal with stress.

- Hamilton (1995) says there is still the problem of why the religious solution to problems arises only in some situations. Why is it the case that sometimes people turn to other mechanisms to deal with things rather than using religious means?

## Marxism

Marxists argue a main role of religion is to prevent social change. In agreement with functionalists, Marxists also see religion as a conservative force. However, Marx did not see that as a good thing. Religion also has an ideological role. As part of the superstructure of society, religious ideas are shaped by the infrastructure. For Marx, religion assists in sustaining an exploitative, oppressive system. It does this through spreading ruling-class ideology. Marxists, therefore, argue that religion benefits the capitalist class, giving them a mechanism to justify their position, and preventing the working class from trying to change its situation of hardship.

Activity 4.15

Consider the following verse that is in the Christian hymn 'All Things Bright and Beautiful'.

> The rich man in his castle
> The poor man at the gate
> God made them high and lowly
> And ordered their estate.

1 Who is responsible for the way society is according to the hymn?

2 How might it affect people wanting to change their situation?

In contrast to functionalists, who stress the part religion plays as an agent of socialisation which brings stability in society, for Marx, this stability comes at a cost. Religion has more of a controlling role. Religion acts as an agent of social control by justifying inequality and exploitation and keeping the working class in their place. Through ideology it promotes the idea that inequality is given and sanctioned by God. For example, under feudalism it was believed that the king had a divine right to power. This concept works well in terms of keeping a system of oppression going, because if people think that is how God meant it to be, then they are unlikely to challenge it. Religion diverts attention from the root cause of social inequality. People do not question the exploitative nature of capitalism; in this way, religion keeps people in their place. Hindus in traditional India, for example, could not change their caste, yet the rewards which go with a caste are unequal. Many religions spread the idea of reward in an after life as long as people lead a 'good' conformist life on earth. No one questions or challenges a system which is god given and where, if they are good, they will be rewarded in. In the case of Christianity, this means heaven. Marxists also point to the way that the established churches supported the *status quo*. They have traditionally had links with the upper class.

Marx regarded capitalism as an oppressive system in which the ruling class exploited the working class. The nature of work in a capitalist system is alienating. This means that people do not feel a part of the process of work. Any desire for creative fulfilment will not be met in this role. Neither do they feel any pride in what is produced. They may only assemble one part of a product and repeat that meaningless task all day and every day. A cog in the production process, the worker is also alienated from their own humanity. Religion comes out of that alienation. Marx saw it as 'the opium of the people', providing relief and comfort. Religion worked like a drug, preventing people from fighting their oppressors, the ruling class. Religion prevented the working class from seeing their problems and trying to change their situation. Religion was also considered as a 'sigh of the oppressed', 'the soul of a soulless world', giving meaning and hope to those most disadvantaged in capitalist societies.

Religion legitimates the capitalist system. According to Marx, it makes people conforming and submissive. It represses any revolutionary tendencies.

Marx saw religion as part of a ruling-class ideology that distorts the oppressive reality in order to benefit the ruling class. The workers are in a state of false consciousness because of the way that this ruling-class ideology is spread, offering false hope and solutions. Religion leads people to think that the privileges of the upper class are 'divinely ordained'; that is, they are God's will, and therefore unquestionable.

## Examples to support Marxism

◆ Leach (1988) supports Marxism in the sense of religion not benefiting ordinary people. He argues that the Church of England should be more in touch with working-class people. He points out that many bishops have been to public school and Oxbridge.

◆ Hook (1990) argues the Church could be doing more with its wealth to help the poor.

◆ There is a close alliance between political and religious elites. The British monarch is crowned by the head of the Church of England.

◆ In times of colonial rule, such as that by the British Empire, indigenous populations were encouraged to adopt Christian belief. This acted as an ideological mechanism of social control, playing a part in the prevention of radical action by the oppressed.

## Evaluation of Marxism

◆ Hamilton (1995) challenges the notion that religion is always ideological and manipulative. He points out that if that were the case it would be expected to originate from the dominant group in society. However, Marx himself recognises that religion can spring from the working class when they are alienated.

◆ Hamilton (1995) is critical of the fact that Marx did not consider that religion might be a means of preserving a sense of meaning and dignity in circumstances of difficulty.

◆ Social action theorists and postmodernists maintain that people are more aware of their position than Marxists allow for. They stress that people are not passive and can act if they choose.

◆ Critics point to the continuation of religion in societies claiming to be communist, such as China and Cuba. Following Marxist logic regarding the role of religion, religion should not be necessary in non-capitalist societies.

◆ Critics point to examples of religions being radical and promoting change, as in Central and South American countries such as Guatemala, Chile and El Salvador. These are examined further below.

## Neo-Marxism

Marxism has developed since the time of Karl Marx's writings. Neo-Marxists such as Maduro (1982) do not agree with the view that religion is always a conservative force; indeed it can sometimes be revolutionary. Neo-Marxists show that religion can be a force for social change. In this respect, Maduro deals with the criticisms directed at Marx in terms of religion preventing change. He refers to Central and South America where some Catholic priests have been active in resistance movements. This merging of Christianity and Marxism is called liberation theology. It grew as a response to poverty and ill treatment, maintaining that it should be supportive of the working class. Liberation theology saw religion as having a role in bringing about social change.

### Activity 4.16

Working in small groups, carry out research on one of the following religious leaders.

- Archbishop Romero
- Martin Luther King
- Leonardo Boff
- Mahatma Gandhi
- Archbishop Desmond Tutu
- Gustavo Gutierrez

Each group should take one leader and comment on the role of religion in relation to social change. Present your findings to the rest of the class.

**Weblink**
You can listen to a BBC interview with modern supporters of liberation theology on a BBC website (see 'Websites' page ii).

# Weberianism

## Weber

According to Weber the aim of religion is to make sense of the world. Religion deals with the problem of theodicy. It provides answers to the big questions in life, such as 'what are we here on this earth for?'. There is a psychological approach at the root of Weber's approach. This social action theory emphasises the pursuit of meaning by the individual. Weber maintained that the ideas developed within religions could influence behaviour. Religious belief could sometimes influence social action, which could challenge the *status quo*. Like Marx, Weber, maintained that groups would use religion to legitimate themselves. However, he also argued that religious beliefs could be used to challenge things too. Thus, in contrast to functionalist and Marxist thinking, religion is not always a conservative force. Rather, it can promote change and revolution. This is illustrated by Weber's classic work *The Protestant Ethic and the Spirit of Capitalism* (1958).

## Calvinist protestantism and capitalism – religion as a force for change

Weber examined the growth of capitalism and how it was encouraged by a particular form of Protestantism called Calvinism. He looked at different countries where there was the potential to develop capitalism in terms of the right economic factors. Where capitalism did flourish, Weber found that Calvinism was present. Weber explains this link in terms of what Calvinists believed and the way of life they practised. Calvinism was about working hard and living simple lives. Ostentation was frowned upon. They were not supposed to spend frivolously.

In terms of faith, Calvinists believed that a select group had been chosen by God to go to Heaven. However, they did not know who had actually been selected, so they looked for signs. They suffered from what Weber called 'salvation anxiety', that is, stress about whether they would be saved and go to Heaven, or whether they would go to Hell. What they took to be a sign has to be understood in the context of the austere lifestyle they had. A sign of being chosen came to be seen in terms of business success. Hence, they worked hard, invested in their work, rather than frittered money away, and a spirit of capitalism flourished. In this context, then, religious beliefs lead to economic change. Nevertheless, Weber did recognise that the material conditions had to be right too. Calvinist Protestantism alone would not have been enough to generate capitalism. There had to be the right economic system too.

## Charismatic leadership

Weber's emphasis on the way that people can act to bring about change is further illustrated by his reference to charismatic leadership. A charismatic leader has very persuasive qualities; people are drawn to him or her. This means that a religious group, under the guidance of a charismatic leader, can make choices about how to act rather than people merely being a product of society. In contrast to functionalists and Marxists, who see individuals as being shaped by society, a Weberian position gives more room for human action. This debate links to the broader theoretical debate between the macro and micro theorists outlined in subsection (i).

Figure 4.5 Srila Prabhupada, Charismatic leader of ISKCON, also known as the Hare Krishna movement, who died in 1977

Weber's ideas do still have relevance today. Beckford (2003) points to contemporary examples that confirm Weber's expectation that religions can both legitimise and challenge the exercise of power. He cites the Iranian revolution of 1979 where various political factions joined forces with the leading representations of the Shia Muslims to expel the Shah and form an Islamic republic.

## Evaluation of Weber

◆ Charismatic leaders – Aldridge (2000) points out that charismatic leadership can be precarious. Many movements collapse when a charismatic leader dies. Aldridge uses the death of the leader of ISKCON to illustrate this. After he died many of his remaining eleven gurus either left the movement or were expelled. This precariousness is also illustrated by the case of the deaths of over 900 members of the People's Temple in 1978 through suicide or execution. Reverend Jim Jones was the charismatic leader. He was put under increasing pressure from the authorities and he and his followers became more and more dependent upon each other. This eventually led to a mass suicide. Jones made his followers take a drink laced with cyanide.

◆ The protestant ethic and the spirit of capitalism – Parkin (1982) is critical of Weber on the grounds that capitalism was late to develop in Scotland in spite of Calvinist Protestantism being present. However, defenders of Weber point to the lack of other necessary conditions in Scotland for capitalism to develop at the time.

### Weblink
To develop your knowledge and understanding of the classical theorists you may want to do some additional reading on the relevant Wikipedia page (see 'Websites' page ii). This summarises the classical theorists.

# Religion in contemporary societies

Religious diversity is characteristic of contemporary societies. Nevertheless there is still an understanding to be gained by the classical theorists. In terms of bringing communities together in the way functionalists maintained religion did, there are still occurrences of consensus. This is often temporary though. Civil religions can bring about social integration.

## Civil religions

Bellah (1975) coined the term 'civil religion' to refer to the way that people are brought together in a secular society. His research took place in the USA where he found arguably religious qualities in rituals such as singing the national anthem at sports events. Supporters of the idea of civil religion point to, for example, the way that God is used in political speeches, how political leaders cite religious texts and the use of public buildings for worship. The idea of civil religion has been developed by functionalists in relation to national rituals. For example, people practice rituals at national events such as street parades; they wave the national flag at national sporting events. English football fans have also began singing *God Save the Queen* at matches. Such practices bring people together in the same way that traditional religious rituals did.

In spite of this application of the classical theorists today, Beckford (2004) highlights three examples of religious conflicts in the contemporary UK which he maintains are not easily understood in the light of the classical theories..

1   Pro-life activists – the use of foetal material for medical research, and anti-nuclear weapons protestors are driven by religious values.

2   Conflict over controversial movements such as the Moonies or Scientologists, where the family of followers argue that relatives have been brainwashed. Anti-cult groups campaign against cults through the media and politics.

3   Conflict between legal requirements and the religious demands of ethnic minorities, for example, the wearing of clothing.

# Postmodernism

## What is postmodernism?

◆ Postmodernism rejects the idea of there being a single universal truth. Truth is not absolute. For postmodernists truth is relative. There is a lot of uncertainty.

◆ Postmodernists will combine ideas from different belief systems. This produces hybridity. Postmodernists have a pick-and-mix of different beliefs and practices.

◆ Postmodernism does not see science and scientific ideas as the only ones having validity.

◆ Postmodernism celebrates the playful and spontaneous.

◆ Postmodernists emphasise choice and consumerism.

Postmodernists see the classical sociologists discussed above in the context of the modern age.

## How do postmodernism and religion link?

Postmodernists are interested in the resurgence of new religion. There is a broad category of new religions. They maintain that some forms of religion are growing. Globalisation has had an impact on religion in postmodern times. Western cultures are influenced by religions from across the globe. Religion becomes a product to be sold and consumed in the 'spiritual marketplace'. Religion is part of a 'pick-and–mix' culture. For example, the New Age movement mixes ideas from ancient religions with contemporary culture.

Lyon (2000) maintains that religion is still present in society; it has just relocated to the sphere of consumption. People can choose what to believe in the same way as they have choice in other areas of their lives – what kind of house they live in or what food they eat. There is increasing choice and this is just as much a feature of religion as anything else.

Beckford (2004) identifies evidence for and against the view that contemporary religious beliefs and practices can be termed 'postmodern' (Table 4.5).

Beckford concludes that, on the one hand, there is evidence of increasing individualisation, hybridity and scepticism about universal truth. But on the other, many people are active in forms of religion that still have key features of traditional religions. He argues that the term 'postmodern' is best used to refer to the fact that there are diversities in religion in contemporary societies rather than it meaning there is a particular form or style of religion.

Table 4.5 Arguments for and against postmodernism

|  | In support of postmodernism | Against postmodernism |
|---|---|---|
| **Combinations** | New Age practices demonstrate postmodern playfulness, e.g. they combine, Zen Buddhism with aromatherapy. Good choice of practices and combinations of religions. | The numbers involved in postmodern practices are very small. |
| **Religious consumerism** | At times of social change group commitments are weaker so people freer to choose a religion to suit them. They can 'pick-and-mix' from the 'spiritual supermarket'. | In reality choices are limited by what is on offer in the spiritual supermarket. |
| **Traditions** | Declining significance of religious traditions which supports the notion that religion in postmodernity abandons traditional truths. | Tradition does not necessarily disappear. It is repackaged in new forms and contexts. |

(Source: adapted from Beckford, 2004, p. 4)

Postmodernism offers incessant choice, which some find threatening.

Bruce (1996) rejects the notion of postmodern religion. He argues that contemporary religion can be understood with the concepts of church, sect, cult and denomination. The term postmodernism is unnecessary.

## Fundamentalism

The issue of fundamentalism is interesting in the light of postmodernism. One way of viewing the rise of fundamentalist movements is as a response to the rise of uncertainty postmodernism brings. In a world of incessant choice it perhaps seems unlikely that religions demanding a strict reading of the sacred text and prescriptive ideas on lifestyle would thrive. However, fundamentalism can be attractive as it offers solutions to what, for some, is a problem of choice. The lack of certainty of a postmodern world where truth is relative can be threatening. Fundamentalism gives a fixed sense of identity, offering certainty and truth.

Fundamentalism is also interesting in terms of the debate about religion and social change. Such religions are trying to change things, but they are conservative in the sense of the kind of society they are striving for, which is traditional.

## Conclusion

It appears that thinking in terms of the binary oppositions presented in the introduction, such as religion being a source of conflict versus consensus, is not that helpful. It is not a clear cut case – an 'either/or' – in contemporary societies. As Beckford (2004) maintains, today religion is rarely a source of complete consensus or conflict. Nevertheless, in some communities religion is still very important, bringing its members together. However, in other circumstances religion provokes conflict. The point is there is a diversity of religions in contemporary societies, and this is certainly true of the contemporary UK, making it difficult to generalise across different faiths.

### Section summary

Use the following key words to copy and complete the summary of this section below. Each word should be used only once.

alienation    collective conscience    charismatic    functions    hybridity    ideology
opium of the people    profane    relative    sacred    salvation anxiety    theodicy
totemsim    value consensus    liberation theology

According to functionalists, there is _____ _____ in society. People have a shared moral order, what Durkheim terms a _____ _____. Religion contributes to society as a whole with its numerous _____ of, for example, maintaining social order, socialisation and promotion of support. Durkheim divides the world into the _____, which is the religious world, and the _____, or non-religious. His work on _____ illustrates the worshipping of the sacred.

For Marx, religion comes out of the _____ experienced by the working class in a capitalist society. Marx saw religion as the _____ ___ ____ _____, acting like a drug to dull the pain of oppression. Religion is part of the ruling class's _____, used to legitimate their position. Neo-Marxists, however, point to some radical leaders trying to change the lives of the poor. The part played by religion in social change is illustrated in _____ _____ , which combines Marxism with Christianity.

Weber shows how religion deals with the problem of _____ , giving explanations to questions such as the meaning of life. He highlights the role of religion in bringing about change in some circumstances. His work on Calvinist protestants experiencing a feeling of _____ _____ shows how, given the right conditions, people can take action. There are examples of leaders with particular qualities who people are drawn to. Weber termed them _____ leaders, who can bring people together with shared meanings of the world, and act accordingly.

Postmodernists see truth as _____ . People pick-and-mix their religious beliefs, dipping in and out of religions, which gives rise to _____ .

## Exam practice

**(a)** Identify and explain two ways in which religion acts as a form of social control.

(17 marks)

**(b)** Outline and evaluate the view that the role of religion in society is to promote stability and consensus.

(33 marks)

# (iii) Religion and social position

## Pause for thought

1   Who do you think are the most religious people in the contemporary UK?

2   Why are some groups more likely to be religious than others?

3   Who do new religious movements and New Age movements appeal to?

Figure 4.6 Sunday service

227

# Religion and social position

In order to explore trends in religiosity, sociologists examine religiosity according to ethnicity, gender, social class and age. However, in making generalisations about religion and social position, it is important to bear in mind that ethnicity, gender, social class and age are not homogeneous categories. For example, regarding ethnicity,.some of those ethnic groups will be middle class, some working class, some men and women, some old, some young. These are divisions *within* as well as *between* the social positions identified. Nevertheless, sociologists need to have some means of classifying and the following social positions are useful to work with.

Another thing to consider is the focus of subsection (i) , which examined the definition of the concept itself. Statistical evidence on the extent to which different ages, ethnic groups, men and women, and different social classes are 'religious' – and the type of religion they adhere to – needs to be regarded with caution. Statistics are a social construction and the way in which they have been compiled needs to be taken into account. For example, in surveys, when people identified with a particular religion, were they religious participants or religious believers, or indeed both? Does saying they are of a particular religious faith have any consequence on their lives?

The 2001 Census was the first census in the UK to ask about people's religion. This was a voluntary question. It asked 'What is your religion?' giving the following options – 'none'; 'Christian'; 'Buddhist'; 'Hindu'; 'Jewish'; 'Muslim'; 'Sikh'. There was also an option to write in 'any other religion'.

Before we look at patterns of religiosity and social characteristics, there are a number of general concepts that might be used to explain religiosity across these characteristics. Weber (1958), for example, explained the appeal of sects to **marginalised** groups. Marginalisation can be experienced by people of a particular class, ethnicity, age and gender. This could be in the form of poverty. However, the concept of **relative deprivation** has also aided sociologists' understanding of religious patterns. Glock (1964) used this to show that it is not necessary to be poor in order to feel deprived. Deprivation is relative to those around you. A sense of

oppression could be significant, whether it is patriarchal, or racism, ageism, class-based, or a combination of these structures that lead people to religion. A lack of self esteem could be another general factor affecting all categories. **Socialisation** is also significant for all groups. For example, it is possible that:

◆ different ethnic groups socialise their young differently in terms of passing on religious values

◆ men and women are socialised differently

◆ the cultural practices of working-class and middle-class people are different in terms of religion

◆ peer groups are socialising particular age groups differently.

# Ethnicity

Key point – Ethnic minorities tend to be more religious than the dominant ethnic group in the UK.

Tables of data need to be interpreted with care. This activity is designed to make you be careful when reading tables.

1 Using Figure 4.7 decide which of the following statements are true or false.

2 In addition to Figure 4.7, what other information might be useful in order to generalise about ethnicity and religion?

True or false?
1 97 per cent of white people in Great Britain are Christian.
2 3 per cent of black people in Great Britain are Christian.
3 91 per cent of Sikhs in Great Britain are Asian.
4 97 per cent of Christians in Great Britain are white.
5 10 per cent of Muslims in Great Britain are white.
6 20 per cent of Buddhists in Great Britain are Chinese.

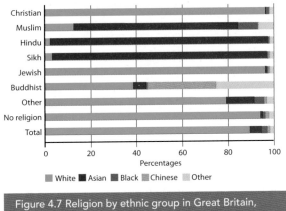

Figure 4.7 Religion by ethnic group in Great Britain, April 2001

(Source: National Statistics Online)

In making generalisations about the composition of a religious group in terms of ethnicity, it is also useful to know the ethnic breakdown of the population as a whole.

The 2001 Census had a change from the previous one in terms of the ethnic categories given. People were able to tick 'mixed' for the first time.

In terms of ethnicity and religious identity, white Christians are by far the largest group with 36 million people, that is, nearly seven out of ten people, describing their ethnicity as 'white' and their religion as 'Christian'. The majority of black people (71 per cent) and people from mixed ethnic backgrounds (52 per cent) also identified themselves as Christian.

The number of people attending Christian churches has been declining since the 1950s. This is examined in subsection (iv) on secularisation. Nevertheless, this overall decline has been slowed as the UK has become more ethnically diverse. In particular there has been a growth of churches with mainly black congregations. In 2005, Christian Research, a religious think-tank, found that 17 per cent of churchgoers were of an ethnic minority background and that 44 per cent of London churchgoers were black.

Black Christianity can be explained in terms of an attempt to gain control where there is a lack of power in society. Beckford (2000) maintains that black evangelicalism can give people a sense of independence and offer hope. It can also help black people become wealthier as black Pentecostalism portrays wealth positively, as something to aim for.

Regarding other religions, the next largest group was Pakistani Muslims. Some faiths have a more

Table 4.6 The UK population by ethnic group, 2001-02

| | UK population | |
| --- | --- | --- |
| | Total population (%) | Minority ethnic population (%) |
| White | 92.4 | n/a |
| Mixed | 0.8 | 11.0 |
| Asian or Asian British | | |
| Indian | 1.7 | 21.7 |
| Pakistani | 1.3 | 16.7 |
| Bangladeshi | 0.5 | 6.1 |
| Other Asian | 0.4 | 5.7 |
| Black or black British | | |
| Black Caribbean | 1.0 | 13.6 |
| Black African | 0.9 | 12.0 |
| Black other | 0.1 | 1.5 |
| Chinese | 0.3 | 4.2 |
| Other | 0.6 | 7.4 |
| Not stated | 0.2 | n/a |
| All minority ethnic population | 7.6 | 100.0 |
| All population | 100 | n/a |
| Unweighted base – 100% | 361644 | 25049 |

(Source: Office for National Statistics, Annual Local Area Labour Force Survey, 2001–2)

1 What proportion of the total population in the UK in 2001 were:

(a) white  (b) of an ethnic minority?

2 Of those ethnic minority groups, what proportion were:

(a) Asian or British Asian  (c) Chinese

(b) Black or black British  (d) other?

U2

4

The sociology of religion

homogeneous ethnic following. For example, 91 per cent of Sikhs were Indian and 97 per cent of Jews were white. If you take ethnic groups as a starting point, and then look at the religious composition of these, again some are more homogeneous than others. The most diverse ethnic group in terms of religion were Indians. A more homogeneous ethnic group in terms of religion were Pakistanis and Bangladeshis – 92 per cent of each was Muslim.

What people say they are in terms of their religion does not tell us anything about the level of religious belief, whether people belong to a religious organisation or how much they practise religion.

## The relationship between religious and ethnic identities

The religion of ethnic minorities in the UK needs to be understood in a historical context. After the Second World War people migrated to the UK from Asia and the Caribbean, bringing their religion with them. In many cases, their religion has been passed down to their children. Religion gave people an important sense of identity as they adjusted to a new country. It brought new immigrants together in a community.

Mitchell (2006) argues the *religious* dimensions of *ethnic* identities have been under-researched. She believes there has been a tendency to characterise religiously demarcated groups as ethnic groups, for example Jewish people are considered by some as a religious group or as an ethnic group. Mitchell contends that in many contexts there is a two-way relationship between religion and ethnicity, that the two stimulate each other rather than ethnicity being at the centre. Identity becomes simultaneously informed by religious as well as ethnic content.

## Muslims in the UK

The British Muslim population has a relatively large number of young people and smaller number of elderly people compared with other religions.

Evidence from the 2001 Census shows that over 33 per cent of British Muslims are under 15 years of age, and 50 per cent are under 25. Jacobson (1998) found that Islam is an important source of identity for young British Pakistanis. Religious identity can be a defensive identity in a racist society. In terms of Mitchell's argument about the relationship between ethnicity and religion, it seems that the religious element of young British Muslims has become prominent over ethnicity. Samad (2006) maintains that for this group there has been a move from an *ethnic* identity where Islam is implicit, to a *Muslim* identity in which ethnicity is implicit. Samed links this to the loss of ethnic languages and the growing strength of a predominantly British identity.

Akhtar (2005) examines why young Muslims are turning to religion, suggesting that it offers a sense of belonging and solidarity. He uses the concept of 'symbolic exclusion'. If young Muslims do not feel part of a wider culture, then they can get that sense of belonging from religion instead. He also draws on the notion of 'othering' maintaining that Muslims have been 'othered' by the West. Akhtar suggests that religion can also provide a means of political mobilisation for individuals who feel constrained in some way by their circumstances. What has happened, though, is that radical groups have turned religion to their own advantage by uniting all the disparate issues faced by Muslims across the globe and building up a simple split of oppressors and victims. Thus oppressive regimes and social, economic and symbolic exclusion are merged together. They are all put under the same banner of discrimination against Islam from 'the West'. Akhtar argues that after 9/11 and the wars in Afghanistan and Iraq, radical Islam groups were able to utilise this return to religion by pushing the division between 'the West' and 'Muslim' to explain all Muslim grievances.

## Gender

Key point – Women are more religious than men.

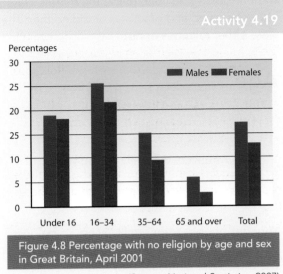

Percentages

Figure 4.8 Percentage with no religion by age and sex in Great Britain, April 2001

(Source: National Statistics, 2007)

Look at Figure 4.8.

1 What does it show in general regarding gender and having no religion?

2 What percentage of males and females had no religion in 2001?

3 Which age group of males and females has the largest percentage with no religion?

# Women are more religious than men

Davie (1994) shows that women make up the majority of Christians in England, Northern Ireland and, especially, Scotland. Women attend religious institutions more often and express greater belief. However, within religious organisations, men tend to be in more senior positions right across the board. Men hold more positions of power and authority. Women and men also see God differently. Davie (1994) found that women see God in terms of love, comfort and forgiveness, but for men God is more about power and control.

## Explanations for women's involvement in religion

◆ Different socialisation – it could be argued that females are socialised into gendered norms compatible with religion, such as, submissiveness, obedience, passivity. They are also taught to be more nurturing.

◆ Gendered roles – women have more time for religious activities because they spend less time in paid employment. Their childcare role also fits well with religion.

◆ Caring roles and biology – Davie (1994) maintains that women reflect more on the meaning of life because they are closer to birth and death.

◆ A compensation for oppression in society – De Beauvoir (1953) argues that women turn to religion as a compensation for their lower status in a patriarchal society.

# Religion and patriarchy

De Beauvoir (1953) wrote what has become a classic feminist text, *The Second Sex*. She regards the relationship between women and religion in a similar way to how Marx sees class and religion: religion is a means of control. For Marx, the upper class was the oppressor; for de Beauvoir it is men. Religion is patriarchal. Religion also compensates women for their suffering with the promise of a better existence in heaven.

El Sadawi (1980) is a Muslim feminist. She argues that it is not religion *per se* that has oppressed women, although it has played a part. Rather it is the patriarchal system at large that is the problem. Men have misinterpreted religious texts and have abused their positions of power. As monolithic religions grew, so too did the religious oppression of women. This has to be understood in the context of the societies at the time which were class ridden and patriarchal. You should also refer to pages 30–41 and 56–65 for useful and relevant examples.

Samad (2006) shows how young Muslim women use feminism in an Islamic framework to improve their situation. He contrasts scriptural Islam with the more oral traditions and customs, explaining how young Muslim women are able to use what is in the texts to argue that they have a right to marry who they want. They also resist family pressure on how they should dress by re-interpreting what is written in the texts about modesty in order to adapt Western fashions. This can be seen today with the hybrid aspect of young Muslims' clothing. For example, a young woman may wear a pair of jeans and shoes with a tunic style top and head covering. She is being modest, her body is covered, but it is not

U2
4

The sociology of religion

the outfit her grandparents may have chosen because of the western fashion element.

The issue of Muslim women wearing a veil has provoked some debate. Some western feminists have interpreted it in what others would criticise as an ethnocentric way, seeing it as oppressive to women because they are not free to dress as they choose. Others, however, regard it as liberating. They are not subjected to the male gaze forced upon other women. It can also be regarded as an assertive act in terms of maintaining an ethnic and gender identity. Ahmed (1992) points out that the veil means that Muslim women can practise modern ways but still retain their modesty.

## Social class

> Key point – The middle class are more religious than the working class

The relationship between religion and social class has become more fragmented in the contemporary UK. However, there are still links. Because of the relationship between the Church and the State, churches have traditionally appealed to the upper class. Denominations have members from all social classes. However, their conservatism can appeal to the middle class in particular. Denominations are varied, though, so it is difficult to make generalisations.

Weber's notion of sects appealing to marginalised groups who do not gain status from other aspects of their lives is relevant to the working class. However, some sects do have a middle class following. It depends on the sect, but there does seem to be a predominantly specific class in each sect. In terms of middle-class sects, these followers can experience relative deprivation. Relative deprivation can also help explain the appeal of Islamic fundamentalism to those who have moved up the social ladder. Bruce (2002b) argues that people selectively remember a past where communities were strong and blame western modernity for their current situation. Although they are materially better off, they feel relatively deprived. Davie (1994) found that the working class are less likely to go to church than the middle class, but may still believe in God. Working class 'believe

without belonging'. She found the middle class either believed and practised or did neither. They were either religious or not.

## Age

> Key point – The young are less religious across religions as a whole. However, Muslims have a relatively strong young following.

Younger people are more likely not to belong to any religion. Among 16–34 year olds in the UK, 23 per cent said they had no religion compared with less than 5 per cent of people aged 65 and over (National Statistics Online). This reflects the growing trend towards secularisation. It is important to remember, however, that not all people who *believe* in a religion *belong* to one. It is also useful to consider different religions in turn in relation to age. It might be the case that specific religions have a younger age profile.

The difference in the age profiles of different religions needs to be considered in terms of the different ethnic make up of different religious groups. Christian and Jewish people are mainly white and have lived in the UK all their lives or migrated before the Second World War, which explains their older age profile. Muslims, Hindus and Sikhs are mostly south Asian. Their younger age profile can be explained in terms of a relatively recent migration to the UK and the fact that they have more children.

Voas (2005) examines the relationship between children's religious beliefs and practices and their parents'. They are critical of the notion that there is what Davie terms belief without belonging today. They argue that, in the UK, evidence shows belief to be declining at a faster rate than attendance. In terms of the impact of parents, they found that two religious parents have a 50:50 chance of passing their belief on to their children. Where there is one religious parent, the children are only half as likely to believe as those families with two believers. Finally, where neither parent is religious it is likely that the children will not be either. They did find, though, that religious parents tend to have more children.

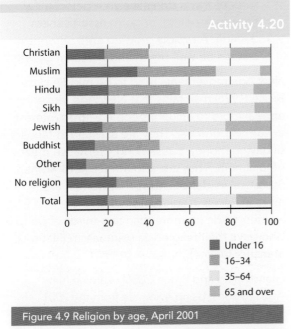

Figure 4.9 Religion by age, April 2001

(Source: National Statistics Online)

Look at Figure 4.9.

1 Which religious group has the youngest age profile of all religious groups in the UK?

2 Which two religious groups have the oldest age profile?

3 What explanations could there be for these trends?

Schools also affect children's religious beliefs. In this environment, children may meet children of different faiths as well as being taught about different religions in the classroom.

Research carried out in 2005 on children and religion, published by the National Children's Bureau for the Joseph Rowntree Foundation, is outlined in subsection (i).

Write a summary in no more than a hundred words of what this research showed on children, religion, and belonging

# New religious movements /New Age movements

It is difficult to determine precise figures on new religious movements. Not all of them have formal registers. Some have their headquarters based abroad, making access difficult from the UK. What attempts to classify them do show, however, is that the membership of most new religious movements is young.

New religious movements can appeal to people who feel deprived in some way,

Weber offers an early explanation for the appeal of sects. He argues they appeal to marginalised groups who do not gain status from other aspects of their lives. This can explain the appeal of sects to women who lack power in a patriarchal society, or to working-class people exploited and alienated at work. Given the variety of sects today, it is difficult to generalise about all of them. Subsection (i) identified different types of sects in terms of Wallis's distinction between world-rejecting, world-affirming and world-accommodating sects. Weber's idea of the appeal to marginalised groups is particularly applicable to some world-rejecting sects. However, it is important to bear in mind that not all marginalised people turn to sects. Many underprivileged groups do not join them. Indeed some are repelled by them; some new religious movements have more appeal to white, middle-class, well-educated young people.

In terms of social class, therefore, there are some new religious movements that are predominantly working class in membership and others that are middle class. Glock's (1964) notion of *relative* deprivation could explain a middle-class feeling of lack of fulfilment. The deprivation need not be economic. Sects can give people a sense of meaning in their lives. It could also be significant as to whether they are world-affirming or rejecting. Scientology, a world-affirming new religious movement, has a well-off membership. So, too, do New Age movements. Barker (1999) maintains that new religious movements are mainly white in terms of ethnicity. Regarding age, Bruce (1995) says that it is the world-rejecting movements, in particular, that appeal to the young. He explains this in terms of disillusionment with youth movements of former decades and a desire for a different path to salvation.

## The New Age

The New Age prioritises the human self, which it sees as essentially good. It tries to strip away the residues of any bad experiences and free the 'self within'. The point of New Age beliefs and practices is self improvement and self-gratification.

Bruce (2002b) explains the popularity of New Age movements in the following way.

◆ They solve the problem of cultural diversity – in a culturally diverse world it would be wrong to insist that one religion is right, so it is better to be a relativist. We can all believe in different 'truths' that are equally valid.

◆ The New Age mirrors the modern emphasis on the right to choose – 50 years ago people accepted the experts' view of 'good' taste, but now personal taste is valued along with individualism.

◆ The New Age empowers the consumer – many New Agers express interest by buying ideas and therapies. People decide what beliefs and practices to buy into in much the same way as they decide which holiday or washing machine to buy.

◆ The New Age interest in personal therapy fits with the modern obsession with self-improvement and pampering. People today are not so accepting of what they have in society. Bruce explains this in terms of changing things. For example, if you are fat, go on a diet, exercise, have cosmetic surgery. If you don't like your personality, have counselling, or go to assertiveness training. A rapidly growing area of tourism centres on well-being and personal growth.

New Age movements tend to be middle class. Bruce (1996) maintains that New Age movements appeal more to affluent people with an interest in human potential. They are satisfied in terms of having money, but seeking alternative means of fulfilment. They are also attractive to women. Statistical evidence shows that women are more involved in spiritualism than men. In 2001 women made up more than two-thirds of people who gave their religion as spiritualism (National Statistics Online).

Glendinning and Bruce (2006) examine New Age religions. Using evidence from the 2001 Scottish Social Attitudes Survey, they found that women were much more likely to use alternative practices than men. Middle-aged middle-class women were the most likely to use them. However, these practices did not necessarily have a spiritual dimension. Women with more advanced educational qualifications were more likely to use complementary or alternative medicines, yoga and meditation; things associated with personal well-being. Younger women with few qualifications were more likely to use horoscopes, fortune telling astrology and tarot cards.

## Section summary

Use the following key words to copy and complete the summary of this section. Each word should be used only once.

> belief without belonging    marginalised    othered    patriarchal
> relative deprivation    symbolic exclusion    socialisation

Religiosity is affected by ethnicity, class, gender and age. These social groups may experience different patterns of _____ from an early age, thereby having different experiences of religion.

Some people, who turn to religion, whilst not poor in absolute terms, may have a feeling of _____ _____. Such groups feel _____ by the wider society. Young people have turned to sects as a result of this. It has also been the case for some ethnic groups. Akhtar, for example, explains that young Muslims can experience _____ _____. He argues that they have been _____ by the West. Religion and gender has been explored in the contest of a _____ society, whereby women are oppressed by men. While women on the whole are more religious than men, it is the latter that hold senior positions in religious organisations.

Working class people are more likely to have _____ _____ _____, than the middle class who are more likely to either believe *and* belong or do neither.

Exam practice

(a) Identify and explain two reasons why young people are less religious than older people.
(17 marks)

(b) Outline and evaluate the view that some ethnic groups are more religious than others in the contemporary UK. (33 marks)

# (iv) The strength of religion in society

## Pause for thought

1   What signs are there of a general decline in religiosity in contemporary society?

2   What signs are there of a growing interest in spirituality?

3   Which religions are growing in the contemporary UK?

Figure 4.10  An alternative use for a church?

## Secularisation

The sections on religion of this book have examined:

◆   the problem of defining and measuring religion

◆   the role of religion in society

◆   religion and social position.

### Activity 4.22

In small groups take one of the above points and identify how it might be relevant in examining secularisation? Discuss with the rest of the class.

Subsection (i) examined inclusive and exclusive definitions of religion. Depending on how you define religion could produce different conclusions regarding secularisation.

## Definition: Secularisation

**Secularisation** broadly refers to the process by which religion is declining. It is the idea that religion is becoming less important in society.

---

Key ways of measuring religion are to consider:

• religious practice

• religious attendance

• religious belief.

Take each of the above points and explain how you would investigate it as a sociologist in order to see whether secularisation was occurring.

---

In Activity 4.23 you have been **operationalising** the concept of secularisation; in other words, making it measurable. As there is no agreement over the concept of secularisation, it is not easy to operationalise. What sociologists do is use *indicators* in order to measure whether secularisation has taken place. However, different sociologists have different views on what the indicators are. In other words, there is some disagreement about what should be regarded as a sign of secularisation having, or not having, occurred. It is a complex debate. The evidence of what are taken as signs for and against secularisation is listed below.

## Evidence for the secularisation of society

◆ Church attendance and membership figures show an overall decline.

◆ The process of modernisation is leading to religious decline.

◆ The Church is less involved in the wider society today.

◆ Religious pluralism is prevalent in contemporary society. There is no longer a single religion which some regard as essential to a truly religious society.

◆ The New Age with its lack of commitment and depth.

## Evidence against the secularisation of society

◆ Problems with statistical evidence on religion – there are problems of reliability in that, over time, one is not comparing like with like, and of validity in that they may not reflect what they claim.

◆ Religious growth – the rise of non-Christian religions and non-traditional Christian religions.

◆ The growth of new religious movements and New Age religions.

◆ The presence of religious belief in contemporary society.

Table 4.7 Sociologists for and against secularisation

| Sociologists in support of secularisation | Sociologists against secularisation |
|---|---|
| Wilson (1976) | Martin (1978) |
| Bruce (1995; 2002) | Davie (1994; 2000) |
| | Stark (1999) |
| | Heelas (1996; 2005) |

## Evidence indicating the secularisation of society

Two main proponents of the secularisation thesis are Wilson (1976) and Bruce (1995; 2002). They maintain that there is a growing indifference to religion.

## Church attendance and membership

Research shows a decline in attendance and membership of religious institutions. Research conducted by the Christian charity Tearfund endorses this view.

> This secular majority presents a major challenge to churches. Most of them – 29.3 million – are unreceptive and closed to attending church; churchgoing is simply not on their agenda.
>
> (Source: *Churchgoing in the UK* – Tearfund, 2007 (www.tearfund.org)

The British Social Attitudes Survey (2006) found a declining trend in the percentage of people who said they belonged to a religion and attended services. In 1964, 74 per cent said that they belonged to a religion, but this fell to 55 per cent in 1983 and fell still further to 31 per cent in 2005.

Research has pointed out that, except for Pentecostal churches, church congregations are composed mainly of older people. This could mean that if churches fail to attract the young, then they will eventually die out.

### Evaluation

It is straightforward to show a long-term decline in participation in church in the UK. What is less straightforward is to interpret what that decline means. Some would say that because fewer people are going to church, therefore religion is declining. However, does a higher church attendance in the past mean that those people going to church were necessarily more 'religious'? Conversely, do fewer people in church today mean that people are necessarily less religious? It is not reasonable to judge whether secularisation is taking place on account of a decline in religious participation, even if the figures on attendance and membership could be taken at face value.

### Activity 4.24

1  Refer back to the different definitions of religion in subsection (i). Which one is more likely to lead to the view that secularisation has taken place? Why?

2  In pairs identify and explain two possible ways of measuring whether secularisation has taken place.

### Activity 4.25

Statistics are a social construction. Think about how church attendance statistics and memberships might have been compiled in the past. Consider how the same information is collected today.

Remind yourself what the following concepts mean:

• reliability

• validity

• representativeness.

Now identify and explain why there might be problems of reliability, validity and representativeness in church attendance statistics.

### Problems

The way that statistics are compiled needs to be considered. Different churches have used different methods. For example, is it the number of people entering the church? Can the same people be included more than once? Are special services such as weddings, baptisms and confirmations included? The people compiling the statistics might have an agenda. For example, if they are put together by a religious organisation, they may need to make their numbers look high.

Higher church attendance in the past may not necessarily mean that people went to church for 'religious' reasons.

A different interpretation of the statistics is given below in the section on evidence against secularisation.

## The processes of modernisation

### Activity 4.26

1  Give an example of how religion might have been used in pre-modern societies where there was a lack of control over events. To prompt you, you might think about the weather, food, sex or childbirth,

2  Using that same example, how is science used in modern times?

U2

4

The sociology of religion

237

Rationalisation was a feature of modernity. There is an argument that rational thought based on science would replace religious thought based on faith in the modern world. The classical sociologists believed that secularisation was an inevitable outcome of modernisation. Weber, for example, thought that increased rationality would lead to a decline in religious belief. Wilson (1976) sees science as important in the rise of secularisation. Bruce (2002b) stresses the rationalisation process. Technology means that people are more in control over the natural world, so do not rely on superstition to give reassurance. However, superstitions do still prevail in modern times. Bruce (2002b) does not contend that increased rationality and less superstition alone produced a decline in Christianity. Rather, it is the combination of a number of processes that emerge with modernity that counts, such as the structural and social differentiation and societalisation outlined below. Rationalisation is important for Bruce, in terms of the increase in routines and procedures it brings.

Modernisation has lead to economic growth. Whereas religion used to help the poor cope with their situation, if people are better off, Bruce (2002b) also argues, there is less need to invest in religion.

### Evaluation

Davie (2000) questions the assumption that secularisation is a necessary part of modernisation. A different view of secularisation is that it is not a universal process.

Postmodernists claim we are now in a time where no one belief system is adequate. They believe there is no absolute truth. Truth is relative. It may have a religious base for some, and a scientific base for others.

## The church is less involved in the wider society today

Bruce (1995) points out that the Church does not have the power that it used to have in relation to society as a whole. The Church and the State are no longer so closely interlinked, so the Church does not have the political influence that it once had. Wilson (1976) argues that religion has lost its influence on people's values. The Church, then, has become disengaged.

1 Identify and briefly explain two functions of religion in the past that have since declined.

2 What kind of community events would the church have been key to in the past?

3 Other than religion, which other agencies of socialisation influence peoples' outlook in the contemporary UK? Illustrate with examples.

### Structural differentiation

This refers to the way that the Church has lost the range of functions that it used to perform. For example, education is now fulfilled by an education system. The Health Service has taken over the Church's caring role.

### Social differentiation

Bruce (1995) points out that in a modern society there is geographical and social mobility. Communities are more fragmented and it becomes harder to sustain religious values as people are introduced to new ways of thinking. Religion becomes a matter of choice rather than being something that is taken for granted.

### Societalisation

Both Wilson (1976) and Bruce (1995; 2002) refer to this process whereby social life becomes fragmented and is no longer centred on the church. Communities decline and religion is no longer a focal point. Community-based activities organised by the church decrease as people turn to other sources.

### Evaluation

Not all sociologists agree with the notion of religious disengagement in contemporary society. People still turn to religion in order to explain seemingly meaningless events such as an early death or pain-inducing illness. Also, it is argued that the Church still has a voice on key debates, such as the age of consent, the use of contraception, abortion, and homosexuality.

Since the 1980s, there has been a privatisation of what were formerly national institutions. This could lead to a need for voluntary organisations, of which churches could be part, playing a more central role in providing services. An example of religion getting involved in economic, political and social life – as opposed to disengaging from it – is Employment Forum UK, which has been involved with employment and regeneration initiatives in the community.

### Weblink

Access the Employment Forum UK website (see 'Websites' page ii) for further details of their work.

## Religious pluralism

Religious pluralism refers to the fact that there is no single faith in contemporary societies. This presents an interesting debate, as some sociologists cite religious pluralism to support the argument for secularisation; they regard a society with a single faith as essential to a truly religious one. However, other sociologists use religious pluralism to argue against secularisation, as outlined in the text below.

There clearly is religious diversity in contemporary societies. Wilson (1976) argues that religion therefore no longer unifies people in society. He sees the growth of new religious movements as evidence of secularisation because he regards them as a response to a society that has no prominent religious values. They are what he considers to be the 'last outpost of religion' in a secular society, predicting that their appeal would diminish. Bruce (2002b) also interprets the growth of sects as supporting secularisation because they undermine the Church's authority on religious truth. Bruce explains the growth in religion of ethnic minorities in terms of the notions of cultural transition and cultural defence.

◆ **Cultural transition**: religion helps people when they arrive in the UK as it gives them contacts to get established. However, Bruce argues this need will decline with new generations of British-born ethnic minorities, thereby supporting secularisation.

◆ **Cultural defence**: religion is a form of identity that can become particularly pronounced when it is under threat. This has been the case between Protestants and Catholics in Northern Ireland.

### Evaluation

It is also possible to see religious pluralism as evidence against secularisation. The rise in new religious movements can be a sign of a religious revival.

## What about the growth in interest in New Age movements?

Activity 4.28

Choose a new religious movement. Present a case for it either supporting or refuting secularisation.

Bruce (2002b) argues that the growth of new religious movements actually makes little difference to the spread of secularisation because he argues that most involvement is shallow. People might dabble in things or take a mild interest in something – reading a few books or listening to a few lectures – but, he maintains, that's as far as it goes. For Bruce, this is far from a religious revival. For example, he stresses that the most popular New Age movements are not to do with magic or the occult, or with the Eastern philosophies. Most New Agers are into relaxation techniques, yoga, massage and meditation. Bruce is dismissive of the significance of these activities, seeing them as an extension of the doctor's surgery, the beauty salon and the gym. His point seems valid when people are keen to take a yoga class because their favourite celebrity is doing it and looks fit, or when they are more concerned with the colour of their outfit than any spiritual enlightenment.

Figure 4.11 Evidence of or a challenge to secularisation?

U2

4

The sociology of religion

239

Bruce challenges the claims of some New Age movements to be 'radical'. He gives the example of the anxious merchant banker, who learns to meditate and goes for a regular shiatsu massage, but does not chance his life and become an eco warrior. He just becomes a happier merchant banker!

# Evidence not indicating the secularisation of society

## A different interpretation of statistical evidence

The section above giving evidence for secularisation provided statistical evidence showing a decline in church attendance and membership. Some sociologists are critical of what higher participation rates in the past actually tell us in terms of the level of religiosity then. Martin (1969), for example, attributes the relatively high church attendance figures in Victorian times to an expression of middle-class respectability. People felt the need to be seen at church. Thus the validity of those figures could be problematic in terms of what they actually present a picture of. They may be fine in giving a picture of attendance, although even this is disputable because of the different recording methods, but they are not a valid picture in themselves of religiosity.

Stark (1999) argues that religion is not in decline because it was never strong in the first place.

Activity 4.29

1  How many clubs or groups are/were you (or a famly member or friend, if you do not belong to any yourself) a member of? Choose one of them. What would your membership, together with that of the other club members, tell an outsider looking at that club? How might any conclusions they draw be problematic?

2  Why might membership of a religious organisation alone be problematic as a way of determining whether secularisation has taken place?

Stark asserts that we are now *more* religious than before. A major critic of Bruce, Stark challenges what higher participation rates in the past really mean. He disputes Bruce's claim that the Middle Ages was a strongly religious period of history. Stark maintains that historical evidence shows that people were generally indifferent to religion. When they went to church, he claims, they went there unwillingly and behaved disrespectfully.

### What does attendance tell us about belief?

Participating in religion through attending a religious institution tells us little about *belief*. It could be the case that people express their religiosity differently in the contemporary UK. Davie argues against secularisation on the grounds that today there is 'believing without belonging'. People can be 'religious' without attending church.

Voas (2005) makes the point that church attendance figures are not consistent throughout contemporary England. He focuses on church attendance statistics at Christmas, identifying three kinds of Christmas predominant in different regions:

◆  real churchgoers and Christmas in church – more common in Hereford

◆  Christmas shopping and parties – found in Manchester

◆  Christmas tourists, people who do not usually attend church going at Christmas – three times greater in Guildford.

## Religious growth – the rise of non-Christian and non-traditional Christian religions

Stark (1999), points to the growth of religion in some parts of the modern world, namely the USA and Western Europe, as a criticism of Bruce's support for secularisation. He claims that church membership in the USA has trebled, not declined. Christian fundamentalism has grown in the USA where it has had more political influence than in the UK. However, it has also been a feature of life in the UK when it developed in the 1980s during the term of the Conservative government

Figure 4.12 A black Pentecostalist church

led by Margaret Thatcher. There was deemed to be a link with the morality advocated by the Conservatives which involved such views as less tolerance towards homosexuality, for example, and a general endorsement of family values.

In terms of Western Europe, Stark acknowledges a decline in *attendance* of religious institutions, but maintains there is still religious *belief*. This notion of belief without belonging is the focus of Davie's (1994) position, which is examined below.

In the UK there is some evidence to show that church attendances are actually growing in places. These increases are occurring in ethnically diverse areas. Christian Research claims that although churches in England have been in a long-term decline since the 1950s, this overall decline has been slowed down as the UK has become more ethnically diverse. It found that a third of churches have rising attendance figures. In particular, there is a growth in those with mainly black congregations. In 2005, Christian Research found that 17 per cent of churchgoers were of an ethnic minority background and that 44 per cent of London churchgoers were black and a further 14 per cent were 'other non-white'. Overall, though, the churches with declining congregations are still losing more people than the churches with increasing congregations are gaining.

### Weblink

Visit the Christian Research website (see 'Websites' page ii) for further information.

## The privatisation of belief

While fewer people are attending religious institutions, it does not necessarily mean that they do not hold religious beliefs People can believe privately in their own homes. In the 2001 Census, 71.6 per cent of people identified themselves as Christian.

Davie (1994) disputes that personal religiosity is in decline. She differentiates between religious *belief* and religious *belonging*. She asserts that people hold religious beliefs in contemporary society, but they do not 'belong' to religions. They are believers without belonging. For Davie, people in the contemporary UK believe in private. Davie refers to the response of the British people to events such as the football tragedy at Hillsborough and the death of Diana, Princess of Wales, which she argues prompt religious questions in relation to why these events happen. She regards trips to the site of Diana's burial and the Anfield football stadium as modern-day pilgrimages. The shrines are not to Gods, but to people. You may also have noticed 'shrines' by the roadside where people have been killed in road traffic accidents.

## Evaluation

Day's (2007) research throws some light on what she terms 'curious anomalies' regarding religiosity in the contemporary UK. For example, 71.6 per cent of people define themselves as Christian but only 7 per cent attend church on Sunday and there is a decline in activities such as baptisms and church weddings. She found the following types of Christians.

◆ Adherent Christians believed in God and went to church.

◆ Natal Christians identified themselves as Christian because of their families, place of birth, and through being baptised.

◆ Ethnic Christians identified themselves as Christian in terms of being English as a way of differentiating themselves from other ethnic groups.

◆ Aspirational Christians believed Christians to be good and respectable.

Her work also contradicts Davie's idea of 'believing without belonging' and those sociologists who maintain that religion has become more privatised. She found that religion is used as 'a public marker of identity'. Religious believers used their beliefs to separate themselves from what they saw as 'others'.

# The growth of new religious movements/New Age movements

## New religious movements

The contemporary UK is a multi-faith society. As the UK has become more ethnically diverse, so too has the range of religions found here. Participation in most Christian religions has declined, but there has been a growth in other religions.

## Evaluation

◆ Wilson (1976) maintained that the popularity of new religious movements would eventually disappear.

◆ Critics such as Bruce (1995) maintain that the growth in some religions does not compensate for the overall decline of religion in general.

## The New Age – a different interpretation

Heelas (1996) refers to the belief in self-spirituality as the central feature of New Age movements. Some sociologists that see religion as still having a significant role in the contemporary world, regard this spiritual dimension as extremely important. Drane (1999), for example, maintained that the modern world could not satisfy people spiritually. New Ageism can fulfil that spiritual need. Heelas and Woodhead's (2005) research in Kendall in the Lake District found that people prefer to call themselves 'spiritual' rather than 'religious' in contemporary times. Davie interprets the growth of the New Age religions as being a sign of the continuing significance of the sacred.

Postmodernists see the growth of New Age beliefs as a rejection of modernity and a rejection of a scientific way of understanding. For postmodernists truth is relative. This fits with the New Age beliefs where science is seen as only one belief system among many others which are regarded as just as valid.

# Conclusion

Secularisation is a complex area. Evidence shows that, in general, religious participation has declined. However, there has been growth is some religions, although supporters would say not enough to compensate for the overall

---

**Activity 4.30**

In small groups, make a PowerPoint or poster presentation either for or against secularisation. You can use visual imagery, cartoons, speech bubbles. The choice is yours.

1 Award each presentation marks out of ten on the basis of clarity, detail, logical structure and use of evidencetation and analysis.

2 Time to reflect. What would you do to improve your own group's presentation?

decline. There is some evidence of religious disengagement, but some evidence to show an active role by religious organisations in the wider society, although there is less evidence of this now than in the past. Rather than trying to simplify all of these debates, it might be safer to conclude that religion is *changing* rather than disappearing. There is an argument for the existence of religious beliefs in contemporary societies, but these have different consequences for people's actions compared with the way they affected people in the past.

## Section summary

Use the following key words to copy and complete the summary of this section. Each word should be used only once.

belief system    belief without belonging    cultural defence    cultural transition
disengaged    modernity    opertionalise    pluralism    rationalisation
secularisation    structural differentiation    social differentiation    societalisation

The concept of _____ broadly refers to the decline of religion. It is a difficult concept to _____, that is put in a form that can be measured. Some see it as an inevitable consequence of the shift to _____ with the rise of science as a new _____ _____. Weber, for example, saw the growth in _____ as challenging religion. The fact that religion has _____ from the wider society is seen as evidence for secularisation. _____ _____, _____ _____, and _____ are all aspects of this. Further evidence comes from religious _____, the idea that there is no longer a single dominant religion. There has been a rise in the religion of some ethnic minorities. Bruce, however, does not see this as a threat to secularisation. He explains these religions in terms of _____ _____ and _____ _____. Davie argues against secularisation. She uses the concept of _____ _____ _____ to explain that people can be religious without active participation.

## Exam practice

(a) Identify and explain two reasons why church attendance figures need to be used with caution. **(17 marks)**

(b) Outline and evaluate the view that religious commitment is declining in the contemporary UK. **(33 marks)**

# The sociology of youth

## (i) Key concepts and the social construction of youth

### Pause for thought

1. At what ages do you think childhood begins and ends?

2. At what point does a person stop being young?

3. Write down the words you associate with youth.

Figure 5.1 A shared youth identity at a music festival

# Youth

**Youth** is characterised as a period of life somewhere between childhood and adulthood. The law in the UK means there is no clear-cut age at which someone becomes an adult – so young people can leave school at 16, marry at 16, learn to drive at 17, but would not be eligible to vote until aged 18. It could be argued that childhood ends at 12 when the teenage years begin, and that the period of youth ends at the age 20, when young people are no longer teenagers and become adults. Many sociological studies consider youth in relation to people between the ages of 15 and 25, although clearly the concept of youth sometimes covers people under the age of 15.

## Activity 5.1

Read the following passage from a newspaper article.

> As the White Stripes took to the stage they looked at first glance like the hottest rock band of the day, playing to a typical young crowd. In red and black outfits and bowler hats, Jack and Meg White strummed to pogoing teenagers. But back in the seated ticket area was a quite different group of fans – contented mid-thirties couples in comfy jumpers and Hush Puppies, old punks, middle-aged and suited blokes straight from the office.
>
> Up the road in a very different venue the crowd was a similar mix of generations for the National Theatre's adaptation of Phillip Pullman's trilogy *His Dark Materials*.
>
> A few years ago youngsters would have done almost anything to avoid being seen out with their parents. Now times are changing. Parents and teenagers are out more and more together-shopping, at the cinema, reading books and seeing plays. Age is no longer a social divide. Growing older does not mean giving up, while youth no longer goes hand in hand with irresponsibility.
>
> (Source: adapted from Arkidge, 2004)

The concept of infantilism has been used in relation to young people who want to grow up too quickly, yet older people are keen to act as if they were still teenagers. If this is the case youth may be an attitude of mind rather than a specific form of behaviour relating to a biological age category. Many people in their thirties and forties relate to the same norms and values associated with youth, albeit at a different stage in their life.

## Activity 5.2

Devise a questionnaire to test the accuracy of the view expressed in the article that parents and teenagers go out together more and more, and that age is no longer a social divide. You must follow these guidelines and should work in pairs or small groups:

- do not use more than ten questions

- the questions may be closed or open-ended

- administer the questionnaires to between 10 and 20 people of different age groups

- write a summary (500 words maximum) explaining why you asked the questions you did and what your findings were.

# Peer group

A peer group is a set of people, belonging to a similar age grouping, who share similar norms and values. Between the ages of 5 and 18, when most young people are in full-time education, peer groups are particularly important in establishing culture and identities. The role of the peer group in the formation and understanding of **youth culture** is therefore very important. Peer group pressure is particularly crucial in the formation of the fashion and music styles that young people adopt.

# Youth culture

The concept of youth culture associates young peer groups with a way of life which is different to that of other age categories such as adults and children. It suggests there are norms and values associated with youth which make them a distinct social group. Norms associated with youth culture centre around music, fashion, schooling and consumption, and values such as freedom and individuality.

Research on youth culture was originally associated with functionalist sociologists such as Abrams (1959) who argued that youth culture was a distinct phase of life which first appeared in the UK in 1950s and was shared by most young people. In this sense youth was almost a transitional stage between childhood and adulthood through which all individuals progress. However, there are criticisms of this view.

1   Young people are not a uniform social group, they differ in a number of ways according to gender, ethnicity and social class. There are different expectations of dress depending on your gender and, sometimes, ethnicity.

2   Many children have norms they share with youth culture. The 'Tweens' are pre-adolescents between the ages of 8 and 12 years old who share a stage of development and are clearly targeted by advertisers, in terms of music, toys and food, in much the same way as young people are.

3   Many adults follow what they consider to be a youth culture. They spend their money on similar consumer goods, ipods, mobile technology, listen to the same music as many young people and value freedom and autonomy, just as they did when they were in their twenties.

## Reasons for the development of youth culture

Much research on youth culture in the UK traces its origins to the post-Second World War period, in the late 1940s and 1950s. However, references to youth as a distinct social group can be found much earlier in the nineteenth century (Pearson, 1983). Youth culture is usually associated with the post-world war society. Britain in the 1950s was a relatively affluent (well-off) society. The economy was in a healthy state and most young people were employed directly after leaving school at the age of 15. They had money to spend on themselves and their disposable income was relatively high. These young people were easy targets for advertisers who were keen for young people to spend their disposable income on consumer products such as music, fashion and leisure.

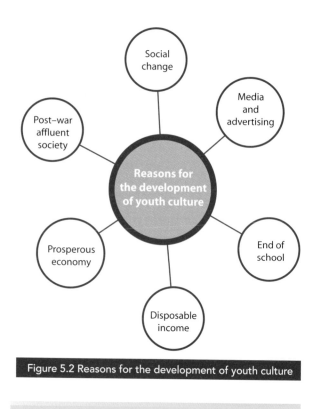

Figure 5.2 Reasons for the development of youth culture

### Activity 5.3

Explain what is meant by youth culture, and outline three problems associated with the concept. You should write between one and two sides of paper, or not more than 500 words.

## Youth subcultures

Youth subcultures refer to the norms and values of distinct groups within youth culture. The concept of subculture refers to a smaller group within a larger one, or a minority section of a majority culture. The concept of youth subculture assumes there are groups of young people who do not follow the same norms and values as each other.

While it may be reasonable to say that most young people enjoy listening to music, there are clear differences in the type of music that young people choose. A similar point could be made about fashion or hobbies; indeed most of the norms associated with youth culture could be broken down to illustrate key differences and similarities between social groups. Some of these differences relate to gender, especially through fashion, although social class and ethnicity are also influential in an individual's choice and preferences.

Examples of youth subcultures in the contemporary UK may include emos, goths, punks, skinheads and chavs. Although these groups are clearly different from each other, they all share the similarity of being distinct social groups who are clearly visible and different to 'ordinary youth' (Willis, 1990). Subcultures are groups of individuals who often develop in opposition to authority and who share norms and values which go against the norms in society.

However, it is worth noting that many young people do not join subcultures. Most young people go to school and are likely to be targeted and give in to some form of advertising and peer pressure.

The concept of subculture can be traced back to a group of sociologists working in Chicago in the 1920s who used the term to describe young people who engaged in delinquent behaviour because they held different norms and values to mainstream youth.

Interactionist ideas have also been useful in exploring subcultures. Labelling is used by interactionist theorists. Becker (1963) proposes that some social groups are more likely than others to be seen as different or deviant, especially if the norms and values they follow differ from those held by the majority group in society. These people become labelled by society because they stand out and their behaviour is different to the accepted norm. Many youth subcultures would claim to have been labelled unfairly by society.

# Spectacular youth subcultures

Much of the work on youth subculture developed from a group of sociologists writing in the 1970s who belonged to the Centre for Contemporary Cultural Studies (CCCS) in Birmingham. They were Marxist-based sociologists who believed that social class was the crucial social division in

---

**Activity 5.4**

Study the images in Figures 5.3 and 5.4 and identify ways in which these two groups differ from one and another.

Figure 5.3 Goths

Figure 5.4 Ordinary youth

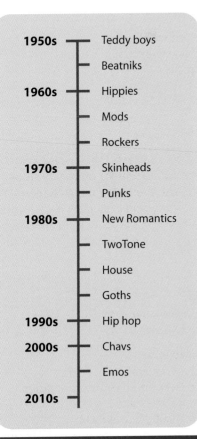

| | |
|---|---|
| **1950s** | Teddy boys |
| | Beatniks |
| **1960s** | Hippies |
| | Mods |
| | Rockers |
| **1970s** | Skinheads |
| | Punks |
| **1980s** | New Romantics |
| | TwoTone |
| | House |
| | Goths |
| **1990s** | Hip hop |
| **2000s** | Chavs |
| | Emos |
| **2010s** | |

Figure 5.5 A timeline of youth subcultures

society and their work showed the importance of social class in the formation and behaviour of youth subcultures. They carried out studies on youth subcultures from the 1950s to the 1970s which have become known as spectacular youth subcultures because of their flamboyant styles and often confrontational attitudes.

In order to explore subcultures we will consider some of the highly visible ones. This subsection will explore at least one from each decade, however, your understanding of youth subcultures will be stronger the more examples you know and can research yourself.

Activity 5.5

Look at the three sets of data about different subcultures in Tables 5.1, 5.2 and 5.3. You need to select one subculture (or another from the time line, Figure 5.5) and create a presentation focusing on the following:

- the main characteristics/features of the subculture
- when and why did this subculture develop?

You can present your work in any form – hand out, talk, PowerPoint®, poster, role-play. Try to access music and clothing to make it extra special.

Table 5.1 1950s Teddy boys

Jefferson (1976) studied the teddy boy culture. His research suggests that teddy boys were relatively affluent (well-off), earned high wages, and came from working-class families. With disposable income to spend they were able to buy Edwardian-style suits which had previously been reserved for the upper middle classes. Through adopting an exaggerated middle-class style of dress they were able to give expression to their changing social situation. The Edwardian style suits worn by the men were expensive, and showed a real interest in style and fashion, which meant that any insults to it were met with aggression and violence in order to reaffirm their masculine status. The teddy girls wore circular skirts and adopted some of the features of American rock and roll culture.

| Music:<br>Billy Cochran<br>Elvis Presley | Attitudes:<br>Desire to shock parents<br>Consumer and style conscious | Hairstyles:<br>Quiffs |
|---|---|---|
| Associated with:<br>Edwardian style dress<br>Working class<br>Dancing and fashion<br>Some racism towards West Indian migrants | Films:<br>*That'll Be the Day*<br>*Friday Night, Saturday Morning* | Websites:<br>Visit the Teddy boy website (see 'Websites' page ii) |

Table 5.2 1960s Hippies

Brake (1980) suggests that hippies in the UK largely came from middle-class families and that it was a popular subculture for university students. There were, however, working-class hippies too. Hippies rejected both the consumer culture which they found offensive and the conservative attitudes of their parents. Hippies were keen to preserve the environment; many were vegetarians; they condemned war, particularly nuclear weapons. Closely associated with taking hallucinatory drugs, such as LSD, the hippies are perhaps best understood by listening to their chilled-out music, during the 1967 Summer of Love.

| Music:<br>Beatles<br>Jefferson Airplane<br>The Grateful Dead | Attitudes:<br>Peace loving, pacifists<br>Anti-consumerism<br>Permissive and liberal society | Hairstyles:<br>Long hair |
|---|---|---|
| Associated with:<br>Make love, not war<br>Flower power and hallucinatory drugs<br>Middle classes<br>Music festivals (Woodstock)<br>Summer of Love | Films:<br>*The Strawberry Statement* | Websites:<br>Visit the hippy website (see 'Websites' page ii) |

Table 5.3 1970s Punks

By adopting a chaotic approach, and claiming to be Anarchists (literally meaning 'without rule'), punks were making a statement targeted at the ruling elite in society. Through adopting an outrageous style of dress based on ripped trousers, lots of zips and safety pins, punks were emphasising their anti-establishment ideas. Interestingly, Frith (1978) suggests that punks were almost entirely working class, and reacting against the social environment of the late 1970s (high unemployment/low wages). Punk was 'dole queue rock', followed by young people claiming unemployment benefit. Other researchers, such as Brake (1980), have explained punk as being 'cross class', drawing followers from the lower middle class and the working class who wanted to shock and make a social and political statement through their style. Frith (1978) studied the punk movement and argued that much of it was an attack on the music establishment which was increasingly dominated by teenage pop bands.

| Music: | | Attitudes: | Hairstyles: |
|---|---|---|---|
| Sex Pistols | Slits | Anarchist | Mohicans |
| Ramones | X Ray Specs | Anti-establishment | Brightly coloured |
| Clash | | Nihilism | dyed hair |

| Associated with: | Films: | Websites: |
|---|---|---|
| Tartan, zips and safety pins | *The Great Rock and Roll* | Visit the punk |
| Anti social behaviour (e.g. spitting at gigs) | *Swindle* (18) | website (see |
| | *Punk: Attitude* (18) | 'Websites' page ii) |

## Reasons for the development of youth subcultures

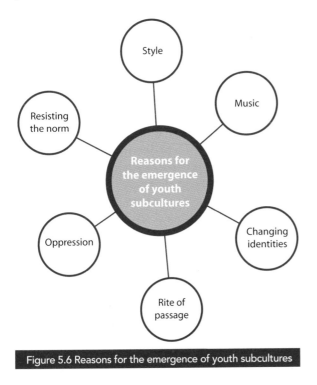

Figure 5.6 Reasons for the emergence of youth subcultures

Research has suggested that a third of people in the UK have been active members of a youth subculture at some point during their lives. The most popular reasons for joining subcultures include providing a sense of identity, allowing individuality to be expressed and being able to bond with like-minded people. Music is a key factor attracting people to different subcultures. When Hodkinson (2004) interviewed goths as part of his ethnographic study into the subculture he found that music was a key attraction to goth culture. A number of goths commented on being attracted to the scene through first hearing bands such as the Cure and the Sisters of Mercy in the 1980s.

### Activity 5.6

Think of examples of youth subcultures in the UK today. Can these be linked to different types of music as much as those from the past can be (see Tables 5.1–5.3)?

## The social construction of youth

As we explored in Unit 1, sociologists believe that society creates culture. If we accept that youth has its own culture and subcultures then it follows that youth is a socially created category, which is related to social issues more than to the biological aging process. As youth cultures change over time, this is further evidence that they must be socially created; as society changes, so do its cultures and subcultures.

The following factors are involved in the social construction of youth:

◆ demographic trends

◆ schooling

◆ the media

◆ the economy

◆ globalisation

◆ consumption

◆ style.

## Demographic trends

Directly after the Second World War there was a baby boom in the UK. With men and women returning from their wartime duties it is probably no surprise that the population grew. The babies born in the mid- to late-1940s were, of course, teenagers in the late 1950s and early 1960s, the time at which youth culture was first noted as a permanent feature of British life. This demographic trend may explain why young people became so visible; quite simply there were more of them.

## Schooling

This growing population of young people may have been a reason why the process of schooling was prolonged. At the end of the Second World War the school leaving age was raised to 15. It was raised again in 1972 to 16, where it remains. There is a strong feeling that in the twenty-first century the government needs to raise it further to 17 or 18 years of age. The trend of raising the school leaving age serves a number of purposes – not only having better-educated young people but also keeping the young out of the workplace or off the unemployment statistics. However, essentially it prolongs the period of compulsory schooling, which for most young people is the period of growing up and socialising without the burden of work, family responsibility and mortgages to consider. In prolonging the school experience, young people have more time to socialise with peers and more time to spend in this transitional stage of maturity and growing up, which prolongs the period of youth.

## The media

The **media** play a crucial role in the creation of youth. From music to fashion, advertising in particular transmits messages and images of different styles and trends. Studies as far back as the 1970s look at the impact of magazines on femininity and show how influential media messages are. The popularity of magazines remains huge today with magazines such as *Cosmogirl* and *Shout* and satellite television channels such as Smash Hits and MTV being aimed primarily at a young audience.

Thornton (1995) claims that the media are largely responsible for the creation of youth culture and subcultures. She uses the concept of subcultural capital (a variation of cultural capital) to explain how young people gain knowledge and experience of different subcultures which brings with it high status. This knowledge comes mainly from different forms of media.

## The economy

One of the reasons why the school leaving age has been extended is because the **economy** benefits from it. A better educated and more mature workforce profits the economy, especially if the alternative is having too many young people looking for too few jobs. The government now pays the Educational Maintenance Allowance (EMA) to young people from families on lower incomes as an incentive to stay in education. Within the economy there is a job market for part-time workers and many young people are ideally positioned to fill these gaps. Therefore, although in education for longer, many young people have money to spend which contributes to the formation of youth culture.

## Globalisation

Modern young people are influenced by global products and trends coming from the available different worldwide styles and the Americanisation of the youth market. This is not a new trend. The 1950s teddy boys and girls borrowed much of their fashion and style from the USA. However, today influences from all over the world are visible: Bhangara music, basketball clothing and the game, PSP (play station portable) technology imported from abroad are all made possible by a global culture and a global market. **Globalisation** plays a huge role in the creation of hybrid subcultures.

## Consumption

Since the 1950s, young people have been targeted by companies because they have spending power; in other words, they have money to spend on consumer and leisure-based goods. The unique position of youth with spending power, parental spending power, accessibility to the High Street and the Internet means that consumption explains many of the reasons why youth culture has not only emerged but has also spread.

## Style

Due to the consumer-led market and process of globalisation, a key feature of the contemporary UK is the importance of style. The UK has always had stylish social groups, long before the emergence of youth culture. However, the accessibility and importance of style in shaping identities is largely a recent trend. Style was critical to the image of the subcultures studied by the CCCS (teddy boys, Mods, hippies, punks). We must remember that these were subcultures and that not all young people were members of these groups. In more recent studies carried out by the postmodern sociologists, we see a society where what you wear, how you wear it and where it is from all matter (Polhemus, 1997).

U2

5

The sociology of youth

### Section summary

Use the following key words to copy and complete the summary of this section below. Each word should be used only once.

| | | | | |
|---|---|---|---|---|
| youth | youth culture | peer group | youth subcultures | spectacular |
| punks | hippies | teddy boys | CCCS | media | rite of passage |
| oppressed | economy | consumption | globalisation | ordinary youths |

_____ is a category lying somewhere between the ages of 12 and 25. It is based on _____ _____ who are thought to share a distinct way of life which separates them from childhood and adulthood. Some sociologists argue that all young people belong to the same _____ _____ and they share in the same norms and values. Other sociologists argue this is an over simplification and ignores factors such as gender, class and ethnicity. The _____ certainly plays an important role in the creation of youth culture.

Marxist sociologists belonging to the _____ are particularly interested in _____ _____. These are smaller cultural groups who are a sub-group of mainstream youth. These sociologists researched the _____ youth subcultures of the 1950s to the 1980s including _____, _____ and _____. Many of the working-class groups in society felt _____, and resented people and institutions in authority.. This was a different view to the functionalists who saw youth culture as a _____ ___ _____ that all young people went through.

We should remember, however, that most young people do not belong to these subcultures and have been described as _____ _____.

There is a strong argument that youth is a socially constructed category, with factors such as _____, _____ and the _____ playing an important role in its formation.

### Exam practice

1 Identify and explain two youth subcultures.
(17 marks)

2 Outline and evaluate the view that youth culture is created by the media. (33 marks)

# (ii) The role of youth culture/subcultures in society

**Figure 5.7 Youth culture or subculture?**

In this subsection we consider different sociological contributions to an understanding of youth culture/subculture in society. Each theory approaches youth culture/subculture in different ways and these differences are highlighted throughout this subsection. There are four theories to consider, which broadly follow their chronological age:

◆ functionalism

◆ Marxism

◆ feminism

◆ postmodern views.

## Functionalism

Functionalists argue that individuals need to be integrated into society, to feel that they belong to communities and social groups. This process of **social integration** happens throughout a person's life. Without social integration, society would begin to break down and experience 'anomie' as individuals would lack a sense of belonging. In the case of young people this integration comes most commonly from family, peers or through school.

Functionalists argue that a key role of youth culture is to promote social integration for young people by offering a **transitory** phase of life which differs from both childhood and adulthood. Functionalists stress the age-related, generational explanation of youth culture.

Parsons (1954), a functionalist, argued that youth culture provides a bridge between childhood and adulthood. This transitional stage enabled young people to become more detached from their parents while achieving their own independence and status as adults. For example, many young people take on a part-time job while they continue with their schooling. The income they earn serves the purpose of enabling a more independent approach to money management which is an important skill needed in modern life. From this view youth culture becomes a **'rite of passage'**, a transitional stage through which all young people journey.

Eisenstadt (1956) suggested that youth culture was an important way of binding young people into society. Through fostering and adopting a shared way of life with their peers, young people would develop feelings of community and togetherness. Furthermore youth culture could provide an outlet for tensions young people face on the road to more independent living. From this view youth culture could enable young people to speak out and react against what they see as unfair – taking part in demonstrations or breaking rules in the home and at school are often tolerated because it is 'what youths do'.

The 1950s are widely accepted within sociology as the time at which the teenage consumer was created. Another functionalist, Abrams (1959), argued the social changes of the time enabled the creation of youth culture, through increased spending power and a consumer economy targeting the youth market. It was around this time that youth became an important part of the economy.

Functionalists tend to see young people as a **homogenous** age group, despite clear differences in personal taste and style between different groups of young people. Functionalists consider that the binding nature of shared norms and values makes youth culture a transitional stage in life. Youth culture was created by social changes of the time, in particular economic changes bringing about a consumer society which enabled the media to target youth as a brand in itself. Functionalists support the view that there is a clear generation gap between

youth and adulthood. The role of youth culture therefore is based on:

◆ drawing boundaries between youth and adulthood

◆ transition, enabling young people to learn to become adults

◆ promoting social integration through youth culture

◆ age and generation.

## Criticisms of functionalism

There are of course criticisms of this functionalist approach.

◆ By emphasising the shared features of youth culture, functionalists are ignoring the clear differences between youth subcultures. According to the Marxists these differences are based on important social class differences within society, which cannot be ignored. In short, functionalists are more interested in the concept of youth culture than subcultures.

◆ By treating youth as an age-specific category the functionalists miss the opportunity to consider youth as a state of mind which can be adopted by children and adults alike.

◆ Functionalists do not consider gender or ethnic-related issues in any way.

◆ Functionalist research is based very much on the same social groups that the writers themselves came from: white, middle-class American males.

## Marxism

Marxist theories of youth culture pay more attention to subcultures than the functionalist ones. Marxist explanations are associated with the CCCS which produced its most influential work on youth culture/subcultures in the 1970s. The work was rooted in traditional Marxist theory by focusing on the important role played by the economy or capitalism in explaining youth culture/subcultures. The CCCS writers argued that social class differences between groups of young people explained the emergence and direction of youth subcultures. They were critical of the functionalist assumption that social class differences were irrelevant in understanding youth culture. For the CCCS writers, social class and the nature of the capitalism at that time (high unemployment, inner-city decay, strikes) were significant in explaining why the youth subcultures were created and the styles they adopted. Furthermore these writers suggested that youth culture was almost a meaningless concept due to the clearly different styles of sub-cultural groups.

The work of the CCCS writers is a type of neo-Marxism ('neo' means new) and considers economic factors and cultural factors to be important in considering social issues. They were interested in studying and trying to 'decode' the different sub-cultural styles of the specific time period in terms of how the economy was operating and the social conditions of different groups at the time. In short, the CCCS argued that youth subcultures were the product of structural explanations (economy, class, employment etc) and not generational (age) explanations. They linked subcultures to the development of capitalism and viewed them as heavily related to different social classes.

The remainder of this section will consider concepts relevant to understanding Marxism: resistance, exaggeration, magical solutions and incorporation.

## Resistance

Hall and Jefferson (1976) argued that youth subcultures react against what was seen as the crisis of capitalism, with high unemployment, low wages, inner-city decline and racist oppression. Through adopting a subcultural style young people were able to resist and therefore reject the dominant hegemonic culture. In this sense youth subcultures can be seen as offering a form of **resistance**. The concept of 'bricolage' explains how different groups re-ordered and rearranged their style to communicate new meanings. Different subcultural styles enable youth to stand out and be differentiated from their peers.

## Exaggeration

Clarke (1976) studied skinhead culture and suggested it represented a cultural style based on an exaggerated version of working-class

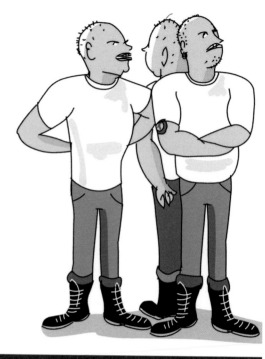

masculinity. Skinheads were around in the late 1960s and early 1970s and they stressed violence ('aggro') and fighting. They wore a distinct style of manual workers' clothing (bovver boots, rolled up jeans and braces). Skinheads were very territorial, they had their local areas which they protected from outsiders, particularly immigrants. Most skinheads came from traditional working-class backgrounds, and the skinhead culture allowed them to exaggerate their working-class masculine backgrounds in order to be distinct and hold on to tradition in the capitalist UK, a society where middle-class values were taking over. Clarke argued that skinheads used their style to recreate the traditional working-class community and to 'magically' recover it from extinction.

### Weblink

For additional information on skinheads watch the film *Made in Britain* (1982), and visit the Skinhead Nation website (see 'Websites' page ii).

Hebdige (1976) claimed that the Mod style was in part a reaction against the boredom of the average working week. At weekends Mods who came from relatively well-off working-class backgrounds would display their style through leisure activities and wearing clothes which were a subverted attempt to reject middle-class style. The Mods had no desire to look like the middle classes, but they did create their own neat and hip style based on Italian styled suits for men, and miniskirts for women. Their economic position of having money combined with wanting to distance themselves from their class origins through style, fashion and leisure combined to explain the Mod subculture.

### Activity 5.7

Watch the film *Quadrophenia*, which is an excellent illustration of Mod culture and tells the story of the clashes between Mods and Rockers in the summer of 1964.

### Activity 5.8

Using the information in this subsection, find two similarities and at least two differences between the functionalist and the Marxist views on the role of youth culture/subculture in society. You may find it useful to use some of these headings:

- gender
- social class
- ethnicity
- generation gap
- resistance
- youth culture or subculture.

Record your findings in a table like the one below.

| Similarities | Differences |
| --- | --- |
| | |
| | |
| | |

## Magical solutions

Brake (1980) suggests that youth subcultures provided '**magical**' solutions to the lives of its members. Membership of a subculture could provide safety from facing the social and economic problems experienced by working-class youths . By forming or joining a subculture young people were given the opportunity to express freedom and experiment with ideas. The subculture allowed them the opportunity to convince themselves that their generation would be different from their parents and that they were solving the social problems of the time. Brake's description of these solutions as being 'magical' illustrates the fact that the solutions are like an illusion, a trick which cannot be sustained in reality.

## Incorporation

Youth subcultures eventually decline to be replaced by others. The concept of incorporation has been used here to describe the way in which new distinct styles eventually find there way into high street stores and popular culture. When this happens the styles lose their cutting edge distinctiveness and eventually they fade away.

To summarise, the Marxist CCCS writers make the following points about youth subcultures in society.

- They arise from and show resistance to the dominant capitalist culture.
- They providing an outlet for some young people who feel oppressed.
- They are based on an exaggerated form of working-class identities.
- They are part of the magical solutions to the economic and social problems faced by many young people.

## Criticisms of Marxist explanations

- Marxists are accused of ignoring the involvement of girls in subcultural groups.
- They do not consider issues of ethnicity; however, their use of oppression and resistance has been applied to ethnicity and subcultures.

- Muggleton (2000) argues that much of the CCCS work assumes that youth subcultures of the 1960s and 1970s came from the working class. While it is clear that some did, it is difficult to understand why advertisers and the media would target the working-class youth market rather than the youth market in general.

- There is an assumption in much of the CCCS work that most young people joined subcultures, which is highly debatable. Perhaps most young people were 'ordinary' youths.

- Maybe the CCCS read too much into the reasons people join and the underlying role youth subcultures play in society. It is possible that young people joined subcultures just for 'fun', a suggestion that the CCCS fail to explore.

- Thornton (1995) argues they have failed to consider the role played by the media in the construction of youth.

## Feminism and gender related issues

Feminists have criticised the Marxist and the functionalist analysis of youth subcultures for largely ignoring the role of females and suggesting that girls were invisible in youth subcultures. Many of the studies considered so far present subcultures as being for males only, with only a brief mention of females in the background or as 'pillion' passengers, as the girlfriends or groupies of males. The idea being that girls 'hung around' the boys and that the boys provided the style and iconic image for the subculture.

However, a detailed consideration of any of the subcultures from the 1950s to the 1980s would show that girls were clearly involved in the music, fashion and any associated forms of social behaviour. For example, there were clearly female hippies, Mods and teddy girls as photographic images from the period show. Since the 1980s, there has been more sexual equality in society and this is shown in images and accounts of more recent youth subcultures such as house, rave and emos, where masculinity and femininity are important aspects of division but in some respects they blend together.

Heidensohn (1985 ) accuses functionalism and the work of the CCCS of being 'malestream'. By this she means that these accounts were written by male sociologists about young male involvement in subcultures. It may be that this is inevitable, after all males are probably more interested in researching male involvement that female involvement, although it could also be the case that making the girls invisible allowed male sociologists to exercise patriarchal dominance in their work.

Blackman (1995) is a male sociologist who carried out an ethnographic study of different youth subcultural groups within a school. He called one of the groups he studied the New Wave Girls. They were a popular academically-able group of ten girls who shared an interest in punk and new wave music and a similar style of fashion; they wore Doc Marten boots, black trousers, T-shirts of various styles and over-sized jumpers. They were from working-class and lower middle-class backgrounds and did not conform to the traditional expectations of femininity; they were able to resist masculine control, parental control and school control. Blackman studied the girls over a period of time, trying to understand the subcultural style and behaviour of the group. He gained access to the girls through a group of Mod boys at the school. Gradually he built up closer relations with the girls through joining them at lunchtime, walking home with them after school, visiting them at their parents' houses, and joining their social activities: going to discos, pubs and on shopping trips with them.

### Activity 5.9

Discuss the issues raised in Blackman's study in relation to male sociologists researching female subcultural groups.

We must remember that women really only entered the workplace permanently in the 1950s and that it would have taken women a long time to gain qualifications on an equal footing with men. Therefore, it was only in the 1970s that female sociologists were being employed as a permanent feature of university life in Britain.

## Bedroom culture

The feminist sociologists McRobbie and Garber (1976) were highly critical of the CCCS work for ignoring the role of females in subcultures. They identified a strong 'teeny bopper' culture among young teenage girls. This culture was based around romance, fashion and the private domestic space of the girls' bedrooms. This has become known as the 'bedroom culture', features of which include:

◆ experimenting with make-up, hair styles and clothes

◆ gossiping with friends about boys they fancied

◆ reading and discussing the contents of *Jackie* magazine.

Essentially the bedroom culture was based around 'codes':

◆ the code of romance

◆ the code of fashion and beauty

◆ the code of personal life

◆ the code of pop music.

McRobbie and Garber studied the images and stories found in a girl's teenage magazine called *Jackie*, which was very important in creating a cult of femininity. They also interviewed a group of girls about their views of the magazines. The study concluded that the girls had subcultures of their own, but that they were lived in the private sphere of the bedroom and not in the streets or parks where many of the boys were more visible.

This idea would link with the work of Smart (1976) who argues that parents exercise different types and amounts of social control on their daughters and their sons. Boys are given more freedom to roam and are more visible in the public spheres of the street or local park. Girls, however, are more protected and have their social space limited to more private or domestic spheres. If this is the case then it becomes another reason to explain why girls have been ignored in sub-cultural studies; because gaining access to them would have been more difficult.

In a recent study, Lincoln (2004) has updated the bedroom culture study. In an ethnographic study of teenage girls' cultural life, Lincoln produces a version of girls' bedroom lives based around zones rather than codes. Lincoln concludes that bedrooms are based around zones, which are shaped by the activities that take place in them. New technologies play a crucial role in these bedrooms, with music and the Internet creating an ethos that the girls wanted. Homework and school life had a zone which was often covered or hidden by more leisure orientated activities, such as magazines or clothes. All of the girls' bedrooms contained some kind of representations of the journey from childhood to youth, through teddy bears and photographs of family members and party nights out.

### Activity 5.10

Have a class discussion or debate on the question of whether girls and boys have different types of social control imposed on them by their parents/guardians. If so, does this differ according to factors such as age or ethnicity? In the discussion, consider issues such as bedtime, access to social activities, expected forms of behaviour.

The concept of girl power could represent a change in the position of girls and youth culture. Instead of being visible only in the shadow of boys or not visible at all because they were chatting, dancing and dressing up in their bedrooms, girl power effectively made young girls highly visible and arguably sexualised in the media. Hollands (1995) studied night life in Newcastle in the 1990s and showed that young women were just as likely as young men to enjoy nights out in the city's pubs and clubs.

## Girl subcultures

Despite the more public role of women there are very few studies of all-girl British subcultures from the 1990s onwards. Females are involved in the more gender neutral movements of recent years – in house, rave, goth and emo subcultures. There are examples of girl subcultures in the USA such as the Riot Grrrls who use powerful image forms of communication to display their anger at feelings of oppression. Equally SK8er girls, often associated with a young Avril Lavigne, have been studied in the US and Canada, but not researched in the UK.

Using the information in this subsection, identify and explain two reasons why girls may be invisible in sociological studies of youth subcultures. Your answer should include at least two sociological studies.

## Criticisms of feminist explanations

◆ Many of the feminist approaches deal only with gender-related issues, neglecting social class and ethnicity dimensions of subcultures.

◆ Recent developments in youth cultures suggest a more androgynous (genderless) development, where the blurring of femininity and masculinity could made gender issues less important in sub-cultural analysis.

◆ The bedroom culture studies assume that girls have their own bedrooms as private space. This may not be the case and raises issues of which girls these studies are representing.

# Postmodern views

Sociological studies in this area of youth subculture since the 1990s have been based largely on postmodern ideas and argue that youth style has become increasingly fragmented and diverse. Postmodern views maintain that a shared attachment is not the norm in the contemporary UK, as most youth styles have become **fluid** and changeable. Youth styles are viewed as increasingly eclectic, and no longer based on factors such as class, ethnicity and gender. In short, the relationship between style, musical taste and identity has broken down. The remainder of this subsection consider concepts relevant to understanding postmodern views of youth subcultures; club cultures, neo-tribes and the supermarket of style.

## Club cultures

The 'clubbing culture', associated with the UK in the late 1980s and 1990s, is one in which young people shared in a collective dance experience regardless of class, gender or ethnicity (Redhead, 1993). Much of this work was carried out at the Manchester Institute of Popular Culture (MIPC) and has been viewed as providing a critique of the work of the CCCS. Club cultures were associated with relatively affluent youths who worked during the week and danced, raved and partied at weekends. It was almost a student leisure-based lifestyle for wage earners. Club culture also had a reputation for drug use in general, and ecstasy in particular. The work of the MIPC depicts youth styles no longer related to factors such as class, gender or ethnicity.

For more information on club culture watch the film *24 Party People*.

## Neo tribes

The club and dance culture is an example of what Bennett (1999) called a 'neo tribe'. He argued that the concept of youth subcultures was no longer suited to the fluid and complex youth styles of the postmodern world. A neo tribe was a more fluid association which people could move in and out of over time, reflecting the transitory and increasingly elongated nature of youth. Other writers have adopted the concept of a 'scene' for both explaining and describing the lifestyle-based youth styles of the 1990s onwards.

## Supermarket of style

Polemus (1997) develops the idea of the fluidity of youth styles and writes about 'the supermarket of style' where youths can choose from different fashions, music tastes and identities – in the same way as supermarket shoppers are offered numerous choices of shampoo or tins of soup. Shopping at the supermarket of style means that different styles are fused together; for example, Britney Spears using Bhangara beats in some of her songs. Polemus also states that young people can wear whatever they choose in creating their own identity, so Nike trainers, with Prada sunglasses and handbag, could be worn alongside Fat Face combat trousers and white T-shirt from M&S.

The postmodern views of youth offer a new view to the CCCS. Their work has been summed up as illustrating the importance of style over substance. This means that youth style is a more crucial feature than what the youths believe in or any shared structural positions. Fluidity and transition are the order of the day.

## Criticisms of postmodern explanations

◆ There are still examples of subcultural groups in society: goths, emos and new metallers would all fit the descriptions of youth subcultures.

◆ The idea of fluidity may be overstated. Most young people do not move in and out of neo tribes over a long time period.

◆ Although there is more choice in youth styles than in the past, young people do have dress conventions to follow.

◆ It could be argued that there are still youth styles associated with different genders, ethnicities and social classes.

### Activity 5.13

1 Create two characters, one with what you would consider to be style and the other without style. You can either draw your characters, describe them or even become them. Think about the following factors:

• dress

• music

• interests

• age/ethnicity/gender.

2 Do all members of your group agree with what makes someone stylish? What does this suggest about the postmodern views?

## Ethnicity and subcultures

Just as the CCCS and functionalist theories lack a gender dimension in their analysis of youth subcultures, they also neglect ethnicity and the impact this has on youth culture and subcultures. Hebdige (1979) claimed there is a clear relationship between black styles of dress, music, dancing and fashion and urban youth cultures, but at no point is this explored in the work of the early theorists.

As far back as the 1940s the influence of Caribbean style can be seen in British youth. From jazz music to reggae, the influence of migrants from the Caribbean in fashion and music cannot be denied. Specific examples of youth subcultures such as the rude boys and the Rastafarians provide a clear link between ethnicity and youth expressed in style, music, fashion and beliefs.

## Rastafarians

Rastafarians are associated with Jamaica and, often, with the music of Bob Marley. Their spiritual leader is Haile Selassie, Emperor of Ethiopia, who was declared a living God (Ras Tafari). They wear the colours of the Ethiopian flag (red, gold and green) with pride, and see white capitalism (which they call the system of Babylon) as an evil which needs to be resisted and reversed. Rastafarian culture is associated with smoking marijuana as they believe that this allows followers to reach a higher spiritual plain. Clearly, subcultural groups such as the Rastafarians illustrate a very clear link between ethnicity and culture, but of course Rastas are not only found in youth groups, there are many older Rastafarians living in Britain. The growth of Rastafarianism in the UK from the 1970s onwards is partially explained by the hostility felt between black and white Britains; subcultures such as Rastafarianism gave political expression to the feelings of oppression felt by many African-Caribbean migrants and their children.

## Bhangra

Bhangra forms an integral part of the culture of Asian neighbourhoods in many British cities. Bhangra is a traditional form of folk music performed in the Punjab, which many Asian immigrants brought to the UK with them. Over time the Bhangra beat has provided young Asians in the UK with a form of music based around the communities of their parents and grandparents. However, Bhangra music has been adapted to fit the lifestyles of the young. A blend of Bhangra, reggae and rap styles has created what is known as popular fusion (Bennett,

Figure 5.9 One of the leading Bhangra artists, Rishi Rich.

2005). Artists such as Apache Indian reflect a multi-ethnic type of music which is based less on resistance and racism and more on using minority ethnic cultures to construct new forms of Asian identity to reflect the everyday experiences of young Asians in contemporary Britain.

## Resistance

It has been argued that black youth cultural groups, such as Rastas, resisted white capitalist cultures. The formation of these subcultural groups around ethnically-shared norms and values was an extension of the colonial struggle as black people tried to break free of white dominance and resist the dominant white capitalist control. Youth subcultures in this sense are related to resistance – a reaction against oppression and a reaction against racism.

## Hybrid subcultures

In the contemporary UK there are specific ethnic-related subcultural groups, such as the Raggamuffins and the Bhangaramuffins, who form around the mixing and merging of different music styles. One very good example of this is hip hop culture with its black roots and origins in the Bronx district of New York in the 1970s, which has clearly been incorporated into mainstream culture in the UK. In the early twenty-first century the most successful rap star in the world was the American, Eminen. There is no better illustration of ethnic hybridity than Eminen and his talent and success played an enormous part in incorporating rap into popular and global culture. Black stars such as Tupac and 50 Cent are iconic symbols for both black and white youth, their music speaking to youth worldwide and adored by millions.

## Ethnocentrism

An ethnocentric view is one which excludes particular cultural viewpoints at the expense of others. It could be argued that the sociology of youth subcultures is ethnocentric. It focusses almost entirely on British white youths. If we look at the work published in the USA at the same time as in the work in this area in the UK, we see much greater attention given to issues of race and ethnicity. Studies of hip hop and Gangsta

Rap were carried out in the USA often written by black sociologists. Recent studies in the UK have begun to explore youth subcultures and ethnicity, and again these are usually written and researched by sociologists associated with that particular subculture or ethnicity. In this sense, as Britain becomes more culturally diverse, we can expect to see more work in this area.

## Section summary

Use the following key words to copy and complete the summary of this section. Each word should be used only once.

transitory    functionalism    homogenous    malestream    feminism    hybridity
pillion    resistance    magical    incorporated    fluid    neo tribe    Marxism
social integration

There are four theoretical approaches to consider when looking at youth subcultures: _____, _____, _____ and postmodern views. Functionalists argue that youth culture plays a _____ role in society, providing a bridge between childhood and adulthood. Young people are all part of the same _____ group, and youth culture promotes _____ _____ binding young people to the society they live in.

Marxists, on the other hand, argue that youth subcultures should be the focus of attention, and that they offer a form of _____ to their members. By joining a subculture young people are able to express their dissatisfaction with their position in society, and the subculture provides them with a _____ solution to the structural barriers they face. However, subcultures are short-lived experiences for young people largely because the ideas of the group become _____ into mainstream and popular culture.

Feminists accuse the other sociological theories of being _____ and of treating females as _____ passengers, hanging on the needs of iconic males. They argue that the study of girls in youth studies has been seriously neglected.

Postmodern theories view youth cultures as being _____, meaning ever changeable. The eclectic nature of contemporary society means that an individual can create their own pick-and-mix style. Bennett used the concept of _____ _____ to describe young people who show attachment to youth styles and identities. These groups also provide evidence of mixed ethnicities and show what is known as _____.

## Exam practice

Outline and evaluate the view that social class is crucial in understanding youth subcultures in the UK.

(33 marks)

# (iii) Youth and deviance

## Pause for thought

1    Have you ever committed a criminal offence?

2    What do you think the concept 'anti-social behaviour' means?

3    What do you understand by the term 'yob culture'?

Figure 5.10 Hoodies

Young people are often associated with criminal or anti-social behaviour. Sometimes this association is through committing the offence and sometimes it is about being the victim. This section will consider some of the sociological ideas surrounding youth crime, and will also focus on the patterns and trends in youth crime in recent years.

## Crime, deviance and delinquency

A crime is a criminal offence which breaks a law. Sometimes crimes are easy to detect; shoplifting, for instance, is quite clear cut, as it is clearly against the law and with reliable evidence it should be possible to decide whether a person is guilty of the offence. Other crimes are less obvious to detect; for example causing a disturbance in a public place may be a crime but who decides what makes it a 'disturbance'?

To further complicate the picture, shoplifting and causing a disturbance in a public place acts may also be described as deviant (behaviour that goes against the norms in society), although not everyone would agree that they are deviant. The difference between crime and deviance is further complicated by the views of society which are far from clear cut. For many people a young boy wearing a hoodie is part of popular culture, and it clearly is not a crime to wear a hoodie. For others, however, wearing a hoodie and hanging out in a public place is behaviour bordering on deviant and anti-social.

Delinquency is a term associated with the criminal and/or anti-social behaviour of young people. First used in the nineteenth century, it is a concept closely related to young people who break the law, although the term delinquent is rarely heard in courts or the legal system. The only use of the term 'juvenile delinquency' in legal terms was in the 1984 Police and Criminal Evidence Act where it was used to describe young offenders between the ages of 10 and 16.

The concepts of crime, deviance and delinquency are often used inter-changeably in sociology although they all focus on aspects of what New Labour have termed anti-social behaviour. Anti-social behaviour is that which causes problems for neighbourhoods and society, and includes both violent and non-violent behaviour. The controversial use of the Anti Social Behaviour Order (ASBO) has become a key features of New Labours approach to tackling the crime problems in society. ASBOs are orders which can be made by the police on anyone over the age of 10 whose behaviour is thought likely to cause alarm, distress or harassment. ASBOs have become a means of social control used by the police in preventing youth crime, deviance and delinquency.

In England and Wales the age of criminal responsibility is ten. Below this age a child cannot be held criminally responsible for the offence they commit. Other European countries have different ages of criminal responsibility, suggesting that agreement on the age of criminal responsibility is not clear cut (Table 5.4).

In the UK anybody aged 18 or above will be treated as an adult in the justice system. The majority of young people (between the ages of 10 and 17) will be treated by the Youth Courts.

Table 5.4 The ages of criminal responsibility in selected European countries

| European country | Age of criminal responsibility |
| --- | --- |
| France | 13 |
| Germany | 14 |
| Greece | 12 |
| Portugal and Spain | 16 |
| Austria | 10 |
| The Netherlands | 16 |
| Poland | 17 |
| Eire | 12 |
| Northern Ireland | 10 |
| Scotland | 8 |
| England and Wales | 10 |

Activity 5.15

Discuss the following issue. You need to think of reasons to justify your views.

At what age do you think young a person can be held responsible for their behaviour?

For the purposes of studying youth deviance we are assuming a young person to be anyone between the ages of 10 and 25. This is in line with much of the available data complied by police records and by the general view of youth in society.

# Researching young people's crime and deviance

Gaining valid and reliable data on young people and crime is difficult because of the sensitive nature of the subject. Much of the information is based on **official statistics** on crime which come from police records of offences reported to and recorded by the police. However, a large number of criminal offences are never reported to the police, and sometimes the police decide not to act on reported offences for a number of reasons, particularly if there are no clear victims or no witnesses.

Activity 5.16

Consider the following offences. Which ones would you report to the police? Give a reason for your choice.

1 You have lost your mobile phone while out shopping.

2 £10 is missing from your wallet.

3 Graffiti has been sprayed on the wall of your house.

4 Someone has scratched the paintwork on your car.

5 Your sociology textbook has disappeared from your locker.

6 You feel you are the victim of sexual or racial harassment at work.

The sociology of youth

In each of the above cases you may have been the victim of a crime, but in reality many of these cases are not reported to the police. This uncovered figure of crime is known as the 'dark figure' and may account for as much as 90 per cent of all crimes committed.

Another way of gaining data on young people and deviance is through the use of self-report studies. In these studies sociologists compile a list of pre-defined offences and ask young people to tick which ones they have committed in the previous 12 months. Respondents are guaranteed anonymity and confidentiality throughout this process. It is thought that young people will be more honest when responding to a self-report study than in an interview situation where 'interviewer effect' will have a major bearing on the quality of the data collected.

Data from a series of self-report studies in 2005 suggest that on occasion young people do behave in ways which might be considered anti-social. In 2004, a quarter of 10–25 year olds surveyed admitted that they had engaged in at least one of four types of anti-social behaviour during the previous twelve months. The most common form of anti-social behaviour was being noisy/rude in a public place (16 per cent), followed by behaving in a way that led to a neighbour complaining (12 per cent). Involvement in graffiti was lower at 3 per cent. Self-report studies suggest that approx 25 per cent of young people are offenders, but we should not ignore that this means 75 per cent are not reporting themselves as offenders.

## Labelling

**Labelling** (Becker, 1963) is a useful concept in the sociology of youth deviance because the definition of whether someone is deviant or not is based largely on whether their appearance and behaviour is different to the norm in society. Some groups of young people claim to have been labelled by people in authority (teachers, police). Labels which focus on criminal behaviour such as trouble makers, yobs, hooligan, and shoplifters are particularly difficult to shake off, and the label can become a 'master status' where the label given precedes all others. For example, when someone labelled as a shoplifter (rightly or wrongly) walks down the street, the label comes

I may as well steal and rob.

Figure 5. 11

to mind straight away and defines how their actions are perceived by others.

Closely related to the concept of labelling is the notion of the self-fulfilling prophecy. Once given a label the person cannot shake it off. They eventually fulfil the label and effectively turn into what they were labelled. In our scenario the boy labelled as a shoplifter actually becomes one because everyone believes he is one anyhow; in effect he believes he has nothing to lose.

## Moral panics

The role of the media is crucial in the labelling of young people. Media such as the Internet, television, magazines, radio and newspapers have the potential to create stereotypical impressions of young people which reaches millions of users. The concept of a **moral panic** refers to the process through which an event or social group are stereotyped by the media with the effect of creating a fear of crime throughout society. The fear is likely to be exaggerated due to the over reporting of the incident.

The concept of the moral panic was first used in the 1970s to describe the process through which an initial concern over drug taking in Notting Hill, London led to the escalation of the problem through specialist drugs squads being set up to target certain social groups. This led to an increase in the number of arrests and, in effect, an 'amplification' of the deviant act. In other words the situation became worse and created a moral panic through society. The concept has also been used by Cohen (1973) to describe the over-reporting by the media of fighting between Mods and Rockers in the summer of 1964. In this case the Mods and Rockers became 'folk devils', popularised as youth sub-cultural groups who were out of control. More recently Thornton (1995) has used the concept in relation to recreational drug taking by young people in the 1990s.

There is a counter argument that the media are not responsible for creating moral panics. This contends that they are simply reporting social reality – life as it is – and that if moral panics do occur this may serve the purpose of alerting society to potential problems, thereby helping to prevent social disorder by reinforcing the difference between right and wrong.

## Weblink
An account of clashes on Brighton beach between Mods and Rockers in the summer of 1964 can be found on the BBC 'On this Day' website (see 'Websites' page ii). It provides some excellent footage of these events, which will improve your understanding of this topic.

### Activity 5.17

1 Can you think of any contemporary events or social groups for which there have been moral panics?

2 Can you think of reasons why the media may choose to exaggerate some stories about young people and crime?

Sociologists treat the official crime figures for young people with caution for all the reasons covered in this section. It is highly likely that these figures are the result of the under reporting of crime, the labelling of young people, and media representing some groups of young people in a negative and stereotypical light. For these reasons sociologists argue that crime statistics are socially constructed – made by the way British society operates.

## Patterns and trends in youth crime

Through various sources such as the British Crime Survey (BCS) it is possible to compile statistical evidence of the nature and extent of crime.

The following is a list of some of the most significant findings from various surveys.

◆ Peak age for offending is 18 for males and 15 for females. However, the over-18s account for three-quarters of all detected crimes.

◆ Theft and handling stolen goods accounts for approximately half of all youth crime in comparison with less than 15 per cent for violence against the person.

◆ Approximately 80 per cent of youth offenders are male.

◆ Between 1992 and 2004 the number of young people convicted or cautioned fell by approximately 20 per cent.

◆ 7 per cent of all young people are classified as 'frequent offenders' (having committed an offence six or more times in the previous year).

◆ Young black males have higher rates of offending than Asian or white youths.

## Age

### Activity 5.18

1 Using the data in Figures 5.12, 5.13 and 5.14 write a short report on the main trends (a trend occurs over time) in relation to young people and crime. You should refer to both the time period and the age group and gender of the offenders.

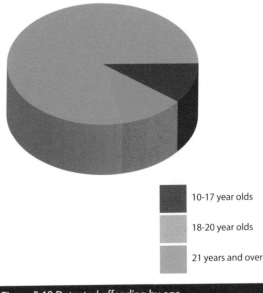

- 10-17 year olds
- 18-20 year olds
- 21 years and over

**Figure 5.12 Detected offending by age**

(Source: Nacro, 2006)

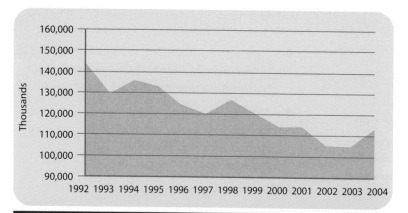

Figure 5.13 Children and young people cautioned, reprimanded, warned or sentenced for indictable offences, 1992–2004

(Source: Nacro, 2006)

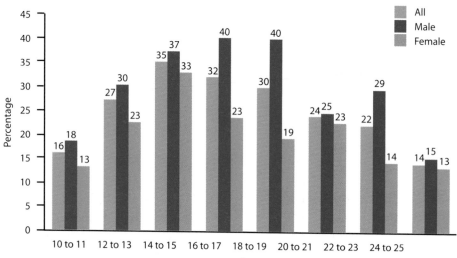

Figure 5.14 Proportion of 10 to 25 year olds committing an offence in the last 12 months by age, 2005

(Source: Offending, Crime and Justice Survey, Home Office, 2005)

## Gender

One of the most significant 'risk' factors for offending is being male. As Figure 5.15 shows, males are more likely than females to have committed criminal offences and although female crime rose during the 1990s it has declined since then. There are a number of possible explanations for these patterns and trends.

◆ Notions of femininity are opposed to criminal and highly deviant behaviour (Muncie, 2004).

◆ For some men, doing crime amounts to being seen as masculine (Messerschmidt, 1993).

◆ Young males have less informal control exercised in their lives (Smart, 1976).

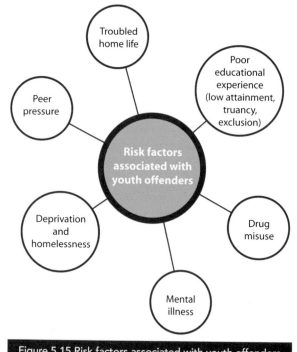

Figure 5.15 Risk factors associated with youth offenders, Nacro, 2006.

The sociology of youth

U2

5

- Young males are more likely to engage in risk-taking behaviour – what has become known as 'edgework'.
- Young males are more likely to be targeted by the police.
- Young males are more likely to be found guilty of criminal offences by the criminal justice system.

These explanations can be supplemented by the feminist explanations covered in the previous subsections.

## Ethnicity

In 2004, MORI carried out a survey of 11–16 year olds in mainstream schools in the UK, with the aim of finding find out accurate levels of offending behaviour. Over 4700 students from 192 schools completed the questionnaire. Table 5.5 shows the different types of offences committed by different ethnic groups.

The over-representation of young black people in the youth justice system remains a cause for concern in the UK. Recent research suggested that the reasons for this over-representation were largely connected to discriminatory treatment and often labelling. Black children were more likely to be charged for offences and had less confidence in the police who they considered as being 'racially stereotyping' and labelling their behaviour.

Other explanations focus on the socio-economic background of the offenders, suggesting that black children are more likely to experience social deprivation and therefore turn to crime as a way of reacting against the system. Clearly, explanations such as these can be related to the work of the CCCS who argued that social class is a key factor in explaining youth subcultural behaviour. However, these explanations do not account for young middle-class offenders from minority ethnic backgrounds, and neither do they explain the patterns of crime which show that different ethnic groups are engaged in different types of crime (Table 5.5). Finally, the media plays a role in the portrayal of the ethnic minority youth criminal, especially in relation to gang behaviour, guns and drug use. While there clearly are examples of criminal gangs based along ethnic divisions in the UK's major cities, there are also gangs based on territorial divisions which are not ethnically related. Alexander (2000) conducted a study into Asian gangs and concluded that the media had created a 'myth of the Asian gang' and that there was no evidence of young groups of Asians terrorising other ethnic groups. Conflict between groups of Asian youths were based around individuals and not a cohesive gang culture.

## Social class

Data on young people, crime and social class are particularly difficult to find probably due to the complexities of operationalising social class. However, it is likely that the nature and the extent of the crime differs according to social class. Messerschmidt (1993) refers to working-class and middle-class males from different ethnic groups being drawn to commit different types of offences; white working-class youth crime takes the form of vandalism, minor theft and alcohol-

Table 5.5 Criminal offences committed by different ethnic groups 2004

| Criminal offence committed | Different types of crimes committed by offenders (%) | | |
|---|---|---|---|
| | Asian | Black | White |
| Stealing | 54 | 72 | 61 |
| Driver and/or passenger in stolen vehicle | 8 | 22 | 13 |
| Assault | 51 | 58 | 49 |
| Handling stolen goods | 24 | 43 | 23 |
| Carrying a weapon | 33 | 41 | 38 |
| Causing criminal damage | 55 | 56 | 56 |

(Source: MORI Youth Survey, 2004, p. 28)

related offences, while minority ethnic group working-class crime is often related to street gangs. Middle-class offences are often reported as being based around recreational drug use.

A study by Nacro (2006) highlights the following risk factors explaining patterns and trends within youth crime. A number of these underscore the likelihood that social class is a key factor in explaining youth crime.

### Weblink
A number of these factors are referred to in a BBC web account of yob culture in the UK (see 'Websites' page ii).

## Sociological explanations of youth crime and deviance, patterns and trends

A number of explanations for these patterns and trends have been offered previously. Now we will apply the sociological theories you have studied already to the topic and consider how they approach the problem of youth crime and deviance.

## Functionalist explanations

The functionalist explanations see a certain amount of youth crime and deviance as a natural and inevitable feature of life in a contemporary society. As young people pass through the transitional phase of youth, on route to achieving the status of adulthood some are bound to deviate and stray from the accepted norm. The explanation offered here should be used in conjunction with the work of Abrarms (1959) and Eisenstadt (1956).

The concept of status frustration has been used to explain why some young working-class males offend. Faced with a gap between the social position they find themselves in (young, lack of money, lack of status) they are drawn into offending behaviour because it provides them with a status and gives them attention. This

concept has been usefully applied to crimes such as graffiti and vandalism as well as crimes with a financial gain. However, as with all of the functionalist explanations, it does not explain young middle-class offenders, female offenders or the different patterns of crime undertaken by young people from different ethnic groups. Other functionalist writers have taken the issue of status frustration further and argued that working-class males were likely to be involved in deviant activities because of living up to the 'focal concerns of masculinity', which included norms and values based on toughness and aggression.

In applying these dated theories to the contemporary UK we can see elements of validity in them as young males seem to be the most likely groups to engage in yob culture, binge drinking and associated criminal activity.

## Marxist explanations

Marxists take a different approach to explaining patterns and trends in youth offending. They focus on social class and the position of young people within the capitalist UK. These explanations come largely from the work of the CCCS. The concepts of exaggeration and resistance can be applied to young offenders who, it is argued, turn to crime and deviance as a way of reacting against and resisting capitalism. Faced with unemployment or working for a low wage in a dead end job provides the necessary fuel to kick back against the capitalist system and one way of doing this is through committing crime. However, these explanations still fail to explain the existence of middle-class young offenders, and only vaguely refer to young offenders from different ethnic backgrounds. Females likewise are largely missing from the Marxist CCCS work.

The concepts of relative deprivation and social exclusion have been used by more recent thinkers in explaining youth crime. In this analysis many of the crimes are motivated by and for money, having an economic and a social basis as many young people who are disadvantaged want the same life opportunities as others. These young people are aware of what they are doing when they commit the offences but the motivation/need for financial gain justifies the action.

# Labelling

Finally, concepts associated with interactionist theory have been referred to in this section and can clearly be applied to the treatment of young people by agencies such as the police and the media. They can also be used as ideas on which to consider the spiraling effect of criminal behaviour for some young people – when given a bad name they live up to the reputation.

## Section summary

Use the following key words to copy and complete the summary of this section below. Each word should be used only once.

labeling     10     dark figure     yob     socially-constructed     master status     moral panic
crime     deviance     self-report studies     official crime statistics     anti-social behaviour

A_____ breaks a law. Behaviour which goes against the norm in society is described as _____. Delinquency is used to describe the _____ _____ behaviour of young people in society.

The age of criminal responsibility in the UK is___, and the period of youth offending officially ends at the age of 18 when young people are treated in the adult courts. Statistical data on crime comes largely from two sources_____ _____ _____ and _____ _____ _____. Both methods have drawbacks and there is a large amount of crime which goes undetected and unreported, known as the _____ _____.

The interactionist concept of _____ is useful in explaining youth crime. Many young people feel this has happened to them and in some cases it can become a _____ _____or lead to a self-fulfilling prophecy. The media is accused of labeling some groups and creating _____ _____. The terms hoodie and ____ culture have been used by the media in over reporting a particular type of youth 'hanging around' behaviour in the UK.

Most sociologists agree that crime and deviance are _____ _____ categories, made by the way British society works.

## Exam practice

(a) Identify and explain two patterns in youth crime.                          (17 marks)

(b) Outline and evaluate the view that labelling explains the youth crime in the contemporary UK.          (33 marks)

# (iv) The experience of youth in education

## Pause for thought

1   What factors have shaped your experience of school?

2   Was gender a factor in your choice of AS level subjects?

3   Are there any groups of students in your school/college who have negative attitudes to school? What kinds of behaviour do you associate with these groups?.

Figure 5.16 Socialising at school

An individual's experience of their school could be considered in many different ways. When you discuss your responses to question 1 above, different people will attach different meanings to their 'school experience'. For many it will be based on the social experiences of mixing with their peer groups, for some it will be based on the extra-curricular activities available at the school, while others will mention the subjects studied, the teachers and their academic achievement in exams and tests. Furthermore an individual's experience of schooling will involve aspects of the **formal** and the **informal** (hidden) curriculum. Figure 5.17 identifies some of the important factors within the school experience.

There is sociological evidence to show that an individual's experience of schooling is influenced by their gender, ethnicity and their social class. The first part of this subsection will consider some of these ideas, before exploring the patterns and trends in subject choice and the explanations for them.

## Experience of schooling by gender

Being male or female is a key factor in an individual's school experience. From attending play group onwards peer groups are formed

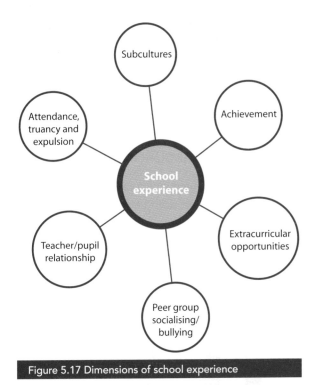

Figure 5.17 Dimensions of school experience

classrooms and playgrounds show how gender-related issues determine friendship groups, opportunities and achievements. A study by Reay (2001) on girls aged 8 in a primary classroom describes four clearly identifiable groups – the nice girls, the girlies, the spice girls and the tomboys – showing that even by the age of 8, gender-related peer groups have formed in school. This subsection considers young people from the age of 12 to 18 which, for most students, covers the years of secondary school where gender is a crucial factor in the experiences of school.

## Academic achievement

The media frequently reports on differences in school experience according to levels of educational achievement at GCSE and at A level, for which boys in recent years lag behind the girls. Many factors have been offered to explain this such as coursework being advantageous to females, boys having too much confidence in their own ability or lacking the social and communication skills of girls.

around issues of masculinities and **femininities**, and it would be misleading to suggest that gender only becomes important during the period of youth. Many studies of primary

Figure 5.18 Educational experience differs by gender, class and ethnicity

However, the pattern of differential educational achievement is not really so clear cut and it is an over simplification to say that gender explains educational achievement. Middle-class boys who attend fee paying schools do very well on the whole, as do middle-class girls. The sizable minority of middle-class boys who do not excel in education are unlikely to form sub-cultural groups but rather to develop feelings of inadequacy, having failed their parents and their social background. However, studies of working class boys who underachieve show how they are more likely to form anti-school subcultures (Willis, 1977) and/or to find an alternative to academic work often through achievement in sport or through workplace-related activities. Similarly the pattern of educational achievement is influenced by ethnicity, where Indian and Chinese students (female and male) on the whole achieve more highly than Pakistani and Bangladeshi groups.

It would seem, therefore, that academic achievement cannot be explained by one set of factors and that social class, gender and ethnicity are all crucial in explaining achievement levels which will impact on students' school experience.

## Changing femininities

A famous study by Sharpe (1976), in which she interviewed a group of working-class girls in the early 1970s, found that girls valued 'romance' and motherhood more than doing well in education and following a career. However, when Sharpe (1994) interviewed another group of girls a decade on she found them to be much more career orientated, seeing education as a route to economic and social success. Two key factors could explain this change.

1    New opportunities for girls in education – schemes which encourage girls to study science and maths such as Women into Science and Engineering (WISE) have had an impact on the experience of some girls in education, encouraging them into new areas previously dominated by boys.

2    The changing class structure which has seen many working-class families becoming socially mobile and wanting their daughters to progress further in education and in life

than they did themselves. A study by Reay et al. (2005) shows how many educationally-successful women stress the support offered by their families and the emotional support of their fathers, in particular, during their latter school years.

## Changing masculinities

Hegemonic (dominant) masculinity is based on the notion of men providing and protecting their female partners and their children. Competing forms of masculinity such as the new man, new lad or homosexual male may challenge the norm. However, evidence would suggest that the attachment a boy has to the dominant values of hegemonic masculinity will influence their experience of schooling. A study by Kehily and Nayak (1997) looked a the use of humour and joking between boys aged 15 and16 in a secondary school and describes 'cussing' where the boys engage in verbal insults, often based around insults about each other's mothers such as 'your mum's a dog' and your mum's got sweaty armpits'. The ability to make such insults brought status within the predominantly working-class peer group. The same study describes a game called punch-'n'-run where young men punched one another and ran away before the opponent had time to retaliate. This was viewed by the researchers as a form of male bonding. The same study reported the importance of humour in establishing heterosexual identity for boys in schools.

The concept of the crisis of masculinity (Mac an Ghaill, 1994) has been used to explain why male achievement patterns in recent years have changed. Faced with an uncertain future and no longer being clear on the male role in society has affected young men who no longer believe that educational success is crucial and are confused about what their role in society is.

### Activity 5.19

In groups make a list of the ways that females and males use break-time and lunch-time. Is there a difference in their use of 'free time'? If there are differences, to what extent do you think gender explains them?

## Resistance

A number of studies of young people in school use the concept of 'resistance' to suggest that students use different types of behaviour as a way of responding to their marginal position in the school/classroom. The early studies on resistance by writers such as Willis (1977) applied the concept to white working-class lads who used sexist and racist jokes as a way of coping with school life. The 'lads' in Willis' study were contrasted with the 'ear 'oles', the academically-able boys who would succeed in their exams. The concept of resistance has been applied to different youth social groups in more recent studies and it is clear that it is not only white working-class boys who 'resist' schooling and the authority of teachers. In a study of year 10 boys in an inner London school called the 'Harkton, boys' resistance to academic achievement and the fear of being seen as a 'swot' was demonstrated.

# Experience of schooling by ethnicity

The concept of resistance has been used in the study of students from ethnic minority groups.

Sewell (2000) used the concept of resistance to explain the behaviour of some groups of African-Caribbean boys in his study. In particular two groups he called the Retreatists and the Rebels resisted the views of teachers and values of the school which they believed had failed to provide for their needs.

Resistance is not only found in relation to boys, Shain (2003) used the concept to explain the behaviour of a group of Asian girls in a secondary school, known as the 'Gang Girls'. The Gang Girls believed they had been the victim of racist bullying by teachers and peers and had developed a 'them and us' attitude to schooling. These girls were very different to the black girls Mirza (1992) found in her study. The black girls displayed a positive self esteem and were focused on achieving academic success. The girls were not labelled negatively by teachers although some teachers had well meaning but misplaced intentions which held the girls back. Mirza found that the Irish girls in her study saw their futures as home-makers, child carers and part-time workers, whereas the black girls anticipated a career, suggesting clear differences in expectations of schooling from different ethnic groups.

## Racism

A number of studies report that racism remains a factor in school experience. Studies on the experiences of black and Asian pupils frequently refer to experiences of racism often in subtle forms from peers and from teachers.

Wright et al. (2006) describe instances of teachers claiming that black boys in their classes were more gregarious (outgoing) and physically expressive than the white boys. Coupled with wearing what some teachers described as a special uniform of dreadlocks and scarves hiding their faces, the teachers felt as though these boys brought attention to themselves which could lead to differential treatment in the classroom. The boys adopted the same behaviour in the classroom as they did outside the classroom and when teachers questioned their behaviour the boys accused them of racism. Whether these instances were a result of racist intentions on behalf of the teachers or not they certainly fuelled negative relations between the black boys and their teachers, and between different groups of peers.

Another important dimension of school experience is exclusion. Each year over 10,000 pupils, mainly black and white working-class boys, are excluded from schools in the UK. Exclusion rates are significantly higher for black males than for any other ethnic group suggesting that the experience of these students is a result of negative attitudes to school or the schools' negative labelling of the boys. Boys are considerably over represented in all these categories.

# Experience of schooling by social class

Social class also impacts heavily on school experiences. Many early studies of school experience centred on white working-class boys, who showed resistance to education and to school, seeing their futures in the work place (Willis, 1977).

In Lees' research (1993) academically or work-orientated girls (also described as pro-school) were typically white females from middle-class homes with strong parental support.

Hatcher (2006) argues that the education system in the UK today does not encourage working-class success and that the experience of working-class pupils differs from middle-class students. The middle classes possess more cultural and economic capital, both key to enjoying the wider benefits of education in the UK. Social class is also an issue in terms of the type of school that a young person attends. Consider the school experience of a year 10 boy at Eton College in comparison with a year 10 boy at a local comprehensive school.

Power et al. (1998) studied 342 academically-able boys and concluded that those not achieving high grades showed resistance to the dominant work ethic in their schools. This finding showed similarities to Aggleton's (1987) study of middle-class students in a sixth form where a group of able boys resisted the middle- class values of academic achievement and wanted to progress without effort; they aimed for 'effortless achievement'.

This subsection has shown that the experience of schooling is related to social class, gender and ethnicity. It would be an over simplification to suggest that any one factor is more important than another. The key issue to remember is that school will be experienced differently according to an individual's social identity.

# Patterns and trends in subject choice

Up to the 1980s boys and girls often followed different educational courses. Boys were often encouraged to study the masculine orientated subjects such as woodwork, metal work and science, while girls were encouraged to study subjects preparing them for their position as a wife and mother or for work in office-based jobs – cookery, needlework and vocational courses involving typing.

The introduction of the 1988 National Curriculum has meant that all students have had to study the foundation subjects of maths, English and science and students have been offered fewer optional subjects. Regardless of their gender, ethnicity or social class all students within a school are basically offered the same subjects up to GCSE level. In post-16 education, choice has remained.

Despite this legal requirement, over time the patterns of subject choice have remained stable, with boys being more likely to study science, maths and technology-related subjects and girls being more likely to opt for modern languages, social sciences and biology. In recent years there has been a slight change in subject choice and, the gender divide is beginning to break down with more girls opting to study A Levels in the physical sciences and more boys choosing subjects in the social sciences.

# What explains the patterns and trends?

## Innate ability

Some research has suggested that boys find maths and science subjects easier , possibly because of their ability to learn facts and figures. Boys tend to perform better at multiple-choice tests. On the other hand, girls may find studying itself a more comfortable activity. They may be able to pay attention to the teacher for longer periods of time and may be in a more favourable position with coursework which requires careful planning over time. These conclusions could be related to the functionalist view that males and females perform different roles in society. These differences may be innate (inbuilt), that is, due to biological factors.

## Subject preferences

It has been argued that the different patterns reflect the different preferences of girls and boys. Some subjects are seen as being more masculine than others (such as maths and computing), while others are seen as more feminine (such as biology and social sciences). Subject choice will of course be influenced by these perceptions. Science, in particular, has been described as a patriarchal subject, dominated by males and aimed at males. The hidden curriculum is a factor in forming these perceptions.

## Socialisation in the home

Parental expectations may have altered over time so that many parents now want their daughters to have the same opportunities in education as

1  Tables 5.6 and 5.7 show the gender breakdown at GCSE and at A Level in the UK in 2006. What patterns can you detect?

2  Carry out an analysis of the gender breakdown in each of the subjects you are studying in your school/college. Are there any patterns? If so what do you think explains them?

3  Are all pupils offered the same subjects at GCSE in your school? If not, what determines the subjects offered?

4  Research the trends in subject choice at A level over the past five years, in your school/college.

Table 5.6 Percentage of students entered for GCSE in selected subjects, 2006

| Subject | Female (%) | Male (%) |
| --- | --- | --- |
| French | 54 | 46 |
| English Literature | 52 | 48 |
| Double Science | 51 | 49 |
| English | 50 | 50 |
| Maths | 50 | 50 |
| D&T | 46 | 54 |
| IT | 50 | 50 |

Table 5.7 Percentage of students entered for A Level in selected subjects, 2006

| Subject | Female (%) | Male (%) |
| --- | --- | --- |
| English Literature | 71 | 29 |
| Social Studies | 69 | 31 |
| Modern Languages | 68 | 32 |
| Biological Sciences | 62 | 38 |
| History | 51 | 49 |
| Chemistry | 51 | 49 |
| Business Studies | 47 | 53 |
| Maths | 40 | 60 |
| Computer Studies | 27 | 73 |
| Physics | 24 | 76 |

(Source: Department for Education and Skills, 2005)

their sons. Thirty years ago women had fewer opportunities in the workplace and the role of provider was an expectation for men. This has now changed and it may be a result of society becoming more meritocratic. This may explain the slight convergence/changes in subject choice in recent years.

## Changing masculinities and femininities

As gender identities are now more flexible young men and young women can follow their chosen educational path with greater ease. It is less of a stigma nowadays to be a woman working in the construction industry or a man working in the catering industry, and this may encourage subject choice to be more fluid and less constrained than in the past. This view is associated with the postmodern theories of individualism and eclecticism.

### Changing expectations in school

Teachers still do have the important role of advising students on subject choice and some teachers may hold sexist attitudes. However, as social expectations have changed, teachers are less likely to label than they were.

Blinkenstaff (2005) suggested that some of following reasons explain why girls are reluctant to opt for Science, Technology, Engineering, Maths (STEM) subjects:

◆ girls lack innate talent in STEM subjects

◆ girls have less interest in these subjects

◆ there are few positive role models

◆ the science curriculum does not interest most girls

◆ teachers give boys more attention in science lessons.

To conclude, the evidence on subject choice shows a relatively stable but slightly fluid picture. It is still fair to say that subject choice at A level is heavily gendered.

# Pro- and anti-school/education subcultures

Throughout this section you have been introduced to a variety of different studies on youth subcultures. This final subsection will focus on examples of subcultures within schools, some of which have a favourable and positive attitude to school and education (pro-education/pro-school), and others which have a negative and often confrontational attitude to school and education (anti-education/anti-school). There are also examples of groups holding a pro-education but anti-school culture, where they value education for 'getting on and getting out' of the working class but they have negative views of school due to their experiences within it. Throughout this subsection the concepts of school and education need to be treated separately; school being the institution and

education being the system in which schools operate.

We are going to consider four studies in turn all of which illustrate different features of subcultures/groups within schools. Each study has already been referred to in this book.

# Example 1: Asian girls

Shain (2003) interviewed Asian girls in a number of different schools in the Manchester area. She identified four different groups of girls; each group used different strategies for coping with school experiences

### Gang Girls

These girls held anti-education and anti-school views. They were confrontational and had developed a 'them and 'us' attitude. These girls felt they had experienced racism in the school and this had led them to form an all Asian female subculture from which white students and teachers were excluded. The girls used survival tactics of resistance through their culture. They had a clear and positive Asian identity which they defended.

### The Survivors

This group were pro-education and pro-school. They defined their school experience in positive terms, worked hard and viewed school and education as a means through which they could better themselves. They were perceived as timid and shy by most teachers, although this was a clever front, a way of avoiding trouble. The girls had all experienced racism and sexism but chose to ignore it. The girls used the tactic of conforming to the expectations of Asian girls (being shy and timid) in order to shape their school experience.

### The Rebels

These girls were pro-education and pro-school, and were a distinct group because they blamed their home background for their differential school experiences. Some of these girls spoke about feeling happier at school than at home and some described their parents' views as 'backward'. These girls rejected the Gang Girls' confrontational attitude and instead often formed friendship groups with white girls. They were seen as rebelling against their parental culture.

## Faith Girls

These girls were pro-education and pro-schooling. They prioritised religion as a source of identity and difference. The girls had positive relations with teachers. They were conformist.

# Example 2: Harkton boys

Archer and Yamashati (2003) studied this group of year 10 boys in a London comprehensive school. They displayed norms and values that were anti-school and anti-education. Style, clothes and accent were crucial parts of their identity in school and in the local area where they wanted to be visible and seen by others. They displayed a strong commitment to their local area and all spoke about the importance of staying 'local' and not moving away when they left school. They enjoyed rap culture, and showed an attachment to the 'bad boy' image. In school they considered reading and education to be 'soft'. They all thought that if they worked hard in class they could be labelled as a 'pussy' and therefore did not want to be seen to make an effort to learn.

# Example 3: Ladettes

Jackson (2006a) researched **ladette** culture in secondary schools and claimed they displayed anti-school and anti-swot characteristics. Their norms and values included acting hard, smoking, swearing, disrupting lessons, being cheeky/rude to the teacher, loud/gobby and open about their (heterosexual) sex lives. These norms and values were displayed in and out of school. The girls were mostly white and working class and were in danger of seriously underachieving in school because of their attitude of 'it's not cool to be clever'.

# Example 4: African-Caribbean boys

Sewell (2000) studied groups of African-Caribbean boys and identified four visible groups.

## Conformists

These boys wanted to achieve academic success and were individually well motivated to succeed. They were pro-education and pro-school.

## Innovators

These boys accepted the goals of schooling but rejected the means of achieving the goals. They were pro-education, but anti-schooling. They thought that schools and teachers had largely failed to provide for their needs.

## Retreatists

These boys rejected the goals of schooling/education and the means of achieving them.

---

Activity 5.21

Use the studies in this section to complete Table 5.8. It will be a useful way of learning the different studies.

Table 5.8 Pro- and anti-school/education subcultures

| Name of group | Norms/values displayed | Examples of pro behaviour | Examples of anti behaviour |
|---|---|---|---|
|  |  |  |  |
|  |  |  |  |
|  |  |  |  |
|  |  |  |  |

They were not confrontational; they just did not like school work.

## Rebels

This groups formed a 'posse'. They followed rap culture and felt school and education had failed them. They were disliked and distrusted by the other three groups.

Having considered these examples we can conclude by summarising the roles subcultures play in schools/education.

◆ To challenge authority.

◆ As a form of resistance, against school, home or society.

◆ To offer members a way of bettering themselves.

◆ To offer expression to group identity, creating a positive or a negative impression.

◆ To provide status.

Activity 5.22

Using the four example studies, which groups would provide examples for each of the five explanations above?

## Section summary

Use the following key words to copy and complete the summary of this section below. Each word should be used only once.

> formal curriculum    informal curriculum    femininities    resistance    ladettes
> STEM    patriarchal    pro-school    anti-school    pro-education
> anti-education    hegemonic masculinity

An individual's experience of schooling is influenced by factors in the _____ _____ such as the subjects they study and grades they achieve and in the _____ _____ through hidden rules of school life. Sociological evidence shows that gender and ethnicity and social class are all important influences on school experience.

There are a range of competing masculinities within a school, and evidence shows that a boy's commitment to _____ _____ will affect his school experience. Similarly there are a range of _____ in school, one example are_____ who display anti-school and anti-swot characteristics. There are clear patterns in subject choice between girls and boys at A Level, with boys being more likely to opt for subjects in physical science and maths, often leading to careers in _____. Girls on the other hand are more likely to choose social sciences or languages to study. One explanation for this is the _____ nature of science.

The concept of_____ has been well used in explaining the school experience of different ethnic groups and different social classes. This is where different groups challenge or subvert the school/education system as a way of resisting teachers and school rules. A number of different groups do this by displaying negative attitudes, known as _____ _____ and _____ _____. Other sub-cultural groups display positive attitudes to school and education, such as the Conformists and the Faith Girls. These are known as _____ _____ and ____ _____.

## Exam practice

(a) Identify and explain two features of anti-school subcultures. (17 marks)

(b) Outline and evaluate the view that pupils' experience of schooling differs according to their gender. (33 marks)

# ExamCafé
## Relax, refresh, result!

## Guidelines for answering questions in Unit 2 (G762)

Your answer will be assessed against three Assessment Objectives (AOs). It is important that you know and understand what these are, and in which questions you need to demonstrate them.

| Assessment objective (AO) | Useful ways of displaying Assessment Objective are through terms such as : |
|---|---|
| 1 Knowledge and understanding: the studies, theories, concepts and contemporary examples you have learned throughout your course | • _____ argued…<br>• A study by_____ explored…<br>• The Marxists would explain this by…<br>• A useful example is_____…<br>• The concept of _____… |
| 2 Interpretation and application: how well you interpret the knowledge and apply it to a given question/point | • This means…<br>• This shows…<br>• Therefore…<br>• In relation to… |
| 3 Evaluation and analysis: judgements, criticisms, appraisals and assessment of sociological knowledge | • However…<br>• On the other hand…<br>• A different view is offered by…<br>• This was criticised by… |

One useful technique to practise is that of KIE (Knowledge, Interpretation, Evaluation):

- Do I *know* this? (K)
- Can I *interpret* this? (I)
- Can I *evaluate* this? (E)

# Answering part a) questions

These questions target knowledge and understanding. Therefore, you need to show what you know in relation to the question.

Here are three general tips to help you.

1   Spend no longer than 15 minutes answering this question. Produce two substantial paragraphs, making it clear to the examiner when one point ends and the next begins.

2   Avoid duplication of material in your two explanations. Select features that are sufficiently different from each other. Sometimes overlap of material is unavoidable but if you can avoid this, do so.

3   Aim to include a study or concepts in each paragraph. Sometimes theory will be applicable and sometimes contemporary examples, but in the main explain the studies and concepts which are relevant.

# Answering part b) questions

These questions target all three Assessment Objectives (AOs). Therefore you are required to show knowledge and understanding, interpretation and application, and evaluation and analysis. These questions require short, essay-like responses.

Here are three general points to help you.

1   Spend no longer than 30 minutes answering the question, with a short introduction of four or five main points (supported with evidence) and a short conclusion. In total you should aim for at least two A4 sides of writing. A very strong answer will probably produce more than this.

2   Plan your answer around the view expressed in the question. Plan arguments for and against the view. One way of doing this is through a clear contrast. It may help to list them in a rough table form like this:

| Arguments for | Arguments against |
|---|---|
|  |  |
|  |  |

In this way you are sure to provide evidence for at least two viewpoints, which should improve your evaluation mark.

3   Keep the question in mind throughout your answer and use the trigger words at the start of this section to highlight the skills you are showing.

# Getting started at AS level

Studying for AS level in sociology will be an extension of what you are used to at GCSE. Most sociology students have not studied GCSE sociology but the skills required in preparing for the AS exams are the same as in most humanities subjects. The key change at AS is that you are required to write longer answers in the exam. This means you need to be able to draw on a range of knowledge and understanding: concepts, studies, theories and contemporary examples and to be able to link them together coherently. One really useful way of preparing for this is to practise planning out longer answers, specifying which theories and studies you can use. The next section, Refresh your memory, shows you one way of doing this.

# ExamCafé
## Relax, refresh, result!

We are going to look at a student response written under exam conditions to the following question.

**Exam question**
(a) Identify and explain two trends in family life in the UK over the past 30 years. (17 marks)
(b) Outline and evaluate the view that the family in the UK is characterised by diversity. (33 marks)

# Relax and prepare

## Ciaran
These questions are OK. I've got enough to write about. I'm not sure I'll know the data for trends over the last 30 years though.

## Jas
I feel quite confident here. I know we've covered both of these in class. I must remember to use studies and theories.

## Angie
Both of these questions seem really wide. I'm worried that I'll have too much to write about.

# Hot tips

# Examiner's tips
- If you are asked to identify two trends from a number of trends, select very different ones which will not overlap too much.
- In longer answers, plan your answer around a key debate to explore between two theories or different studies/viewpoints. This can be used to structure your answer, as it will increase your evaluation marks.
- If you can comment on social policy issues in (b) answers, this will offer a different angle.

# Refresh your memory

## Revision checklist

You might find it useful to use a table like the one below to check your knowledge, and record your own sources of information

| Topic | Studies | Do I know this? | Look here |
|---|---|---|---|
| **Trends in family life:** divorce, marriage, family size, lone parents. | Williams; Allan and Crowe | | |
| **Different types of family diversity:** class, sexual, regional, cultural, organisational | Rapoport and Rapoport; Roseneil and Budgeon | | |
| **Theories:** Functionalism New Right views Feminism Postmodernism | | | |

# Get the result!

## Model answers

**Examiner says:**

Angie has used some accurate data to show that she clearly understands a trend occurs over time. Her use of a study is also good practice although the point made about the rise in divorce leading to lone-parent families does need explaining. The use of Sharpe is a clever use of material from Unit 1, which is to be encouraged. However, Sharpe's work actually showed that girls were still interested in being a mother although they wanted to delay that part of their lives while they secured a career.

## Angie's answer to part (a)

The first trend is the increase in the number of lone-parent families in the UK. There are now three times as many children living in lone-parent households as in 1972. Allan and Crowe argue this is due to factors such as an increase in divorce and a rise in the number of women who have children without getting married or cohabiting. For these women, having a child is a positive experience that they want for themselves without any intention of sharing the experience with the child's father. This could be linked to Sharpe's work where she argued that young girls in the 1990s were less interested in being

(Angie's answer continued . . .)

family orientated and more interested in having careers than they were in the 1980s.

Another trend is that women are choosing to have their children later in life. The average age for having their first child has increased by three years. There are lots of reasons for this; according to Williams the high cost of childcare is a major factor. He argues that for many women delaying the age of having their first child is a positive choice as they give priority to their careers. This can again be linked to Sharpe's work.

# Angie's answer to part (b)

Diversity is the concept that recognises differences within the family. Family diversity means the organisational differences between families such as lone parents, same sex couples, married couples and reconstituted families (Rappaport and Rappaport)

According to the New Right and the functionalists, the dominant type of family in the UK is the nuclear family. The nuclear family consists of two heterosexual adults who are married, have dependent children and who have traditional conjugal roles: the male breadwinner and the female homemaker whose responsibilities are domestic labour and childcare. New Right supporters such as Dennis argue that the nuclear family is in decline but they reject the view that diversity is a positive feature of contemporary life. Functionalist writers such as Parsons argue the family has two functions: the primary socialisation and the stabilisation of adult personalities. According to both Dennis and Parsons, men are suited to their role as breadwinner and women are suited to being homemakers.

Feminists and Marxists have criticised the nuclear family saying that many women are not happy fulfilling their stereotypical gender role and that the nuclear family exploits women. They refer to the high levels of depression and illness that many housewives suffer from. This feminist perspective has been criticised for ignoring the positive experiences of family life.

The postmodernists see life as a 'supermarket', where people can choose the types of relationship they form and the structure of the family they live in. Stacy argues that the postmodern family is characterised by diversity, and Beck uses the concept of individualisation when explaining family life in the UK. This perspective has been criticised for emphasising choice too much; for example, most lone-parents do not choose to be in that position. .

Evidence for the view that the family is characterised by diversity are family trends. Marriage rates are in decline, and rates of cohabitation are increasing although it could be argued that even though marriage is in decline, this is because people value marriage more. Divorce rates have also increased over the past 30 years. Lone parent families are also increasing, with 24 per cent of children now being socialised in these families. These trends suggest that diversity is typical in the contemporary UK. The UK also allows same-sex couples to be married and to adopt children, showing a clear acceptance of diversity from a legal point of view. However, these families are sometimes seen as going against the norm in society and we can ask if they are treated in the same way as traditional nuclear families are.

There also diversity in family life based on social class, with higher social classes possessing more cultural capital from their families. Brannen describes the beanpole family in the UK, where family members have more contact between generations than within a generation.

(Angie's answer continued . . .)

There are also a range of culturally-diverse practices seen in families in the UK. Some ethnic groups are more religious than others and this is evident in their family practices, where the expectations placed on girls and boys differs as is the case in some Sikh families. Evidence also shows that women in African Caribbean families are more likely to be lone parents than any other ethnic group.

It is clear from this evidence that families in the contemporary UK do show diversity. It could be argued this is due to various government policies. The New Right governments of the 1980s tried to make it harder for people to divorce, and were reluctant to offer the same legal rights to same-sex couples as New Labour have. New Labour does seem to promote diversity and choice, which can be seen as a feature of postmodern life in the contemporary UK.

**Examiner says:**

This is a useful conclusion as it answers the question and brings in a social policy angle as new material. This shows that Angie does understand the theoretical divisions and the importance of social policy in bringing about change.

Overall, Angie's introduction and conclusion both show clear sociological insight, and suggest she is a very able AS student. She initially makes the mistake of answering the question related to diversity but not focused wholly on it. It is almost as though she knows too much and hasn't taken the time to plan the answer out in a way that would improve the coherence and her grade. The answer would be stronger if it was structured around the Rapoports and the range of evidence on different types of diversity: cultural, class, organisational. She could use Roseneil and Budgeon in evaluation, before exploring the functionalist and New Right arguments that diversity is not a permanent feature of life in the UK. This is a good response but not likely to achieve the highest grade at AS.

# ExamCafé
## Relax, refresh, result!

We are going to look at a student response written under exam conditions to the following question.

**Exam question**
(a) Identify and explain two differences in morbidity patterns according to gender. (17 marks)
(b) Discuss the view that inequalities in health and illness between different ethnic groups are caused by cultural factors. (33 marks)

## Relax and prepare

### Hot tips

**Keely**

This is OK. I've revised gender and ethnicity and know what to do.

**Rob**

I know the theories for (b) but I'm not sure I know enough patterns for either part.

**Sean**

We did loads in class on ethnicity and gender, so there is plenty to write about.

### Examiner's tips

- Remember to evaluate every theory/argument you put forward.
- Relate the points you make to the actual question.

## Revision checklist

You might find it useful to use a table like the one below to check your knowledge, and record your own sources of information.

| Topic | Do I know this? | Look here |
|---|---|---|
| Morbidity patterns | | |
| Explanations for gender inequalities:<br>• biological<br>• artefact<br>• cultural<br>• structural | | |
| Patterns of health and illness by ethnic group | | |
| Explanations for gender inequalities:<br>• biological<br>• artefact<br>• cultural<br>• structural<br>• racism | | |

Health

# Get the result!

## Model answers

## Keely's answer to part (a)

**Examiner says:**

Keely correctly defines morbidity and gives a clear difference, backed up with a study and some examples of different illnesses. The answer is focused too heavily on women and would improve with some discussion of the illnesses associated with men. This could draw on factors relating to the workplace or to the risky lifestyle of some men.

It has been said that 'men die quicker while women get sicker', suggesting there are differences in morbidity (illness) and mortality (death) rates according to gender.

The first difference is that women and men suffer from different types of illness. Cancer is a good example; women develop breast cancer and men develop prostrate cancer. This is due to biological differences between men and women but may also be due to social factors. The development of all types of cancer has been linked to biological factors and lifestyle issues. Annandale and Field argue that a woman's production of oestrogen, for example, is influenced by biological factors and lifestyle. The menstrual cycle and women's ability to give birth both contribute to higher patterns of morbidity for women.

Another difference in morbidity patterns is that women seek advice from their GPs more than men do. This is important because it suggests that not only do men and women suffer from qualitatively different types of ill-health, they also suffer from different quantities of it too. Women's nurturing role may account for their tendency to visit their GPs more often than men do. Banks argues that men are less likely to visit their GPs because independence and stoicism are defining features of masculinity.

# Keely's answer to part (b)

There are clear differences in health and illness according to ethnic group. This essay will outline what these differences are, before exploring the cultural factors which may explain them. These will be evaluated by the artefact and structural explanations.

Whitehead (1987) and Mares (1987) suggest that members of minority groups die from the same diseases as the majority population — heart disease and cancer. However, a detailed analysis of patterns of morbidity and mortality show some differences between ethnic groups. For example, African-Caribbeans have higher rates of strokes than other ethnic groups, and Tay-Sachs disease is associated with Jewish people. However, it is difficult to accept that genetic differences alone explain differences in patterns of health and illness, as most Jewish people do not develop Tay-Sachs and most African Caribbean people do not suffer from strokes.

The cultural/behavioural explanations suggest it is the norms, values and social behaviour of an individual/social group that determines the level of their health. Sometimes this is due to lifestyle choices,

## Examiner says:

This is another feature and Keely does well in displaying her knowledge and understanding of the terms qualitative and quantitative. The paragraph needs more detail and more development, especially the points relating to women's nurturing role and the importance of masculinity, both of which should be developed.

## Examiner says:

This introduction sets out clearly what Keely is going to do. If you struggle with essay structure, this type of introduction can help you to focus directly on the question. As you become more a confident writer, you will probably find different and more interesting ways of doing this. The obvious point to make in this introduction is the danger of treating ethnic groups as distinct; gender, class and age cut across them.

## Examiner says:

This is a knowledge-giving paragraph, and serves the purpose of stating some of the patterns. It would improve with further development of all of the points made. For example, what are the implications of Whitehead's and Mares' suggestions for this actual exam question?

traditions and cultural values. Cultural explanations focus on factors such as diet, smoking and exercise patterns which do differ between different ethnic groups. For example, Bangladeshi men are the most likely group to smoke cigarettes (44 per cent compared with 27 per cent of the general population). This may account for some of the illnesses they suffer from. Similarly, the relatively high rates of heart disease suffered by Asians have been attributed to the use of cooking fats such as ghee. The majority ethnic group in the UK has many illnesses relating to high intakes of alcohol, and associated risky behaviours.

The cultural explanations have been criticised for making sweeping generalisations about different ethnic groups; treating the cultures of 'Asian' groups as being shared, whereas, in fact, there are huge differences between Indian and Chinese groups, without even focusing on social class differences. Many sociologists focus on cultural factors alongside other issues, such as poverty and biological/genetic differences, as giving a more valid explanation of patterns of ill health. Structural/material explanations focus on the quality of life and material surroundings as explanations of ill health. It may be the position of a social group in the social class structure and their material wealth which determines their health. As ethnic groups such as Pakistanis experience higher levels of unemployment than other groups, this is likely to affect their social class position and their living conditions. Victor studied the homeless who were placed in B&B accommodation and who showed higher levels of depression, stress and hospital visits. Most of these people were from the minority ethnic groups. The low income experienced by some ethnic groups also contributes to a lack of a healthy diet and a lower quality of living. These structural approaches suggest that it is not ethnicity (or the culture of ethnic groups) alone which accounts for the differences in health and illness patterns, but also that socio-economic factors play a part.

Racism has also been given as an explanation for patterns of ill health. McNaught suggest that racism at both a personal level and at an institutional level results in ethnic minorities receiving a poor

Health

**Examiner says:**

Overall, despite being mechanical, Keely's introduction and conclusion both show sociological understanding of this debate. Her conclusion would be stronger if she referred to the socially-constructed nature of health, illness and wellbeing. The whole answer is sound but needs further development of the points made: racism, structure, artefact and culture.

(Keely's answer continued . . .)

level of care from the NHS. Bowler showed that midwives on maternity wards held stereotypical views of Muslim Asian women, which may have affected the quality of care the patients received. Evidence shows that children born to Pakistani mothers are more likely to die in the first week of their lives than if they were born in other ethnic groups. This may be explained by racism or cultural differences, or there may be a genetic explanation.

A final explanation is the artefact one, which suggests there are no real differences in the patterns of ill health by ethnic group. The statistical evidence shows a distorted picture of health due to the methodological difficulties or artificial differences. Ethnic groups are also gendered, social class and age stratified so how can ethnicity alone be shown to be the crucial factor.

This is clearly a complex area, made worse by the genetic differences between some social groups which may explain some of the differences in health and illness patterns. Cultural explanations may play a part, however, the weight of evidence suggests it would be limiting to consider culture alone. Structural and biological/genetic differences are also important.

# Exam Café
## Relax, refresh, result!

We are going to look at a student response written under exam conditions to the following question.

**Exam question**
(a) Identify two ways in which individuals show their religious commitment in the contemporary UK. (17 marks)
(b) Outline and evaluate the Weberian view of the role of religion in society. (33 marks)

## Relax and prepare

### Hot tips

**Brendan**

Part (a) seems easy and I remember Weber was writing about religion and social change so (b) should be OK too.

**Sayma**

Part (b) is a bit scary. I worry that I'll get the theories confused.

**Michaela**

I can think of loads of ways for (a) but I'm not sure I'll have the evidence to back them up.

### Examiner's tips

- Make sure you cover the main aspects of the theory/view in the main body of the essay. Bringing something new into a conclusion is good practice but not if it should be an integral part of the essay.
- Always try to provide an evaluative point for each theory and question the assumptions or key points it makes. Even if you don't have a named study to call on, use your sociological awareness and question key ideas.

Religion

## Revision checklist

You might find it useful to use a table like the one below to check your knowledge, and record your own sources of information.

| Topic | Do I know this? | Look here |
|---|---|---|
| Church attendance | | |
| NRMs – why people join | | |
| Weber on social change (Calvinism) | | |
| Weber on charismatic leaders | | |
| Marx on religion as social control, ideology, Neo-Marxism | | |
| Beckford on religious diversity/postmodern views | | |
| Hamilton on the ideological role of religion | | |

# Get the result!

## Model answers

### Brendan's answer to part (a)

**Examiner says:**

This is focused on one way, and Brendan used class and age to illustrate his point with regard to status. He does initially confuse religious identification with attendance but his answer ends up making a valid point about status, attendance and identity.

One way is through attending a place of worship (church/mosque) and identifying themselves with a religion. The 2001 Census figures show that 71 per cent of people in the UK identified themselves as Christian, and approximately 25 per cent had no religion at all. The most obvious way to show this commitment is through attending a place of worship. However, church attendance in the UK is only 7 per cent. Most people who attend church are middle class; the group

(Brendan's answer continued . . .)

least likely to attend are youths. The middle classes may feel they should attend church to show thanks for all they have in life. Also it could be that it makes them look like good solid citizens — church attendance is often associated with a high status. This may be one of the reasons why so many leading politicians attend church as it is a social expectation. Youths are the least likely group to attend because they have so many other things to do with their time. There are other ways in which youths can gain status than by attending church (which may give them a low status). So my first way in which individuals show their religious commitment is by identifying with a religion and attending religious services in order to improve their social status.

Another way individuals show their religious commitment is by joining New Religious Movements. There is a growth in these types of movement because of their appeal, achieved by mixing elements of traditional religions with more individual views and ideas. Many NRMs contain elements of 'self improvement' and, together with New Age Movements, they appeal to young adults in particular. By joining a NRM people show their dedication as some of these groups require a large amount of commitment in terms of time and energy.

**Examiner says:**

By ending the paragraph stating what his 'way' is, Brendan makes sure the examiner knows he is answering the question.

**Examiner says:**

The focus on NRMs to illustrate commitment is a good. However, this answer would benefit from an example or a study.

## Brendan's answer to part (b)

**Examiner says:**

It is good practice to show theoretical divisions in questions which clearly require it, and Brendan knows this. To be more precise, however, functionalism is related to the concept of social stability more than Marxism is.

The Weberain view on the role of religion in society is that it promotes social change rather than promoting social stability. The opposing view is associated with Marxists who argue religion is a force of social stability.

Weber's view is that religion can bring about change in society as it is a very strong force. He uses the historical example of Calvinism in which followers lived a minimalist lifestyle, working hard and achieving high standards because the Calvinist religion taught them that only some people were part of the chosen select few. Weber was influenced by Social Action theory arguing that religious ideas could influence social behaviour. In this way the religious ideas associated with Calvinism promotes capitalism. This shows that religion is a force for change in promoting a capitalist economy.

There are, however, arguments against the view that religion is a force of social change, provided by the Marxists. Marx is associated with the quote 'religion is the opium of the people'. I interpret this as meaning religion has a very powerful influence upon individuals, almost like a drug, dulling the pains experienced by life. In this way religion does not promote social change, it promotes social conformity and can be viewed as a form of social control.

The Church of England provides a good example of this; there is a clear link between the church and the monarchy, and the prime minister appoints the bishops who have a place in the House of Lords, making laws for the UK. In this sense, religion could be said to illustrate the power of the ruling class in society and can be seen as a source of social control.

Religion can provide relief and comfort from feelings of alienation and worthlessness associated with many working-class jobs. For Marx, religion legitimises the capitalist system and holds back any revolutionary tendencies in society. In short, religion keeps people in their place in the capitalist system; it acts a force of social control.

The debate between Weber and Marx should not be considered as starkly opposite viewpoints. The neo-Marxist, Maduro, argues that Marxism should not be presented in such a one-dimensional way. For Maduro, under certain circumstances religion can promote change. The case of Libertarian theology in Latin America is a good example of where the Catholic Church, working alongside Marxist-based thinkers, has brought about a change in the living conditions of many of the world's poorest people. Similarly, it has been stated that Weber did not say religious ideas alone will bring about social change; the economic and social conditions need to be ripe for change to occur. Religion however does play a part.

(Brendan's answer continued . . .)

Weber provides a classic account of the role of religion in society and his contribution should not be neglected. Even though his theories are dated, Beckford states they are still valid. The contemporary UK is a religiously diverse society and it is difficult to conceive how religion cannot be concerned with bringing about change in some ways, while operating as a force of social control in other ways. His work on the role of charismatic leaders in fostering change is also important and can be applied to religious gurus worldwide who encourage change and resistance often drawing on their own leadership styles and visions.

**Examiner says:**

The first part of this conclusion is good; it uses Beckford, religious diversity and the contemporary UK. The reference to Weber and charismatic leaders should come earlier in the main body of the essay as the point is wasted in the conclusion. Perhaps Brendan should have planned it out better, or perhaps he just remembered this as he wrote the conclusion?

On the whole this is a good attempt at an answer and would achieve one of the higher grades. The strength of the answer lies in using the theories and some studies/examples to show engagement with the question throughout. Following the examiner tips would improve it still further.

Religion

# Exam**Café**
## Relax, refresh, result!

We are going to look at a student response written under exam conditions to the following question.

**Exam question**
(a) Identify and explain the features of any two youth subcultures. (17 marks)
(b) Outline and evaluate the view that spectacular youth subcultures are no longer important in the contemporary UK. (33 marks)

## Relax and prepare

### Hot tips

**Jodie**

I revised a range of subcultures so that I could write about the ones I knew best if a contrast or compare question came up.

**Lisa**

I know I must take the time to read the questions carefully and really think through how I can apply what I have learned when it comes to writing answers.

**Stephen**

We spent a lot of time on CCCS work in class so I thought it was worth taking time to revise this in detail, and most of the longer (b) questions need theory in them.

### Examiner's tips

- In answering the question, choose two subcultures that are very different from each other, selected, for example, from different decades.
- In answering (b) questions, think theoretically. Which theories did you cover in class and which are relevant?
- The question asks you to evaluate, so you should consider at least two opposing views. One way of doing this is to focus on different theories or approaches to the question.

## Revision checklist

You might find it useful to use a table like the one below to check your knowledge, and record your own sources of information.

| Topic | Do I know this? | Look here |
|---|---|---|
| Norms, values and features of youth subcultures including: dress, hobbies, values, music and behaviour | | |
| Examples of spectacular youth subcultures of the past | | |
| Examples of youth subcultures of today (goths) | | |
| CCCS | | |
| Functionalism | | |
| Marxism (CCCS) | | |
| Postmodern views | | |

Youth

# Get the result!

## Model answers

## Jodie's answer to part (a)

**Examiner says:**

Jodie has correctly identified two different subcultures and has used the first paragraph to outline the features of mods. This is good technique as it allows her to focus clearly on the features of one subculture at a time.

Two examples of youth subcultures are mods and hippies. Mods were working class but they tried to look middle class. They earned money because they all worked and many drove scooters. They wore tailored jackets and spent their money on looking good and living the mod lifestyle. Mods were trying to look more middle class and during, the week (when they were at work), they had normal jobs and many people did not know they were mods. At the weekend they would change. Many mods hung around together and they did not get on with rockers. Male mods often got into fights with rockers, but female mods were encouraged to stay out of fights. An example of mods and rockers fighting was at Clacton.

**Examiner says:**

Jodie's answer considers a range of features: social class background, dress codes, work situation, mode of transport, friction and fighting with rival rockers. Again, this is good practice as it shows breadth. However, at no point does Jodie give a reference for the features and this is a serious weakness of the answer. Where does she get her evidence from? Similarly, although mods did wear tailored suits, stronger answers might focus on the Italian designs from Saville Row which mods favoured. Mods did ride scooters but chose Vespas and Lambrettas in particular. Jodie could have made reference to Stan Cohen's study which is based on mods and rockers. If Jodie has watched the film *Quadrophenia*, she could have referred to this as a source of evidence.

Jodie has offered a good range of features here, and her use of examples enhances the answer. She may have been better selecting a second subculture from a different decade, but she has answered the question.

The range of features in this answer is good and Jodie does as the question asks and focuses on features of two different subcultures. However, to achieve the highest grade Jodie would need to refer to at least one more study or concept. There is sufficient evidence to draw from on mods and hippies and without this further reference, she will be struggling to achieve high marks in a question like this.

(Jodie's answer continued . . .)

Hippies, however, were different. Like the mods they were around in the 1960s but they were a very different subculture. They were interested in peace, love and rejecting war and consumerism. They are also associated with taking psychedelic drugs (LSD) and magic mushrooms. Brake, who studied hippies, said it was easy for them to be anti-consumerist because most of them came from middle-class backgrounds which had given them consumerism already and they could always go back into it.

# Jodie's answer to part (b)

**Examiner says:**

The groups cited as spectacular are correct, but this is not a strong introduction. Jodie needs to set out the views she is going to explore.

**Examiner says:**

Jodie uses the concept of incorporation with some accuracy, although it could be applied much more fully to the work of the CCCS than it is, or even to the concepts of globalisation or consumer culture. The reference to the pick and mix society is accurate, but again should be linked to postmodern theory and Jodie could have developed this point much further. Just because something is created from other 'pieces' does this really mean it cannot be spectacular and highly visible?

Spectacular youth subcultures include groups like skinheads, who all had shaved heads, and punks who had outrageous colours in their hair, piercing, tattoos and clothes they had made themselves. Subcultures may be less important today than they were in the past because it is getting harder to shock people and to stand out. The concept of incorporation is relevant here, which is when new subcultures come around, their distinctive style becomes incorporated into mainstream culture, for example punk clothes being sold in Top Shop. This means that the subculture becomes less important and spectacular because everyone can buy into it, wear the clothes and listen to the music. Many people think there is now a 'supermarket of style' in which people can 'pick and mix' from different styles so that, instead of making a new spectacular subculture, they just choose and mix bits from previous ones. This means that the subcultures are less spectacular today. The work of the CCCS

(Jodie's answer continued . . .)

(Marxist) sociologists shows the importance of spectacular youth subcultures in the past. The Marxists argue that youth subcultures develop due to structural and cultural factors and that social class plays a crucial role in their formation.

The spectacular youth subcultures of the past were very class based, for example hippies were mainly middle class. In the contemporary UK, social class is not as important as it used to be. Hodgkinson studied goths and couldn't relate them to a particular social class; they are almost cross-class. Bennet believes that subcultures no longer exist and there are now neo-tribes, which are more fluid and eclectic. However, there are still some subcultures in the UK such as emos and skaters, but these are not as spectacular as in the past. They don't have fights like the mods and rockers used to; actually in my experience these groups get on quite well. Overall, as the amount of subcultures has decreased I think they have become less spectacular and visible.

**Examiner says:**

This whole paragraph would be better if it focused only on postmodern ideas and neo-tribes. Jodie has not explained what they are, although her use of concepts is accurate. The discussion of social class needs to be made separately and tied more directly to the question of spectacular youth subcultures.

**Examiner says:**

This final paragraph shows some evaluation of the view in the question. It is pleasing to see the use of some contemporary subcultures. Again, reference to Hodgkinson's goth study would help here and would make it sound less like the material was based on commonsense observation.

Overall, Jodie writes a mid-level response to this question. Her part (a) is stronger on the whole than her (b). Although she clearly understands the issues, she has not provided the depth of knowledge necessary for a high-level response, and in particular the detailed work of the CCCS is largely missing from (b). Jodie could improve her performance in all three assessment objectives by following the advice given in the examiner comments on these pages.

# Glossary

The glossary includes terms that may be of value in further reading, in addition to those terms that have been highlighted in the text.

**access** how to get in touch with the target population or a sample of the target population

**achieved status** a status which someone works for and earns

**affective neutrality** the attitude whereby someone will not let personal views or interests affect the way they carry out their professional duties

**ageing population** a population where an increasing proportion of the population is over 65

**agency** the ability to exercise choice about the actions one takes and the way these shape identities

**alienation** a term used by Marxists to refer to the dissatisfaction experienced by workers

**anti-social behaviour** a New Labour concept to describe behaviour which causes a disturbance to others

**ascribed status** a status which someone is born into or inherits

**binary opposition** seeing the world in terms of two opposing positions, for example East versus West

**chronic illness** illness that continues for a long time

**chronological** by order of date

**code switching** the way in which some ethnic groups behave differently with family and with their peer groups; also described as wearing a white mask

**cohabitation** couples in a relationship living together without being married

**collective conscience** a collective set of norms, values and morals

**common culture** sharing of culture in societies, shared norms and values

**conflict** disagreement; Marxists and feminists are conflict theorists

**consensus** agreement; functionalists are consensus theorists

**consumer culture** a culture based on what we buy and consume, often based on spending and material goods

**cult** a religious group to which individuals are loosely affiliated. The features of a cult correspond closely to world-affirming movements discussed by Wallis (see Table 4.4 on page 216)

**cultural capital** refers to the cultural advantages held by the upper and middle classes

**cultural diversity** a society with culturally-embedded differences

**culture** a concept with many definitions, commonly thought of as 'a way of life'

**deconstruct** a postmodernist practice involving challenging taken-for-granted categories, such as class or ethnicity. and recognising difference within them

**definition of the situation** a term used by social action theorists for when people have their own interpretation of an event and give their own meaning to it

**discourse** the power of language which affects the way people think

**disease** a specific biological or mental abnormality which usually involves medically-diagnosed symptoms

**disengagement** the process of detaching oneself from something

**dual identity** refers to having more than one identity

**economic capital** income and wealth leads to power and privilege

**economy** the material/monetary base of a society

**emotion work** the supportive caring work that women do in looking after family members

**ethics** what is seen as morally right and wrong when conducting research, such as confidentiality, anonymity, privacy and the right to withdraw

**ethnicity** cultural heritage

**ethnocentric** judging other cultures as inferior from the standpoint of your own culture

**expressive role** a caring, nurturing role

**extended family** a family of three generations, or two generations including relatives from at least one partner

**femininities** the different ways of being female

**fluid** ever changeable; not fixed

**formal curriculum** the subjects studied within a school

**functional** a term used by functionalists to look at the contribution of an institution such as the family to society as a whole

**fundamentalism** the reassertion of traditional religious values when they are seen as under threat

**gatekeeper** the person or persons who provide the sociologist with access to the groups they wish to research

**gender roles** the set of behaviours attached to being male or female

**generalisability** the ability to make claims about the target population from the research findings

**globalisation** the process where national boundaries become less relevant and the world becomes a smaller more interconnected place

**hegemonic masculinity** the dominant type of masculinity

**high culture** cultural practices of the upper class, such as opera, classical music, and theatre

**homogenous** a group who are together and have a sense of sameness

**household** a dwelling where one or more persons live

**hybridity** a coming together of cultures, styles and identities resulting in the formation of new ones

**hyper-reality** a term used by postmodernists to refer to the way in which media images become another 'reality'

**iatrogenesis** illness and disease caused by medical treatment

**ideology** a partial picture of reality that is presented as the only way of seeing things

**illness** the subjective experience of *feeling* unwell or ill

**incessant choice** the increasing options available to people in their everyday lives

**informal curriculum** what is learned in school without it being taught; often called the hidden curriculum

**instrumental role** a practical role of provider

**interpretivist** a sociologist who seeks meanings and motives of those being researched

**kinship** ties through blood or marriage

**labelling** the process through which some groups are assumed to behave in particular ways, without clear evidence

**ladettes** a female subculture within school which is often anti-education

**lay definitions/people** those not trained in or not having a detailed knowledge of a particular subject; non-professional; non-expert views

**macro theories** look at society as a whole, recognising the structural constraints upon individual action; examples are functionalism, Marxism and feminism

**malestream** feminist concept to describe male-dominated sociological work

**marginalised** where people are excluded from full participation in mainstream society, closely related to New Labour's social exclusion

**masculinities** different ways of being male

**media** technological communications such as newspapers, television, radio, the Internet

**medicalisation** human experiences which were once seen as a normal part of being human have now been brought under medical scrutiny and control

**micro theories** theories which believe that individuals construct society: for example, social action theories

**middle age** a stage in life for reflection, associated with people in their forties and fifties

**misogynist** someone who does not like women

**modernity** an age of science and reason

**moral panic** the media creates anxiety through over-reporting or exaggerating events

**morbidity** illness and disease

**mortality** death

**multicultural society** a society where different cultures co-exist

**nation** a group with a common culture and history, often linked to place

**nature** biological/genetic makeup of an individual

**negotiation** refers to the fact that meanings are not fixed and develop through interaction

**New Age** not a true religious movement, but a loose collection of individuals and groups which share a belief in self-spirituality

**non-random sampling** a systematic approach to selecting a sample

**norm** an agreed common form of behaviour

**normative femininity** a view that there is a socially acceptable way for women and girls to dress and act

**nuclear family** a family consisting of two generations: parents and children

**nurture** behaviours that are a result of socialisation

**objectivity** the ability to explore/research the social world without bias; to be as scientific as possible; an approach favoured by positivists

**official statistics** data from government records giving the official picture

**operationalise** to put a concept into a measurable form by using indicators

**opium of the people** a Marxist term referring to the way religion dulls the pain of oppression thereby preventing people from acting to change things

**oppression** a Marxist-based concept for feelings of exploitation

**organic analogy** a comparison between the way the institutions of society work together with the organs of the human body; used by functionalists

**othering** a process of defining a group in the negative, where the self is defined in a positive way and the other is defined in terms of what it is not, therefore being inadequate

**passive femininity** acceptance of traditional female behaviours and roles

**patriarchy** male dominance

**peer group** a group of people who share similar norms and values and a common age category

**peer group pressure** acting in a particular way because others encourage you to

**popular culture** cultural practices with mass participation, such as soap operas, pop music, and Hollywood movies; the culture of the masses

**positivist** a sociologist who argues the social world can be studied in a logical, systemic, objective, scientific way

**primary socialisation** socialisation by the family in the early stages of life

**race** a biological category referring to such things as skin colour

**racialised masculinities** forms of male behaviour which combine gender and ethnicity as dimensions of identity

**random sampling** a non-systematic approach to selecting a sample

**rationalisation** refers to something based on reason

**reconstituted family** stepfamilies, formed when new families come together after former families split up

**relative deprivation** lacking economically and/or socially in comparison to the group people identify themselves with

**relative/relativity** the view that definitions are not fixed and absolute; rather they reflect differences between and within societies and over time

**reliability** the ability to repeat research and gain the same or similar results, i.e. consistent results

**representative** the extent to which the sample selected is a fair reflection of the target population

**resistance** a way of preventing something or reacting against it; often associated with social class and Marxism

**rite of passage** an event/time period which each member of a shared group goes through in their life

**role** a pattern of behaviour and routine carried out in action

**role models** individuals held as examples to others

**secondary socialisation** socialisation from the age of 5 onwards from education, media, peer group, religion and workplace

**secularisation** broadly refers to the decline in the importance of religion

**social capital** networking and helping each other out informally

**social closure** a means of maintaining a high position in the status hierarchy by restricting membership to a limited group of people

**social control** the means by which society controls its members

**social integration** a functionalist idea of binding people to a social structure

**socialisation** the learning of a culture's norms and values

**socially constructed** the way a society makes a situation through its own internal processes and structures

**societalisation** the process through which social life becomes fragmented and ceases to be locally based

**status** social standing within society

**subculture** a group with shared norms and values; a distinct group within the majority culture

**target population** the group(s) or people the sociologist would like to research

**triple shift** the three areas of work women do: paid work, housework and childcare

**universalism** the value that ensures that all people are treated similarly

**validity** where the data provide a true picture of the social reality of those being researched

**value** general principle/belief that people agree on

**value consensus** a term used by functionalists to refer to agreement over, and sharing of, values

**value free** research carried out without the values of the researcher intruding on the research design or the analysis of the data

**work / life balance** a situation where people have control over when and how they work and are fulfilled in their work time and in their leisure time

**youth** a period of life between childhood and adulthood between the ages of 15 and 30

**youth culture** the norms and values associated with young people

# References

Abbott, P. and Wallace, C. (1990) *An Introduction to Sociology: Feminist Perspectives*, London: Routledge

Abrams, M. (1959) *The Teenage Consumer*, London: London Press Exchange

Acheson Report (1998) *Independent Inquiry into Inequalities in Health*, London: HMSO

Adkins, L. (1995) *Gendered Work: Sexuality, Family and the Labour Market*, Maidenhead: Open University Press

Aggleton, P. (1987) *Rebels Without a Cause: Middle Class Youth and the Transition from School to Work*, Lewes: Falmer Press

Ahmed, L. (1992) *Women and Gender in Islam: Historical Roots of a Modern Debate*, New Haven and London: Yale University Press

Akhtar, P. '(Re)turn to Religion and Radical Islam', in Abbass, T. (Ed.) (2005) *Muslim Britain: Communities under Pressure*, London: Zed Books

Alcock, C., Payne, S. and Sullivan, M. (2000) *Introducing Social Policy*, Harlow: Pearson Education

Aldridge, A. (2000) *Religion in the Contemporary World: A Sociological Introduction*, Cambridge: Polity Press

Aldridge, A. (2004) 'Defining religion', *Sociology Review*, 14 (2)

Alexander, C. (1996) *The Art of being Black*, Oxford: Oxford University Press

Alexander, C. (2000) *The Asian Gang: Ethnicity, Identity, Masculinity*, Oxford: Berg Publishers

Ali, M. (2003) *Brick Lane*, London: Doubleday

Allan, G. and Crow, G. (2001) *Families, Households and Society*, Basingstoke: Palgrave Macmillan

Amin, K. (1992) *Poverty in Black and White: Deprivation and Ethnic Minorities*, London: CPAG with the Runnymede Trust

Ammerman, N.T. (2003) 'Re-awakening sleeping giant: Christian fundamentalist in late twentieth century US society', in Ter Haar, G. and Busuttil, J.J. (Eds) *The Freedom to do God's Will: Religious Fundamentalism and Social Change*, London: Routledge

Annandale, E. and Field, D. (2007) 'Socio-economic inequalities in health', in Taylor, S. and Field, D. (Eds) *Sociology of Health and Health Care*, 4th edn, Oxford: Blackwell

Ansley, J. (1972) *The Growth and Structure of Human Populations*, Princeton: Princeton University Press

Arber, S. and Thomas, H. (2001) 'From women's health to gender analysis of health', in Cockerham, W.C. (Ed.) *The Blackwell Companion to Medical Sociology*, Oxford: Blackwell

Archer, L. (2003a) 'Race, masculinity and schooling: Muslim boys and education', in Epstein, D. and Mac an Ghaill, M., *Educating Boys, Learning Gender*, Oxford: Oxford University Press

Archer, L. (2003b) *Race, Masculinity and Schooling: Muslim Boys and Education*, Maidenhead: Open University Press

Archer, L. and Francis, B. (2006) 'Challenging classes? Exploring the role of social class within the identities and achievement of British Chinese pupils', *Sociology* 40 (1), 29–49

Archer, L. and Yamashati, H. (2003a) 'Theorising inner-city masculinities: race, class and gender in education', *Gender in Education*, 15 (2), 115–32, London: Routledge

Aridge, J. (2004) 'The vanishing generation gap', *Observer*, 1 February.

Armstrong, K. (2001) 'The war we should fight', *Guardian*, 13 October

Back, L. (1996) *New Ethnicities and Urban Culture*, London: Routledge

Bajekal, M. et al. (2006) (Eds) *Focus on Health: Office for National Statistics*, Palgrave Macmillan; National statistics website: www.statistics.gov.uk

Banks, I. (2001) 'No man's land: men, illness and help seeking', *British Medical Journal*, 323, 1058–60

Banton, M. (2000) 'Ethnic conflict', *Sociology*, 34 (3), 481–98

Barker, E. (1999) cited by Barter, J. (2007) *Sociology of Religion*, Philip Allan, p. 106

Barker, C. (2003) *Cultural Studies: Theory and Practice*, London: Sage.

Barker, E. (1985) 'New religious movements: yet another great awakening?', in Hammond, P.E. (Ed.) *The Sacred in a Secular Age*, Berkeley: University of California Press

Barnes, C. (2003) 'What a difference a decade makes: reflections on doing "emancipatory" disability research', *Disability and Society*, 18(1)

Barrett, M. and McIntosh, M. (1982) *The Anti Social Family*, Verso London

Barrett, M. and Roberts, H. (1978) 'Doctors and their patients', in Smart, H. and Smart, B. (Eds) *Women, Sexuality and Social Control*, London: Routledge & Kegan Paul

Barter, J. (2007) *Sociology of Religion*, Oxfordshire: Phillip Allan

Beck, U. (1992) *Risk Society*, London: Sage Publications

Beck, U. and Beck-Gernsheim, E. (1995) *The Normal Chaos of Love*, Cambridge: Polity Press

Becker, H.S. (1963) *Outsiders: Studies in the Sociology of Deviance*, New York: Free Press

Beckford, J. (2000) *Dread and Pentecostal: A Political Theology for the Black Church in Britain*, London: SPCK

Beckford, J. (2003) 'Religion: consensus and conflict', *Sociology Review*, November.

Beckford, J. (2004) 'Religion and postmodernity', *Sociology Review*, 14 (2)

Bell et al. (2004) cited by Duncan, S. (2006) 'What's the problem with teenage parents?', *Sociological Review*, 51(2), 199–217

Bellah, R.N. (1975) in Macionis, J. and Plummer, K. (2002) *Sociology A Global Introduction*, Harlow: Pearson Education

Bellah, R.N. (1992) *The Broken Covenant: American Civil Religion in Time of Trial*, 2nd edn, Chicago: University of Chicago Press

Bennett, A. (1999) 'Subcultures or neo-tribes? Rethinking the relationship between youth, style and musical taste', *Sociology*, 33 (3), 599–617

Bennett, A. (2005) *Cultures of Popular Music*, Buckingham: Open University Press

Bennett, A. (2006) 'Punk's not dead: the continuing significance of punk rock for an older generation of fans', *Sociology*, 40 (2), 219–35

Berger, P.L. and Luckmann, T. (1966) *The Social Construction of Reality*, London: Allen Lane, Penguin

Bernades, J. (1997) *Family Studies*, London: Routledge

Bernstein, B. (1961) 'Social class and linguistic development: a theory of social learning', in Halsey A.H et al., *Education, Economy and Society*, New York: The Free Press.

Berthoud, R. et al. (1997) *Ethnic Minorities in Britain: Diversity and Disadvantage*, London: Policy Studies Institute

Bivins, R. (2007) *Alternative Medicine? A History*, Oxford: Oxford University Press

Black Report (1980) in Townsend, P. et al. (1992), *Inequalities in Health: The Black Report and The Health Divide*, London: Penguin

Blackburn, C. (1991) *Poverty and Health: Working with Families*, Milton Keynes: Open University Press

Blackman, S. (1995) *Youth: Positions and Oppositions: Style, Sexuality and Schooling*, Aldershot: Avebury

Blackman, S. (1998) 'The school: "Poxy Cupid"', in Skelton, T. and Valentine, G. (Eds) *Cool Places: Geographies of Youth Cultures*, London: Routledge

Blaxter, M. (1990) *Health and Lifestyles*, London, Tavistock-Routledge

Blinkenstaff, J.C. (2005) 'Women and science careers: leaky pipeline or gender filter?', *Gender in Education*, 17 (4), 369–86

Bond, R. and Rosie, M. (2006) 'Routes into Scottishness', in Bromley, C. et al. (eds) *Has Devolution Delivered?*, Edinburgh: Edinburgh University Press

Bose, R. (2003) 'Families in transition', in Lou, A. (Ed.), *Southern Asian Children and Adolescence in Britain*, London: Whurr

Bourdieu, P. (1990) *The Logic of Practice*, Cambridge: Polity Press

Bourdieu. P. (1986) *Distinction*, London: Routledge

Bowler, I. (1993) 'They're not the same as us: midwives stereotypes of South Asian descent maternity patients', *Sociology of Health and Illness*, 15 (2), 157–78

Bradley, H. (1996) *Fractured Identities: Changing Patterns of Inequality*, Cambridge: Polity Press

Brah, A. (Ed.) (1999) *Thinking Identities, Ethnicity, Racism and Culture*, London: Macmillan Press

Brake, M. (1980) *The Sociology of Youth Culture and Youth Subcultures*, London: Routledge & Kegan Paul

Brannen, J. (2003) 'The age of beanpole families', *Sociology Review*, 13 (1), 6–10

British Social Attitudes Survey (2006), *The Twenty-third Report*, London: Sage Publications

Brown, G. and Harris, T. (Eds) (1989) *Life Events and Illness*, London: Guilford Press

Brown, G. et al. (1995) 'Loss, humiliation and entrapment among women developing depression: a patient and non-patient comparison', *Psychological Medicine*, 25, 7–21

Browne, K. and Bottrill, I. (1999) 'Our unequal, unhealthy nation: class inequality, health and illness', *Sociology Review*, 9 (2)

Bruce, S. (1995) *Religion in Modern Britain*, Oxford: Oxford University Press

Bruce, S. (1996) *Religion in the Modern World: From Cathedrals to Cults*, Oxford: Oxford University Press

Bruce, S. (2002a) 'God and shopping', *Sociology Review*, 12 (2)

Bruce, S. (2002b) *God is Dead: Secularisation in the West*, Oxford: Blackwell

Brundson, C. (1997) *Screen Tastes: Soap Opera to Satellite Dishes*, London: Routledge

Bryman, A. (2004) *Social Research Methods*, 2nd edn, Oxford: Oxford University Press

Burdsey, D. (2004) 'One of the lads?: Dual ethnicity and assimilated ethnicities in the careers of British professional footballers', *Ethnic and Racial Studies*, 27 (5), 757–9

Butler, C. (1995) 'Religion and gender: young Muslim women in Britain', *Sociology Review*, 4 (3), 18–22

Bytheway, B. (2005) 'Age identity and the celebration of birthdays', *Ageing and Society*, 25 (4), 463–78

Calnan, M. (1987) *Health and Illness: The Lay Perspective*, London: Tavistock

Carvel, J. (2007) 'C. difficile outbreak which killed 90 patients may trigger criminal charges', *Guardian*, 11 October

Cater, S. and Coleman, L. (2006) *'Planned' Teenage Pregnancy: Perspectives of Young Parents from Disadvantaged Backgrounds*, Joseph Rowntree Foundation, Bristol: Policy Press

Chandler, J. et al. (2004) *Sociological Research Online*, 19 (3)

Charles, N. (2002) *Gender in Modern Britain*, Oxford: Oxford University Press

Clarke, A. and Warren, L. (2007) 'Hopes, fears and expectations about the future: what do older people's stories tell us about active ageing?' *Ageing in Society*, 27 (4), 465–88

Clarke, J. (1976) 'The skinheads and the magical recovery of community', in Hall, S. and Jefferson, T. (Eds) *Resistance Through Rituals: Youth Subcultures in Post-War Britain,* London: Hutchinson

Cleaver, E. (2003) in Heath, S. (2004) 'Transforming friendship', *Sociology Review*, 14 (1)

Cohen, S. (1973) *Folk Devils and Moral Panics: The Creation of Mods and Rockers*, London: MacGibbon & Kee

Connell, R.W. (2002) *Gender*, Cambridge: Polity Press

Connelly, J. and Crown, J. (Eds) (1994) 'Homelessness and ill-health', in Senior, M. and Viveash, B. (1998) *Health and Illness*, Basingstoke: Palgrave Macmillan

Coulthard, M. et al. (2004) *Focus on Social Inequalities*, Office of National Statistics, National statistics website: www.statistics.gov.uk

Council of Europe (2002) cited on Women's Aid website, www.womensaid.org.uk

Creswell, J.W. (1994) *Research Design: Qualitative and Quantitative Approaches*, London: Sage Publications

Creswell, J.W., Trout, S. and Burbuto, J.E. (2002) 'A decade of mixed methods writing: a retrospective', available from http: //aom.pace.edu/rmd/2002forum/retrospect.pdf (accessed June 2007)

Currie, D.H. (1999) *Girl Talk: Adolescent Magazines and their Readers*, Toronto: University of Toronto Press

Curtice, J. and Heath, A. (2000) 'Is the British lion about to roar?', in *Focussing on Diversity: The British Social Attitudes Seventeenth Report* (2000-1 edn), London: NCSR/Sage Publications

D'houtard, A. and Field, M.G. (1984) 'The image of health: variations in perceptions by social class in a French population', *Sociology of Health and Illness*, 6, 30–60

Dale, A. et al. (2004) *Labour Market Trends*, 12 (4), 13

Davey Smith, G. et al. (2002) 'Ethnic inequalities in health: a review of UK epidemioloigcal evidence', in Nettleton, S. and Gustaffson, E. (Eds), *The Sociology of Health and Illness Reader*, Cambridge: Polity Press

Davie, G. (1994) *Religion in Britain since 1945: Believing without Belonging*, Oxford: Blackwell

Davie, G. (2000) *Religion in Modern Europe: A Memory Mutates*, Oxford: Oxford University Press

Davies, T. (1994) 'Disabled by society?', *Sociology Review*, 3 (4)

Day, A. (2007) 'A sociology of belief', *Sociology Review*, 16, (4)

De Beauvoir, S. (1953) cited in Haralambos, M. and Holborn, M. (2004) *Sociology Themes and Perspectives*, London: HarperCollins, p. 413

Dench, G. et al. (2006) *The New East End: Kinship, Race and Culture*, London: Profile Books

Dennis, N. (1993) *Rising Crime and the Dismembered Family*, London: IEA Health and Welfare Unit

Denscombe, M. (2003) *The Good Research Guide*, 2nd edn, Maidenhead: Open University Press

Department for Education and Skills (2005), *Education and Training Statistics for the UK*, available from http://www/eoc.org.uk/pdf/facts_about_GB_2006.pdf (accessed January 2008)

Department of Health (1999a) *Saving Lives, Our Healthier Nation*, Labour Party White Paper, Cm 4386, London: HMSO

Department of Health (1999b) *Health Survey for England: The Health of Minority Ethnic Groups*, available from www.dh.gov.uk (accessed January 2008)

Department of Health and Social Security/ Department of Education and Science (1977) *Prevention and Health*, Labour Party White Paper, Cmnd 7047, London: HMSO

Department of Work and Pensions (2002), available from www.statistics.gov.uk (accessed January 2008)

Dermott, E. (2003) 'The "intimate father": defining paternal involvement', *Sociological Research Online*, 8 (4), available from http://www.socresonline.org.uk/8/4/dermott.html (accessed August 2007)

Dermott, E. (2006) 'What's parenthood got to do with it?: Men's hours of paid work', *British Journal of Sociology*, 57 (4), 619–34

Derrington, C. and Kendall, S. (2004) *Gypsy Traveller Students in Secondary Schools: Cultures, Identity and Achievement*, Stoke on Trent: Trentham Books

DeVault, M. (1991) *Feeding the Family: The Social Organization of Caring as Gendered Work*, Chicago: University of Chicago Press

Devine, F. et al. (2005) *Rethinking Class: Culture, Identities and Lifestyle*, Basingstoke: Palgrave Macmillan

Dobash, R. and Dobash, R. (1979) *Violence Against Wives*, London: Open Books

Dobash, R. and Dobash, R. (2000) 'Evaluating criminal justice interventions for domestic violence', *Crime Delinquency*, 46, 252–70

Doyal, L. (1985) 'Women and the National Health Service: the careers and the careless', in Lewin, E. and Oleson, V. (Eds) *Women, Health and Healing*, London: Tavistock

Drane, J. (1999) *What is the New Age saying to the Church?*, London: Marshal Pickering

Dubos, R. (1987) 'Mirage of health', in Davey, B. et al. (Eds) (2001) *Health and Disease: A Reader*, 3rd edn, Maidenhead: Open University Press, pp. 8–9

Duncan, S. (2006) 'What's the problem with teenage parents?', *Sociological Review*, 51(2), 199–217

Duncombe, J. and Marsden, D. (1995) 'Women's "triple shift": paid employment, domestic labour and "emotion work"', *Sociology Review*, (4)

Dunne, G. (1997) *Lesbian Lifestyles: Women's Work and the Politics of Sexuality*, London: Macmillan

Durkheim, E. (1912) cited in Aldridge, A. (2004) 'Defining religion', *Sociology Review*, 14 (2), 8

Edgell, S. (1980) *Middle Class Couples*, London: Allen & Unwin

Eisenstadt, S. (1956) *From Generation to Generation: Age Groups and Social Structure*, New York: Free Press

El Sadawi, H. (1980) *The Hidden Face of Eve: Women in the Arab World*, London: Zed Books

Eversley, D. and Bonnerjea, L. (1982) 'Social change and indications of diversity', in Rapoport, R. et al. (Eds) *Families in Britain*, London: Routledge & Kegan Paul

Fenton, S. (2003) *Ethnicity*, Cambridge: Polity Press

Finch, J. and Mason, J. (1993) *Negotiating Family Responsibilities*, London: Routledge

Foster, J. (1990) *Villains : Crime and Community in the Inner City*, London: Routledge

Foucault, M. (1973) *The Order of Things: An Archaeology of the Human Sciences*, New York: Vintage/Random House

Fox, K. (2004) *Watching the English*, London: Hodder & Stoughton

Francis, B. (2000) *Boys, Girls and Achievement: Addressing the Classroom Issues*, London: Routledge/Falmer

Francis, B. and Archer, L. (2006) 'Triad: British Chinese pupils constructions of laddism', *Sociological Review*, 53 (3), 495–521

Friedson, E. (1970) *The Profession of Medicine*, New York: Dodd Mead

Frith, S. (1978) *The Sociology of Youth*, Ormskirk: Causeway Press

Frosh, S. et al. (2002) *Young Masculinities: Understanding Boys in Contemporary Society*, Basingstoke: Palgrave Macmillan

Gabb, J. (2005) 'Lesbian motherhood: strategies of familial-linguistic management in lesbian parent families', *Sociology*, 39 (4), 585–603

Garrod, J. (2005) 'Campaigns for fathers' rights', *Sociology Review*, 14 (3)

Garrod, J. (2006) 'Children and religious belief', *Sociology Review*, 15 (3)

Garrod, J. (2007) 'Parents, children and society', *Sociology Review*, 16 (3)

Gatrell, C. (2006) 'Whose child is it anyway? The negotiation of paternal entitlements within marriage', *Sociological Review*, 55 (2), 352–72

Gauntlett, D. (2002) *Media, Gender and Identity: An Introduction*, London: Routledge

Geetz (1966) cited in Kidd, W. et al. (1998) *Readings in Sociology*, Heinemann

General Register Office for Scotland, *Census 2001*

Giddens, A. (1992) *The Transformation of Intimacy: Sexuality, Love and Eroticism in Modern Societies*, Cambridge: Polity Press

Giddens, A. (2006) *Sociology*, 5th edn, Cambridge: Polity Press

Gill, R. and Herdieckerhoff, E. (2006) 'Rewriting the romance: new feminist chick lit?', Feminism, *Media Studies*, 6 (4), 487–504

Gillborn, D. (1990) *Race, Ethnicity and Education: Teaching and Learning in Multi Ethnic Schools*, London: Routledge

Glendinning, T. and Bruce, S. (2006) 'New ways of believing or belonging; is religion giving way to spirituality?', *British Journal of Sociology*, (57), 3

Glock (1964) cited in Dawson, L. (1998) *Cults in Context; Readings in the Sociology of New Religious Movements*, Transaction Publications, p. 142

Goffman, E. (1968) *Asylums*, Harmondsworth: Penguin

Graham, H. (2002) 'Socio-economic change and inequalities in men and women's health risk in the UK', in Nettleton S. and Gustaffson, U. (Eds), *The Sociology of Health and Illness Reader*, Cambridge: Polity Press

Grundy, E. and Henretta, J. (2006) Between elderly parents and adult children: a new look at the intergenerational care provided by the "sandwich generation"', *Ageing and Society*, 26, 707–22

Hall, S. (Ed.) (1992) 'New ethnicities', in Rattansi, A. and Donald, J., *Race, Culture and Difference*, London: Sage Publications

Hall, S. and Jefferson, T. (Eds) (1976) *Resistance Through Rituals: Youth Subcultures in Post-War Britain*, London: Hutchinson

Hamilton, M. (1995) *The Sociology of Religion*, London: Routledge

Hantrais, L. (2006) 'Changing family life in Europe', *Sociology Review*, 6 (1), 28–31

Haralambos, M. and Holborn, M. (2004) *Sociology Themes and Perspectives*, London: HarperCollins

Hardill, I. et al. (1997) 'Who decides what? Decision making in dual career households', *Work, Employment and Society*, 11 (2), 313–26

Hatcher, R. (2006) 'Social class and schooling: differentiation or democracy?', in Cole, M. (Ed.), *Education, Equality and Human Rights*, Oxford: Routledge

Hatter, W. et al. (2002) 'Dads on dads: needs and expectations at home and at work', MORI Social Research Institute, London: Equal Opportunities Commission

*Health Statistics Quarterly* (2007), National statistics, available from www.statistics.gov.uk (accessed January 2008)

Heath, S. (2004) 'Transforming friendship', *Sociology Review*, 14 (1)

Hebdige, D. (1976), 'The meaning of mod', in Hall, S. and Jefferson, T. (Eds) *Resistance Through Rituals: Youth Subcultures in Post-War Britain*, London: Hutchinson

Hebdige, D. (1979) *Subculture the Meaning of Style*, London: Methuen

Heelas, P. (1996) *The New Age Movement: The Celebration of the Self and the Sacralization of Modernity*, Oxford: Blackwell

Heelas, P. and Woodhead, L. (2005) *The Spiritual Revolution: Why Religion is Giving Way to Spirituality*, Oxford: Blackwell

Heidensohn, F. (1985) *Women and Crime*, London: Macmillan

Helman, C.G. (1978) 'Feed a cold, starve a fever: folk models of infection in an English suburban community, and their relation to medical treatment', *Culture, Medicine and Psychiatry*, 2, 107-37

Hewitt, R. (1996) *Routes of Racism*, Stoke-on-Trent: Trentham Books

Hodkinson, P. (2002) *Goth, Identity, Style and Subculture*, Oxford: Berg Publishers

Hodkinson, P. (2004) 'The Goth scene and (sub) cultural substance', in Bennett, A. and Kahn Harris, K. (Eds) *After Subculture, Critical Studies in Contemporary Youth Culture*, Basingstoke: Palgrave Macmillan

Holden, A. (2006) *The Burnley Project: Evaluating the Contribution of Interfaith Dialogue to Community Cohesion*, available from http://www.lancs.ac.uk/fass/religstudies/research/projects/burnley.htm (accessed January 2008)

Hollands, R. (1995) *Friday Night, Saturday Night: Youth Cultural Identification in the Post-Industrial City*, Department of Social Policy, University of Newcastle

Hook, S. (1990) *Convictions*, New York: Prometheus Books

Hope, T. and Jones, I. (2006) 'Locating contemporary British paganism as late modern culture', *Journal of Contemporary Religion*, 21 (3), 341–54

Howlett, B.C. et al. (1992) 'An explanation of white, Asian and Afro-Caribbean people's concepts of health and illness causation', *New Community*, 18 (2), 281–92

Hunt, S. and Lightly, N. (1999) 'A healthy alternative? A sociology of fringe medicine', *Sociology Review*, 8 (3)

Hyde, M. (2001) 'Disabled people in Britain today: discrimination, social disadvantage and empowerment', in *Sociology Review*, 10 (4)

Illich, I. (1976) *Limits to Medicine: Medical Nemesis*, London: Boyars

Illich, I. (2002) *Limits to Medicine, Medical Nemesis: The Expropriation of Health*, London: Boyars

Illsley, R. (1980) 'Professional or public health?', Nuffield Provincial Hospitals Trust, London, in Taylor, P. et al. (1996) *Sociology in Focus*, Ormskirk: Causeway Press

Jackson, C. (2006a) 'Wild girls? An exploration of "ladette" cultures in secondary schools', *Gender in Education*, 18 (4), 339–60

Jackson, C. (2006b) *Lads and Ladettes in School: Gender and a Fear of Failure*, Maidenhead: Open University Press

Jackson, S. and Scott, S. (2002) *Gender: A Sociological Reader*, London: Routledge

Jacobson, J. (1997) 'Religion and ethnicity: dual and alternative sources of identity among young British Pakistanis', *Ethnic and Racial Studies*, 20 (2), 238–56

Jagger, E. (1998) 'Marketing the self, buying another: dating in a post modern consumer society', *Sociology*, 32, 795–814

Jefferson, T. (1976) 'Cultural responses of the Teds: the defence of space and status', in Hall, S. and Jefferson, T. (Eds) *Resistance Through Rituals: Youth Subcultures in Post-War Britain*, London: Hutchinson

Jenkins, R. (2004) *Social Identity*, London: Routledge

Jhally, S. (1992) *Enlightened Racism: The Cosby Show, Audiences and the Myth of the American Dream*, Boulder: Westview Press

Johal, S. and Bains, J. (1998) *Corner Flags and Corner Shops: The Asian Football Experience*, London: Orion

Jordan, B., Redley, M. and James, S. (1994) *Putting the Family First*, London: UCL Press

Karlsen, S. and Nazroo, J. (2004) 'Fear of racism and health', *Journal of Epidemiology and Community Health*, 58, 1017–18

Karpf, A. (2002) 'Alternative medicine is practically mainstream now – should we cheer?', *The Guardian*, 8 May 2002

Kehily, M. et al. (2001) 'Boys and girls come out to play: making masculinities and femininities in school playgrounds', *Men and Masculinities*, 4 (2), 158–72

Kehily, M.J. (2007) *Understanding Youth: Perspectives, Identities and Practices*, London: Sage Publications

Kehily, M.J. and Nayak, A. (1997) 'Lads and laughter: humour and the production of heterosexual hierarchies', *Gender and Education*, 9 (1), 69–88

Kettley, N. (2006) 'It's cool to be clever: the marginal relevance of gender to educational practices and attainments at AS/A Level', *Evaluation and Research in Education*, 19 (2), 126–44

Koffman, J. et al. (1997) 'Ethnicity and the issue of psychiatric beds: a one day survey in North and South Thames regions', *British Journal of Psychiatry*, 171, 238–41

La Valle, I. et al. (2002) *Happy Families? Atypical Work and its Influence on Family Life*. Policy Press with Joseph Rowntree Foundation

Laslett, P. (1991) *A Fresh Map of Life: the Emergence of the Third Age*, Cambridge, Massachusetts: Harvard University Press

Lawrence, F. (2006) *Guardian*, 16 January.

Lawson, T. et al. (2000) *Advanced Sociology through Diagrams*, Oxford: Oxford University Press

Leach, E. (1967) cited in Haralambos, M. and Holborn, M. (2004) *Sociology Themes and Perspectives*, London: HarperCollins, p. 494

Leach, E. (1988) *Culture and Communication*, Cambridge: Cambridge University Press

Leavis, F.R. (1933) *Culture and the Environment*, London: Chatto & Windus

Lees, S. (1986) *Losing Out: Sexuality and Adolescent Girls*, London: Hutchinson Education

Lees, S. (1993) *Sugar and Spice: Sexuality and Adolescent Girls*, Harmondsworth: Penguin

Leighton, G. (1992) 'Wives' paid and unpaid work and husbands' unemployment', *Sociology Review*, 1 (3)

Lewis (2001) cited in Shipman, B. and Smart, C. (2007) 'It's made a huge difference: recognition, rights and the personal significance of civil partnership', *Sociology Research Online*, 12 (1)

Lincoln, S. (2004) 'Teenage girls' "bedroom culture": codes versus zones', in Bennett, A. and Kahn Harris, K. (Eds) *After Subculture, Critical Studies in Contemporary Youth Culture*, Basingstoke: Palgrave Macmillan

Lishman, G. (2005) 'Ageing is an opportunity not a burden', *The Edge*, Issue 20, p. 18

Lissauer, T. (1994) in Connelly, J. and Crown, J. (Eds) *Homelessness and Ill Health: Report of a Working Party of the Royal College of Physicians*, London: Royal College of Physicians

Littlewood, R. and Lipsedge, M. (1982), *Aliens and Alienists: Ethnic Minorities and Psychiatry*, Harmondsworth: Penguin

Lobstein, T. (1995) 'The increasing cost of a healthy diet', *Food Magazine*, 31, p. 17

Lury, C. (1996) *Consumer Culture*, Cambridge: Polity Press

Lyon, D. (1994) *Postmodernity*, Oxford: Oxford University Press

Lyon, D. (2000) *Jesus in Disneyland. Religion in Postmodern Times*, Cambridge: Polity Press

Mac an Ghaill, M. (1994) *The Making of Men: Masculinities, Sexualities and Schooling*, Maidenhead: Open University Press

MacDonald, R. and Marsh, J. (2005) *Disconnected Youth? Growing up in Britain's Poor Neighbourhoods*, Basingstoke: Palgrave Macmillan

Macfarlane, A. (1990) 'Official statistics and women's health and illness', in Roberts, H. (Ed.) *Women's Health Counts*, London: Routledge & Kegan Paul

Macintyre, S. (1993) 'Gender differences in the perceptions of common cold symptoms', *Social Science and Medicine*, 36 (1), 15–20

Madell, D. (2006) 'An online survey of UK young people's use of mobile phones', *Research & Development Bulletin* 4 (2), 21–8

Maduro, O. (1982) *Religion and Social Conflicts*, New York: Orbis Books

Malinowski, B. (1922) *Argonauts of the Western Pacific: An Account of Native Enterprise and Adventure in the Archipelagos of Melanesian New Guinea*, London: Routledge & Kegan Paul

Malinowski, B. (1915) cited in Haralambos, M. and Holborn, M. (2004) *Sociology Themes and Perspectives*, London: HarperCollins, p. 408

Marsh, J. and Millard, E. (2003) *Literacy and Popular Culture in the Classroom*, Reading: National Centre for Language and Literacy

Martin, C. et al. (1987) 'Housing conditions and health', *British Medical Journal*, 294, 1125–7

Martin, D. (1969), cited in Haralambos, M. and Holborn, M. (2004) *Sociology Themes and Perspectives*, London: HarperCollins

Martin, D. (1978) *A General Theory of Secularisation*, Oxford: Blackwell

Martin, G. (2000) 'New Age Travellers', *Sociology Review*, 9 (4)

Mason, D. (2005), *Race and Ethnicity in Modern Britain*, Oxford: Oxford University Press

McDowell, L. (2003) *Redundant Masculinities: Employment Change and White Working Class Youth*, Oxford: Blackwell

McGlone, F. et al. (1996) cited in Haralambos, M. and Holborn, M. (2004) *Sociology Themes and Perspectives*, London: HarperCollins, p. 489

McKeown, T. (1976) *The Role of Medicine: Dream, Mirage, or Nemesis*, Oxford: Blackwell

McKingsley, E. (2001) *The Spiritual Dimensions of Ageing*, London: Jessica Kingsley Publishers

McKinlay, J. (1984) *Issues in the Political Economy of Health Care*, London: Tavistock

McLoone, P. (1996) 'Suicide and deprivation in Scotland', *British Medical Journal*, 312, 543–4

McLuhan, M. (1989), *Global Village*, Oxford: Oxford University Press

McRobbie, A. (2007) *Gender, Culture and Social Change: The Post-Feminist Masquerade?*, London: Sage Publications

McRobbie, A. and Garber, J. (1976) 'Girls and subcultures', in Gelder, K. and Thornton, S. (Eds) *The Subcultural Reader*, London: Routledge

Medhurst, A. (1999) 'The Royale Family', talk given at the Material Cultures Conference, Coventry

Messerschmidt, J.W. (1993) *Masculinities and Crime: Critique and Reconceptualisation of Theory*, Lanham, Maryland: Rowman & Littlefield

Miller, A.S. and Hoffman, J.P. (1995) 'Risk and religion: an explanation of gender differences in religiosity', *Journal for the Scientific Study of Religion*, 34 (1), 63–75

Millerson, G. (1964) *The Qualifying Association*, London: Routledge

Mills, C. Wright. (1959) *The Sociological Imagination*, Oxford: Oxford University Press

Mirza, H. (1992) *Young, Female and Black*, London: Routledge

Mitchell, C. (2006) 'The religious content of ethnic identities', *Sociology*, 40 (6), 1135–52

Mitchell, W. and Green, E. (2002) '"I don't know what I'd without our mam": motherhood, identity and support networks', *Sociology*, 41 (2), 277–93

Modood, T. (2005), *Multicultural Politics: Racism, Ethnicity and Muslims in Britain*, Edinburgh: Edinburgh University Press

Modood, T. et al. (1997) *Ethnic Minorities in Britain: Diversity and Disadvantage*, London: Policy Studies Institute

MORI (2002) '"Dads on dads": needs and expectations at home and at work', available from www.eoc.org.uk (accessed January 2008)

MORI (2004) Youth Survey, available from http://www.yjb.gov.uk/Publications/Resources/Downloads/YouthSurvey2004.pdf (accessed August 2007)

Morris, J. (2007) available from www.bbc.co.uk/bbcfour/documentaries/profile/profile_jan_morris.shtml (accessed January 2008)

Muggleton, D. (2000) *Inside Subculture: The Postmodern Meaning of Style*, Oxford: Berg Publishers

Muncie, J. (2004) *Youth and Crime*, 2nd edn, London: Sage Publications

Murdoch, G.P. (1949) cited in Haralambos, M. and Holborn, M. (2004) *Sociology Themes and Perspectives*, London: HarperCollins, p. 6

Nacro (2006) 'Detected offending by age: some facts about children and young people who offend' (2004), Youth Crime Briefing, available from www.nacro.org.uk (accessed January 2008)

Nacro (2006) *Children and Young People Cautioned, Reprimanded, Warned or Sentenced for Indictable Offences, 1992–2004*

Navarro, V. (1979) *Medicine under Capitalism*, London: Croom Helm

Nayak, A. (2006) 'Displaced masculinities: chavs, youth and class in the post-industrial city', *Sociology*, 40 (5), 813–31

Nazroo, J. (1997) *Ethnicity and Mental Health*, London: Policy Studies Institute

Nettleton, S. (2006) *The Sociology of Health and Illness*, 2nd edn, Cambridge: Polity Press

Niebuhr, R. (1929) cited in Thompson, I. (1986) *Religion*, Longman

O'Dea, T. (1966), cited in Hamilton, M. (1995) *The Sociology of Religion*, Harlow: London: Routledge

Oakley, A. (1974) *Housewife*, London: Allen Lane

Oakley, A. (1984) *The Captured Womb: A History of the Medical Care of Pregnant Women*, Oxford: Blackwell

Oates, C. and McDonald, S. (2006) 'Recycling and the domestic division of labour: is green pink or blue?', in *Sociology*, 40 (3), 417–33

Offending, Crime and Justice Survey (OCJS) (2005) 'Proportion of 10 to 25 year olds committing an offence in the last 12 months by age, 2005', available from http://www.homeoffice.gov.uk/rds/offending_survey.html (accessed January 2008)

Office for National Statistics (2000) 'Psychiatric morbidity among adults living in private households, 2000', available from www.statistics.gov.uk (accessed January 2008)

Office for National Statistics (2001) *Annual Local Area Labour Force Survey, 2001–2*, London: HMSO

Office for National Statistics (2001) *Census 2001*, London: HMSO

Office for National Statistics (2002), available from www.statistics.gov.uk (accessed January 2008)

Office for National Statistics (2004–5) *General Household Survey, 2004–2005*, London: HMSO

Office for National Statistics (2005a) *Quarterly Labour Force Survey, December 2005–February 2006*, London: HMSO

Office for National Statistics (2005b) *Population Trends – Autumn 2005*, London: HMSO

Office for National Statistics (2004) *General Household Survey 2004/05*, available from http://www.statistics.gov.uk/downloads/theme_compendia/GHS05/GeneralHouseholdSurvey2005.pdf (accessed June 2007)

Office for National Statistics (2004/2005) *Labour Force Survey, 2004 and 2005*, available from http://www.statistics.gov.uk (accessed January 2008)

Oliver, M. (1996) *The Politics of Disablement*, London: Macmillan

Osler, A. and Vincent, K. (2003) *Girls and Exclusion: Rethinking the Agenda*, London: RoutledgeFalmer

Pahl, J. (1989) *Money and Marriage*, Basingstoke: Macmillan

Pakulski, J. and Waters, M. (1996) *The Death of Class*, London: Sage Books

Parekh, B. (2006) *Rethinking Multiculturalism*, Basingstoke: Palgrave Macmillan

Park, A. et al. (Eds) (2001) *British Social Attitudes: The Eighteenth Report, Public Policy, Social Ties*, London: Sage Publications

Parker, D. and Song, M. (2006) 'New ethnicities online: reflexive racialisation and the internet', *Sociological Review*, 54 (3), 575–94

Parkin, F. (1982) cited in Slattery, M. (2003) *Key Ideas in Sociology*, Cheltenham: Nelson Thornes, p. 64

Parsons, T. (1951) 'The social system' in Taylor, S. and Field, D. (Eds) (2007) *Sociology of Health and Health Care*, Oxford: Blackwell

Parsons, T. (1954) *Essays in Sociological Theory*, Glencoe: Free Press

Parsons, T. (1959) cited in Kirby, M. at al. (2000) *Sociology in Perspective for OCR*, Oxford: Heinemann, p. 88

Parsons, T. and Bales, R.F. (Eds) (1955) *Family, Socialisation, and Interaction Process*, Glencoe, Illinois: The Free Press

Pearson, G. (1983) *Hooligan: A History of Respectable Fears*, London: Macmillan

Perren, K. et al. (2004) 'Neighbouring in later life: the influence of socio-economic resources, gender household composition on neighbourly relationships', *Sociology*, 38 (5), 965–84

Pill, R. and Stott, N.C.H. (1982) 'Concepts of illness causation and responsibility: some preliminary data from a sample of working-class mothers', *Social Science and Medicine*, 16, 43–52

Plummer, G. (2000) *Failing Working Class Girls*, Staffordshire: Trentham Books

Polhemus, T. (1997) 'In the supermarket of style', in Redhead, S., Wynne, D. and O'Connor, J. (Eds) *The Clubcultures Reader: Readings in Popular Cultural Studies*, Oxford: Blackwell

Popay, J. and Bartley, M. (1989) 'Conditions of labour and women's health' in Martin, C. and McQueen, D. (Eds) *Readings For a New Public Health*, Edinburgh: Edinburgh University Press

Power, S. et al. (1998) 'Schoolboys and schoolwork: gender identification and academic achievement', *Journal of Exclusive Education*, 2 (2), 135–53

Power, S. et al. (2003) *Education and the Middle Classes*, Maidenhead: Open University Press

Prior, L. et al. (2002) 'Beliefs and accounts of illness: views from two Cantonese communities in England', in Nettleton, S. and Gustaffson, U. (Eds) *The Sociology of Health and Illness Reader*, Cambridge: Polity Press

Punamaki, R. and Aschan, H. (1994) 'Self care and mastery among primary health care patients', *Social Science and Medicine*, 39 (5)

Rapoport, R. et al. (Eds) (1982) *Families in Britain*, London: Routledge & Kegan Paul

Reading, R. and Reynolds, S. (2001) 'Debt, social disadvantage and maternal depression', *Social Science and Medicine*, 53 (4), 441–53

Reay, D. (1998) *Class Work: Mother's Involvement in their Children's Primary Schooling*, London: Routledge

Reay, D. (2001) 'Spice girls, "nice girls", "girlies" and "tomboys": gender discourses, girls' cultures and femininities in the primary classroom', *Gender and Education*, 13 (2), 153–66

Reay, D. (2005) *Degrees of Choice*, Stoke on Trent: Trentham Books

Redhead, S. (1993) *Rave Off: Politics and Deviance in Contemporary Youth Culture*, Aldershot: Avebury

Renold, E. (2007) 'Primary school "studs": (de)constructing young boys' heterosexual masculinities', *Men and Masculinities*, 4 (3), 275–97

Rogers, A. and Pilgrim, D. (2005) *A Sociology of Mental Health and Illness*, Maidenhead: Open University Press

Rogers, A. et al. (1999) *Demanding Patients?*, Buckingham: Open University Press

Roseneil, S. and Budgeon, S. (2004) 'Beyond the conventional family: intimacy, care and community in the 21st century', *Current Sociology*, 52 (2), 180

Rosenhan, D. L. (1973) 'On being sane in insane places', *Science*, 179, 250–8

Ross, C. et al. (2001) 'Powerlessness and the amplification of threat: neighbourhood disadvantage, disorder and mistrust', *American Sociological Review*, 66, 568–91

Said, E.W. (1995) *Orientalism*, Harmondsworth: Penguin

Samad, Y. (2006) 'Muslims in Britain today', *Sociology Review*, 15 (4)

Saunders, P. (1996) *Unequal but Fair?*, London: Institute of Economic Affairs.

Savage, M. (1992) *Property Bureaucracy and Culture: Middle-class Formation in Contemporary Britain*, London: Routledge

Savage, M. et al. (2005) 'Local habitus and working class culture', in Devine, F. et al. (Eds) *Rethinking Class: Culture, Identities and Lifestyle*, Basingstoke: Palgrave Macmillan

Scheff, T. (1966) *Being Mentally Ill: A Sociological Theory*, Chicago:Aldine

Seidler, V.J. (2006) *Young Men and Masculinities: Global Cultures and Intimate Lives*, London: Zed

Selfe, P. and Starbuck, M. (1998) *Religion*, London: Hodder & Stoughton

Seligman, M.E.P. (1975) *Helplessness: On Depression, Development and Death*, San Francisco: W.H. Freeman

Seligman, M.E.P. (1990). *Learned Optimism*, New York: Knopf.

Senior, M. (1993) 'Health, illness and postmodernism', *Sociology Review*, 6 (1)

Senior, M. and Viveash, B. (1998) *Health and Illness*, Basingstoke: Palgrave Macmillan

Sewell, T. (2000) *Black Masculinities and Schooling: How Black Boys Survive Modern Schooling*, 2nd edn, Stoke on Trent: Trentham Books

Shain, F. (2003) *The Schooling and Identity of Asian Girls*, Stoke on Trent: Trentham Books

Shakespeare, T. and Watson, N. (2002) 'Well, I know this is going to sound very strange to you, but I don't see myself as a disabled person: identity and disability', *Disability and Society*, 17(5), 509–29

Sharma, U. (1992) *Complementary Medicine Today*, London: Routledge

Sharpe, S. (1976) *Just Like a Girl: How Girls Learn to be Women*, Harmondsworth: Penguin

Sharpe, S. (1994) *Just Like a Girl: How Girls Learn to be Women*, 2nd edn, Harmondsworth: Penguin

Shaw, M. (2002) 'A matter of life and death: How can we reduce inequalities in health?', *Sociology Review*, 11 (4)

Shaw, M. and Davey Smith, G. (2005) 'Health inequalities and New Labour: how the promises compare with real progress', *British Medical Journal*, 330, 1016–21

Shearer, A. (1981) *Disability: Whose Handicap?*, Oxford: Blackwell

Sheeran, Y. (1995) 'Sociology, biology and health', *Sociology Review*, April, 8–10

Showalter, E. (1991) *The Female Malady: Women, Madness and English Culture 1830–1980*, London: Virago Press

Singh, R. (2003) 'Religious beliefs and practices among Sikh families in Britain', in Lou, A. (Ed.) *Southern Asian Children and Adolescence in Britain*, London: Whurr

Skeggs, B. (1997) *Formations of Class and Gender*, London: Sage Publications

Skelton, C. (2001) *Schooling the Boys: Masculinities and Primary Education*, Maidenhead: Open University Press

Skelton, C. and Francis, B. (2003) *Boys and Girls in the Primary Classroom*, Maidenhead: Open University Press

Smart, C. (1976) *Women, Crime and Criminology*, London: Routledge

Smart, C. (1999) *Divorce in England 1950–2000: A Moral Tale*, paper prepared for CAVA workshop, available from www.leeds.ac.uk/cava/papers/wsp2.pdf (accessed January 2008)

Smart, C. et al. (2000) *New Childhoods: Children and Co-Parenting after Divorce and Objects of Concern? Children and Divorce*, Centre for Research on Family, Kinship and Childhood, University of Leeds

Smart, N. (1969) *The Religious Experience of Mankind*, New York: Scribner

*Social Trends* (2007), National statistics, available from www.statistics,gov.uk (accessed January 2008)

Somerville, J. (2000) *Feminism and the Family: Politics and Society in the UK and USA*, Basingstoke: Macmillan

Song, M. (2003) *Choosing Ethnic Identity*, Cambridge: Polity Press

Sproston, K. and Mindell, J. (Eds) (2006) *Minority Ethnic Groups: Health Survey for England 2004*, London: HMSO

Stacey (1996) cited in Macionis, J. and Plummer, K. (2002) *Sociology A Global Introduction*, Harlow: Pearson Education

Stanley, L. (2002) 'Should "sex" really be "gender" – or "gender" really "sex"?', in Jackson, S. and Scott, S. (2002) *Gender: A Sociological Reader*, London: Routledge

Stanley, L. and Wise, S. (2002) 'What's wrong with socialisation?', in Jackson, S. and Scott, S. *Gender: A Sociological Reader*, London: Routledge

Stansfeld, S.A. et al. (2003) 'Social inequalities in depressive symptoms and physical functioning in the Whitehall II study: exploring a common cause explanation', *Journal of Epidemiology and Community Health*, 57, 361–7

Stark, R. (1999) cited in Wallis, J. (2002) 'The secularisation debate', *Sociology Review*, September

Stark, R. and Bainbridge, W.S. (1985) *The Future of Religion: Secularization, Revival and Cult Formation*, Berkeley: University of California Press Berkeley

Storey, J. (2003) *Cultural Studies and the Study of Popular Culture*, Edinburgh: Edinburgh University Press

Strinati, D. (1995) *An Introduction to Theories of Popular Culture*, London: Routledge

Szasz, T. (1971) *The Manufacture of Madness*, London: Routledge & Kegan Paul

Taylor, P. et al. (1996) *Sociology in Focus*, Ormskirk: Causeway Press

Taylor, S. and Field, D. (2007) (Eds) *Sociology of Health and Health Care*, Oxford: Blackwell

Tearfund (2007) *Churchgoing in the UK – Tearfund UK 2007* (www.tearfund.org)

Thomas, K.J. et al. (2003) 'Trends in access to complementary or alternative medicines via primary care in England, 1995-2001: results from a follow-up national survey', *Family Practitioner* 20 (5), 575–7 (abstract)

Thompson, M., Vinter, L. and Young, V. (2005) *Dads and their Babies*, London: Equal Opportunities Commission, available from http://83.137.212.42/sitearchive/eocwelsh/PDF/dads_and_their_babies_executive_summary_wales_eng.pdf (accessed January 2008)

Thornton, S. (1995) *Club Cultures: Music, Media and Subcultural Capital*, Cambridge: Polity Press

Tolmac, J. and Hodes, M. (2004) 'Ethnic variation among adolescent in-patients with psychotic disorders', *British Journal of Psychiatry*, 184, 428–31

Townsend (1999) in Browne, K. and Bottrill, I. 'Our unequal, unhealthy nation: class inequality, health and illness', *Sociology Review*, 9 (2)

Troeltsch, E. (1931) cited in Haralambos, M. and Holborn, M. (2004) *Sociology Themes and Perspectives*, London: HarperCollins, p. 422

Turner, B. (1987) *Medical Power and Social Knowledge*, London: Sage Publications

Tyrer, P. (2000) *Personality Disorders: Diagnosis, Management and Course*, Oxford: Butterworth-Heinemann

Victor, C. (2005) *The Social Context of Ageing*, London: Routledge

Vincent, N. (2006) *Self Made Man*, London: Atlantic Books

Voas, D. (2005) 'Religion: for life or just for Christmas?', in *Sociology Review*, 15 (2)

Voas, D. and Bruce, S. (2006) 'Is religion giving way to spirituality?', in *Sociology Review*, 15 (4)

Voas, D. and Crockett, A. (2005) 'Religion in Britain: neither believing nor belonging', *Sociology*, 39 (1), 11–28

Vogler, C. and Pahl, J. (1994) 'Money, power and inequality within marriage', *Sociological Review*, 42, 263–88

Vogler, C., Brockmann, M. and Wiggins, R. (2006) 'Intimate relationships and changing patterns of money management at the beginning of the twenty-first century', *British Journal of Sociology*, 57 (3), 455–82

Wadsworth, M. (1986) 'Serious illness in childhood and its association with later life achievement', in Wilkinson, R.G. (Ed) *Class and Health: Research and Longitudinal Data*, London: Tavistock

Waldron, I. (1983) 'Sex differences in illness incidence, prognosis and mortality: issues and evidence', *Social Science and Medicine*, 17, 1107–23

Wallis, J. (2002) 'The secularisation debate', *Sociology Review*, September

Wallis, R. (1984) *The Elementary Forms of the New Religious Life*, London: Routledge

Wanless Report (2002) *Securing Our Future Health: Taking a Long-Term View*, available from http://www.hm-treasury.gov.uk/Consultations_and_Legislation/wanless/consult_wanless_final.cfm (accessed January 2008)

Ward, J. and Winstanley, D. (2005) 'Coming out at work, performativity and the recognition and negotiation of identity', in *Sociological Review*, 53, 3, 447–75

Warner, J. (2005) *Perfect Madness: Motherhood in the Age of Anxiety*, San Francisco: Riverdeep

Weber, M. (1922) cited in Aldridge, A. (2004) 'Defining religion', *Sociology Review*, 14 (2), 8

Weber, M. (1958) *The Protestant Ethic and the Spirit of Capitalism*, New York: Scribner

Weeks, J. et al. (1999) 'Everyday experiments: narratives of non-heterosexual relationships' in Silva, E. and Smart, C. (Eds) (1999) *The New Family?*, London: Sage Books

White, C. et al. (2003) 'Trends in social class differences in mortality by cause, 1986 to 2000', *Health Statistics Quarterly*, 20, 25–37

Williams, J. (2006) 'Households and marriage', *Sociology Review*, 16 (1)

Williams, R. (1983) *Keywords*, London: Fontana

Williamson, H. (2004) *The Milltown Boys, Revisited*, Oxford: Berg Publishers

Willis, P. (1977) *Learning to Labour: How Working-class Kids get Working-class Jobs*, Farnborough: Saxon House

Willis, P. (1990) *Common Culture: Symbolic Work at Play in the Everyday Cultures of the Young*, Milton Keynes: Open University Press

Wilmott, P. (1988) 'Urban kinship past and present', *Social Studies Review*, November

Wilson, B.R. (1976) *Contemporary Transformations of Religion*, Oxford: Oxford University Press

Witz, A. and Woodward, K. (Eds) (2000) *Questioning Identity: Gender, Class, Nation*, London: Routledge

Woodhead, L. (2007) cited in Pigott, R. *Lifting the Veil on Religion and Identity*, ESRC Society Today, available from http://www.esrcsocietytoday.ac.uk/ESRCInfoCentre/about/CI/CP/the_edge/issue24/veil1.aspx?ComponentId=18739&SourcePageId=18760 (accessed November 2007)

Woodward, K. (2000) *Questioning Identity: Gender, Class, Nation*, London: Routledge

Wright, C., Weekes, D. and McGlaughlin, A. (2006) 'Gender-blind racism in the experience of schooling and identity formation', in Arnot, M. and Mac an Ghaill, M., *Gender and Education*, London: Routledge

Wynne, D. (1998) *Leisure, Lifestyle and the New Middle Class*, London: Routledge

Young, J. (2005) 'Illness behaviour: a selective review and synthesis', *Sociology of Health and Illness*, 26 (1), 1–3

Young, M. and Willmott, P. (1957) *Family and Kinship in East London*, London: Routledge

Young, M. and Willmott, P. (1973) *The Symmetrical Family*, Harmondsworth: Penguin

Zaretsky, E. (1976) cited in Best, S. et al. (2000) *Active Sociology*, Harlow: Longman, p. 302

# Index

Index